First Edition, First Printing: 2020
ISBN: 978-1-7340189-8-1-52500
The Paideia Institute for Humanistic Study, Inc.
www.paideiainstitute.org

Andrew Dinan is an Associate Professor of Classics & Early Christian Literature at Ave Maria University, where he has taught since 2004. He began his study of Latin in the public schools of northern Virginia and his study of Greek at the University of Notre Dame, from where he graduated with a degree in Liberal Studies. After earning a graduate degree in Theology from the John Paul II Institute for Studies on Marriage and Family (Washington), he did graduate work (MA and PhD) in Greek and Latin at the Catholic University of America. His publications, in the fields of patristics, liturgical Latin, and Neo-Latin studies, have appeared in *Humanistica Lovaniensia, The Classical Journal, Vigiliae Christianae, Journal of Early Christian Studies, American Catholic Studies, Antiphon,* and others. His particular interest is the role of Latin within American history and culture. He is currently working on an annotated transcription and translation of the Latin correspondence between the nineteenth-century American prelates Francis Patrick Kenrick (1797–1863) and his brother Peter Richard Kenrick (1806–1896).

CONIUGI AMANTISSIMAE ET INCOMPARABILI
LIBERIS DILECTISSIMIS

AMERICANA LATINE

LATIN MOMENTS IN THE HISTORY OF THE UNITED STATES

ANDREW C. DINAN

PREFACE

Latinists in the United States seem to be at a disadvantage when compared to their peers in Europe. Readers in northern and western Europe who take up Caesar's *Commentaries*, for example, are reading *in situ;* they are reading about events that took place in or near where they live. If they wish to do so, they can walk in the steps of Caesar's army; they can pinpoint locations of rivers, mountains, and forts that he mentions; in short, they can see what Caesar saw, at least in outline.

This is the case not only for historical writing. What reader of Cicero or Horace would not benefit from visiting places these authors mention? If we broaden our scope to take in patristic or medieval Latin, the possibilities proliferate. The literary remains from these later periods are vast—immensely vaster, indeed, than what survives from the classical period—but the geographical scope expands to include countries beyond the Roman Empire, and it deepens to include places not much mentioned by classical authors or that have taken on new significance. A visitor to Ostia, for example, can read the ninth book of the *Confessions* conscious of being at or near the site of St. Augustine's mystical conversation with his moribund mother. This same visitor—to use a lesser known and more mundane example—can read the *Octavius* of Minucius Felix while glimpsing the surf into which the protagonists of that dialogue saw young boys playfully skipping stones.

Such immediacy seems elusive in the Americas, especially in the United States, which stands several steps removed from the Romans in terms of language, if not culture. However much we push back the date of the first European entrance into this hemisphere, this land was *terra invisitata atque incognita* for the Romans and their immediate successors. To be sure, Latinists in the United States are aware of their country's classical tradition. They are likely to be acquainted with the correspondence of the colonial era, marked by frequent classical allusion; with the curricula of early schools and colleges, replete with the study of the classics; and with the classical substrate to our Constitution, law, architecture, and literature. Yet for various reasons—geographical, cultural, historical, and, particularly for English speakers, linguistic—a suspicion nevertheless remains that Latin is ineluctably foreign; it is Europe's history, onto which we have been fastened and against which we have occasionally protested; we can perhaps appropriate elements of this heritage, but this appropriation is more deliberate and conscious than organic and instinctive.

Yet there is much Latin that has been written by Americans, to Americans, in the Americas, or about the Americas. As early as Columbus's first voyage—in fact even earlier—a robust, diverse, and valuable body of what might be called American Latin, or *Americana Latine,* began to develop, and it continued until well into the nineteenth and even into the twentieth century. This literature concerns nearly every region in the Americas, from Veracruz to Vancouver, from San Francisco to Newfoundland, from Bolivia to the Hudson Bay. Recent years have seen remarkable interest in the Latin literature emanating from Latin America, especially Mexico, Peru, and Brazil. Canadian Latin too has begun to receive attention. The present volume, however, is devoted primarily to the Latin of lands that would eventually comprise, or are currently part of, the United States.

Latin writings composed in or about the United States come from men, and occasionally women, of various ethnicities. Some of this literature was written by well-known personages; much, however, was written by men and women whose names typically do not grace history textbooks. Numerous genres are represented, and the subjects range from the pedestrian to the sublime. Some of this literature is in an elevated style; much, however, is in a common idiom. What unites this diverse body of literature is that Latin was used for the purpose of communication. With few exceptions, these writings were not school exercises or museum pieces, nor were they uninspired concessions to an antiquated tradition. Each text was written or spoken with the intention of delighting, informing, or motivating some person or group.

The present volume is offered for the delight of Latinists and indeed of all who desire to glimpse some of the ways that the Latin language has permeated the history of the United States.

Ave Maria University
Die Apparitionis Beatae Mariae Virginis de Fatima MMXX

COVER MAP

America Septentrionalis
divisa in suas principales partes et status
seu dominatus regis
Galliae, Castiliae, Angliae,
Sueciae, Daniae, et Batavorum
P.D. Sanson Geographum Regis Galliae ordinarium

Iohann Hoffmann
excudit.

Library of Congress
Geography and Map Division

https://www.loc.gov/resource/g3300.ct007331/?r=0.089,0.222,0.727,0.369,0

ACKNOWLEDGEMENTS

Living in Southwest Florida has many advantages, but proximity to archival fonds or historical records is not one of them. This can be compensated to some extent by the increasingly abundant resources available online, not only through Google Books, Internet Archive, and HathiTrust, but also through state historical societies, universities, the Library of Congress, subscription newspaper sites such as GenealogyBank and Newspapers.com, collaborative sites such as Find a Grave, or privately maintained sites such as Catholic-Hierarchy. But over the last seven years I have enjoyed the gracious assistance of dedicated and generous librarians and archivists who have not only responded to my queries but have also enabled me to see images of documents that are difficult to obtain in published form or that have never been published.

Additionally, I am grateful to the organizers and attendees of the Neo-Latin section of the Kentucky Foreign Language Conference for their encouragement of my project and for providing a forum in which I could share some of my research. Colleagues, staff, and students at Ave Maria University have generously supported my efforts, and more importantly they have fostered a culture in which both research and teaching are promoted and valued. I am grateful as well to the anonymous reader of my manuscript and to the staff at The Paideia Institute, especially Marco Romani, who shepherded this work through publication. Finally, my deepest gratitude is to my family—my wife, son, and three daughters, as well as my siblings, parents, and now-deceased grandparents—who have lovingly fashioned homes that have made the research and writing of this book not only possible but meaningful.

CONTENTS

INTRODUCTION

Johan Printz, born in southern Sweden in 1592, received a liberal education before joining the Swedish army and rising to the rank of Lieutenant Colonel. In 1640 he was forced to surrender a stronghold in Saxony during one of the battles of the Thirty Years War (1618–48), and a few years later he ended up as Governor of New Sweden, a small tract of land along the Delaware River comprising portions of present-day Pennsylvania, Delaware, and New Jersey. It was Printz's job to protect Swedish interests in the face of English and Dutch settlements in the mid-Atlantic and further north. He succeeded. An early twentieth-century historian remarks that under his governorship (1643–53) "New Sweden saw its best days."[1]

Fifteen months after his arrival in Delaware, Printz sent a report home to the Noble West India Company describing the status of New Sweden. In the middle of this report, originally written in Swedish, he makes a surprising request. He explains that he often receives official letters in Latin, and that he would prefer to respond in Latin, but since he has spent the previous twenty-seven years with "the musket and the pistol in [his] hands" rather than "Tacitus and Cicero," he finds it too difficult to "sit and laboriously collect together an epistle;" therefore he asks that a Latinist be sent over, who might also serve as an advisor and diplomat. His plea went unheeded, for three years later, in his 1647 report, he repeats this request, declaring that he receives Latin letters "from all parts" and even attaching one such letter to his report.[2]

Latin, it is well known, remained the universal language of scholarly communication in Europe throughout the Middle Ages, the Renaissance, and well into the early modern period, but Printz's request reveals that the use of Latin was not confined to the European continent, nor was it restricted to learned treatises. Latin, it seems, was of practical value for some persons in early North America.

A century and a half later, on the opposite coast, the German surgeon Georg von Langsdorff (1774–1852), traveling on a Russian ship, arrived in San Francisco harbor where he was met by a contingent from the Presidio that included the Franciscan friar José Uria. Von Langsdorff later recalled: "As not one of our party understood Spanish, the conversation was carried on, in Latin, between me and the Franciscan friar, this being the only medium by which we could make ourselves intelligible to each other."[3] Three decades later the Russian Orthodox priest John Veniaminov (1797–1879) had a similar experience when visiting the Franciscan missions in California.[4]

Such anecdotes abound in early American history. Beginning in the late 1740s the Rev. Jonathan Ashley (1712–80), a Congregational minister in Deerfield, Massachusetts exchanged Latin letters with Jean Baptiste De Saint-Pé (1686–1770), a Jesuit priest in Canada, because this was their only common language.[5] Two decades earlier François Seguenot (1644–1727), a Sulpician priest in Montreal, wrote Christine Baker (1689–1773), now in Boston, to persuade her to return to the Catholic Church. He requested that any response be made to him (by way of her ministers or others) in Latin or Greek, if not in French. He would then reply in Latin or Greek, since, as he said, he did not know English or Dutch.[6]

At times, to be sure, Latin was not enough. The Dutchmen Jasper Danckaerts (1639–c. 1703) and Peter Sluyter (1645–1722), members of the Labadist sect, were able to converse with the Puritan minister John Eliot (1604–90) "partly in Latin, partly in English."[7] The Italian Jesuit Philip Rappagliosi (1841–78), who ministered in Montana, humorously describes the circuitous nature of conversation on his Atlantic crossing: "The four of us have no common language, it's a comedy: I speak Latin with him [the Irishman]. Brother Melchers wants me to speak Italian so that he can then translate for our third companion in German; this way *after five minutes* the four of us understood what we wanted to say to one another."[8]

Evidently, then, at times Latin was used in North America for communication—written and oral—when there was no common modern language. But other anecdotes suggest that Latin was not simply a back-up. Friends who shared a vernacular, and even family members, have employed Latin when communicating with each other.[9]

In 1646 eighteen-year-old Samuel Winthrop (1627–*c.*1677), having left Harvard prior to graduation in order to pursue a business opportunity in Europe, wrote a Latin letter of explanation from the island of Teneriffe addressed to his father, Governor John Winthrop (1588–1649).[10] Samuel was following a Winthrop tradition. Still extant is a Latin letter that Forth Winthrop (1609–30), Samuel's half-brother, wrote to their father, as well as two Latin letters that Forth wrote to his older brother John Winthrop, Jr. (1606–76).[11] These date from the 1620s, when the Winthrops were still in Europe, and they reflect the pedagogical aims and methods of Tudor and Elizabethan schools, when letter-writing in Latin, following classical (Cicero, Horace, and Ovid) and humanistic (Erasmus) models, was a regular practice.[12] But Samuel's letter indicates—and this should not be a surprise—that Europeans retained these classical aspirations when they crossed the Atlantic.

But familial Latin, as well as Latin between friends, was not a phenomenon restricted to colonial America. Julius Peter Garesché (1821–62), who was killed at the Battle of Stones River, Tennessee while fighting for the Union, is said to have corresponded for many years in Latin with a former Georgetown classmate; additionally, at least one of Garesché's Latin letters to his father has survived.[13] Thomas Ewing Sherman (1856–1933), the son of General William Tecumseh Sherman, wrote his grandfather at least one letter in Latin.[14] A few decades earlier the Massachusetts-born Oliver Alden Taylor (1801–51), a graduate of Union College and Andover

Theological Seminary, wrote his uncle as well as his brothers Latin letters.[15]

Sometimes familial Latin letters were pedagogic exercises or proofs of learning. During the Civil War Friedrich Muench (1799–1881), one of the so-called Latin Farmers of the American Midwest, wrote his son letters from Jefferson City, Missouri, where he was serving as state senator, and he asked his son to translate between English, German, and Latin.[16] John Witherspoon (1723–94) wrote his son David in Latin and French, by way of encouraging him to keep up his studies in these languages.[17]

But at other times the motivation for familial Latin letters was something different from pedagogy. The Jesuit Philipp Segesser (1689–1761), who eventually ministered in Sonora, north and south of today's Mexico-Arizona border, wrote seven Latin letters to a brother and uncle in Switzerland, none of which apparently was motivated by language learning.[18] The Irish-born Francis Patrick Kenrick (1797–1863), the Bishop of Philadelphia and then Archbishop of Baltimore, carried on a three-decade-long correspondence in Latin with his brother Peter (1806–96), eventually the Archbishop of St. Louis; though the Latin is elegant, the subject matter of the Kenricks's letters is far from riveting, consisting largely of details of ecclesiastical administration, personnel issues, and scholarly projects.[19] It is possible that at times they valued Latin because it safeguarded confidentiality, but regardless of the motive, it is clear that Latin for them was a natural, everyday means of communication.

Somewhat different are the Latin letters that the Jesuit Johann Jacob Baegert (1717–72) wrote from Baja California to his family back home in Alsace. On September 26, 1761 Baegert began to write his brother George, a fellow Jesuit, in German, but finding this "too difficult" he switched to Latin. He completed the letter and sealed it, but, as he explains:

> "alas, a desire overcame me to write some verses in praise of the California country. It has not been of any trouble for me to do so, though I have been far away from Parnassus for a long time. With this I send you these stanzas, partly that you may see what leaps my poetic blood can still make, partly because they contain in short almost everything that may be said and written about California . . . And now follows the Latin song."[20]

Regrettably the original Latin of this letter does not survive, but it offers an intriguing glimpse into phenomena that are almost unknown today, viz., Latin as a language of intimacy—even more intimate than the vernacular—and poetry as a cherished component of this intimacy. This is all the more surprising when one considers that Baegert was far removed from a university setting or from a community in which the composition of such poetry formed an integral part. Latin, it seems, was a way of maintaining or reinforcing a connection with such a community or culture.

At times Latin has even been used in North America when communicating not with other persons but with, or for, oneself. In 1645, while traveling through New England in search of a location for his iron works, John Winthrop, Jr. kept a Latin diary in which he described the weather, topography, stopping places, and conversations. Winthrop's choice of Latin, it has been surmised, was due to his desire to maintain proficiency.[21]

But Latin diaries, like the Latin letters or conversations mentioned above, are not exclusive to the colonial era. They too are found well into the nineteenth century. For example, John Reveley Guerrant (1865–1930), later a medical doctor, kept at least two Latin diaries in the 1880s, first while he was a high school student, then while he was studying at Washington and Lee University in Lexington, Virginia.[22] Moreover, as in the case of familial Latin letters, not all of these diaries can be explained on pedagogical grounds. Joseph Crétin (1799–1857), the first Bishop of

St. Paul, Minnesota, left an informal diary in Latin, to be used, he said, when compiling the annals of his diocese.[23] Joseph Rosati (1789–1843), the first Bishop of St. Louis, kept two diaries in Latin, one of which contained notes of official acts, the other detailed comments of a private nature (*Ephemerides Privatae*). The editor of the latter diary notes that this practice was typical of American bishops of the time, for whom "Latin was like a second mother tongue."[24] Adrian Hoecken (1815–97), a Jesuit missionary in Montana, kept a book that was part diary and part "catch-all, the entries of which are in English, French, Dutch, Indian dialects, and Latin."[25] The Jesuits, in particular, were fond of Latin diaries: others that have survived include ones by Christian Hoecken (1808–51), a missionary to the Sioux, and Maurice Gailland (1815–77), who worked in Montana.

The present book is an attempt to showcase the active use of Latin exhibited in the above-mentioned instances and in countless others. This book is the fruit of an investigation into *who* was using Latin, *when*, *where*, and *how* it was being used, and especially—although this is often difficult to discern—*why* it was being used.

This topic is related to two broader themes, both of which have been much studied in recent decades, viz., the classical influence upon American culture and the rise of Classics as an academic discipline within the United States.[26] After all, every speaker or writer of Latin stands in some way in relation to the classical tradition, and most speakers and writers of Latin have emerged from, and many are connected to, a college or university. Yet the subject of this book is nonetheless distinct from those two themes. One can be influenced by the classics but not necessarily speak or write Latin. Not all professional classicists, indeed, have been speakers and writers of Latin. Conversely, not all speakers or writers of Latin have been professional classicists. This book will therefore reveal a new dimension to the classical tradition within the United States, one that has received comparatively little attention.

The first survey of what might be called the Latin of the United States was made by James Luce Kingsley (1778–1852), a professor at Yale, in the context of his review of Francis Glass's sensational *Georgii Washingtonii Vita*. Although Kingsley was intrigued by the phenomenon of American Latin, he considered the corpus small, "as the occasions for its use have been much less frequent here, than in Europe."[27]

The credit for being the first to document in a systematic manner the corpus of Latin in the United States belongs to Leo M. Kaiser (1919–2001), a long-time professor at Loyola University in Chicago. In two major articles Kaiser catalogued, respectively, Latin poetry and prose; elsewhere he offered studies of individual authors and texts; he also initiated a compilation of original Latin inscriptions found in the United States; and he produced an annotated anthology of Latin verse.[28] Kaiser's scholarship remains the starting point for all students of the field, yet his work has been contextualized and extended by the surveys of Josef IJsewijn, Ann M. Blair, and John Gallucci,[29] and it has been supplemented by Stuart M. McManus.[30]

Today those interested in the Latin of the United States enjoy ready access to numerous texts that these and other scholars have identified, some of which have been transcribed, edited, and translated. Yet this field of study is still in its early stages, and a comprehensive treatment remains several years away. The Latin literature of Latin America, by contrast, is much better known and has been more extensively studied.[31]

Many Latin writings from the United States, especially those from the nineteenth and twentieth centuries, have yet to be discovered, and others lie untranscribed in university, municipal, and ecclesiastical archives, not all of which are in the United States. Kaiser's work, after all, extended only to 1800 for prose and 1825 for poetry. Yet the amount of American Latin from 1800 to the present far exceeds the American Latin from the prior two centuries. Despite considerable changes in America's engagement with the classics in the nineteenth century, Latin continued to be spoken and written, particularly within and between religious and academic communities. Still to be investigated thoroughly are nineteenth-century American newspapers, materials relating to commencement exercises, programs for civic celebrations or academic convocations, memoirs, academic monographs, the manuscripts in the Library of Congress, governmental publications, as well as classical journals, journals of religious communities, of medical societies, and of schools, colleges, and universities, to name some of the most promising sources. One contribution of the present volume, it is hoped, is the identification of new texts, authors, and sources.

I have structured this book chronologically, from the first mention of continental America in the eleventh century to the middle of the twentieth century, attempting when possible to connect each text to a significant, though not necessarily well-known, person or event. Indeed, looking at the history of the United States in conjunction with the Latin language will, it is hoped, introduce readers to previously unknown persons and events, or perhaps yield new perspectives on already known persons and events.

I have sought to highlight the diversity and range of genres that characterize the Latin of the United States. Selections are from treatises, formal and informal letters, diaries, inscriptions, decrees, reports, orations, translations, as well as poems. Special attention has been given to what might be called ordinary Latin, i.e., compositions that would not be considered *belles lettres*, in order to showcase the role of Latin as an everyday, even perfunctory means of communication. I have not included works that were written primarily as school exercises, unless these were published for an audience beyond the classroom. Morevoer, with one exception, I have not included poems that already appeared in Kaiser's *Early American Latin Verse.*

I have not succeeded in providing a Latin text for each of the fifty states, but at least every region of the United States is represented. Only a small number of the texts included here originated from, or directly concern, New England. Instead, the majority were written from or about the so-called Spanish Borderlands, New France, New Sweden, New Netherland, the mid-Atlantic, the upper Midwest, or the Pacific Northwest, and a few concern primarily Mexico and Canada. Several selections involve an author in one region of the Americas writing to someone in another region. Latin, after all, has been a transnational language, and this remained the case in this hemisphere. Additionally this book will, I hope, foster a richer perspective on the history of the United States than is usually presented in textbooks, which justly emphasize the early-seventeenth-century English settlements at Jamestown and Plymouth. The collection of documents presented here will enable readers to situate these English efforts within a larger context. Moreover, some of these texts poignantly depict the impact that European efforts in America had upon indigenous peoples, and some directly address the practice of slavery and its consequences, both of Native Americans and of Africans.

I hope that this selection of texts suggests in some way the value of Latin for the study of American history. It may also yield new perspectives on the literary tradition of the United States.[32] Above all, I hope that readers will find delight in seeing the classical (or medieval) idiom employed in new and often unexpected places, close to home.

NOTE

A particular challenge in the presentation of later Latin texts is orthography. In this volume I have added diphthongs and made some effort to standardize spelling in accordance with classical convention, although in a few instances I have retained irregular spellings that seemed pertinent to the author, genre, or text.

Some of the passages included in this volume have not been published previously, but none is to be considered a diplomatic text.

Finally, at times the notes are uneven, which reflects my uneven competence and experience. In general, the notes provide historical details rather than classical allusions.

1 Vinland (11th century)

The earliest known reference in any European language to mainland America is found in the eleventh-century *Gesta hammaburgensis ecclesiae pontificum* of Adam of Bremen, a *magister scholarum* and canon in northern Germany, and it occurs in the context of the Christian evangelization of Scandinavia. In 1053 Pope St. Leo IX (*r.* 1049–54) had appointed Adalbert, the Archbishop of Hamburg-Bremen (*r.* 1043–72), to be papal legate and vicar of Nordic nations, and the city of Bremen, "the Rome of the North," was to be the basis for missionary efforts.[33] Adalbert asked Adam to assist him. To make inquiries into the political and ecclesiastical history of the lands to be evangelized, Adam visited Sven Estridsen, the King of Denmark (*r.* 1047–76). The king became one of Adam's principal sources for the *Gesta hammaburgensis*, whose scope extends from the end of Charlemagne's reign to the time of the Holy Roman Emperor Henry IV (*r.* 1084–1105). Adam's work has been likened to the Venerable Bede's *Historia ecclesiastica gentis Anglorum* for its "width of perspective, accuracy of account, and historical wit."[34] Yet although he took Sallust as his stylistic model, Adam's Latin has been deemed to be "obscure and difficult," with "a number of Germanisms" as well as "positive grammatical errors."[35]

In the fourth book of *Gesta hammaburgensis*, titled "Descriptio Insularum Aquilonis," Adam relates Sven Estridsen's knowledge of lands to the west and north of Scandinavia (4.39).[36] The king apparently was aware of an island to the west of Iceland that was called Vinland, where wild grapes and crops abounded. The exact identity of Vinland has been the subject of considerable speculation, with possible locations ranging from the Chesapeake region to northern Canada. Most scholars today locate Vinland in northeastern Newfoundland at a site called L'Anse aux Meadows, which was excavated by the Norwegian couple Helge Instad and Anne Stine Ingstad in the

1960s and is thought to be the site of Leif Ericsson's settlement in the first decade of the eleventh century.[37]

Praeterea unam adhuc insulam recitavit[38] a multis in eo repertam oceano, quae dicitur Winland, eo quod ibi vites sponte nascantur, vinum optimum ferentes.[39] Nam et fruges ibi non seminatas abundare non fabulosa opinione, sed certa comperimus relatione Danorum. Post[40] quam insulam, ait,[41] terra non invenitur habitabilis in illo oceano, sed omnia, quae ultra sunt, glacie intolerabili ac caligine inmensa plena sunt. Cuius rei Martianus ita meminit:[42] Ultra Thilen,[43] inquiens, navigatione unius diei mare concretum est.

Source: Bernhard Schmeidler, *Adam von Bremen, Hamburgische Kirchengeschichte*, 3rd ed. (Hanover: Hahnsche Buchhandlung, 1917), 275–76.[44]

1.1 Greenland (12th–15th centuries)

It is difficult to know whether to consider colonial Greenland a part of America or Europe. Politically, it belongs today to Denmark, and David Quinn argues that the Norse colony in Greenland was "a projection of Europe." Accordingly, he notes: "It is possible to incorporate the history of the Greenland colony integrally into a history of northern Europe: it is possible also virtually to exclude it from a history of America." Yet, as Quinn remarks, the Greenland settlements also "faced west" and were in contact, albeit "tentatively and intermittently" with continental America. He concludes: "Modern continental and national allegiances cannot remove the reality that the Greenland colony was in a sense an 'American' experience for Europeans."[45]

Responding to President Donald Trump's bid to purchase Greenland, the Prime Minister of Denmark, Mette Frederiksen, stated in August 2019: "Greenland is not for sale. Greenland belongs to Greenland."

No texts relating to Greenland are included in this volume, but readers may be interested to consult the following Latin documents, most of which are letters pertaining to the challenges of sacramental life and ecclesiastical administration in a land so distant from mainland Europe. Texts 2–8, photographs of which were incorporated into the Vatican's exhibit at the 1904 World's Fair (Louisiana Purchase Exposition) in St. Louis, can be found in *The Flatey Book and Recently Discovered Vatican Manuscripts Concerning America as Early as the Tenth Century* (London: Norroena Society, 1906), 131–76.

1 *Orderici Vitalis . . . Historiae Ecclesiasticae Libri Tredecim*, ed. Augustus LePrevost, vol. 4 (Paris: Julius Renouard et socii, 1852), X.6.

2 Pope Innocent III to the Archbishop of Nidaros (Norway), February 13, 1206.

3 Pope John XXI to the Archbishop of Nidaros, December 4, 1276.

4 Pope Nicholas III to the Archbishop of Nidaros, January 31, 1279.

5 Pope Nicholas III to the Archbishop of Nidaros, June 9, 1279.

6 Pope Martin IV to the Archbishop of Nidaros, March 4, 1282.

7 Pope Nicholas V to the Bishops of Shaoltensus and Olensus, September 20, 1448.

8 Pope Alexander VI to the Church of Garda (Greenland), early in his pontificate.

2 Columbus's First Voyage (1492)

In 1492 Christopher Columbus succeeded in obtaining from Queen Isabella of Castile (*r.* 1474–1504) permission to undertake an expedition westward toward what he thought would be India. The details of the agreement between Columbus and the crown were negotiated during the early months of that year, and they are contained in eight documents known collectively as The Capitulations of Santa Fe (April 17 and 30, 1492). Two of these were in Latin, and they are presented below. The first is a letter of recommendation written by King Ferdinand II of Aragaon (*r.* 1479–1516). Columbus carried several copies of this letter with him, and according to Bartolomé de las Casas, the blank space in the letter was to be filled in with the name(s) of the ruler(s) into whose land(s) Columbus arrived. The second is Columbus's passport, which reveals that Columbus's destination was India.[46]

The third text below is taken from the letter that Columbus sent to Barcelona from Lisbon upon returning from his first voyage. Although Columbus had facility with Latin—his library contained several Latin works in whose margins he had made Latin annotations—he wrote this letter in Spanish.[47] Dated February 15, 1493 and originally addressed to Luis de Santángel, the secretary of the royal treasury and one of Columbus's supporters, this letter, or a copy, was sent to Rome where it was translated into Latin by Leander de Cosco. The translation, dated "tertio kalendas Maii MCCCCXCIII," was published in an eight-page pamphlet by Stephen Plannck and disseminated throughout Europe where it became, to paraphrase a modern historian, something like a best-seller.[48] Thus, although not originally written in Latin, this letter nevertheless reveals the importance of Latin for international communication in late fifteenth-century-Europe. It "ranks as the first significant American document."[49] Very few copies of the so-called Plannck edition of this letter survive. One copy was recently found in the Library of Congress, but it was returned to the Riccardiana Library in Florence, from where it was determined to have been stolen.[50] The excerpts given below describe: a) landfall in the Bahamas; b) initial attempts at trading; c) Columbus's intentions towards indigenous peoples.

I

Serenissimo Principi _______________, amico nostro carissimo, Ferdinandus et Elisabet, rex et regina Castellae, Aragoniae, Legionis, Siciliae, Granatae, etc., salutem et prosperorum successuum incrementa. Ex nonnullorum subditorum nostrorum relatibus et aliorum qui e regnis et partibus istis ad nos venere, laetanter intelleximus quam boni animi et optimae voluntatis estis erga nos statumque nostrum, quantaque animi affectione de rebus nostris secundis cupitis certiorari:[51] quare decrevimus nobilem capitanum nostrum Christoforum Colon praesentiarum latorem ad vos mittere, a quo bonam valetudinem statumque felicem nostrum et alia quae sibi iussimus et nostra ex parte vobis referat intelligere poteritis. Rogamus itaque vos et eius relatibus indubiam fidem perinde ac nobis habere velitis; quod nobis pergratissimum ad modum erit, beneplacitis vestris promptos quidem et paratos nos offerentes. Ex civitate nostra Granatae XXX Aprilis anno domini millesimo CCCCLXXXXII.

Yo El Rey

Yo La Reyna

II

Mittimus in presentiarum nobilem virum *Xpōforum*[52] *Colon* cum tribus caravelis[53] armatis per maria oceana ad partes Indiae pro aliquibus causis et negotiis servitium Dei ac fidem orthodoxae augmentum concernentibus.

III

Tricesimo tertio die postquam Gadibus discessi, in mare Indicum perveni,[54] ubi plurimas insulas innumeris habitatas hominibus reperi, quarum omnium pro felicissimo Rege nostro, praeconio celebrato, et vexillis extensis, contradicente nemine, possessionem accepi:[55] primaeque earum Divi Salvatoris nomen imposui,[56] cuius fretus auxilio tam ad hanc quam ad ceteras alias pervenimus; eam vero Indi Guanahanyn vocant.[57] Aliarum etiam unamquamque novo nomine nuncupavi, quippe aliam insulam Sanctae Mariae Conceptionis, aliam Fernandinam, aliam Isabelam, aliam Ioannam et sic de reliquis appellari iussi.[58]

Quamprimum in eam insulam (quam dudum Ioannam vocari dixi) appulimus;[59] iuxta eius litus occidentem versus aliquantulum processi, tamque eam magnam nullo reperto fine inveni, ut non insulam sed continentem Cathai provinciam esse crediderim;[60] nulla tamen videns oppida municipiave in maritimis sita confinibus praeter aliquos vicos et praedia rustica, cum quorum incolis loqui nequibam; quare simul ac nos videbant, surripiebant fugam . . .

Maximum erga omnes amorem prae se ferunt; dant quaeque magna pro parvis, minima licet re nihilove contenti. Ego attamen prohibui, ne tam minima et nullius pretii hisce darentur, ut sunt lancis, paropsidum vitrique fragmenta: item clavi, lingulae; quamquam si hoc poterant adipisci, videbatur eis pulcherrima mundi possidere iocalia. . . Item arcuum, amphorae, hydriae, doliique fragmenta bombyci et auro tamquam bestiae comparabant; quod quia iniquum sane erat, vetui, dedique eis multa pulchra et grata, quae mecum tuleram, nullo interveniente praemio, ut eos mihi facilius conciliarem, fierentque Christicolae, et ut sint proni in amorem erga Regem, Reginam principesque nostros, et universas gentes Hispaniae, ac studeant perquirere et coacervare, eaque nobis tradere quibus ipsi affluunt et nos magnopere indigemus.

Nullam hi norunt idololatriam; immo firmissime credunt ommem vim, omnem potentiam, omnia denique bona esse in caelo, meque inde cum his navibus et nautis descendisse, atque hoc animo ibi fui susceptus postquam metum repulerant. Nec sunt segnes aut rudes, quin summi ac perspicacis ingenii; et homines, qui transfretant mare illud, non sine admiratione uniuscuiusque rei rationem reddunt; sed nunquam viderunt gentes vestitas, neque naves huiusmodi. Ego statim ac ad mare illud perveni, e prima insula quosdam Indos violenter arripui, qui ediscerent a nobis, et nos pariter docerent ea quorum ipsi in hisce partibus cognitionem habebant, et ex voto successit: nam brevi nos ipsos, et hi nos, tum gestu ac signis, tum verbis intellexerunt, magnoque nobis fuere emolumento. Veniunt modo mecum,[61] tamen qui semper putant me desiluisse e caelo, quamvis diu nobiscum versati fuerint, hodieque versentur, et hi erant primi, qui id quocumque appellabamus nuntiabant, alii deinceps aliis elata voce dicentes, Venite, venite et videbitis gentes aethereas.

Sources: I Henry Vignaud, *Histoire Critique de la Grande Enterprise de Christophe Colomb* (Paris: H. Welter, 1911), 2: 582.
II This text, which is in the Archivo de la Corona de Aragón, and can now be seen online through PARES, has been reproduced by several twentieth century authors.[62]
III Richard H. Major, *Select Letters of Christopher Columbus, with other original documents, relating to his four voyages to the New World* (London: Hakluyt Society, 1847), 1–3, 7–9.

3 The World Divided (1493)

News of Columbus's voyage exacerbated an existing struggle between Spain and Portugal concerning authority over newly-discovered lands. Earlier disputes concerning Guinea and various Atlantic islands had prompted papal efforts to delineate areas of ownership. Similarly, Columbus's voyage occasioned papal briefs from Pope Alexander VI (*r.* 1492–1503) that are known as the Bulls of Donation. The first of these, *Inter caetera* (May 3, 1493), granted the Spanish sovereigns authority over any newly-discovered lands in the west not yet under the dominion of a Christian prince. The third of these, also called *Inter caetera* and dated one day later (May 4, 1493), established a line of demarcation 100 leagues west of the Azores or Cape Verde Islands, with Spain being granted dominion over lands to the west of this line.[63] Excerpts from the May 4 *Inter caetera* are given below.

Investigations in the latter nineteenth and early twentieth centuries brought to light many details of the compilation and the motivation for the second *Inter caetera*.[64] A consideration of the document's source, the identity of the scribe (or *abbreviator*), the date of the tax assessed by the *rescribendarius*, and the date of the document's arrival in Spain (July 19), enabled Herman Vander Linden to demonstrate that this second brief was in fact backdated, and that it was written at the prompting of the Spanish sovereigns who were seeking, through their ambassadors in Rome, a more favorable settlement than had been given in the first *Inter caetera* (May 3, 1493). Moreover, it is considered likely that Columbus himself suggested the famous line of demarcation in preparation for a subsequent voyage.

Once the Spanish monarchs received this bull, they conveyed a copy to Columbus and urged him to publish it and to take it with him "so that all the world may know that no one can enter into these regions without authorization from us."[65]

Alexander episcopus, servus servorum Dei:
carissimo in Christo filio Fernando regi,
et carissimae in Christo filiae Elisabeth
reginae Castellae, Legionis, Aragonum, Siciliae,
et Granatae, illustribus,
salutem et apostolicam benedictionem.

. . . omnes insulas et terras firmas inventas et inveniendas, detectas et detegendas versus occidentem et meridiem, fabricando et constituendo unam lineam a polo Arctico scilicet septentrione ad polum Antarcticum scilicet meridiem, sive terrae firmae et insulae inventae et inveniendae sint versus Indiam aut versus aliam quancunque partem, quae linea distet a qualibet insularum, quae vulgariter nuncupantur de los Azores et Caboverde,[66] centum leucis versus occidentem et meridiem,[67] ita quod omnes insulae et terrae firmae repertae et reperiendae, detectae et detegendae, a praefata linea versus occidentem et meridiem, per alium regem aut principem Christianum non fuerint actualiter possessae usque ad diem nativitatis Domini nostri Iesu Christi proximae praeteritum a quo incipit annus praesens millesimus quadringentesimus nonagesimus tertius, quando fuerunt per nuntios et capitaneos vestros inventae aliquae praedictarum insularum, auctoritate Omnipotentis Dei nobis in beato Petro concessa, ac vicariatus Iesu Christi, qua fungimur in terris, cum omnibus illarum dominiis, civitatibus, castris, locis et villis, iuribusque et iurisdictionibus ac pertinentiis universis, vobis heredibusque et successoribus vestris, Castellae et Legionis regibus, in perpetuum tenore praesentium donamus, concedimus, et assignamus, vosque et heredes ac successores praefatos illarum dominos cum plena, libera, et omnimoda potestate, auctoritate, et iurisdictione, facimus, constituimus, et deputamus; decernentes nihilominus per huiusmodi donationem, concessionem, et assignationem nostram nulli Christiano principi, qui actualiter praefatas insulas aut terras firmas possederit usque ad praedictum diem Nativitatis Domini nostri Iesu Christi, ius quaesitum sublatum intelligi posse aut auferri debere. . . Datum Romae apud Sanctum Petrum, anno Incarnationis Dominicae millesimo quadringentesimo nonagesimo tertio, quarto nonas Maii, pontificatus nostri anno primo.[68]

Source: Frances Gardiner Davenport, ed., *European Treaties Bearing on the History of the United States and its Dependencies to 1648* (Washington, DC: Carnegie Institution of Washington, 1917), 72, 74.

4 America Placed and Named (1507)

That the New World is called "America" is due to the Latin passage included here, taken from the 1507 work *Cosmographiae Introductio* by the German mapmaker Martin Waltzmüller, or Waldsee-müller (c. 1470–c. 1522). To illustrate his work Waltzmüller produced a map that reflected the knowledge of the New World gained from explorations thus far. By "daringly" depicting two large land masses between Europe and Asia, Waltzmüller "changed the world, or at least the appearance of it on the map."[69] Additionally, Waltzmüller labeled the southern land mass America, after the Italian navigator Amerigo Vespucci (1451–1512), who beginning in 1497 made several voyages to South America (and perhaps to Central and North America as well) under the patronage of the Spanish crown.

It has been suggested that Waltzmüller may have had reservations about using the name "America," because subsequently he dropped it in favor of the expression "Terra Incognita," and later he referred to South America as "Terra Nova" and North America as "Cuba."[70] But "America" was picked up by other early sixteenth-century mapmakers, and it became standard nomenclature for referring to both continents in the western hemisphere.

According to Henry Harrisse, the bibliographer of early Americana: "But for this little work the Western Hemisphere might have been called 'The Land of the Holy Cross,' or 'Atlantis,' or 'Hesperides,' or 'Iberica,' or 'Columbia,' or 'New India,' or 'The Indies,' as it is designated officially in Spain to this day" (Harrisse was writing in 1866).[71]

The only surviving copy of Waltzmüller's map, which has been called "America's birth certificate," was acquired by the Library of Congress in May 2003 for $10,000,000. It was discovered in 1901 by the Jesuit Joseph Fischer in the library of Prince Waldburg, located in the castle of Wolfegg.[72]

Nunc vero et hae partes sunt latius lustratae et alia quarta pars per Americum Vesputium (ut in sequentibus audietur) inventa est quam non video cur quis iure vetet ab Americo inventore sagacis ingenii viro Amerigen[73] quasi Americi terram sive Americam dicendam: cum et Europa et Asia a mulieribus sua sortita sint nomina.

Source: Henry Harrisse, *Bibliotheca Americana Vetustissima: A Description of Works Relating to America Published Between the Years 1492 and 1551* (New York: George P. Philes, 1866), 94.

5 Sebastian Cabot (1508)

Apart from private fishing expeditions, the first English-sponsored voyages to America were those of John Cabot (c. 1450–c. 1499) and his son Sebastian (c. 1484–1557). A citizen of Venice, though born in Genoa, John Cabot attempted unsuccessfully to obtain royal patronage in Portugal and Spain and eventually came to England and settled in Bristol. On March 3, 1496 he received a patent from King Henry VII (*r.* 1485–1509) which, in spite of the papal line of demarcation (see section 3), granted Cabot and his sons the ability to annex to the English crown any lands that they might discover on their westward voyages.

John Cabot departed Bristol in May 1497 on the *Matthew*, and on June 24 he sighted land, which was perhaps Cape Breton (northern Nova Scotia),[74] although he believed that he had reached the northern lands of the Great Khan. He is thought to have perished during a second voyage that departed in May 1498. In 1508 his son Sebastian attempted to find a northern route to Asia.

The passage below concerns Sebastian's voyage. It is taken from Peter Martyr d'Anghiera (1457–1526), an Italian priest who spent much of his career in Spain, serving as papal prothonotary, prior of Granada, and from 1511 as chronicler of the newly established Council of the Indies, a position that granted him privileged access to Spanish activity in the New World. His most famous work, *De orbe novo decades*, begins with Columbus's first voyage and treats European expeditions through Magellan, Davila, and Cortés.[75] At the time Peter Martyr published the first edition of this work, Sebastian Cabot was living in Spain and in fact was Peter Martyr's friend and occasional dinner-guest.

According to his twentieth-century English translator, Peter Martyr "handled Latin as a living, not as a dead language," yet his style—"vigorous, terse, vitalised"—was offensive to the increasingly prevalent "cultivated ears of Ciceronian Latinists," and the renowned humanist Antonio de Nebrija (1441–1522) was responsible for adding "polish" to the first edition of *De orbe novo* before it was published in 1516.[76]

Peter Martyr relates Cabot's voyage in the context of his discussion of ocean currents.

Scrutatus est eas,[77] Sebastianus quidam Cabottus, genere Venetus, sed a parentibus in Britanniam insulam tendentibus, uti moris est Venetorum, qui commercii causa terrarum omnium sunt hospites, transportatus paene infans. Duo is sibi navigia propria pecunia in Britannia ipsa instruxit et primo tendens cum hominibus tercentum ad Septentrionem, donec etiam Iulio mense vastas repererit glaciales moles pelago natantes, et lucem fere perpetuam, tellure tamen libera gelu liquefacto.[78] Quare coactus fuit, uti ait, vela vertere et Occidentem sequi, tetenditque tamen ad Meridiem litore sese incurvante, ut Herculei freti latitudinis fere gradus aequarit[79] ad Occidentemque profectus tantum est, ut Cubam insulam a laeva longitudine graduum paene parem habuerit. Is ea litora percurrens quae Bacallaos[80] appellavit, eosdem se reperisse aquarum sed lenes delapsus ad Occidentem ait, quos Castellani Meridionales suas regiones adnavigantes inveniunt, ergo non modo verisimilius, sed necessario concludendum est, vastos inter utramque ignotam hactenus tellurem iacere hiatus,[81] qui viam praebeant aquis ab Oriente cadentibus in Occidentem, quas arbitror impulsu caelorum circulariter agi in gyrum circa terrae globum, non autem Demogorgone[82] anhelante vomi absorberique ut nonnulli senserunt, quod influxu et refluxu forsan assentire daretur. Baccallaos Cabottus ipse terras illas appellavit, eo quod in earum pelago tantam repererit magnorum quorundam piscium, tynnos aemulantium, sic vocatorum ab indigenis, multitudinem, ut etiam illi navigia interdum detardarent. . . Familiarem habeo domi Cabottum ipsum et contubernalem interdum, vocatus namque ex Britannia a Rege nostro Catholico[83] post Enrrici maioris Britanniae Regis mortem[84] concurialis[85] noster est, expectatque indies ut navigia sibi parentur, quibus arcanum hoc naturae latens iam tandem detegatur. Martio mense anni futuri millesimo quingentesimo decimo sexto, puto ad id explorandum discessurum.[86]

Source: *De Orbe Novo Petri Martyris ab Angleria Mediolanensis Protonotarii Caesaris senatoris decades* (Alcalá de Henares: Michael de Eguía, 1530), fol. 46 (3rd decade, chapter 6).

6 Florida (1513)

Although evidence from early maps suggests that the peninsula of Florida may have been known to Europeans since about the year 1500,[87] Spanish interest during the decades following Columbus's voyages was directed primarily to the west and south of the Caribbean islands. The first well-substantiated European landing in Florida is that of Juan Ponce de León (1474–1521).[88] Ponce, who had accompanied Columbus on his second voyage and recently had been deposed as Governor of San Juan del Puerto Rico, received a contract from King Ferdinand (February 23, 1512) to discover and settle the island of Binini (also known as Bimini, Bimine, or Beinini), which was thought to be north of Puerto Rico.

Ponce first sighted Florida somewhere on the upper east coast—most likely between St. Augustine and Jacksonville—on Easter Sunday (March 27) in the year 1513 and he came ashore on April 3. He then turned south and rounded the Keys (which he called Los Martires) and sailed along the Gulf Coast. He landed perhaps near the mouth of the Caloosahatchee River (present-day Ft. Myers), where he briefly skirmished with the Calusa natives, who most likely had been forewarned about the Spanish by Cuban natives seeking refuge in Florida from the growing Spanish presence.[89] After he left Florida Ponce sailed to the Bahamas and attempted to search for Binini, which was thought to possess not only wealth but also, some said, a regenerative spring.

Eight years later, in 1521, Ponce undertook a second and much larger voyage to Florida, but he was mortally wounded, likely near the site of his original Gulf Coast landing, and he died shortly after retreating to Cuba.

Over the next four decades several Spanish expeditions reached Florida—Lucas Vásquez de Ayllón (1526), Pánfilo de Narváez (1528), Hernando de Soto (1539), the Dominican priest Luis Cáncer de Barbastro (1549), and Tristán de Luna (1559–61). Of these, only Luna in

Pensacola was successful in establishing some sort of permanent settlement, but after one month this was beset by a devastating hurricane and it survived for only two years. Not until the late summer of 1565 was a more lasting Spanish settlement established in Florida, at St. Augustine.

The first passage below is taken from the second decade, or book, of Peter Martyr's *De Orbe Novo* (see section 5). Peter Martyr only briefly touches upon Ponce's exploits. Notably, he offers a description of Ponce's failed slave-raiding expedition to the island of Guadaloupe, but he was not yet aware—at least at the time he wrote the initial decades—of Ponce's Florida expeditions. The passage included here refers instead to the infamous fountain of youth, which has been dubbed North America's oldest legend.[90] This passage is, in fact, the "earliest explicit reference to this fountain," yet there is no indication in this first passage that it was in Florida; it was rather said to be located on an island 325 leagues north of Hispaniola named Boiuca or Agnaneo, but in subsequent years this spring became identified with Bimini and Florida, which had themselves become conflated. Thus in the seventh decade of *De Orbe Novo*, Peter Martyr specifically, "and for the first time in print," locates the Fountain of Youth in Florida.[91] The second passage below relates the restoration of an old man who had visited this spring.

The third passage is an excerpt from Francesco Sacchini's five-volume history of the Jesuits, *Historiae Societatis Iesu*. Sacchini (1570–1625) taught humanities and rhetoric in Rome and for many years served as the secretary to the Father General of the Jesuits, Marius Vitelleschi, a résumé that suggests that he was one of the more fluent Latinists of his era.[92] Moreover, by virtue of his secretarial position as well as the early Jesuit involvement in Florida (see section 11), Sacchini had access to numerous first-hand accounts of the initial explorations of Florida. The volume from which this excerpt is taken was written prior to 1622. Here he describes the geography of Florida and the origin of its name.

The fourth Latin passage below is the inscription on Ponce de León's tomb, which is in the cathedral of San Juan Bautista in San Juan, Puerto Rico.

I

Inter quas[93] ad leucas ab Hispaniola quinque ac viginti supra tercentum unam esse insulam fabulantur, qui eam explorarunt ad intima, nomine Boiuca, alias Agnaneo, fonte perenni adeo nobilem, ut eius fontis aqua epota senes reiuvenescant.[94] Nec arbitretur Beatitudo tua[95] hoc dictum iocose aut leviter, ita serio rem hanc per curiam universam ausi sunt spargere, ut populus omnis et ex iis quos virtus aut fortuna secernit a populo, non pauci rem esse veram arbitrentur. Ego vero si quid sentiam interrogaveris, naturae rerum genitrici non me tantum tribuere respondebo, sibique servasse Deum hanc praerogativam pro non minus propria, quam scrutari corda hominum aut privationi dare accessum ad habitum existimo, nisi Colchia forte fabula de renovato Aesone Erythreae Sibyllae fuisse folia crediderimus.[96]

II

De re hac unum dedit exemplum decanus.[97] Lucaium[98] habet familiarem, Andream cognomine barbatum, quod barbatus ipse inter suos imberbes evaserit. Patrem hic habuisse dicitur senecta gravi iam pressum. Ex propinqua Floridae regioni sibi natali insula, fontis eius fama impulsus, et longioris vitae captus amore, praeparatis viatico necessariis, uti ad Puteolana balnea[99] ex urbe vel Neapoli solent nostri valetudinis recuperandae gratia, profectus est ad eius fontis optatos haustus. Ivit, moratus est, lotus et epotus per plures dies cum statutis per balnearios remediis, viriles tulisse domum vires et virilia quaeque exercuisse fertur.

Nupsisseque iterum et filios genuisse, huius rei testes praestat filius e transvectis ab eius patria Lucaia, plures qui virum decrepita fere gravatum, dein florentem et viribus ac robore corporis pollentem se vidisse asserunt.[100]

III

Est Florida provincia perampla, finitima Novae Hispaniae. Qua parte haec nostrum orbem respicit, partibus triginta ab Aequatore in Septentrionem elata,[101] ex eademque boreali regione sinui Mexicano praetenta, Ioannes Pontius Leonius cum e vicinis solvisset insulis, in eam primum salutis anno millesimo quingentesimo duodecimo incidit,[102] quo die victoris Christi ad vitam reditus colebatur. Quod quia Pascha florum Hispani appellant; inde nomen inventae regioni Floridae indiderunt: tanquam felices creandorum ab se coronas Martyrum simul diei, quo inventa est, et nominis auspicio praemonstraret.[103]

IV

Mole sub hac fortis requiescunt ossa Leonis,
Qui vicit factis nomina magna suis.

Sources: I, II *De Orbe Novo Petri Martyris ab Angleria Mediolanensis Protonotarii Caesaris Senatoris Decades* (Alcalá de Henares: Michael de Eguía, 1530), fols. 35, 97 (2nd decade, chapter 10, 7th decade, chapter 7).
III Franciscus Sacchinus, *Historiae Societatis Iesu Pars Tertia sive Borgia* (Rome: Typis Manelfi Manelfii, 1649), 86.
IV Washington Irving, *Voyages and Discoveries of the Companions of Columbus* (London: John Murray, 1831), 305.

7 Verrazzano in New York (1524)

The Florentine navigator Giovanni Verrazzano (*c.* 1485–*c.* 1528) is the first recorded European to enter New York harbor, eighty-five years before Henry Hudson.[104] The first of Verrazzano's three voyages to the New World—he died on the island of Guadeloupe in 1528 during his final one—was sponsored by Italian bankers, French silk merchants, and King François I of France (*r.* 1515–47). He was in search of a route to China.

Departing in January 1524 on the caravel *La Dauphine*, Verrazzano took a more northerly course than Columbus had taken, and about March 20 he sighted land, which was likely south of Cape Fear, North Carolina. Having ventured south along the coast for about fifty leagues in search of a harbor, he turned back north and came ashore where he had initially sighted land. Then he sailed northeast along the Outer Banks of North Carolina, the Delmarva Peninsula, and the coast of New Jersey before anchoring in New York Harbor. According to Verrazzano's letter (in Italian) to King François, the mouth of what would later be called the Hudson was "a very agreeable place between two small but prominent hills."[105] Eventually Verrazzano sailed north as far as Newfoundland and arrived back in France on July 8 of the same year.

The following is taken from a Dutch work written about a century after this voyage by Johannes de Laet, a scholar as well as one of the directors of the Dutch West India Company (see section 16).

Franciscus I Franciae Rex, prosperis Hispanorum ad insulas et Americae continentem expeditionibus permotus, Ioannem Verazzanum Florentinum, cum una navi, qua quinquaginta navales socii vehebantur, ad Septentrionalis Americae partes lustrandas ablegat.

Is anno MDXXIV mense Ianuario ab insulis Canariis

solvens et primo cursum recta in occidentem dirigens, aura ab oriente prospere afflante, viginti quinque dierum spatio, circiter quingentas leucas enavigavit; horrenda dein tempestas illum supra modum afflixit; qua remittente, cursum nonnihil versus Septentrionem flexit et post totidem dierum navigationem, novas conspexit terras, ad latitudinem triginta quattuor graduum ab aequatore versus Arctum,[106] litoribus inter Austrum et Septentriones productis . . .

Centum circiter milliaria (ut ipsi visum) ab hoc loco pulcherrimus amnis[107] in oceanum effluebat, a quo rursus ora quinquaginta milliaria versus ortum convertebatur, donec ad insulam quandam perventum esset, triangulari forma, quae decem milliaria a continenti videbatur disiuncta, et in nemorosa iuga consurgebat, quam *Claudiam* appellarunt.[108]

Porro quindecim ab hac milliaria provecti portum subierunt ad altitudinem unius et quadraginta graduum et XL scrupulorum[109] cuius fauces austro expositae, medium milliare patebant, intus lateribus utrimque recedentibus in modum freti, paene viginti milliaria ambitu suo capit et versus boream ad duodecim milliaria in longitudinem porrigitur, aliquot minores insulas arboriferas et mire delectabiles interluens. Ab accolis satis humaniter hic sunt accepti: Regulus illorum cervina pelle induebatur, aes ipsis notum erat et in pretio.

Hinc ora, editior multo, ad orientem flectebatur paene quinquaginta milliaria:[110] rursusque versus Arctum recedebat, sed hic populus vere barbarus et immanis moribus, nullis rationibus ad mutuum congressum aut colloquium adduci poterat: Ursorum, lutrarum et phocarum pellibus tecti, vitam piscibus et ferina tolerare visi, nulla frumenti notitia, nulla serendi cura: ipsumque solum illorum quae seruntur maligne patiens, immanes ubique saltus et montes, et aeris aliorumque metallorum haud obscura indicia.

Source: Johannes de Laet, *Novus Orbis seu descriptionis Indiae occidentalis Libri XVIII* (Leiden: Elsevier, 1633), 64.

8 The Rights of Native Americans (1537)

On at least one occasion during his first voyage Columbus curtailed the maltreatment of indigenous peoples in Hispaniola by some members of his crew, but he himself nevertheless seized perhaps two dozen natives and brought them back to Spain (see section 2).

From the beginning, the practice of abducting, and enslaving, indigenous peoples in the New World met with opposition, notably from Queen Isabella. The Spanish sovereigns issued an edict in 1500 that prohibited the enslavement of Native Americans, yet the three exceptions that were subsequently given were much exploited.[111] Opposition to the increasingly widespread slave-raids in the Caribbean also came from members of the Dominican Order, notably from Bartolomé de las Casas (1484–1566), who in 1550–51 at Valladolid debated the humanist Juan Ginés de Sepúlveda (1494–1573) concerning the rights of Native Americans and the justice of the conquest of the Americas. But Las Casas was preceded by the Dominican Antonio de Montesinos (d. 1545), who preached an emphatic anti-slavery sermon on the fourth Sunday of Advent in 1511 on the island of Hispaniola.

It was the advocacy of two other Dominicans, Bernardino de Minaya de Paz (*c.* 1485–*c.* 1565) and Bishop Julián Garcés of Tlaxcala (New Spain), that seems to have prompted Pope Paul III (*r.* 1534–49) to issue the bull *Sublimis Deus* (June 2, 1537), which is excerpted below. This document stipulates that indigenous peoples are not to be enslaved or deprived of their possessions. Moreover, in declaring Native Americans capable of receiving the Christian faith, the Bull underscores that they are rational human beings and therefore not to be coerced but rather invited to the Christian faith by means of word and example.[112] Those who regard Native Americans as "muta animalia" are said to be henchmen ("satelites") of the devil.

Yet as recent works have shown, the enslavement of Native Americans was pervasive and lucrative, and it perdured for centuries.[113] According to one estimate, between 2.5 and 5 million Native Americans were enslaved between Columbus's arrival and the end of the nineteenth century.[114]

Paulus Papa tertius universis Christi fidelibus praesentes litteras inspecturis salutem et Apostolicam benedictionem.

Nos igitur, qui eiusdem Domini Nostri vices, licet immeriti, gerimus in terris, et oves gregis sui nobis commissas, quae extra eius ovile sunt, ad ipsum ovile toto nixu exquirimus. Attendentes Indos ipsos, ut pote veros homines, non solum Christianae Fidei capaces existere, sed ut nobis innotuit, ad fidem ipsam promptissime currere. Ac volentes super his congruis remediis providere, praedictos Indos et omnes alias gentes ad notitiam Christianorum imposterum deventuras, licet extra Fidem Christi existant sua libertate ac rerum suarum dominio privatos, seu privandos non esse. Immo libertate et dominio huiusmodi, uti et potiri, et gaudere, libere et licite posse, nec in servitutem redigi debere. Ac si secus fieri contigerit irritum et innane. Ipsosque Indos et alias gentes verbi Dei praedicatione et exemplo bonae vitae ad dictam Fidem Christi invitandos fore . . . decernimus et declaramus.

Datum Romae Anno Domini millesimo quingentesimo trigesimo septimo. Quarto nonas Iunii Pontificatus nostri, Anno tertio.

Source: Francis A. MacNutt, *Bartholomew de las Casas: His Life, Apostolate, and Writings* (Cleveland: Arthur H. Clark, 1909), 426, 428, 430.

9 Coronado in Kansas (1541)

Early Spanish interest in northern Mexico was particularly piqued by two episodes, the extraordinary adventure of Álvar Núñez Cabeza de Vaca (d. 1559), who after reaching Florida with Pánfilo de Narváez's expedition, had wandered for several years across sea and land all the way into Mexico, and the report of the Franciscan Friar Marcos de Niza (d. 1558), who told of a northern region called Cíbola that contained seven cities of gold.

Eager to ascertain the truth of these claims, the first Viceroy of New Spain, Antonio de Mendoza (*r.* 1535–50), commissioned Francisco Vásquez de Coronado (1510–54) to undertake an expedition north.[115] In February 1540 Coronado set out from Nueva Galicia in command of a massive contingent of Europeans, Native Americans, and some Africans. He was also accompanied by some Franciscan friars.[116] When Coronado reached Háwikuh, the first of the famous cities of Cíbola (south of Gallup, New Mexico), he was disappointed to discover that it was not as large as he had expected. Coronado subdued the pueblo and made this the basis of several exploratory missions that he despatched to Arizona and northern New Mexico.

The following year, enticed by reports of another wealthy land to the east, Coronado crossed the panhandle of Texas and Oklahoma and reached the region of Quivira, which is thought to have been in central Kansas (near Salina), but he was again disappointed, and he belatedly discovered that the tale of wealthy Quivira was a ruse to lure him away from Pueblo settlements in New Mexico. In the spring of 1542 Coronado set out to return to Mexico, but the friars Luis de Úbeda (a brother) and Juan de Padilla (a priest) remained behind to evangelize, the former in Cicuique (San Miguel County, New Mexico), the latter back in Quivira, where he was killed.

According to the chronicler Castañeda de Nájera, who was present on the expedition, these early explorers of

Quivira were like Hercules in southern Spain, paving the way for Julius Caesar to follow. In the same way, Castañeda anticipated, others would eventually follow Coronado into the Great Plains.[117]

The following is taken from the last volume of a massive history of the Franciscan order, *Annales Minorum*, composed by the prolific Irish-born friar Luke Wadding (1588–1657).[118] The *Annales* treats the history of the Franciscans until the year 1540. The excerpt given here, then, was one of the last to be recorded.

Anno Christi 1540; Caroli V Imper. Occid. Anno 22; Pauli III anno 6; Religionis Minorum Anno 333.[119]

Prodierat, uti diximus anno praeterito,[120] Franciscus Vasquez Coronado, opulentissimam Cibolae provinciam,[121] quam primus Frater Marcus Nicenus Minorita[122] explorandam edocuit, subiugaturus, et sacrorum curatores comites adhibuit Ioannem de Padilla Sacerdotem, ac Ludovicum de Escalona sanctissimae vitae laicum,[123] Minoritas, provinciae Baeticae alumnos; quorum primus multum fructum attulit in nova Hispania, dum Guardianum ageret in conventu Tulantzingico, et deinde in coenobio Sapotlanensi.[124] Cum autem ad Quivirae provinciam aeris temperie, aquarum bonitate, camporum amoenitate laudatissimam, a Cibola leucas ducentas versus Ortum divergentem, pervenisset, et ultra paulisper ad Azuteas proficisceretur, uxoris revisendae cupidus,[125] rediit ad novam Galetiam unde profectus est, relicto Padilla, et socio apud Azuteas, qui populi conversioni, et martyrio subeundo valde inhiabant. Ubi illic, et in provincia Tiguez[126] aliquantulum cum iuvenculo interprete, et aliquot barbaris Mechuanis, itemque Andrea de Campo Lusitano substitissent, et nonnihil profecissent, ac denuo Quiviram reverterentur, in itinere ab indigenis fuerunt trucidati, illamque regionem suo sanguine primi consecrarunt.[127] Tanta fuit in veneratione apud Coronadum militiae Praefectum Ludovicus, ut militibus praeceperit, quotiescumque eius nomen audirent, toties capite inclinato, eius vitae sanctitatem venerarentur.

Source: Luke Wadding, *Annales Minorum*, vol. 8 (Rome: Peter Collins, 1654), 656.

10 Hunting and Sport in Florida (1565)

The French Admiral Gaspard de Coligny (1519–72) made two attempts to establish an overseas colony for French Huguenots, first in Brazil (1555) and then along the southeastern coast of the present-day United States (1562). In addition to religious motives, the expedition to Florida had strategic objectives. French settlements would encroach upon Spain's empire and provide a base for attacks upon Spanish shipping.

On May 1, 1562, following a two month voyage, three ships and 150 men under the command of Capt. Jean Ribault (1520–65) made landfall near the mouth of the St. John's River (modern-day Jacksonville, Florida), which they called River May. To indicate French dominion, they erected two stone markers. Having sailed north to Port Royal (present-day Parris Island, South Carolina), Ribault established Charlesfort, but after one year this was abandoned due to lack of food. On June 22, 1564 René de Laudonnière (*c.* 1529–82) led another group of Huguenots to the mouth of the St. John's, where he established Ft. Caroline. In two battles in the fall of 1565 Pedro Menéndez de Avilés (see section 6) seized this fort and captured and killed most of the French inhabitants.[128]

Among the survivors of Menéndez's attack was the court artist Jacques LeMoyne de Morgues (*c.* 1533–88), who subsequently wrote and illustrated an account of the French settlement, which was published, with engravings of LeMoyne's drawings, by Theodore DeBry (1528–98). The images as well as the text from this volume were influential in shaping European consciousness of North America. The images, in particular, were "types" used by artists and illustrators for well over a century,[129] although scholars today are cautious about accepting them as accurate depictions. The following selections describe two customs of the Timucua people.

Cervorum venatio

Industria ad cervos capiendos utuntur Indi, numquam a nobis ante conspecta: maximorum quos capere potuerunt cervorum pelles ita corpori applicare norunt, caput suo capiti accommodantes, ut per oculorum foramina, tamquam per larvam, conspicere possint; ita compti quam proxime possunt, ad cervos nihil metuentes accedunt; prius tempore observato, quo cervi ad flumen bibendi causa eunt; eos, arcum et sagittam manu tenentes, facile figere possunt, cum frequentes sint admodum in ea regione: arboris tamen cortice sinistrum bracchium muniunt, ne ab arcus nervo laedantur a natura ita edocti. Pelles vero cervis detractas, non chalybe, sed conchis adeo accurate parare norunt, ut mirum sit, nec quemquam in universa Europa inveniri existimo, qui tanta arte eas parare queat.

Iuventutis exercitia

Apud illos cursu adulescentes exercentur, constituto inter ipsos certo praemio, quod, qui diutius cursuram continuare potest, aufert: arcu etiam frequenter exercentur. Deinde pila ludunt in hunc modum: in media area praefigitur arbor octo aut novem orgyias[130] alta, et summo fastigio quadrum quoddam e viminibus contextum sustinens, quod qui pila se exercendo tetigerit, praemio decoratur. Delectantur praeterea venationibus et piscationibus.[131]

Source: Theodore de Bry and Jacques Le Moyne, *Indorum Floridam Provinciam Inhabitantium Eicones* (Frankfort: Joannis Wechel, 1591), plates 25, 36.[132]

11 Virginia Before Jamestown: A Spanish Jesuit Mission (1570)

In 1565 the successful sea-captain Pedro Menéndez de Avilés (1519–74) received from King Philip II of Spain the title *Adelantado* (Governor) of La Florida. At the time, La Florida extended well beyond today's peninsula and panhandle to include a vast and undefined expanse of land stretching west towards Mexico and north towards Newfoundland. As a basis for Spanish settlement and to defend Spanish ships traveling back to Europe along the Gulf Stream, Menéndez established a string of coastal forts from Tampa around the peninsula to present-day South Carolina, and he intended to station priests in each of these locations in order to minister to Spanish settlers and to evangelize indigenous tribes. Initially he sought priests from the Dominican order, but later he secured the consent of the Jesuits to send missionaries.

The Jesuit experience in La Florida lasted only six years, and it was bloody.[133] Of the approximately twenty Jesuits who spent time there between 1566 and 1572, nine were killed and a tenth died of natural causes. Only a few weeks after he came ashore in September 1566, Fr. Pedro Martínez, the first superior of the Florida mission, was killed near present-day Jacksonville by members of Saturiwa's tribe. His two companions, Fr. Juan Rogel and Br. Francisco Villareal, attempted without much success to establish missions in the southwest (near present-day Ft. Myers) and in Tequesta (present-day Miami), while they awaited reinforcements from Spain.

In the late summer of 1570, frustrated not only with the slow progress of evangelization but also by repeated conflict with Menéndez and Spanish soldiers, the new Vice-Provincial of the Florida mission, Fr. Juan Bautista Segura (1529–71), opted to initiate a mission far to the north, in a region known as Ajacán, only a few miles from the later English settlement at Jamestown. This region was not altogether unknown to the Spanish.

At one time, in fact, Menéndez had considered establishing the capital of La Florida near the Chesapeake Bay (which the Spanish named Bahía de Santa María). Moreover, in 1561 a Spanish vessel that had been blown off course ended up in the Chesapeake, and the sailors either abducted or took with his or his family's consent a native of the region named Paquiquineo, who was brought to Spain and presented before the King. The following year Paquiquineo was taken to Mexico where he became sick and received baptism, having taken the name Luís after the Viceroy (Luís de Velasco). Now several years later Don Luis, as the Spanish called him, offered to assist the Jesuits in the evangelization of his tribe in Ajacán, and he accompanied Segura and seven other Jesuits on this mission.[134] Also accompanying the Jesuits was a young man named Alonso Olmos, the son of settlers of Santa Elena (present-day Parris Island), who was to serve Mass and assist in constructing the mission.

When the Jesuits arrived in Ajacán in September of 1570, they built a small house with a chapel, and they attempted to evangelize the neighboring peoples. Yet the region was in the grip of a famine, and the Jesuits did not receive the expected assistance from Don Luis, who abandoned them and returned to live among his tribe. Repeated attempts to persuade him to return met with failure. In early February 1571, Don Luis and some companions ambushed the Jesuits on multiple occasions, killing them all. The lone survivor was Alonso, who was protected by a neighboring chief. In August 1572 Alonso was rescued by Menéndez and other Jesuits who sailed to the Chesapeake to ascertain what had happened to the mission.

Most of the early sources about this event are in Spanish, but the first text below is a notable exception, and it has been overlooked by recent historiography.[135] It is an excerpt from the *Litterae Annuae*, the annual report that Jesuit missions sent back to Rome. These missives were often redacted, read aloud in Jesuit houses, and published, and their Latinity is usually quite elevated. This particular excerpt comes from the 1573 letter sent by the Jesuits from their new mission in Mexico. This letter, then, provides an excellent example of the international (transatlantic and hemispheric) use of Latin during this era: Jesuits in Mexico communicating to Rome information that they had received about events that recently transpired in the Chesapeake region.

The remaining selections below are poems by the Belgian-born Jesuit Gerardus Montanus (1584–1632), who taught eloquence in Madrid and published works of rhetoric and poetry.[136] These poems, which commemorate two of the Jesuits who died in Ajacán, are taken from his *Centuria Epigrammatum in Martyres Societatis Iesu.* In keeping with early precedent (viz., St. Ambrose, Pope St. Damasus, Prudentius), religious congregations such as the Jesuits promoted Latin martyrial poetry. Also in keeping with early precedent these same communities maintained detailed and often eloquent menologies or martyrologies, i.e., books that commemorated deceased community members whose lives or deaths were considered edifying. Some of this material involves events that transpired within the future United States.[137]

I

De nostris,[138] qui mortem initio ab Indis passi sunt ea in regione, quae ad septentriones vergens Florida dicitur, haec liquidius intelleximus; fuisse quippe Indum quendam, cui nomen Ludovicus, quem interpretem, pluresque civitates esse atque oppida in Florida mentientem, Hispani milites sequerentur.[139] Ab his, cum liberius viverent, quam promulgatio evangelii postularet, sacerdotem[140] nostrosque recessisse, et in regionem interiorem cum interprete solos penetrasse[141] quem inde quindecim passuum millibus ad domesticos suos[142] digressum, cum nostros per binos socios accessisset, hos ab interprete statim, postera deinde die ante lucem sacerdotem reliquosque nec opinantes occisos.[143] Cumque qui cum interprete venerant, sacris inter sese vestibus distributis calice ad ebrietatem abuterentur, duos tresve ad arcam nostrorum accessisse ut raperent si quid reperissent, sed imaginem Crucifixi conspicatos repente mortuos cecidisse.[144] Reliquos perterritos nec appropinquare quidem ad arcam ausos. Haec retulit unus[145] e novem in quem ut natu minorem cruentas manus non iniecere. Quae res non exiguam spem facit fore ut fuso illorum sanguine frigida efferae gentis corda caelestem ignem aliquando concipiant, aliorumque conversionem pariant.

II

Ioanni Baptistae Segurae in Florida passo.

Te quoque purpureis cinctum Segura coronis
    Candida sublimem tollit in astra fides.
Te pudor, et niveo comitatur gratia vultu,
    Te charis et pietas, te decor omnis amat.
Sis violis cumulata licet, sis Florida acanthis,
    Martyre floridior non potes esse tuo.

Aloysso Quiros, cuius arculam scrutantes barbari et cilicium crucemque intuentes stupore mortui sunt.[146]

Tegmina vulnificis dum barbarus hispida setis,
    Et pugilum exuvias, et flagra saeva legit.
Et non paestanis[147] detexta Rosaria sertis,
    Et Crucis haud ullas iam nisi cernit opes.
Haeret hians, lethoque cadens miratur oborto.
    Semideosque homines, semihominesque deos.

Sources: I Felix Zubillaga, *Monumenta Mexicana*, vol. 1 *(1570–1580)* (Rome: Monumenta Historica Societatis Iesu, 1956), 94. I have altered punctuation and orthography on the basis of my personal inspection of the digitized manuscripts of this text, which are preserved in Archivum Romanum Societatis Iesu.
II Gerardus Montanus, *Centuria Epigrammatum in Martyres Societatis Iesu* (Madrid: Melchior Sanchez, 1645), 205 (#12, 13).

12 Sir Francis Drake in California and Florida (1579, 1586)

After Ferdinand Magellan (and his successor Elcano), the next voyager to circumnavigate the globe was Sir Francis Drake (c. 1540–96). Passing through the straits of Magellan on the *Golden Hind*, Drake entered the Pacific and raided Spanish towns along the coasts of Chile, Peru, and Mexico. He continued north along the coast of present-day California and perhaps beyond, until he turned west in late July 1579 and sailed across the Pacific. He arrived back in Plymouth Harbor in September 1580, having been gone for more than thirty-three months.

The exact location of Drake's landing on the upper west coast of the United States has long been a matter of dispute. Some have suspected that the English intentionally obfuscated their itineraries so as to induce anxiety among the Spanish, who considered the Pacific to be their sea—"a Spanish lake"[148]—and who feared that the English presence in the Pacific would threaten the security of their recently-discovered trade route with the Philippines. Rumors even arose that Drake had discovered the western access to the famed Northwest passage. Drake's voyage was one of the factors that prompted the Spanish to seek settlements in Alta California.

In 1875 a geographer identified a bay thirty miles north of San Francisco as Drake's likely landing spot, and today this remains the conventional, though not univerally accepted opinion.[149] In October 2012 the United States Department of the Interior designated this body of water, known as Drake's Bay, as a National Historic Landmark.

Much of the uncertainty about Drake's voyage and about his landing spot is due to the absence of original accounts of the voyage. His journal is not extant, and an early account published by Richard Hakluyt is thought to contain propaganda.[150] The Latin text printed here, published by Theodore De Bry, is from a translation made by Gotthard Arthus of a Dutch text.

Five years later, in September 1585, Drake set out from Plymouth on a larger expedition, containing, according to Walter Bigges, one of Drake's captains, twenty-five ships and some 2500 men. Over several months Drake captured and raided Spanish towns in the Cape Verde Islands, South America and the West Indies, and in June of 1586 he besieged St. Augustine, burning the town (which at the time had about 300 inhabitants) as well as the fort and destroying the nearby fields.[151] The English entrance into the fort at St. Augustine is the subject of the second passage below, which is taken from a text published in Leiden in 1588 that was based upon an account of this voyage written by Bigges and continued by another member of the expedition following Bigges's death in Cartagena.[152] Following the siege of St. Augustine, Drake sailed north in search of Santa Elena, and in early June he came ashore and rescued General Ralph Lane and the remnants of the Roanoke colony.

I

Quinta Iunii, cum esset sub 42 gradu versus polum arcticum,[153] eiusmodi frigus expertus est, ut socii ipsius tolerare id amplius non possent. Quare terram aliquam investigare ibique appellere cogebatur. Prima ergo quam conspexit regio ita nivibus obruta erat, ut navibus egredi non luberet. Progressus igitur ulterius sub 38 gradum lineae pervenit, ibi pulchrum et amoenissimum sinum maris ingressus anchoras eiecit.[154] Quo facto statim ad eum accolae illius regionis accelerarunt, aedes horum proxime ad litora extructae erant. Hi Ducem suis muneribus afficiebant, et visis pulcherrimis atque pretiosissimis istis rebus, quas Draco et socii secum attulerant, ultra modum commirati sunt . . .

Cum deinde populus omnis ab eo discessisset, Draco cum sociis suis in terram longius exspatiatus, ferarum maximum numerum invenit, inprimisque cervos quasi mille ubique congregatos. Tota vero regio cuniculis abundabat, qui ex utraque menti parte sacculum gestabant, quo cibum suum sibi colligebant. Pelles horum animalculorum apud ipsos sunt in maximo pretio, ea de causa quod Regi vestes praebeant. Insulam hunc [sic] Draco Novam Albionem vocabat,[155] ob scopulos albos, et quia aliquam cum Anglia, quae olim Albion dicta fuit, conformitatem habeat. Hoc in loco vix glebam aliquam attinges, quae non aliquid auri aut argenti admixtum habeat. In eius autem rei memoriam, quod ibi fuisset, ipsique datum esset ius et titulus imperii nomine Reginae suae, in portu quodam monumentum quoddam argenteum extruxit, cui nomen Reginae, diem adventus et voluntariam spontaneamque illam oblationem huius regni insculpsit. In pede eius dimidium solidum sive assem Anglicanum, una cum Reginae pictura et insigniis adfigebat. In basi suo nomine asscripto.[156] Hispanos in hanc regionem unquam penetrasse, verosimile non est.

II

Sic iam vix milliare integrum progressi, propugnaculum quoddam nuper ab Hispanis extructum ad alteram amnis ripam, indeque milliari altero distans oppidum moenibus nullis munitum, aedificiisque ligneis temere constructum, in conspectu habuimus.[157] Hic tormenta nostra ad disiciendum propugnaculum paravimus, unumque ex iis ante vesperam e regione eiusdem collocavimus. Primus globus ab ipso Vicario Generali in vexillum hostium emissus fuit, qui id medium transvolavit: quemadmodum e Gallo quodam qui ab illis ibi aliquandiu in carcere detentus fuerat,[158] post intelleximus. Tormentum deinde alterum in inferiorem propugnaculi partem, quae e tigno ligneo erat, direximus. Eadem illa nocte Vicarius Generalis cum quattuor vexillis militum flumen traicere, suosque ibi loco fossis undique munito tam vicinos propugnaculo ipsi, ut ad id inde sclopetarii nostri facile pertingere, et quemcumque caput ibi altius erigentem percellere possent, collocare; item tormenta etiam sua in hostes statim dirigenda eo transvehere decreverat: sed cum navales socii ad ducendas fossas praesto non essent; negotium illud omne in proximam noctem delatum fuit. . .

Quorum neminem, ut in terram descendentes propugnaculum statim intravimus, post ibi offendimus. Muri autem huiusce propugnaculi e malis navalibus trabibusque ligneis aliis, in modum Palissadorum (ita hodie genus quoddam loci muniti vocamus) constructi: fossae vero quae extra eos, necdum ad finem omnino perductae erant, quas, ut et propugnaculi eiusdem partes alias, spatio quattuor mensium ante nostrum adventum, perficere non potuerant. Et idcirco id diutius tenere, nostris adventantibus, aut defendere non poterant.[159] Quod etiam ideo non temere ab illis desertum fuisse, existimandum est: quia praeterquam quod facile expugnari, haud difficulter etiam incendi potuisset. Tormenta ibi, quattuordecim numero, super aggeres e truncis pineis sibi invicem superpositis et in modum rotae connexis, terrae aliquam multo hic illic intersperso, collocata erant.[160] Arca etiam adhuc clausa in qua pecuniae Regiae, de qua stipendia militibus illic numerari consueverant, duo millia librarum Sterlinarum nostratium erant, reperta ibi nobis fuit.[161]

Propugnaculo igitur Sancti Ioannis (ita id vocabant) ad eum modum occupato, oppidum quoque ipsum adire tentavimus.

Sources: I Theodore De Bry, ed., *Americae Pars VIII* (Frankfort: M. Becker, 1599), 11–12, 13.[162]
II Walter Bigges, *Expeditio Francisci Draki Equitis Angli in Indias Occidentales Anno MDLXXXV* (Leiden: Fr. Raphelengium, 1588), 17–19.[163]

13 New Mexico (1582)

In June 1581, about four decades after Coronado's expedition to Quivira (see section 9), the Franciscan Agustín Rodríguez, led a party north from Chihuahua along the Conchos and Rio Grande Rivers up into New Mexico, as far as Santa Fé and Taos. This has been dubbed "The Second Spanish Expedition to New Mexico."[164] In addition to Rodríguez, a native of Niebla (Spain) who had already spent time among the Chichimeca people, and several soldiers who were commanded by Capt. Francisco Sánchez (also known as Chamuscado), the party included the friars Francisco López and Juan de Santa María as well as nearly twenty Native Americans. The Franciscans's objective was to establish missions in the north. Some Spaniards, however, saw in these northern regions a labor-source for the rich silver mines of northern Chihuahua. In New Mexico they encountered the Piro and Tigua peoples, distinguished by elaborate dwellings and clothing as well as advanced agricultural practices.

Eventually all three friars died on this expedition. Fray Santa María decided to return to Mexico and was killed en route, in mid-September 1581. The other two friars were killed by some of the Tigua in early 1582 when they opted to remain behind in New Mexico rather than return to Santa Bárbara with Capt. Sánchez. A party initially sent out under Antonio de Espejo to rescue them—before all were known definitively to be dead—led to further exploration eastward into the Great Plains and westward into Arizona. The following is an account of the death of Fray Santa María written by Francisco Gonzaga, who was elected Minister General of the Franciscans in 1579.[165]

Praeterea anno Domini 1580, frater Augustinus Rodriguez, qui a Provincia Sancti Evangelii[166] erat valde remotus, ac per aliquot annos in regione Zacatecarum, inter Indos Chichimecas[167] peregrinatus fuerat,[168] zelo salutis animarum actus in pium conversionis barbarorum illorum infidelium opus ad ipsam Provinciam perveniens, ex eadem fratres quandoque assumpsit, ut illuc rediret. Quippe qui fervens spiritu et animarum conversionem anhelans indagare explorareque studuit an in regione, quae ulterius atque intimius Aquilonem versus extenditur, aliqui Indorum populi reperirentur. Idque quamplurimis diebus perquirens, gentesque innumeras plebeiosque multos turbidos atque confusos reperiens, Mexicum adiit ut pro eorum conversione fratres secum adduceret.[169] Cum eo igitur frater Franciscus Lopetius et frater Ioannes a Sancta Maria sacerdotes atque Minoritico in conventu Mexicano sacrae Theologiae studiis incumbentes profecti, sui itineris socios 12 milites Hispanos habuere.[170] Praedictus autem frater Franciscus ceteris fratribus praeerat. Qui animarum zelo per montana loca de Zacatecas transeuntes, atque a civitate Mexico Aquilonem versus viae stadia quadringenta ambulantes, ad maximam tandem Indorum multitudinem pervenerunt, hoc est ad distinctos quadraginta sive quinquaginta populos circa sex milia domorum inhabitantes regionemque seu provinciam illam novum Mexicum nominarunt.[171] Illi autem populi fratres ipsos benigne susceperunt, de eorumque adventu gratulati sunt.

At ubi frater Ioannes a Sancta Maria hac naturali bonitate et comitate a nova Indorum natione reperta tam humaniter se vidit receptum, nulla eorum obiecta contradictione, immo multa de fratrum praesentia exorta laetitia, secumque reputans gentem ipsam salutari Evangelicae doctrinae praedicatione perfacile fore instruendam, solus Mexicum redire de tantaque Indorum suavitate et humanitate Mexicani conventus fratres certiores facere decrevit, unde et verbi Dei ministros pro recentium populorum conversione ex eis eligere sive assumere secum posset.[172]

Sicque is animarum zelo accensus iter arripuit (diversum tamen a primo) ut Mexicum peteret vixque trium dierum viam confecerat, cum infidelium opera sub dio ex longo itinere fessus dormiens pergravi magnae molis pondere pressus ac respirare nequiens, spiritum emisit iterque divertit in caelum, ubi sui laboris conatus, ardentisque ac pii desiderii praemia plene consequeretur.[173] Hic vero natione Cathalanus robustus iuvenis erat, ac florescente iuventute Religionis habitum in hac Sancti Evangelii Provincia suscepit. Optimae praeterea indolis fuit, semperque religiosis moribus praeditus, spectabilis vitae, magnaeque virtutis indicia praebuit atque incrementa.

Hispani milites, qui fratrum (ut meminimus) comites fuerant, ad propria sunt pariter reversi, Proregi quae gesta fuerant referentes.

Source: Franciscus Gonzaga, *De origine seraphicae religionis franciscanae* (Rome: n.p., 1587), 1278–79.

14 "Nothing but Solitude" in Newfoundland (1583)

A bronze plaque on Water Street in St. John's, Newfoundland commemorates the beginning of Britain's "Overseas Empire." Since the early 1500s the banks off the Newfoundland coast had been a haven for European fishing expeditions, but by the 1570s the English sought to displace their competitors, and on August 5, 1583 Sir Humphrey Gilbert (c. 1537–83) claimed Newfoundland for England. The following are excerpts from a Latin letter written from St. John's, Newfoundland by the Hungarian-born Stephen Parmenius, who was on board Gilbert's expedition.[174]

Born in Buda to Protestant parents, Parmenius (d. 1583) set out sometime after 1579 to finish his education in various European universities, and he came eventually to Christ Church College, Oxford where he became aquainted with a circle of outstanding Latinists devoted to humanistic studies.[175] Parmenius shared a room with Richard Hakluyt the younger (1552–1616), a lecturer in geography, who along with his cousin (also named Richard Hakluyt) was a major proponent and publicist of transatlantic exploration. It was the younger Hakluyt who introduced Parmenius to Gilbert.

Perhaps since the early 1560s Gilbert had had an interest in America, particularly in the possibility of a Northwest passage to Asia, and on June 11, 1578 he was granted a six-year patent by Queen Elizabeth to settle regions not yet held by a European power. By the time Parmenius met him in 1582, Gilbert had already made one aborted attempt to reach America and he was preparing another venture, most likely to the south of Newfoundland, in present-day New England, where he hoped to establish a colony. Hakluyt was publicizing Gilbert's expedition. To assist with this publicity, Parmenius composed a 319-line Latin ἐπιβατικόν, which is well known to Neo-Latinists.[176] Eventually, hoping to commemorate the expedition in a Latin epic, Parmenius opted to come along himself. Yet Parmenius's stay in Newfoundland was brief. On August 20 he departed for England on the *Delight*, and he perished in a shipwreck, most likely on Sable Island or Cape Breton.

Parmenius never composed his Latin epic, but his Latin letter, written from St. John's and addressed to Hakluyt, reached England. The choice of Latin for the letter is not altogether surprising. As Parmenius's modern editors note, even when corresponding with fellow Englishmen, the scholars with whom Parmenius was associated in Oxford and London often wrote in Latin.[177]

Ornatissimo viro,
Magistro Richardo Hakluyto
Oxonii in Collegio aedis Christi,
Artium et Philosophiae Magistro,
amico, et fratri suo.[178]

... Undecimo Iunii ex Anglia revera tandem et serio solvimus, portu et terra apud Plemuthum simul relictis. Classis quinque navibus constabat, maxima, quam frater Amiralii [sic] accommodaverat, ignotum quo consilio, statim tertio die a nobis se subduxit.[179] Reliqui perpetuo coniunctim navigavimus ad 23 Iulii, quo tempore magnis nebulis intercepto aspectu alii aliam viam tenuimus; nobis seorsim prima terra apparuit ad Calendas Augusti, ad gradum circiter 50[180] cum ultra 41 paucis ante diebus descendissemus spe Australium ventorum, qui tamen nobis suo tempore nunquam spiravere. Insula est ea, quam vestri Penguin vocant, ab avium eiusdem nominis multitudine.[181] Nos tamen nec aves vidimus, nec insulam accessimus, ventis alio vocantibus. Ceterum convenimus omnes in eundem locum paulo ante portum in quem communi consilio omnibus veniendum erat, idque intra duas horas, magna Dei benignitate et nostro gaudio. Locus situs est in Newfoundlandia, inter 47 et 48 gradum, divum Ioannem vocant.[182] Ipse Admiralius, propter multitudinem hominum et angustiam navis, paulo afflictiorem comitatum habuit, et iam duos dysentericis doloribus amisit; de ceteris bona spes est. Ex nostris (nam ego me Mauricio Browno vere generoso iuveni me coniunxeram[183]) duo etiam casu quodam submersi sunt.[184] Ceteri salvi et longe firmiores. Ego nunquam sanior. In hunc locum tertio Augusti appulimus;[185] quinto autem ipse Admiralius has regiones in suam et regni Angliae possessionem potestatemque vendicavit, latis quibusdam legibus de religione et obsequio Reginae Angliae.[186] Reficimur hoc tempore paulo hilarius et lautius. Certe enim et qualibus ventis usi simus, et quam fessi esse potuerimus tam longi temporis ratio docuerit, proinde nihil nobis deerit. Nam extra Anglos, 20 circiter naves Lusitanicas et Hispanicas nacti in hoc loco sumus: eae nobis impares non patientur nos esurire. Angli etsi satis firmi, et a nobis tuti, authoritate regii diplomatis omni obsequio et humanitate prosequuntur.

Nunc narrandi erant mores, regiones, et populi. Ceterum quid narrem, mi Hakluyte, quando preater solitudinem nihil video? . . .

Ursi circa tuguria nonnunquam apparent, et conficiuntur: sed albi sunt, ut mihi ex pellibus conicere licuit, et minores quam nostri. . .

Aer in terra mediocriter clarus est; ad orientem supra mare perpetuae nebulae. Et in ipso mari circa Bancum (sic vocant locum ubi quadraginta leucis a terra fundus attingitur, et pisces capi incipiunt) nullus ferme dies absque pluvia. Expeditis nostris necessitatibus in hoc loco, in Austrum (Deo iuvante) progrediemur, tanto indies maiori spe, quo plura de iis quas petimus regionibus commemorantur. Haec de nostris. . .

In Newfundlandia apud portum Sancti Iohannis 6 Augusti 1583.

Stephanus Parmenius Budeius, tuus.

Source: Richard Hakluyt, *The Principall Navigations* (London: George Bishop and Ralph Newberie, 1589), 697–98.

15 The English in Maine (1607)

On April 10, 1606 King James I granted the Virginia Company a charter to establish colonies between 34° and 45° latitude. "For the more speedy accomplishment" of these settlements, the charter directed a London-based group of "knights, gentlemen, merchants, and other adventurers" to settle land between 34° and 41° (roughly from today's North Carolina to New York City) and a Bristol/Exeter/Plymouth group to settle land between 38° and 45° (roughly from today's northern Virginia to the Canadian border). The results of the southern venture in Jamestown are well known, but the northern effort, which gave rise to a settlement in present-day Maine, is little known today.[187]

Known as the Sagadahoc, or Popham, Colony, this short-lived northern settlement was sponsored by a group of well-connected investors and promoters, notably Sir John Popham (*c.* 1531–1607), a former Speaker of the House of Commons and Attorney General who at the time was Lord Chief Justice and acting Lord Chancellor of England. Popham's nephew George (1550–1608) served as the President of the colony, and he commanded the *Gift of God*, one of two ships that departed Plymouth on June 1, 1607.[188] Another ship, the *Mary and John*, was commanded by Raleigh Gilbert, the son of Sir Humphrey Gilbert (see section 14) and the nephew of Sir Walter Raleigh. On board the two ships were about one hundred settlers and crewmembers as well as two Native Americans who had been kidnapped two years earlier in Maine during a prior English attempt at colonization.

Popham's expedition reached the coast of Maine on August 7, 1607, and he settled near the mouth of the Kennebec River.[189] His colony was marred, it has recently been argued, by diplomatic missteps and inexcusable treatment of the native population (primarily the Etchemin tribe), which fostered a residue of mistrust and suspicion. These poor relations, along with the death of the elder Popham, an unusually cold winter, scarcity of food, and the lack of consistent leadership—the younger Popham died in February, and Gilbert planned to return to England to claim his inheritance—led colonists to disband the settlement in September 1608.[190]

The following is a Latin letter written in December 1607 by George Popham and addressed to King James I (*r.* 1603–25).[191] In what has been called "barbarous Latin,"[192] Popham effusively highlights the esteem in which the natives held King James, the favorable prospects for extending the British empire, the commercial opportunities present (involving nuts, spices, wood, berries, and ambergris), and the existence of a sea about seven days journey to the west that would lead to China. In the light of the known difficulties of the settlement at the time, one recent study has described this letter as a "thinly veiled cry for help."[193] The King, for his part, was a fluent Latinist, having been tutored by the celebrated Scottish humanist George Buchanan (1506–82). As the King famously lamented: "They gar me speik latin ar I could speik Scotis."[194]

Ad pedes serenissimi regis sui humillime se proiecit Georgius Pophamus, Praesidens secundae Coloniae Virginiae.

Si divinae Maiestatis Tuae placuerit patientiae, a servo observantissimo ac devotissimo, quamvis indigno, pauca recipere, ab Altitudinis Tuae claritate vel minimum alienare arbitror; quoniam in Dei gloriam, Sublimitatis Vestrae amplitudinem, et Britannorum utilitatem redundare videantur. Peraequum igitur iudicavi Maiestati Tuae notum fieri, quod apud Virginios et Moassones,[195] nullus in orbe terrarum magis admiratur, quam Dominus Iacobus, Britannorum Imperator, propter admirabilem iustitiam ac incredibilem constantiam, quae istarum provinciarum nativis non mediocrem perfert laetitiam; dicentibus insuper nullum esse Deum vere adorandum, praeter illum Domini Iacobi; sub cuius ditione atque imperio libenter militare voluerint. Tahanida, unus ex nativis qui Brittaniae adfuit, Vestras laudes ac virtutes hic illis illustravit.[196]

Quid et quantum, in his negotiis subeundis et illorum animos confirmandis, valerem, eorum sit iudicium, qui domi volutarunt scienter; agnoscens omnes conatus meos perire, cum in comparatione officii debiti erga Principem habeantur. Optima me tenet opinio, Dei gloriam facile in his regionibus elucescere, Vestrae Maiestatis imperium amplificari, et Britannorum rempublicam breviter augmentari.

Quod ad mercimonium attinet, omnes indigenae constanter affirmant, his inesse provinciis nuces amisticas,[197] maciam et cinnamomum; praeterea bitumen, lignum Brasiliae, cochinelam et ambergetie, cum multis aliis magni momenti et valoris; eaque maxima quidem in abundantia.

Insuper affirmative mecum agunt, esse mare aliquod, in adversa vel occidentali huius provinciae parte, non plus[quam] septem dierum itineris spatium a praesidio nostro Sancti Georgii in Sagadahoc, amplum, latum et profundum; cuius terminos prorsus ignorant: quod aliud esse non potest nisi Australe, tendens ad regiones Chinae, quae longe ab his partibus procul dubio esse non possunt.

Si igitur placuerit divinos habere occulos Tuos apertos in subiecto certificationis meae, non dubito quin Celsitudo Vestra absolvet opus Deo gratissimum, magnificentiae Vestrae honorificum, et reipublicae Tuae maxime conducibile, quod ardentissimis precibus vehemeter exopto; et a Deo Optimo, Maximo, contendo ut regis mei Domini Iacobi Maiestatem quam diutissime servet gloriosam. In praesidio Sancti Georgii, in Sagadahoc de Virginia, 13° Decembris 1607.

Servus Vestrae Maiestatis omnimodis devotissimus

Georgius Pophamus

Source: Edward Ballard, *Memorial Volume of the Popham Celebration, August 29, 1862* (Portland, ME: Bailey & Noyes, 1863), 221–23.[198]

16 The Beginning of New Netherland (1609–15)

The English navigator Henry Hudson, working for the Dutch East India Company, sailed into New York harbor in 1609, where Verrazzano had anchored some eighty-five years earlier (section 7). Hudson was searching for a northern passage to Asia. Dutch settlers began to arrive in America the following decade, forming the settlements of Ft. Nassau (Albany) and New Amsterdam (Manhattan). Recent years have seen a renewed interest in this consequential period.[199] An enormous cache of documents from this era, most of which are in Dutch, are currently being translated and published. Yet there are also Latin writings about the Dutch settlements.

The first passage given below, which describes Hudson's voyage, is taken from Book III of *Novus Orbis*, a history of New Netherland, or Novum Belgium, as it was called. The author was Johannes de Laet (1581–1649).[200] Born in Antwerp but reared in Amsterdam, where his Calvinist parents had relocated, De Laet studied philosophy and the classics at Leiden, where he became acquainted with an erudite school of humanists that included the poet and classicist Daniel Heinsius (1580–1655) and the learned historian and linguist Joseph Scaliger (1540–1609). De Laet and Scaliger were lasting friends; eleven letters (in Latin) from Scaliger to De Laet survive, and De Laet was one of the few intimate friends who was invited to take books from Scaliger's library following his death. As for Heinsius—he wrote a Latin ode in honor of De Laet, which formed an epigraph to the *Novus Orbis.*

In addition to his numerous scholarly activities, De Laet was a major fundraiser for the newly-formed Dutch West India Company, and he became one of its directors. In connection with this work, he published *Provisionele Ordere* (1624) and *Nieuwe Wereldt ofte Beschrijvinghe van West-Indiën* (1625). These were the only two of his many learned publications written in Dutch rather than Latin, which, it has been said, suggests that they were principally intended for businessmen rather than scholars. The latter of these works, the first extended description in Dutch of the Americas, was based not only on previously published histories but also on logbooks and De Laet's own conversations with those who had traveled there, and it offers a detailed discussion of geography, complete with maps and illustrations. So successful was this work that a second edition appeared in 1630 and a Latin edition, revised and translated by De Laet himself, was published in 1633, as part of the *Respublica* series sponsored by the Leiden publisher Elsevier.[201] The first passage below contains excerpts from this Latin version.

De Laet never visited the New World, although in 1630 he became a shareholder in two Dutch colonies on either side of the Hudson River (Rensselaerswyck, Laetsburgh). His daughter Johanna lived for more than two decades in New Amsterdam (1653–76).

In the 1640s De Laet became involved in a contentious debate with Hugo Grotius (1583–1645) regarding the origin of Native Americans.[202] Grotius maintained that the peoples of North America had emigrated from Scandinavia during the Middle Ages, while De Laet argued that Europeans—primarily Scythians—had migrated to North America at a much earlier date by means of a land bridge. The second passage below is an excerpt from De Laet's response to Grotius. Although the debate largely involved geography and history, Grotius found fault with De Laet's Latinity, which he mocked in the following epigram: Latius haud Latius satis est: nec scribere cessat/ Latius; ut sileat Latius, est satius.[203]

I

Societas quippe Indiae orientalis, *Henricum Hudsonum* Anglum cum celoce miserat versus aquilonares Americae regiones, ut aditum ad Tartariam et Sinenses aperiret; quod quum frustra tentasset, mutato cursu[204] novam Franciam primum adivit ad altitudinem quattuor et quadraginta graduum et quindecim scrupul.[205] Deinde versus Africum flectens ad altitudinem quadraginta et unius graduum et XLIII scrupul.[206] terram conspexit,[207] et insulam opinatus, *Novam Hollandiam* nominavit, verum partem esse Continentis, atque adeo promontorium *Blancum* sive *Cod*, paulo post patuit, et subducta cursuum ratione ab ipsis iudicatum, promontorium hoc circiter septuaginta et quinque milliaria magis ad occasum remotum esse ab Europaeis regionibus, quam vulgo in hydrographicis tabulis describatur. Porro postquam oram maritimam variis locis conspexissent, inde a trigesimo septimo gradu (hucusque enim ad Austrum inviti an sponte declinaverant) ad quadragesimum[208] usque litorum ductum secuti, sinum amplum adierunt et pone humile et arenosum cornu anchoras fixerunt: duo hic barbari alcium pellibus amicti illos visitarunt et satis humaniter exceperunt: aditaque Continenti, pruna caerulea iam matura ab illis lecta; pulcherrimaeque quercus, populi, aliaeque arbores passim ab ipsis conspectae. Dein sublatis anchoris flumen ipsum subierunt et ad quadragesimum tertium gradum latitudinis septentrionalis ascenderunt,[209] ubi alveus iam angustior et vadosior maiora navigia haud amplius sustinet, indubiis signis patuit numquam ante illum diem Europaeos aut flumen ingressos aut huc usque ascendisse. Quare quum Hudsonus cum celoce sua Amstelodamum sub finem Autumni rediisset, et quae de hoc flumine compererat (quod a barbarorum, qui fauces illius accolunt, nomine *Manhattes* appellaverat) edisseruisset, statim anno MDCX mercatores quidam Amstelodamenses, eo navem cum variis mercibus destinarunt: et diplomate ab Illust. D. Ordinibus confoederati Belgii impetrato, quo ipsis solis hoc flumen et vicinas regiones commerciorum gratia adire permittebatur, sequentibus annis hic cum barbaris commercia exercita fuerunt et a nostris quoque hibernatum: demumque anno MDCXV munimentum auspiciis eorumdem D.D. Ordinum hic structum et praesidio militum aliquandiu servatum, uti paulo post dicemus. Hisce initiis huic Continentis septentrionalis parti NOVI BELGII nomen quaesitum, hodieque perennat. . .

Ideoque vix ullam Americae regionem coloniis e nostro caelo deducendis aptiorem esse existimo; praesertim quum nihil hic desit, quod ad vitam humanam sustentandam necessarium iudicatur, et uberius labore et industria parari possit. Sola armenta atque iumenta hic desiderantur, quae levi negotio huc transportari, et ob pabuli paene ubique copiam commodissime ali possunt. Vites autem si cultura accederet, et vini uberem proventum videntur polliceri.

II

Ego autem ita iudico quum America tam late pateat quam noster orbis, et non minus habitata fuerit, quam aut Europa aut Asia, aut Africa, omnino credendum esse non ab annis quingentis aut mille primum habitari coepisse, sed statim post confusionem linguarum et dispersionem illam familiarum etiam in Americam migratum fuisse: nam alias non video quomodo idonea ratio reddi possit tantae ubique per Americam incolarum multitudinis: et infinitarum ferme diversarum linguarum, et a se invicem et ab Europaeis toto caelo discrepantium. Neque tamen negandum puto, etiam subsequentibus saeculis novos advenas accessisse, sive casu, sive ex instituto in has aut illas partes successerint. Post Christi fidem susceptam id accidisse in animum inducere non possum, quia ne levissima quidem Christianismi vestigia in hisce partibus, usquam inventa. Caret autem ut puto, exemplo, nationem aliquam aut populum post sacra Christiana rite accepta, ita ea denuo obliterasse ut nihil eius esset reliquum. Quod autem aliquae provinciae aut regiones quae aliquando Christianos habuere nunc nullos habeant, id factum quia aut locum mutarunt incolae, aut penitus ab advenis excisi sunt. Deinde imprimis dispiciendum existimo per quas vias intrare potuerint; nam aut terra venerunt aut mari; et quidem mari illis primis temporibus aut dudum post, venire non potuisse arguit navigandi primis illis saeculis imperitia; quare terra potissimum venisse credendum, et diligenter inquirendum, divortium inter Asiam et Americam utrum ullum sit, aut quantillum sit: itemque in illam connexionem terrae Australis cum nova Guinea. Nam aliis partibus nimis vastum divortium facit Oceanus uterque. Ad haec observandae historicorum indicationes, quum de gentium aliquarum migrationibus, seu voluntariis, seu coactis agunt. Coniecturis hic minime fidendum puto, nisi quae valde probabiles sunt.

Sources: I J. De Laet, *Novus Orbis seu descriptionis Indiae occidentalis Libri XVIII* (Leiden: Elsevier, 1633), 70–71, 74–75.
II J. De Laet, *Notae ad dissertationem Hugonis Grotii de Origine Gentium Americanarum* (Paris: William Pele, 1643), 70–72.[210]

17 New France in Maine (1613)

On May 22, 1611, following a four-month voyage, the Jesuit missionaries Pierre Biard (1567–1622) and Enemond Massé (1575–1646) arrived in Acadia, in modern-day Nova Scotia, where a few years earlier Samuel de Champlain (d. 1635) and Pierre de Gua (*c.* 1558–1628) had established the settlement of Port Royal. The Jesuit mission did not last long. Conflict with the new French commander, Jean de Biencourt de Poutrincourt (1557–1615), and his son, Charles de Biencourt (1591/2–1623/4), prompted the Jesuits in May 1613 to relocate across the Bay of Fundy to Saint-Sauveur (Mount Desert Island, Maine).[211]

On July 2, 1613 the new settlement at Saint-Sauveur was besieged unexpectedly by Captain Samuel Argall (1580–1626), who had sailed from Jamestown with a royal commission to evict the French from territory claimed by the English. Argall captured and raided the French ships and invaded the nascent settlement. In the ensuing struggle one Jesuit brother, Gilbert du Thet (c. 1575–1613), was killed. Some of the surviving French settlers, along with Massé, were allowed to return to France. Biard and another Jesuit, Jacques Quentin (1572–1647), were among fifteen prisoners taken to Virginia, where they were ordered to be hanged. Their lives were spared, however, and subsequently they were taken back north in order to supply information to help the English destroy the French settlement of Port Royal. Eventually Biard and Quentin were conveyed back to France, by way of the Azores, Wales, and England, and they were released.

The following extract is from Biard's account of these events, dated May 26, 1614, one month after he had returned to France. It is addressed to the Jesuit General in Rome, Claudio Acquaviva (1543–1615).

Born near Grenoble, Biard had entered the Jesuits in 1583, and following his 1599 ordination he taught in Tournon and then in Lyon, but beginning at least as early as 1602 he wrote repeatedly to the Jesuit General, requesting permission to go to the foreign missions. Biard is one of the major sources for the early history of the Port Royal settlement and for the early Jesuit mission to New France. He is especially known for his lengthy *Relation de la Nouvelle-France* (Lyon 1616). Additionally, more than twenty letters to and from him have survived, some of which are in Latin.[212]

Eramus, ut Vestra Paternitas scit in Nova Francia quattuor omnino e societate, anno superiore 1613.[213] Et quidem tunc primum incipiebamus novam moliri commodo loco habitationem, novam coloniam, etc.[214] Ecce subito nescio quo casu (casus certe fuit, non consilium) iniecti nostrum in litus Angli Virginienses,[215] magno furore navem nostram invadunt, omnibus prope defensoribus in terra occupatis. Pugnatum tamen est aliquandiu, sed necessario facta est non multo post deditio. In certamine duo e gallis occisi,[216] quattuor vulnerati et insuper frater noster Gilbertus Duthet, vulneratus ad mortem fuit. Is postridie inter manus meas religiose expiravit.[217]

Capta navi et rebus omnibus direptis, multum nobis fuit, nobis inquam sacerdotibus et Iesuitis, non occidi. Verum et hoc ipsum non occidi, si solum fuisset, omni nece atrocius erat. Nam quid sane ageremus in locis omnino desertis et incultis rerum omnium nudi et egentes? Sylvatici quidem ad nos clam et de nocte ventitabant,[218] infortunium nostrum complorabant, quae poterant pollicebantur et magno certe animo et fideli. Verum ea erat locorum rerumque conditio ut nusquam nisi mors, aut calamitosior morte miseria occurreret. Et eramus omnino triginta in his angustiis. Una res molliores reddebat Anglos, quod videlicet una e nostris scapha ipsis nequicquam observantibus evaserat;[219] hanc quia fore testem nostrae oppressionis non dubitabant, vitae nostrae parcere cogebantur. Timebant enim talionem et regem nostrum.[220]

Ergo tandem (magnum scilicet beneficium) nobis triginta qui supereramus unam aiunt sese velle scapham relinquere quo per eam circumeamus oram maritimam si quam forte navem gallicam reperiamus quae nos in patriam revehat. Demonstratum est in eam scapham plures quam quindecim ingredi non posse. Verum aliud nihil obtineri potuit, nec de nostris quidem navigiis. Ne morer in hac difficultate sibi quisque ut potuit consuluit: P. Enemundus Massaeus in eam quam dixi scapham ingressus est cum aliis quattuordecim; eique favit Deus uti iam Vestra Paternitas cognovit. Ego ducem anglum adii obtinuique pro me et P. Jacobo Quentino socio meo,[221] itemque pro Joanne Dixon qui admissus erat in societatem[222] et servo item uno[223] ut deveheremur ad insulas vicinas in quibus Angli piscari solent,[224] inibique ut Anglis illis piscatoribus commendaremur. Quo per eos in Angliam delati inde, quod facile est, in Galliam rediremus.

Obtinui hoc quidem inquam verbis, sed verbis fides non fuit. Nos enim, una cum reliquis gallis qui restabamus in universum quindecim detulerunt ipsi recta in suam Virginiam longe ab eo loco in quo capti fueramus leucis facile ducentis quinquaginta. At in Virginia, novum periculum. Etenim qui ibi praeest[225] suspendi nos omnes volebat, sed in primis iesuitas. Sed restitit is qui nos ceperat capitaneus, fidemque datam opposuit. Et valuit tandem vel fides vel regis timor.

Source: Reuben Gold Thwaites, ed., *Jesuit Relations and Allied Documents,* vol. 3 (Cleveland: Burrows Bros., 1898), 4, 6, 8.

18 Maryland (1634)

The English settlements in Maryland arose from the desire of George Calvert (?1580–1632), the Baron of Baltimore, to develop a colony in British North America that was hospitable for Catholics. The first attempt at this was made in 1621 in Newfoundland, but this settlement, named Avalon, was unsuccessful.[226] In June 1632, following Calvert's death, his son Cecil (1606–75) attained a royal charter from Charles I for the colony of Maryland. Unlike earlier English settlements, Maryland was to guarantee freedom of religion: all free men, Catholic as well as Protestant, could vote and hold public office.

The following are excerpts from the *Declaratio Coloniae Domini Baronis de Baltimore in Terra Mariae prope Virginiam* (1633), one of three documents written to promote the Maryland settlement. The author, Andrew White (1578?–1656), was a Jesuit priest who accompanied the initial voyage of the *Ark* and the *Dove* to Maryland, and he ministered there for a little over a decade until he was seized and deported in 1645 by the Puritan Richard Ingle. White, educated in France and Spain, had previously been a professor of theology, Scripture, and Hebrew at universities in Belgium, but his unusually strict devotion to the thought of St. Thomas Aquinas incurred the opprobrium of his colleagues and he was removed from his position. In 1633 White was selected to undertake missionary work in America.

The *Declaratio*, as well as the better known *Relatio Itineris in Marilandiam*,[227] was discovered in the Jesuit archives in Rome in the early 1830s by William McSherry (see section 54), who at the time was Provincial of the Jesuits in Maryland.[228] The text below has been taken from Thomas Hughes's four-volume history of the Jesuits in the mid-Atlantic, which contains numerous Latin documents from the early colonial period.[229]

Provincia est prope coloniam Anglicanam in Virginia, quam honoris causa a Maria coniuge sua,[230] Serenissimus Rex Angliae[231] Terram-Mariae vel Marylandiam voluit appellari. Hanc nuper provinciam idem Serenissimus rex pro sua magnificentia, mense Iunio 1632, Domino Baroni de Baltamore et heredibus suis in perpetuum donavit; quam donationem publico totius regni sigillo munivit ac ratam habuit.[232] Idcirco illustrissimus Baro iam statuit in eam regionem coloniam ducere, primo et praecipue ut in eandem ac loca finitima lucem evangelii ac veritatis invehat, quo nullam hactenus veri Dei notitiam affulsisse compertum est; tum etiam eo consilio ut socii omnes itinerum ac laborum in partem quaestus et honoris vocentur, regisque imperium latius propagetur. . .

Consilium primum ac summum Illustrissimi Baronis est, quod aliorum etiam qui in eadem navi fuerint esse debet, ut in terra tam frugifera non tam frugum atque arborum quam religionis ac pietatis semina spargantur. Consilium enimvero dignum christianis, dignum angelis, dignum Anglis,[233] quo nobilius nullum aut gloriosius tot antiquis Anglia victoriis nobilitata suscepit. Ecce regiones sunt albae ad messem, paratae ad evangelii semen gremio fructifero recipiendum. Indi ipsi mittunt undique nuntios ad conquirendos idoneos homines qui incolas doctrina salutari instruant et sacro fonte regenerent.

In confesso est situm regionis optimum esse ac commodissimum, quippe quae ad 38 vel 40 gradum in aquilonem porrigitur, situ loci Hispali, Siciliae, Hierusalem[234] et optimis Arabiae Felicis plagis et Chinae haud absimilis. Aer serenus ac mitis, nec ardoribus Floridae vel antiquae Virgineae infestus, nec Novae Angliae frigoribus exustus, sed mediam quandam inter utramque temperiem obtinet,[235] utriusque fruitur bonis ac mala nescit. Ab oriente oceano alluitur, ab ocidente infinito prope continenti obiacet, qui in mare Chinense protenditur. Duo aestuaria habet sane magna; utrinque sinus piscium fecundissimi. Alterum cui nomen Chesa-peack 12000 passuum latum binisque interfusum regionibus, ab austro centum et sexaginta millia passuum in aquilonem volvitur;[236] magnarum capax navium, discretum variis iis amplis ac pascuosis insulis, in quibus piscium quos Largos vocant copiosa piscatio; alterum appellant Pilawase,[237] ubi integro anno asellorum piscatio est,[238] sed non adeo commoda, nisi mensibus tantum frigidioribus, nam calidiores sale condiri vetant.

Source: Thomas Hughes, *History of the Society of Jesus in North America, Colonial and Federal: Documents,* vol. 1, part 1 (London: Longmans, Green, 1908), 145, 146, 147.[239]

19 Latin or French in New York? (1643)

The Jesuit priest Isaac Jogues (1607–46), a native of Orléans (France), was an early missionary to the Hurons, who gave him the name Ondessonk (Bird of Prey).[240] While returning from a mission to Québec in August 1642, Jogues, along with a band of Huron natives and French companions, was ambushed by the Iroquois a day's journey outside of Trois Rivières. He was held captive in Ossernenon, the present-day town of Auriesville, New York, for more than a year, suffering various tortures, including running the gauntlet, having his fingernails torn off, and having his fingers gnawed and mutilated. Eventually he escaped to Manhattan with the help of the Dutch and returned to France, arriving on Christmas Day of 1643, unrecognizable to his fellow Jesuits in Rennes. That spring he opted to return to New France, having received an indult from the Pope enabling him to celebrate Mass with mutilated fingers. He was killed with a tomahawk by the Iroquois on October 18, 1646. In 1930 he was canonized along with seven other French missionaries to North America.

While still in captivity, Jogues wrote a letter to his provincial superior in France, Fr. Jean Filleau (1573–1642). This letter, which fills 30 pages of a modern volume, recounts in detail his captivity. The first passage below is the beginning of this letter, in which Jogues gives two reasons why he has written in Latin rather than in French. The use of Latin is perhaps counterintuitive today, for Jogues explains that he has opted for Latin not only to facilitate his citation of Sacred Scripture, but also because he desires his letter to be "minus commune." Jogues's modern editor paraphrases this latter reason: "It is an intimate document, which justifies the use of Latin."[241] The second passage presented below describes Jogues's capture.

Jogues was educated at the recently-founded Jesuit college in Orléans and then at La Flèche and Paris (Clermont), and according to his biographer he acquired a "thorough knowledge of Latin and Greek" and was able to write "in a smooth flowery style." Still extant are his Latin accounts of some of his dreams.[242] Only recently has this letter, and other Latin letters from New France, begun to receive attention from Latinists.[243]

Volenti mihi ad Reverentiam Vestram scribere, quanam lingua id facerem primum dubium fuit, utriusque enim sermonis post tam longam intermissionem paene oblitus, tam in uno, quam in altero difficultatem patiebar. Verum hae me duae rationes, et quod liberius Sacrae Scripturae verba usurpare potero, quae mihi maximo solatio semper fuerunt in tribulationibus, quae invenerunt me nimis, et quod minus communem cupio esse hanc epistulam nostram, minus communi sermone ut scriberem impulerunt. Dabit veniam eximia illa vestra Caritas, quae peccatorum nostrorum multitudinem alias cooperiebat, si quid sit ab homine, iam ab annis octo, usu, consuetudine, immo nunc habitu et vestitu barbaro, contra leges officii aut sermonis peccatum.

Peractis negotiis quae nos illuc adduxerant, celebratoque S.P.N.[244] Ignatii festo,[245] 1 Augusti nos rursus itineri Huroniam versus, committimus. Secundus a discessu nostro dies illuxerat, cum summo mane, e sociis nostris aliqui recentia in litore vestigia conspiciunt; cumque ex his aliqui inimicorum, alii amicorum esse contendunt, Eustachius Ahatsistar,[246] cui omnes ob egregia in bello facta primas deferebant, hostium, inquit (sint licet in iis fortissimi) quantum ex vestigiis conicio, non amplius quam tres canoae sunt, nos vero eo sumus numero, qui talem hostium manum non pertimescamus: eramus autem circiter 40, aliqui enim se nobis adiunxerant. Igitur coeptum prosequentes iter, vix milliare unum confeceramus, cum in hostes incidimus, qui nos partito agmine ex utraque fluminis ripa opperiebantur 70 numero, canoae 12.

Hi in herbis et arundinibus latitantes, ubi ad eum locum pervenimus, in quo nobis insidias paraverant, bombardas, quas satis magno numero habebant, exploserunt, occiderunt tamen neminem. Ad primos bombardarum ictus Hurones paene omnes, relictis Canois (ad litus enim, quod medio in alveo concitatior sit amnis, adnavigabamus) concitata fuga se in penitissimas silvas abdiderunt. Relicti igitur nos Galli quattuor cum paucis, partim Christianis, partim Catechumenis, praemissa ad Christum oratione hosti resistimus. Sed cum pauci, id est vix duodecim aut quattuordecim cum triginta confligimus, obruimur numero: pugnamus tamen, donec videntes socii nostri alias canoas ex adversa fluminis ripa sibi imminere, animis cadentes aufugerunt. Tunc Gallorum unus, qui inter primos decertabat, Renatus Goupil nomine,[247] et aliqui ex Huronibus capti sunt. Ego autem haec videns, nec fugere volui, nec potui; quo enim nudis pedibus fugissem? potuissemne Gallorum unum aliosque Hurones iam captos aut capiendos non baptizatos relinquere? Itaque cum hostes, ut fugientes insequerentur, me in loco ubi pugnatum fuerat stantem praeteriissent, unum ex his qui ad captorum custodiam remanserat, advoco, moneoque me captivum captivo Gallo adiungat, velle me sicut itineris, ita etiam periculorum et mortis ipsius esse socium; ille vix credens, multumque sibi timens accedit, meque iam captivis coniungit.

Source: Mathias Tanner, *Societas Iesu usque ad sanguinis et vitae profusionem militans* (Prague: Typis Universitatis Carolo-Ferdinandeae, 1675), 511, 512.[248]

20 New World Diplomacy I: New Sweden and New England (1644)

Among the affairs that the Governor of New Sweden, Johan Printz, may have had in mind when he requested that a Latinist be sent over to assist him (see the Introduction to this volume) was a dispute involving George Lamberton, one of the two leaders of the Delaware Trading Company based in New Haven. This company, established to promote trade in fur in the mid-Atlantic, came into conflict with the Dutch as well as the Swedes.

In June of 1642 Lamberton purchased from Native Americans land at the mouth of the Schuylkill River (in present-day Philadelphia) and a year later he purchased land at Varkens Kill (on the Salem River in present-day New Jersey). The Dutch responded to the former purchase by burning the English trading house, arresting the traders, seizing their wares, and compelling Lamberton to pay restitution for engaging in illegal trade. Following the second purchase Printz, who had arrived in New Sweden that February, arrested Lamberton and put him on trial at Fort Christina before a jury consisting of Dutch officers and Swedish officials and settlers. Printz disputed Lamberton's claim to the tract at Varkens Kill, and he also claimed that Lamberton had no right to trade with Native Americans of the region and that Lamberton had bribed the Native Americans to kill the Swedes and the Dutch. Although he was found guilty of this last charge, Lamberton was released, but some of his crewmembers later lodged a complaint in New Haven, and the matter was eventually taken to the General Court in Boston. Subsequently John Winthrop (*c.* 1587–1649), the Governor of the Massachusetts Bay Colony and President of the Commissioners for the United Colonies of New England, wrote Printz a letter of complaint.[249] This initiated an exchange of letters between the two governors, one of which, Winthrop's brief and cordial reply to Printz, is given here.

The Latin from New Sweden remains to be explored.[250]

Litteris tuis humanissimis (colendissime Domine) aliter respondendi, in praesentiarum non datur facultas, quam, quod acceperim, et in illis, erga nos et Anglorum gentem, benevolum amicissimumque animum gratanter perceperim: unde, et ex antiqua arctissimaque illa inter Anglos et Suecos necessitudine, facile sibi persuasum habeat Dominus Gubernator Suecorum, se[251] suosque omnes Anglos in hisce terris, pari studio et benevolentia prosequi, et in honore habere, semper curaturos. Quod vero litterarum tuarum et exemplarium partes attinet, responsum plenum et particulare, a proxima Comissionaria conventione exspectare possis. Interim spero (quod etiam a Dominatione tua peto) ut omnia, inter vos et confoederatos nostros Neuhauenses, summa pace et concordia, transigantur negotia. Vale. Tuae Dignitatis amicissime studiosus, J.W.

Source: Frederic Kidder, *The Swedes on the Delaware and their Intercourse with New England* (Boston: David Clapp & Son, 1874), 10.[252]

21 New World Diplomacy II: New France and New Netherland (1658)

The following is a letter from the Jesuit missionary Simon Le Moyne (1604–65) addressed to Peter Stuyvesant (1610–72), the director of the Dutch settlement in Manhattan.[253] Le Moyne, who arrived in Canada in 1638, lived among the Hurons for many years, but he also at times performed diplomatic roles, undertaking several peace missions from the French to the Iroquois between 1654 and 1662. During the winter of 1657–58, while he was living among the Mohawks in Ossernenon, he traveled to New Amsterdam to minister to some Catholics there and also to thank the Protestant minister Jan Megapolensis for his kindness toward Le Moyne's fellow Jesuit Isaac Jogues (see section 19). The Dutch in turn asked Le Moyne to obtain permission from the Governor of New France for their ships to trade in the St. Lawrence. Le Moyne, having obtained this permission,[254] wrote the Dutch the following letter dated April 7, 1658 from Fort Orange, near present-day Albany.[255]

Fort Orange, 7 Avril, 1658.

Domine Illustrissime:—

Mitto ad te, lubens, quas accepi Kebeco litteras; gallico illas quidem idiomate, hoc est aperto et amico.[256] Noluit, opinor, latine scribere, qui nomen suum epistulae subscripsit vir nobilissimus iuxta ac eruditissimus, Dominus Dailleboust;[257] fortassis quia plures apud vos gallice sciunt quam latine; immo quia Gallorum una res agebatur et eorum qui Gallos unos amant.

Porro is scripsit qui hodie vices gerit Pro-regis nostri absentis, quique et ipse fuit quondam Pro-rex noster.[258]

Quod ergo felix, faustum, fortunatumque sit. Agite sulcis, Manatenses amicissimi, Kebecum nostrum; aliquando invisite uti post modum Canadenses nostri ad vos, Deo duce, appellant felicissime. Etsi enim non est integrum mihi, vobiscum hoc anno, quod speraveram, navigare, quia silvestres[259] meos habebo nautas mecum; tamen in posterum et comitem vobis spondeo et famulum.

Ignosce, si places, Domine Illustrissime, et accipe hoc totum, quod paulo liberius fluit e calamo, tamquam certissimum sensus in Hollandos tuos et amoris in Te testimonium, quippe qui sum ex animo, Tibi, Domine Illustrissime,

Servus addictissimus idem et obsequius,

Simon le Moyne, e Soc. Iesu

Source: E. B. O'Callaghan, *History of New Netherland; or, New York under the Dutch*, 2nd ed. (New York: Bartlett and Welford/Appleton, 1848), 2.364.

22 The Mississippi (1673)

The exploration of the Mississippi River was due to religious and commercial motives: the French desire to evengelize Native American tribes and to find a warm-weather port accessible from Canada. In 1672 Frontenac, the Governor of New France, commissioned Louis Jolliet (1645–1700) to follow the Great River (the Mississippi) to its mouth. In this quest Jolliet was joined by the Jesuit priest, Jacques Marquette (1637–75).

Born in Laon (France), Marquette arrived in New France in 1666 and spent a year with fellow Jesuit Gabriel Druillettes (1610–81) studying native languages. During the next five years Marquette visited or established missions at Sault Ste. Marie, La Pointe du Saint-Esprit (on the western edge of Lake Superior), and Saint-Ignace (just north of Mackinac Island). In May 1673 he departed with Jolliet to explore the Mississippi. Eventually they reached latitude 33° 40', just north of the Arkansas river, far enough to establish that the Mississippi flowed into the Gulf of Mexico rather than westwards to the Gulf of California.

The first selection below is an account of this voyage written by the Jesuit Claude Dablon (1619–97), dated October 25, 1674, copies of which were sent to the Jesuit General in Rome and to the Jesuit Provincial in Paris. It was Dablon, as superior of the Jesuit missions in New France, who assigned Marquette the task of exploring the Mississippi.[260]

The second selection below is a letter written by Marquette during his return up the Mississippi in the summer of 1673. During their voyage downriver, a bit south of present-day Memphis, Marquette and Jolliet had encountered a Native American tribe—most likely Chickasaw—whose possessions gave evidence of European trade. On his return upriver Marquette left with this tribe a Latin letter which, he hoped, would eventually reach these (likely Spanish) trading partners. Instead, the letter evidently reached Colonel William Byrd (1652–1704) of Virginia, and then, perhaps by way of William Penn, it ended up in Welbeck Abbey in England, in possession of the Duke of Portland. What exists today is not the original but a transcription purportedly made by Byrd.

I

Post repertum ante duos annos a Patre Albanel septentrionis mare,[261] spem dederamus fore ut mare item meridionale detegeremus. Detexit hoc anno Pater Marquette, qui inde feliciter reversus est vere hoc ultimo. Dici potest expeditionem illam omnium quae adhuc istis in regionibus factae sunt, periculosissimam esse simul et iucundissimam. Mense Iunio anni 1673, cum tandem Pater Marquette celebrem illum fluvium reperivisset, de quo barbari tam multa dixerant et tam miranda, distantem plus centum leucis ab Outaouacis[262] ubi hiemaverat, navigavit in eo flumine usque ad 33 gradum elevationis,[263] ac pro certo habet venisse se ad Floridam, ac si 40 aut 50 praeterea leucas progressus esset, venturum fuisse se ad sinum mexicanum. Sed illinc redire maluit ne socios suos coniceret in Hispanorum manus, quos non procul abesse audiebat.[264] Omnis ea regio per quam iter habuit pulcherrima est, pratis ac silvis pariter distincta, plus quinquaginta oppida numeravit. Affabiles sunt populi maximam partem ac dociles, a quibus benigne auditus est cum apud eos de Christiana fide verba fecit. Itineris illius narratio plena erat rebus exquisitis iisque non levibus. Sed qui eam afferebat (Jolliet), cum prope Montem regium cymbam corticeam fregerit naufragus, quascumque habebat chartas ipsi perierunt.[265] Aliud eiusdem narrationis exemplum exspecto anno proximo a patre Marquette, qui remansit apud Outaouacos, ut sit in procinctu ad suscipiendam missionem apud Illinikeos.[266]

II

In cuiuscunque manus hae literae venerint Salutem in Domino.

Cum misera oboedientia nullus fuerim, quaerebam alios qualescunque ad Christum Salvatorem nostrum adducere, forte accedit quod, ut captus ex Spiritualium impetu, hos barbaros quorum familiarem esse credo cum Europaeis consuetudinem, offenderem: Verum cum ab ipsis nihil intelligerem, gratissimum mihi fuerit, si qui sitis, quae urbis vestrae latitudo et longitudo, qui sint hi barbari, me feceritis certiorem.

Interim hoc a me accipite, ad Societatem Iesu vocavit me Dominus, vultque ut in Canadensi regione propter barbaros (quos sanguine suo redemit) vitam peragam, unde certum est mihi, si Immaculata Virgo, Dei Mater, mihi adfuerit in hisce locis, licet miserrimis, vitae spiritum reddere, cum pro nobis Christus tanta tulerit tormenta, non sane voluit ut ei quam nobis conservat parceremus, qua dum fruimur, Deum oremus ut (si nunquam in terris) in caelo nos coniungat.

Datum ad Fluvium Convectionis[267] ad altitudinem Poli 35[d] ad Longitudinem forte 275[d]

4th August 1675[268]

Servus in Christo Iesu et Immaculata Virgine

Iacobus Macput,[269] Societatis Iesu

Sources: I Camille de Rochemonteix, *Les Jésuites et la Nouvelle-France au XVII[e] siècle* (Paris: Letouzey et Ané, 1896), 3.11.

II C.W. Alvord, "An Unrecognized Father Marquette Letter," *American Historical Review* 25 (1920): 676.

23 Strange Dreams in Massachusetts (1677, 1685)

At times Latin has been used in America to communicate or record matters of great sensitivity or intimacy, including dreams. The following two selections are taken from the diary of Samuel Sewall (1652–1730). In addition to holding various judicial positions in the Massachusetts Bay Colony, Sewall was a successful merchant and a member of the Board of Overseers of Harvard College. He was also, infamously, one of the judges at the Salem witch trials.

Sewall was an accomplished Latinist. Leo M. Kaiser has catalogued several of his surviving elegiac distichs, whose themes range from laments for his still-born son to celebration of the destruction of a crucifix in Québec (see section 30). Sewall preserved some of these poems in a diary that he kept between the years 1674–1729. This diary also contains an account of his father-in-law's fit of anger on February 14, 1677 as well as a dream that Sewall had during the stormy night of Wednesday, June 3, 1685. These accounts may have been written in Latin so that his wife, Hannah Hull, would not be able to read them.[270] A modern translator ascribes the Latin of the second passage, at any rate, to "Sewall's delicacy of feeling."[271]

Feb. 14, 13th Meeting at Goodman Davis's, where G. Tappin and Cousin Savage[272] spake to 1 Peter 1.6.[273] By which words I seriously considered that no godly man hath any more afflictions than what he hath need of: qua meditatione mihi quidem die sequente usus fuit; nam socer[274] (iam paene fervidus propter avenas sibi inconsulto oblatas) de stipite aequo grandiore quem in ignem intempestive (ut aiebat) conieci mihi iratus fuit, et si ita insipiens forem dixit se mihi fidem non habiturum, et ventosam mentem meam fore causativam. Deus det me sibi soli confidere, et creato nulli. Psal 37.3. 4. 5,[275] principium huius psal. canebam conscius, quem propter ea quae dicta sunt maestus petivi.

In somniis visum est mihi, me rediisse Novoburgo[276] vel alio aliquo oppido; et me absente, uxorem mortuam esse Roxburiae vel Dorcestriae;[277] quam narrationem aegerrime tuli Nomen saepius exclamans. Dum percontarer ubi esset socer dixerunt eum in Angliam profecturum; Filia scilicet mortua liberum esse ei ut iter faceret quo vellet. Hanc mortem partim ex incuria mea et Amoris indigentia accidisse Elizabetha[278] susurravit quod adhuc me gravius pressit. Excusso somno pro gaudio uxorem quasi nuper nuptam amplexus sum.

Source: "Diary of Samuel Sewall 1674–1729, vol. 1, 1674–1700," *Collections of the Massachusetts Historical Society*, 5th ser., vol. 5 (Boston 1878), 35, 79.

24 Native American Poetry (1678 and beyond)

An important component of the Jesuit plans to evangelize Florida in the mid-1560s was the establishment of a school in Havana to educate the sons of *caciques* of Florida tribes (see section 11).[279] Latin, most likely, would have been a part of this curriculum. Certainly Native Americans studied Latin in the Jesuit-run colleges established in Mexico in the 1570s.[280] But as early as 1537 Native Americans were learning Latin from the Augustinians in Mexico City, and Native Americans were enrolled at the Franciscan College of Santiago Tlatelolco, which opened its doors on January 6, 1536 and where courses were taught in Latin. It has recently been shown that graduates from Tlatelolco were responsible for most of the extant Latin writing by Native Americans in Mexico.[281] At times Native Americans were said to surpass Spaniards in their facility with Latin and to have attained Ciceronian levels—"hablan tan elegante el latín como Tulio."[282] The names, the occupations, and the levels of proficiency in Latin for several Nahua men in the late 1500s and early 1600s have been preserved.[283]

By comparison, fewer examples of early Native American Latin from within the land that would become the United States are known. The following elegiac poem, preserved in Cotton Mather's *Magnalia Christi Americana*, is one of the few to have survived. The author, Eleazar, was one of five Native American students at Harvard's Indian College, founded in 1656.[284] The poem commemorates the death of Rev. Thomas Thacher (1620–78), the pastor of Boston's Old South congregation as well as a physician.[285] Until a few years ago, only one other Latin work by a student from Harvard's Indian School had been known, a Latin oration by Caleb Cheeshateaumauk ("Honoratissimi Benefactores"), but in the fall of 2013 two Harvard graduate students announced the discovery of a Latin poem by the Native American student Benjamin Larnell, which has subsequently been published.[286]

The Native American engagement with Latin in the United States in later centuries remains to be explored. A natural focal point of such a study would be the various Indian schools founded in the nineteenth century, some of which sponsored a classical curriculum. For example, the curriculum of the Cherokee Male Seminary in Tahlequah, Oklahoma (then known as Indian Territory) was based on those of Latin schools in the northeast, particularly Boston Latin.[287] Similarly, students taking the High School course at the Cherokee Female Seminary (also in Tahlequah) took Latin for eight semesters.[288] One graduate from the Cherokee Female Seminary, Cora Archer, is said to have recited "an original Latin ode" at a wedding reception in Tennessee in July 1884.[289] Several decades earlier, Cherokee students studied the classics at a Connecticut seminary established by the American Board of Commissioners for Foreign Missions (founded 1810).[290] It seems likely that graduates from these institutions composed Latin poetry, which remains to be discovered.

In obitum Viri vere Reverendi D. Thomae Thacheri,
qui ad Dom. ex hac vita migravit,
18. 8. 1678.

Tentabo illustrem, tristi memorare dolore,
Quem lacrimis repetunt tempora nostra, virum.
Memnona sic mater, mater ploravit Achillem,
Iustis cum lacrimis, cumque dolore gravi.
Mens stupet, ora silent, iustum nunc palma recusat
Officium. Quid? Opem tristis Apollo negat?
Ast, Thachere, tuas conabor dicere laudes,
Laudes virtutis, quae super astra volat.
Consultis rerum dominis, gentique togatae
Nota fuit virtus, ac tua sancta fides.
Vivis post funus; felix post fata; iaces tu?

Sed stellas inter gloria nempe iaces.
Mens tua iam caelos repetit; victoria parta est:
Iam tuus est Christus, quod meruitque tuum.
Hic finis crucis; magnorum haec meta malorum;
Ulterius non quo progrediatur erit.
Crux iam cassa manes; requiescunt ossa sepulchro;
Mors moritur; vitae vita beata redit.
Quum tuba per densas sonitum dabit ultima nubes.
Cum Domino rediens ferrea sceptra geres.
Caelos tum scandes, ubi patria vera piorum;
Praevius hanc patriam nunc tibi Iesus adit.
Illic vera quies; illic sine fine voluptas;
Gaudia et humanis non referenda sonis.[291]

Source: Cotton Mather, *Magnalia Christi Americana*, vol. 1 (Hartford: Silas Andrus, 1820), 448.

25 Mission to California (1681, 1701)

One of Arizona's two contributions to National Statuary Hall in the United States Capitol commemorates Eusebio Francisco Kino (1645–1711), a Jesuit missionary priest who spent three decades in northwestern New Spain.[292] Born in northern Italy (Segno), Kino celebrated his recovery from a near-fatal illness while he was a student by taking the name Francisco (in honor of St. Francis Xavier), entering the Jesuits (in the upper Germany province), and dedicating himself to missionary work. Originally he hoped to work in China, and he studied astronomy, mathematics, and cartography in anticipation of this destination, but instead he was selected to explore (Baja) California. After an initial expedition there in 1683, he spent two and a half decades in Pimería Alta, which comprised the Mexican state of Sonora as well as portions of present-day Arizona. From his base at Mission Nuestra Señora de los Dolores in Sonora (not far south of Nogales), he founded missions throughout the region, one of which, San Xavier del Bac (founded 1700), still stands south of Tucson.

The first passage below is an excerpt from a letter that Kino sent shortly after arriving in Mexico in 1681, when he was still uncertain of his ultimate destination—China, California, or elsewhere. The letter is addressed to Maria de Guadalupe de Lencastre (1630–1715), the sixth Duchess of Aveiro and Duchess of Arcos and Maqueda. Born in Portugal, the Duchess spent most of her life in Spain, and her Madrid house was a sort of "information center"[293] for the Catholic missionary work that she subsidized in the Far East, the Mariana Islands, and the Americas. She was able to read Portuguese, Spanish, French, Italian, Latin, and to some extent German, and she composed some Latin verses. Among Kino's twenty letters to the Duchess, eight are in Latin, one is in Italian, and the others are Spanish. In this letter Kino comments on an earthquake, which he relates to a comet that had appeared the previous year (Newton's Comet or the Great Comet of 1680). Kino submitted a treatise he wrote on this comet to the Hieronymite nun and sometime-Latin poet, Sor Juana Inés de la Cruz (d. 1695), who in turn wrote a (Spanish) sonnet to Kino.[294] (Sor Juana also wrote a Spanish poem for Kino's patron, the Duchess of Aveiro.[295])

The second passage below is a letter from a Czech Jesuit, Wenceslaus Eymer (1661–1709), congratulating Kino on his (re)discovery that Baja California was a peninsula.[296] Although very eary Spanish maps correctly depict it as a peninsula, by Kino's day Baja California was thought to be an island. In a series of expeditions Kino realized that it was a peninsula, and he made a map depicting this. Kino includes this letter in his account of Pimería Alta.

I

Excellentissima Domina Ducissa:

Pax Christi Iesu, et Divini Amoris incendia!

Iam ante mensem, et primis fere diebus mei huc Mexicum adventus litteras ad Suam Excel^{am} dedi de toto nostro itinere ac navigatione Indica. Fortassis illae litterae una cum istis simul ad Suae Excellentiae manus pervenient. Omnes enim consignavi R^{do} P^{tri} Balthasaro de Mansilla Procuratori Philippinarum et Marianarum[297] includendas cistae regiae, quae Mexico Madritum mittitur. . .

Agit quoque R.P. Balthasar de me in Chinam mittendo, ac propterea iam ante plures dies hac de re cum R.P. Provinciali huius Mexicanae Provinciae[298] locutus est, conatus me pro suo oriente obtinere. R.P. Provincialis vero, (qui cogitat me cum alio Patre missionario veterano[299] in Californiam mittere, dum post paucos menses Deo volente naves et milites ac insignis expeditio, ad illam sive insulam, sive paeninsulam amplissimam et vastissimam melius quam hactenus detegendam dirigetur) nondum R^{do} P^{tri} Balthasaro ultimatum consensum dedit. . .

Die 23 Iunii hora 6ta vespertina hic habuimus magnum terraemotum. Plures hic publicae comprecationes instituuntur, pro obtinendis pluviis. Ego suspicor has extraordinarias siccitates esse aliquem cometae[300] effectum, quibus quandoque succedunt inundationes aquarum. Divina clementia sua nos pietate custodiat ac tueatur semper incolumes. . .

Nisi flota citius ex portu Verae Crucis discedat, conabor Suam Excel^{tiam} proxime edocere per alias adhuc litteras de missione ad quam me R.R. P.P. Superiores missuri sunt, et sive in orientem me mittant, sive in missionibus huius Novae Hispaniae, seu pro California me retineant, Sua Excel^{tia} me semper habebit sibi obstrictissimum et obsequiosissimum ac in precibus et Missae sacrificiis sui continuo memorem; memoriam autem quotidianam facile excitabit vel illa sacra B.V. MARIAE imago, quam suo nomine insignitam Sua Excel^{tia} mihi Madrito Gades submittere dignata est, et in meo Breviario gesto.[301] Hisce SS^{mis} Suae Excel^{tiae} et dulcissimorum liberorum[302] precibus ac toti Sacrae Familiae me et missiones tam orientis, quam occidentis, praesertim vastissimam Chinam devotissime ac ardentissime commendo.

Mexici, 4 iulii 1681.

Suae Excel^{tiae} Obstrictissimus in Christo Servus,
et Capellanus Eusebius Franciscus Kinus S.J.

II

Quod bonum, felix, fortunatumque sit, et ad maiorem Dei Deiparaeque sine labe conceptae[303] honorem, Ecclesiae Sanctae incrementum, Fidei orthodoxae dilatationem, animarumque salutem eveniat, California sub auspiciis Reginae Lauretanae,[304] sudore apostolico et labore indefesso P.P. Ioannis Mariae[305] et Francisci Eusebii continens feliciter inventa est. Eat nunc cum suo Draco[306] Anglia,[307] et digitum ori imponat temeritas Britanica, quae inani fabula in Atlante Californiarum[308] Californiam a se circumnavigatam iactat. Gratulor igitur Reverentiae Vestrae, et uberrima Dei auxilia precor, quibus munitus bellum idolatriae Californiae indicat cruentum cum palma victoriam gloriosi occinimus.

Sources: I Transcribed from Huntington Library, San Marino, California, HM 9972.[309]
II H. E Bolton, *Kino's Historical Memoir of Pimería Alta* (Cleveland: Arthur H. Clark, 1919), 1.300–1.

26 The French in Louisiana (1682, 1700)

The explorations of Marquette and Jolliet (see section 22) were resumed by Robert Cavelier, sieur de La Salle (1643–87), who finally reached the mouth of the Mississippi in early April 1682. A formal ceremony marked the occasion. On April 9 a wooden column, along with a cross, was erected near the site of present-day Venice, Louisiana, and at its base was buried a lead plate that contained on one side the arms of the French King and on the other side the first Latin inscription given below.

La Salle, motivated by concerns that the English would move west across the Appalachian mountains, favored a line of forts in the Mississippi Valley that would protect French settlements and claims. He himself did not see this plan realized—he perished sometime in early 1687 in Texas—but others continued the quest to establish French control of the interior of the continent, particularly Pierre LeMoyne, sieur d'Iberville (1661–1706). A native Canadian who is considered the founder of Louisiana, d'Iberville was instructed by King Louis XIV to establish a French colony at the mouth of the Mississippi. At this time the French were especially anxious about the question of succession to the Spanish throne and the possible threats to French interests from Spanish settlements in Florida.[310] Accordingly, during the winter of 1700 d'Iberville constructed a fort (Fort de la Boulaye) along the Mississippi thirty miles south of present-day New Orleans.[311] The second text below was inscribed on a cross placed in the cemetery of this fort on Sexagesima Sunday of that year (which fell on February 14) by the Jesuit missionary, Paul Du Ru (1666–1741), who accompanied d'Iberville's 1700 expedition.

I

LVDOVICVS MAGNVS REGNAT NONO APRILIS, MDCLXXXII. ROBERTVS CAVELIER CVM DOMINO DE TONTY, LEGATO,[312] R.P. ZENOBIO MEMBRE, RECOLLECTO,[313] ET VIGINTI GALLIS PRIMVS HOC FLVMEN INDE AB ILINEORVM PAGO ENAVIGAVIT, EIVSQUE OSTIVM FECIT PERVIVM, NONO APRILIS ANNI MDC LXXXII

II

D. O. M.
GALLI CUM HUC VENISSENT PRIMI,
PRIMÛM EX CANADENSI PLAGA
DUCE DE LA SALLE, AN. 1682:
SECUNDÙM EX EODEM LOCO
DUCE DE TONTY, AN. 1685:
TERTIUM EX ORIS MARITIMIS
DUCE D'IBERVILLE, AN. 1699.
QUARTÙM EX EODEM LOCO,
ET EODEM DUCE, AN. 1700
HANC CRUCEM HOC IPSO ANNO 1700
14 FEBR. POSUERUNT.
AD CUJUS PEDEM ARÂ CONSTRUCTÂ
EODEM ANNO ET DIE
FECIT SACERDOS È SOCIET^E JESU
ATQUE HOC SEPTUM MORTUORUM SEPULTURAE
RITÈ DEVOVIT.

Sources: I Thomas Falconer, *Memoir of M. Cavelier de la Salle,* printed with *On the Discovery of the Mississippi, and on the South-western, Oregon, and North-western Boundary of the United States* (London: Samuel Clarke, 1844), 43.
II *Relation ou journal du voyage du R. P. Jacques Gravier, de la Compagnie de Jésus, en 1700* (New York: Cramoisy, 1859), 68.[314]

27 A Father Seeks His Son in Pennsylvania (1699)

In 1681, to satisfy a debt, King Charles II (*r.* 1660–85) granted William Penn (1644–1718) a massive tract of land west of New Jersey and north of Maryland. Penn thereby became proprietor of Pennsylvania. Having suffered persecution in England for being a Quaker, Penn was determined that his new colony would be tolerant not only of Quakers but also of other persecuted sects. Among those Europeans attracted to Penn's "holy experiment" was Francis Daniel Pastorius (1651–1719), an erudite German lawyer and member of the Pietists, a sect seeking to reform Lutheranism.[315] Pastorius became Penn's agent in Frankfort, facilitating the passage to Pennsylvania of those who sought to emigrate, and he continued to exercise this role after he himself arrived in Pennsylvania in 1683.

Pastorius was an accomplished Latinist. As a student at the gymnasium in Windsheim he had been required to speak Latin because the teacher, a Hungarian, did not know German. Pastorius studied at several universities in France, Germany, and Switzerland.[316] Onboard ship to America, Pastorius spoke Latin with Thomas Lloyd (1640–94), later Pennsylvania's Lieutenant-Governor, because it was their only common language. Above Pastorius's Philadelphia home was the following inscription: "Parva Domus, sed amica bonis, procul este profani." He was an avid writer, and he is said to have composed (but not published) several Latin works, including *Lingua Latina or Grammatical Rudiments*, *Melligo Sententia Latine*, and *Latinae primordia Linguae*. He has also been credited with writing the first anti-slavery tract in the American colonies (1688).[317]

In June 1698 Pastorius's father, Melchior Adam Pastorius (1624–1702), anxious about his son's safety, wrote Penn from Germany (in Latin) seeking confirmation that his son was still alive. Penn was in England at the time. The passage below is Penn's Latin response.

A Monsieur Monsieur Melchior Adam Pastorius President, à Windsheim in Franconia.

Observande mi in Iesu Christo Amice,

Ex intimo amoris affectu te saluto praesentemque tibi et futuram exopto felicitatem, quae constat in fida oboedientia in Lucem et Cognitionem illam quam tibi per Christum Iesum impertiit Deus.

Nuper adhuc in vivis fuit filius tuus, et iam nunc Philadelphiae agit. Irenarcha hoc anno est, aut nuperrime fuit,[318] alias vir sobrius, probus, prudens et pius audit, spectatae inter omnes, inculpataeque famae, familiaspater est, quot vero filiorum, ignoro.[319] Amoris tui pignus, cum litteris valetudinis tuae nuntiis pergratum illi accideret.

Brevi Provinciam istam iuvante Deo visurus sum,[320] interea temporis quid velis et quid de eo expetas vel ad ipsum scribas vel in litteris ad me dandis exprimas.

Cum votis itaque ut Deus una cum salutis suae demonstratione dignetur seniles tuos annos[321] sicuti olim Simeoni[322] prolongare, valere te iubeo sincerus tibi ex animo amicus, William Penn.

Bristolii die 20 Mensis 12 vulgo Februarii 1699.

Source: Francis Daniel Pastorius, *Umständige Geographische Beschreibung der zu allerletzt erfundenen Provintz Pensylvaniae* (Frankfurt: Andreas Otto, 1700), 96.[323]

28 Latin Poetry for Property (1703)

The College of William & Mary, the second oldest institution of higher learning in British North America (1693), was established by royal charter to be "a certain place of universal study, or perpetual College of Divinity, Philosophy, Languages, and other good Arts and Sciences." It was to have a President, six professors, and about one hundred students. The British crown granted the College twenty thousand acres, but an unusual condition was attached. Every year on November 5 (Guy Fawkes Day) "two copies of Latin verses" were to be delivered to the house of the Governor or Lieutenant Governor of Virginia. This would suffice "for the time being, for ever, in full discharge, acquittance, and satisfaction of all quit-rents, services, customs, dues and burdens whatsoever, due, or to be due, to us, or our successors."[324] The following poem, which dates from 1703, was written to satisfy this stipulation. Other such verses, from the 1770s, have already been published.[325]

The poem is addressed to Francis Nicholson (1655–1728), the Governor of Virginia from 1698 to 1705.[326] Born in Yorkshire, Nicholson received a commission in the Holland Regiment and participated in campaigns in Flanders and North Africa before being sent to America in 1686, where he had a lengthy career as colonial administrator. In addition to governing Virginia, Nicholson served at times as Governor of four other regions: New England with authority over New York (1688–89), Maryland (1694–98), Nova Scotia (1712–15), and South Carolina (1721–25). Despite initial success in Virginia, Nicholson eventually incurred significant opposition, and he clashed in particular with James Blair (*c.* 1655–1743), William & Mary's first president. Along with other members of the Governor's Council, Blair sought and obtained Nicholson's removal from office in April 1705, seventeen months after this poem was submitted.

The script is difficult to read in places, and a few of the words printed below are conjectures.

Iuventus Virginiensis Collegii illustris alumni
Se Suaque Studia gratumque animum,
haecque qualiacunque Carmina
Francisco Nicholson Armigero Virginiae Proregi,
Fauteri [sic] et Macenali [?] Suo munificentissimo
humillime offert

Quas grates dignas memori de pectore promam
Quasve referre parem donis, Clarrissime, tantis
Totque tuis, a Te, tam prompte in me cumulatis?
Tu mihi musarum Sedem Duo predia magna
Ditia, bis decies mille arvi iugera opima[327]
Muneribusque amplis nactus Diploma refertum
Cimeriis tenebris ego dum cooperta cubarem
Artis virtutis morumque ego dum rudis essem
Ars Virtus probitas a Te moresque modesti
Dumque reluctarent multi mihi reddita prompte
Non alias alio posthac sub Sole repostas
Et procul a Patria trans pontum quaerere terras
Musarumque Domus, doctas et Apolinis urbes
Ut doctas Artes discam lustrare necesse est
Artes namque domi ingenuas disco, doctasque Sorores
In Patria veneror, Tibi quod dignissime caelo
Debitur[328] verum avertat nobis Deus omen
In caelum Serus redeas Virginia longum
Gymnasium, Clerusque Ecclesia, Te potiatur
His Gaudens adsis, reddens laetam undique gentem.
Nonis Novembris MDCCIII

Source: Students of the College of William & Mary, Latin poem to Governor Francis Nicholson, 1703 November 5, MS 43.04, Francis Nicholson Papers, John D. Rockefeller Jr. Library, The Colonial Williamsburg Foundation, Williamsburg, VA, with permission.

After this section was written, I encountered a transcription and discussion of this poem in Julian Ward Jones, "A 'New' Latin Quitrent Poem of the College of William and Mary," The Virginia Magazine of History and Biography 96 (1988): 491–504.

29 Isolation in the Mississippi Valley (1707)

The following are excerpts from a letter dated March 6, 1707, written by the missionary Jacques Gravier (1651–1708) and addressed to the Jesuit General Michelangelo Tamburini. Gravier, a native of Moulins (France) who arrived in Canada in 1684, is considered the "founder of the Illinois misson," which he initiated in 1689.[329] His dictionary of the Illinois language is preserved in the library of Trinity College (Hartford). In 1700 he was in Louisiana with Jean-Baptiste Le Moyne de Bienville. But in the fall of 1705 he was wounded in the arm by an arrow shot by a member of the Peoria tribe. Having unsuccessfully sought treatment in Mobile, he set out for Paris, where he wrote this letter. He died somewhere near Mobile on his way back to the Illinois.

This text is taken from the *Jesuit Relations and Allied Documents*, a massive collection of original texts and translations, with extensive annotations, that was compiled by Reuben Gold Thwaites (1853–1913), who for many years was director of the State Historical Society of Wisconsin.

Non ita pridem huc[330] adveni ex nostris missionibus indorum vulgo Illinois dictorum, positis iuxta magnum flumen Mississipaum quod in sinum mexicanum influit . . . Confeci vero in navi plus quam 2000 leucarum non eo animo ut extrahentem ex medio bracchio cui infixus inhaeret ad reliquam vitam sagittae lapis inveniam, (quattuor enim aliae quas in me idem barbarus in odium fidei vibraverat, praeter auriculam transverberatam, vixdum me laeserant,) confeci autem valde sollicitus de obtinendis a Reverendo Patre Generali operariis quibus maxime indigent missiones nostrae et de casuum imprimis illorum ad Vestram Paternitatem missorum resolutione. Eorum enim qui spectant ad matrimonium fidelis cum infideli contrahendum, sunt maximi momenti pro stabiliendo christianismo . . .

In meo pago[331] qui quingentis leucis Quebec distat, quique tribus circiter animarum millibus constat, si absente pastore non fuerint dispersae oves ad tempus, solus sine collega, sine socio, immo saepe sine famulo novemdecim abhinc annis solus fere semper vixi. Iam sex supra quinquaginta annos natus. Solus quoque P. Gabriel Marest[332] agit in sua missione eiusdem nationis cui vix datur per diem integrum locus aut recitandi breviarium aut edendi aut brevem somnum media noctis parte capiendi. Vix quoque collegae suo P. Ioanni Mermet,[333] iam consumptis prae nimio zelo viribus cassam per valetudinem agere licet, illis autem vix est respirandi locus propter maiorem numerum neophytorum et fervorem maximum, nam ex ducentis supra mille animabus quibus constat pagus vix quadraginta reperiantur qui non profiteantur maxima pietate et constantia catholicam fidem. Distamus autem ab invicem 120 leucas, vixque semel uno et altero anno illum adeundi mihi locus datur.

Source: Reuben Gold Thwaites, ed., *Jesuit Relations and Allied Documents,* vol. 66 (Cleveland: Burrows Bros., 1899), 120, 122.

30 Latin Grammar in Rural Maine (1720)

According to a recent history: "No priest was hated or feared more in New England in the early eighteenth century than Father Sebastien Ralé."[334] A native of Pontarlier (France), Ralé (1657–1724) arrived in America in 1689 and apart from two years with the Illinois in Kaskaskia he worked among the Abenaki people in northern New England and eastern Canada.[335] Among other achievements, he compiled a French-Abenaki dictionary, which is preserved at Harvard University.[336] Ralé, whose name is also spelled Râle, Rasle, or Rasles, came into repeated conflict with the English, who suspected that he was inciting the Abenaki against them. English soldiers burned his church in Norridgewock (present-day South Madison, Maine) and made several attempts to arrest him. Eventually Ralé was shot by the English in August 1724. His death occasioned a Latin epigram from Samuel Sewall (see section 23), dated September 5, 1724: Dum Cererem et Bacchum meditaris, Ralle sacerdos/ Vitam disperdis, victima iusta cadis.[337]

Earlier, to counteract Ralé's influence, the Governor of Massachusetts had sent the Protestant clergyman Joseph Baxter (1676–1745) to minister on Arrowsic island, further down the Kennebec river from Norridgewock. Baxter and Ralé exchanged letters in Latin. In addition to doctrinal issues, their correspondence, surprisingly, involved points of Latin grammar and syntax.[338] The following is the beginning of Baxter's second letter to Ralé. The original spelling, capitalization, and punctuation (including underlining) have been retained.

Reverende Domine

Delectaris Procul dubio Reprehendendo, Ideoque ea culpas Quae non sunt Reprehensione digna. Et in culpando Tuipse Crimina admittis. Dicis enim mihi, Tu Anglice Loqueris, utendo verbis Latinis. In his verbis Domine Tibi ipsi contradicis. Si Quis enim verbis Latinis utitur, Quamvis non Rhetorice tamen Latine & non Anglice Loquitur. Quisquis Anglicè Loquitur verbis Anglicanis utitur. Quid si sincere sonat Anglice est verbum vere Latinum.

Dicis, Amicum est Substantium, nec potest esse Adiectivum. Sed non Recte dicis. Certissime datur Tale Adiectivum Apud Latinos. Amicus Animus,[339] est Latina Locutio, & vale Lumen Amicum.[340] & Humor Pratis Amicus &c:[341]

Ais, Commercium in hoc est Barbarum Quid. Sed Quis Tuae Dictioni credet absque Probatione. Ipse dixit[342] non valet.

De multis Aliis etiam dicis non sunt Latina sed Barbara. At non valet Authoritas Tua. Certissime Talia verba saepe Inter Latinos adhibentur.

Dicis, merere est sollescismus, Illud verbum est Deponens, non Activum, scribe mereri. Sed aiunt Docti datur mereo, merere. aeque ac mereor mereri. Merere culpam in infinitivo est Latina Locutio,[343] & merere salutem[344] etc:

Dicis Mola est Lapis, non aedificium: Sed Docti aiunt Mola est aedificium, Lapis qui ponitur in mola, Lapis Molaris est.[345]

Dicis, Domus habet in Accusativo Plurali Domos, non Domus. Sed Quare non habet Domos, & Domus?

Multa Alia etiam reprehendis Quae non sunt vituperanda. Et si Te Imitarer Possem dicere, Tu Minister! Tu e Societate Jesu! & Haec non non Intelligis. Dicis verba mea non sunt Intelligibilia. Quare non intellegis verba Quae saepe apud Latinos adhibentur? sed exemplum Christi Jesu sequi malo, Qui Convitiis Affectus non vicissim convitiabatur: Quum Malis Afficeretur, non minabatur. & est 1 Pet 2.23[346] & Isti monitioni, vel Mandato Auscultabo: in Prov: 26.4. ne Responde stulto secundum stultitiam[347] ejus ne adaequeris ei Tu quoque.

Manifeste patet Te reprehendere multa Quae non sunt

culpanda. Tamen concedo Errata sunt in Scriptione mea Quam Praepropere scribebam. viz: Existimaris virum pro vir, & movent pro movet &c:

Et in Tuis scriptionibus equidem multa sunt Errata (Quamvis fuisti (ut inquis) Professor Rhetoricae, & Linguae Graecae in urbe nemausensi)[348] Ego nunquam fui Professor Rhetoricae, & Tamen Errata video, Quot Errata tum posset Criticus, & vir Perdoctus reperire in Epistolis Tuis? Imo in Epistola Quam Gloriosissime scribebas. Falsissime me accusabas dicendo Tu Te Iactitas Apud Silvestres Te apprime scire Linguam Latinam. nunquam enim Iactavi Inter Silvestres. non unum verbum Locutus sum Silvestribus de Lingua Latina: sed Tu maxime Iactabas in secunda Epistola, & Tamen in ea scribebas Intelligit, & accurate scribit Latina. In hac Dictione Quidem Tu non Accurate scribis Latine nam Accusativus Casus sequitur verbum scribit. Scripsisse Te oportuit Accurate scribit Linguam Latinam, vel accurate scribit Latine.

Source: My transcription from the facsimile in James Phinney Baxter, *The Pioneers of New France in New England, with contemporary letters and documents* (Albany: Joel Munsell's Sons, 1894), after p. 146.[349]

31 French Expedition into the Rocky Mountains (1743)

In the early months of 1913 newspapers around the country carried thrilling reports of the discovery in Fort Pierre, South Dakota of a lead plate bearing a Latin inscription.[350] The discovery had been made on February 16 by schoolchildren playing near a hospital. The plate had lain in the earth since the spring of 1743, when it had been buried by the Vérendrye brothers. The existence of this plate had long been known, because the Vérendryes had mentioned its burial in their journal, but its exact location had not been known. Moreover, for the first time the text of the inscription could be read. In fact some newspapers printed the Latin in their reports of this finding.

In the spring of 1742 the Vérendrye brothers—Joseph (1717–61) and François (1715–94)—undertook an expedition to the west in search of a water route to the Pacific.[351] For several years their father, Pierre Gaultier de Varennes et de la Vérendrye (1685–1749), had been attempting to do the same, and another brother had made it perhaps as far as Nebraska.[352]

They departed Fort La Reine, about sixty miles west of present-day Winnipeg, on April 29, 1742, and after spending time among the Mandan tribe in present-day North Dakota they perhaps reached the Rocky Mountains, in northwest Wyoming. On their return east, in March of 1743 they reached present-day Pierre, South Dakota—some sixty years before Lewis and Clark—and prior to departing they set up a lead plate with the inscription printed below. The plate has been called "one of the most valuable monuments of the history of the west."[353]

Anno XXVI Regni Ludovici XV[354] Prorege,
Illustrissimo Domino, Domino Marchione[355]
De Beauharnois MDCCXXXXI
Petrus Gaultier de La Verendrie Posuit[356]

Source: Verendrye Site at nps.gov.

32 Journal of the Seven Years War (1759, 1762)

Henry True (1726–82), the first pastor of the Protestant congregation in Hampstead, New Hampshire, was a chaplain to a New Hampshire regiment that saw action in upstate New York during the Seven Years War.[357] During the war True kept a journal, partly in Latin, in which he records the weather, troop movements, conversations, religious experiences, as well as his affection for his wife and children back home. It extends from June 1 to October 18, 1759 and again from June 29 to October 16, 1762.

The first passage included below is from Tuesday, July 3, 1759, when his company reached Lake George. A year earlier the British had suffered a serious defeat at Ft. Ticonderoga (also known as Ft. Carillon), where Lake George empties into Lake Champlain. Control of this fort was essential to the British effort to penetrate the Champlain Valley and reach Montreal and Quebec. This year, however, the French offered little resistance. On July 27, 1759 British forces under the command of General Jeffrey Amherst took Ft. Ticonderoga, having suffered few casualties.[358]

The second and third passages are from August 1762, when the New Hampshire regiment had moved across the state to Oswego.

The spelling and punctuation are printed as they appear in the printed transcription.

Tuesday, July 3d.—Ab Edvardo[359] removebamus ad Lacum Georgii cum bis milibus hominum, cum magnis instramentis Belli, secundum octavam Horam noctis fecimus itineris finem et nobis Lacus Georgii apparuit, beneficio Dei omnes venimus salvi, hac nocte ventus fuit altus, pulvis in Aethere volitabat, Locus vidibatur deformis, Hiemi cubuimus, sed gratia Dei valitudine fruibar, de Domo putavi, eos Dei providentia protegit.

Saturday, August 18th.—Dies Serenus visi Robert Makane,[360] colloquium habui cum eo de eternis. Dixit mortem non terrere eum, in secreto preces habuit ab eneunte Aetate, circiter Decimam horam expiravit, Juxta tertiam horam P. M. Sepelitus, Postia nostra tabunacula trans flumen—movebamus, ubi castra Aedificant.

Sabbath, August 19th.—Dies Serenus habui sermonem apud milites—post meridiem Arma virumque canerem, habui aliquam mitigationem in mea anima, visum est mihi habere cor—ut tolleretur ad Deum pro meo populo, familia, amicis exercituique, O utinam me illum Diem videre quando proficiscar ad meum populum familiamque, eis Deus benedicat hac nocte pluebat tonabat cum acuto fulgore.

Source: *Journal and Letters of Rev. Henry True of Hampstead, New Hampshire* (Marion, OH: Star Press, printed for Henry True, 1900), 7, 13.

33 Latin Letters among Friends (1765)

Dr. Benjamin Rush (1746–1813), a leading doctor in colonial America and a signer of the Declaration of Independence, was a vigorous opponent of classical education. In a famous 1789 essay he delineated a series of practical and philosophical objections to an educational system based on the study of the Greek and Latin languages.[361] He was sanguine, but realistic, about his prospects for reform. He "expect[ed] to prevail in the United States in [his] attempt to bring the dead languages into disrepute,"[362] but he likened himself to David, attempting to slay Goliath.[363]

When challenged on his views by John Adams, he responded: "Who are guilty of the greatest absurdity—the Chinese who press the feet into deformity by small shoes, or the Europeans and Americans who press the brain into obliquity by Greek and Latin?"[364] One of his most serious charges was that the languages conspired against the democratic ethos. As he wrote in the same letter to Adams: "Do not men use Latin and Greek as the scuttlefish emit their ink, on purpose to conceal themselves from an intercourse with the common people?"[365] The classics not only "consume the flower of human life" but they induce readers to permit or to perpetrate "ancient crimes."[366] Nor did he believe that the study of the classics improved one's proficiency with English. As he explained, the correction to his own pompous and affected vernacular had come from reading Hume and Swift.[367] In short, the classics, like "Negro slavery and spirituous liquors," were obstacles to "the progress of morals, knowledge, and religion in the United States."[368]

In his later years Rush continued to press the attack. In 1810 he taunted Adams: "Were every Greek and Latin book (the New Testament excepted) consumed in a bonfire, the world would be the wiser and better for it." The linguistic hegemony of Rome, Rush averred, like Rome's earlier military and religious prowess, was "unjust." He pronounced: "'Delenda, delenda est lingua Romana' should be the voice of reason and liberty and humanity in every part of the world."[369]

Rush himself had received a classical education, first at West Nottingham Academy (in Rising Sun, Maryland) and then at the College of New Jersey (later Princeton). Following an apprenticeship with a Philadelphia physician, he pursued medical studies in Edinburgh and was awarded the M.D. in 1768 following the successful defense of his thesis, *De coctione ciborum in ventriculo*, which is said to be characterized by "elegant latinity."[370] He later served as Surgeon General of the Continental Army and as professor at the College of Philadelphia, and he was one of the founders of Dickinson College.

The following letter dates from the summer of 1765. In anticipation of his matriculation at Edinburgh, Rush had been studying the classics, taking "great pleasure in reading Latin authors" and reading "more physic in Latin than ever."[371] During this same summer Ebenezer Hazard (1744–1817), Rush's classmate at the College of New Jersey who had recently moved to New York, proposed initiating a Latin correspondence with Rush.[372] But after a few letters Rush begged off: "Public commotions and calamities are increasing too fast to admit of a communication of sentiments in Latin." (This, evidently, is a reference to the crisis precipitated by the Stamp Act of 1765). Rush allowed, however, that they might resume a Latin correspondence once "the restoration of peace and tranquillity to our distressed country gives us more time to pursue that useful branch of improvement."[373]

One of Rush's Latin letters to Hazard has already been printed.[374] The following letter, however, has never been printed, so far as can be determined. The original spelling for the most part has been retained.

Charissime Amice /

Tesseram tui amoris recipi, cui ago tibi gratias maximas. Incipisti methodum scribendi a quo spero nos in futuro multum prodesse. Lingua latina est digna cultu, praesertim a me quia apud Edinburgum compulsus ero scribere Thesem vel Dissertationem inauguralem de aliquo morbo lingua Romana, aut laureae Collegii temporibus meis nunquam cingent.[375]

Hanc Litteram per pastorem tuum Reverendum recipies Dom: Rodgers.[376] Laetis pectoribus, et bracchiis expansis non dubito quin gratulabamini Adventum Urbe Novi Eboraci. Diu vivat ornamentum Ecclesiae, fulcrum religionis verae, approbatus Deo, amatusque populo. Nobis concionem optimam praedicavit die solis postrema de officiis et gloria Iesu mediatoris, a tertio capite Revelationis Sancti Iohannis et versu 7[ma].[377]

Pastor noster celeberrimus Murray omnibus nunc placet.[378] Apud funerem nuper loquebatur, tametsi tam strenue modum opposuit. Apologiam fecit quando apud locum sepulchri provenit funus. Narravit a quibus causis praeiudicia oriebantur, sed (Deo monstranti viam) iam nunc utilititas [sic] innocentiaque modi patifecere—tunc de peccato originali—de imperio inexorabili pallidi mortis, et incerta adventu eius solemniter praedicavit. Parentes mortui infantis refocillebat a promissis divinis. Ubi Christus parvulos illi venire obsecrat, nam ab talibus caelum constare.

Dom: Brainerd nuper uxorem ducebat, vid: Dom:[m] Price.[379] "Connubio iunxit stabili, propriamque dicavit"[380] Dominus Murray. Ceremoniae nuptiales cito peracti fuerant, nam tantum iubebat illos peragere promissa, officiaque quae (non dubitavit) ambobus diu ex quo praenosceri.

Nullam parum Latinam tua littera video. In uno loco habes "ulla mea epistola" nonne magis elegans si mea epistola in casu genitivo numeri pluralis positae fuissent? In fine sententiae secundae habes quoque producet quod lectione tua magis erit dignum. Quocum substantivo concordat dignum? Certe non cum ulla mea epistola. Obsecro per omnem mihi amicitiam ut monstres meos quoque errores, scribendo, proxima occasione.[381]

Vale, iterumque vale ab imo pectore—Tempus celerrime fugit. Eheu horae fugaces![382] O bene vivemus hoc mundo, ut cum Deo aeternum vivemus posthac.

Medicus eximius Morgan praefulget medicis omnibus nostris.[383] Decus et gloria loco natali. Est enim quid Horatius de amico suo narrat in itinere ad Brundusium "Homo factus ad unguem"[384]

Valde cupio videre te.

—"Dextram iungere dextrae,
et veras audire et reddere voces"[385] Virg:

Amorem praesente medico Treat[386] [ne]c non Chirurgico McLane. Scribam si possim medico Treat.

Denuo vale. Diu vivas. Saluta matrem, sororem[387] et Thomam Hazard[388] nomine meo. Soror tua Maria valet. Domina Flint[389] vobis omnibus amorem largitur. Hodie illam, heri sororem vidi. —

Tuus sum amantissimus quondam condiscipulus semper amicus.

Philad[a]: Officina nostra, Iulii die decima quinta 1765.

Benjaminus Rush

Source: Library Company of Philadelphia, Rush Family Papers: Benjamin Rush Papers, Box 1, folder 19, Philadelphia, Pennsylvania.

34 Vale California! (1767)

In 1773 the papal brief *Dominus ac Redemptor* mandated the universal dissolution of the Jesuits, but this was the culmination of a series of individual decrees enacted by European nations, beginning with Portugal in 1759. In 1767, by order of King Charles III (r. 1757–88), the Jesuits were banished from Spain and from all Spanish territories, including those in the Americas.

The following Latin passage indicates that the consequences of the expulsion were wrenching. It is taken from *Relatio Expulsionis Societatis Iesu Ex Provincia Mexicana, Et Maxime e California*, by Francis Bennon Ducrue (1721–79).[390] At the time of the banishment Ducrue, who was born in Münich and arrived in Mexico in 1749, was Superior of the (Baja) California missions, working in particular at Santa María de Guadalupe. On Christmas Eve of 1767 Ducrue was ordered by Captain Don Gaspar de Portalá to summon the sixteen Jesuits then working in the California missions—six Spaniards, two Mexicans, and eight Germans—for departure to the mainland, followed by an overland trip to Veracruz, and then overseas to Europe. Each Jesuit was permitted to carry only provisions for the journey, but allowance was made for three books.[391]

Ducrue sent his account of the expulsion along with a brief dictionary of some terms from the native Californian language (*Specimina linguae Californicae*) to the German Protestant scholar Christoph Gottlieb von Murr (1733–1811), who published them in his Nuremberg-based *Journal zur Kunstgeschichte*.[392] The first part below describes the enforcement of the order of expulsion. The latter portion contains excerpts from a farewell speech to Native Americans that was given by one of the Jesuits. Following the expulsion, Ducrue returned to Münich.

Annus agebatur salutis nostrae millesimus septingentesimus sexagesimus septimus, quo universa Societas Iesu non solum ex Hispania Europea, sed et ex omnibus Americae utriusque regnis et provinciis exsulare regio decreto compulsa fuit. Res autem tanti momenti diu ante cum multo silentio tractabatur, donec destinatus exsecutioni dies adventaret. Erat autem dies hic ipsi SSmo Cordi Iesu sacer, et vel ideo aureis characteribus cordibus nostris perpetuo imprimendus, quod tali die (inciderat enim in feriam sextam[393]) quo Dominus et Dux noster Iesus pati dignatus est, etiam Societas illius passionem suam inchoaverit.

In hunc finem summo mane in omnibus civitatibus, ubi Societas nostra collegium habebat, omnes colles, et praesertim quae ad collegium ducebant, a numeroso milite occupatae fuere, quin vel ipsi insoliti huius apparatus finem divinare possent. Hora vero quarta, dato ad surgendum signo, urbium praefecti collegii campanam pulsare, et aperta porta cum armata manu irruere, ac omnia simul cubicula occupare aggressi sunt; tum demum patres omnes ad sacellum domesticum, vel ad triclinium convocabantur. Somniare sibi videbantur patres, nec quid cum illis ageretur, sciebant. Hinc timere omnes, alii etiam mortem iam vicinam exspectare, alii omnino semianimes corruere, alius denique, licet mente captus, rei insolentia perterritus e fenestra se praecipitare visus, quo lapsu etiam vitam prius finivit, quam rei eventum viderit . . .

. . . Et hinc illa suspiria, hinc denique intensissimus ille dolor, quem explicare aut credere nullus alius poterit quam illi, qui quantum laboris ac sudoris illae animae constiterint, experti, et inde tam irreparabile damnum dimensi fuerint.

At nihil iam lacrimae, nihil lamenta. Regis urgent imperia,

abeundum, nec aliud iam superest solatium, quam nostra innocentia et maxime inscrutabilia Dei iudicia. Valete ergo pauperculae oviculae! Valete carissimi in Christi filioli! Dei suprema dispositio est. Nolite dubitare de illius misericordia. Nolite timere! Super nos enim, non super vos, haec tempestas exorta est. Habetis Patrem, nempe caelestem, qui vobis electis Abrahae filiis providebit. Veniet vobis praesto pastor et doctor, qui vos per easdem aeternarum veritatum semitas, quas nos vobis demonstravimus, ad caelestem patriam perducat. Servate fidem, quam recepistis. Servite Deo, quem cognovistis, et sperate in illius misericordia infinita, nos denuo coniungendos in Patria. Valete! Aeternum valete!

Dixit haec Pater fracta iam voce, (nec plura permisit dolor) et conscenso equo inter stupendos miserorum eiulatus et copiosum lacrimarum imbrem discessit . . .

Verum non valet ratio, ubi vinctas manus et respectus et auctoritas tenent. Discedendum iam, et illorum umeris efferendi ad cymbam patres quos hi paulo ante suis tamquam perditas oviculas ad ovile Christi detulerant. Vale ergo, dilecta California! amandissimi longe Indi, valete! Non nostra voluntate a vobis avellimur sed superiori dispositione; at licet corpore separemur, cordibus tamen nostris vos inscriptos tenemus, nulla umquam aetate, oblivione nulla, nec ipsa morte delendos. Cessate iam a lacrimis, cessate a lamentis; frustra haec. Nolite flere super nos; imus enim gaudentes, quoniam digni habiti sumus pro nomine Iesu contumeliam pati. Adiuvimus vos, quantum per divinam providentiam licuit, et adduximus vos ad semitas vitae aeternae.

Dixere haec et similia Patres, dum cymbae imponerentur, moxque Litanias lauretanas[394] alta voce recitavimus, usque dum navim non procul a portu distantem sub medium noctis conscendimus.

Source: Benno Francisco Ducrue, "Relatio Expulsionis Societatis Iesu ex Provincia Mexicana, et maxime e California A. 1767, cum aliis scitu dignis notitiis," *Journal zur Kunstgeschichte* 12 (1784): 217–18, 226–27, 237–38.[395]

35 Electric: Benjamin Franklin in Germany (1767)

During Benjamin Franklin's eighteen years in Europe he made one brief visit to Germany. In mid-June 1766, after he had presented to the English House of Commons the American case against the Stamp Act, Franklin set out from London for the continent with Sir John Pringle (1707–82), a prominent physician and professor of moral philosophy in Edinburgh. In a letter to his wife, Franklin described the trip as his necessary annual vacation, and he alleged that his health had been compromised the previous year by his failure to take such an excursion.[396] After spending some time in France, Franklin and Pringle visited Göttingen and Hanover.

Franklin later spoke of being "impress'd" with the "Learning and Politness" of the professors at Göttingen,[397] and he signed a copy of his *Experiments and Observations on Electricity made at Philadelphia in America* (London 1769) to the professoriate there. Additionally, he and Pringle were elected foreign members of the Königliche Akademie der Wissenschaften. It has been argued that Franklin's brief encounter with the young research university in Göttingen prompted Americans to take an interest in German universities and may also have influenced Franklin's own plans for the College of Philadelphia (later the University of Pennsylvania).[398] In Hanover Franklin met Johann Friedrich Hartmann, the head of the Royal Hospital in that city, who had recently published *Elektrische Experimente im luftleeren Raum* (Hanover 1766). It may have been from Hartmann, in fact, that Franklin obtained a pulse-glass, a hand-held device for boiling water.[399] In the aftermath of his visit, Franklin received the following Latin letter from Hartmann.

For his part, Franklin knew Latin well. In fact, in his *Autobiography* he claims that after one year of formal study at South Grammar School (Boston Latin) he had "neglected" Latin entirely, but that at a later date he nonetheless was able to read "a Latin Testament" with some facility due to his intervening study of French, Italian, and Spanish.[400] Indeed, based on his own experience, Franklin advocated an educational reform: rather than making Latin a propaedeutic for modern languages, the sequence should be reversed.

An extended treatment of Franklin's engagement with the Latin language remains to be written.[401] His massive correspondence contains, in addition to the one presented here, numerous Latin letters from European scholars and scientists.[402] Notable, too, is his own publishing house's edition of James Logan's annotated translation of *De Senectute*, which Franklin hailed as the "first Translation of a *Classic* in this *Western World*."[403]

In the following letter Hartmann refers to Franklin's work on the lightning rod, which led to Franklin being honored at home and abroad. Harvard and Yale awarded him honorary degrees in 1753, and he received the Copley Prize from the Royal Academy in London, the first non-British resident to win this honor. Immanuel Kant considered Franklin a "new Prometheus" for bringing fire down from heaven, and Turgot (1727–81), following Manilius, penned the following hexameter celebrating Franklin's achievements: *Eripuit coelo fulmen sceptrumque tyrannis*.[404] Another tangible indication of Franklin's international reputation is that his writings on electricity were translated into Latin, most likely sometime in the late 1760s.[405]

Viro Summe Reverendo, Franklino, S. P. D.
Ioannes Friedericus Hartmannus

Saepe mihi rediit iucundissima eius recordatio diei, quo visere te atque colloqui tecum primum licuit. Vehementer, crede mihi, de eo doleo, quod, utut tum erant temporis locique rationes, et machinas electricas et experimenta ita tibi conspicienda offerre non poteram, ut digna tanti tamque docti viri observatione essent. Noli existimare, in me aliquid culpae positum fuisse. Princeps Schwarzburg Rudolstadiensis,[406] qui pro suo in litteris amore epistolarum mecum habet commercium, cum accepisset, te in itinere per Germaniam constitutum esse, nihil magis in votis habuit, quam ut colloqui tecum copia sibi fieret; eaque de causa virum quemdem doctum, amicum suum, Gottingam miserat, te ut suo nomine salutaret. Iste vero ipso die primum Gottingam pervenit, quo tu urbem istam reliqueras; itaque spe tui visendi deiectus est.

Inter haec quidam in Germania Princeps a me expetiit, ut machinas ad deducenda ex aedificiis fulmina in suis terris construendas curarem; qua de re summis abs te precibus contendo, ut eam rationem, qua tu in America hunc in finem usus es,[407] accuratius describas. Ita fiet, ut popularibus meis valde prosis; et summum ceteros apud illos adipiscaris honorem.

Animus mihi est, historiam Electricitatis,[408] quantum ego valeo, plenam conficere. Iam cum hac in re nemo fere maius te nomen habet, communices mecum velim, quae de experimentis atque inventionibus tuis imprimis memoria digna videntur. Equidem non nego, valde audacter me ex te petere, sed semper timido mihi succurrit humanitas tua, et, quod in summa felicitatis meae parte posuerim, animus tuus in me propensus.

Si quid ego te iuvare possim, promptum me habebis atque paratissimum. Ita vale faveque.

Dabam Hannoverae, MDCCLXVII. Calendis Octobris.

Source: Jared Sparks, *The Works of Benjamin Franklin*, vol. 7 (Boston: Hilliard and Gray, 1840), 326–27.[409]

36 Loyalist Latin in New York (1777)

John MacKenna (1743–89) was a Catholic chaplain to Loyalist regiments during the Revolutionary War.[410] Born in County Meath (Ireland), MacKenna had been a parish priest in Glengarry, Scotland before he joined a group of 300 Highlanders (largely from the McDonnell clan) who sailed to America in 1773 and settled in New York's Mohawk Valley, many as tenants on the vast estate of Sir William Johnson (d. 1774). These immigrants, who had taken an oath of loyalty to the British crown upon their settlement in America, did not share the revolutionary sympathies of their neighbors, and eventually the Continental Congress directed General Philip Schuyler to strip them of their weapons, and six of them were taken as hostages to Lancaster, Pennsylvania. Increasingly isolated in New York, many of the Highlanders, including MacKenna, sought refuge in Canada, and once there some of them joined Loyalist regiments. MacKenna was chaplain to two of these regiments—the Royal Highland Emigrants and the Royal Yorkers—as well as more generally to any Catholic soldiers, regardless of nationality, who were under the command of Governor General Guy Carleton. MacKenna was, according to a modern biographer, "unquestionably the most active chaplain on the Canadian station."[411]

MacKenna wrote the Latin letter printed below to Étienne Montgolfier (1712–91), the superior of Sulpician priests in Canada and the Vicar General for the Bishop of Québec. Montgolfier, for his part, was a committed loyalist, following the events of the war closely.[412] At the time of this letter, MacKenna was accompanying Lt. Col. Barry St. Leger who, in an attempt to split the American colonies in two, had marched across central New York and was engaged in a protracted siege of Ft. Stanwix (also known as Ft. Schuyler), located at the site of present-day Rome, New York.[413] Ultimately St. Leger's quest to take the fort was unsuccessful, but during the siege the British and their Mohawk and Seneca allies won an engagement in the nearby town of Oriskany, defeating four patriot regiments and their Oneida allies en route to relieve the fort.[414]

Little is known for certain about MacKenna's education, although some sources indicate that his seminary formation took place at the Irish College in Louvain. Moreover, it is unclear why he opted to write in Latin. He knew French (in addition to German, Gaelic, and English).

Due to poor health MacKenna returned to County Meath in 1778, and he died eleven years later, having attempted on more than one occasion to seek increased compensation from the British government for his losses during the war.

The letter was written from Wood Creek, located to the west of Fr. Stanwix, and it is dated August 10, 1777.[415]

Reverende ac perdilecte Domine, tandem aliquando pervenimus ad arcem fort stanikx, quae brevi in nostra possessione, Deo adiuvante, erit, cum omnino a regalibus circumcincta sit, septima huius[416] Dominus johnson baro,[417] cum octoginta (80) ex propriis copiis, et quingentis (500) sylvestribus, mille bostonenses[418] tribus fere leucis ab arce[419] fort staninkx aggressus fuit, obtinuit Dominus johnson victoriam, occisi fuerunt ducenti bostonenses inter quos fuerunt ipsorum generalis Harkiman[420] et multi ex principalibus officialibus, Dominus johnson perdidit tantum quatuor officiales, sex milites, et viginti indos, triginta in toto occisi.[421] Dominus st Leger imperat semper ad arcem fort stanikx. Dominus Roywell[422] st ours, salebyry,[423] vasal, Bazin[424] et omnes alii canadenses recte valent. omnes bono animo sumus. valde difficile est mihi quotidie dicere missam propter bellum et nihil desuper est tam omni veneratione in christo humillimus et obedientissimus Rae Dois vae[425]

Joannes MacKenna.

Digneris partiri salutem omnibus Reverendis Dominis seminarii atque patri well.[426] Capti fuerunt bostonenses triginta tantum in bello propter angustias temporis pauca scripsi.

Source: Excerpt from "Father John McKenna: A Loyalist Catholic Priest" by Peter Guilday, published by *The Catholic World*, Vol. 133, © 1931.[427]

37 American Medicine: A Proposal at Williamsburg (1782)

On June 15, 1782 the Episcopalian clergyman James Madison (1749–1812), the eighth president of the College of William & Mary, wrote his cousin James Madison (1751–1836), the future United States President, to report on life in Williamsburg in the immediate aftermath of the Revolutionary War. (The surrender at Yorktown, only thirteen miles distant from campus, had occurred eight months previously.) In particular Rev. Madison described an event that had brought "the greatest Respect . . . to our University." Three days earlier, the eminent French physician Jean François Coste (1741–1819) was awarded an M.D. degree by William & Mary, one of the first institutions in the (future) United States to confer this degree.[428] To commemorate the occasion Coste had delivered a Latin oration that was well received by the generals and officers in attendance.[429] All told, Madison pronounced, it was "a very brilliant Appearance," and it was a sign that the young colonies did not neglect science, "tho' it seemed to want the Arm of our Ally, as much as our unfortunate Country did some Time past."[430]

Coste, born in Villes and educated in Paris and Valence, had been a military doctor in France and Switzerland, and he had been recommended by Voltaire to oversee a hospital in the short-lived utopian city of Choiseulville near Lake Geneva.[431] He published widely, and in 1774 he became a member of the Royal Academy of Sciences. In July 1780 he accompanied Count de Rochambeau to the British colonies to serve as First Physician to the French army. On board ship he composed *Compendium Pharmaceuticum*, a handbook of formulae for prescriptions, which was published in Newport upon his arrival.[432] During the siege at Yorktown Coste supervised a field hospital, and following the British surrender he set up a hospital for French and Continental troops on the grounds of William & Mary, an action that won him an elegant commendation from an appreciative General Washington.[433] Back in Europe, Coste served as the first elected mayor of Versailles and then as chief medical officer for Napoleon's coastal armies.

The following Latin passages are: 1) the brief preface to Coste's *Compendium Pharmaceuticum*; 2) the dedication of his published Williamsburg oration, and 3) selections from his Williamsburg oration in which he sketches a program for "philosophic medicine" in the young American republic. Coste holds out the wartime experience in Williamsburg as a paradigm—just as soldiers were treated on the college campus, so too medical education in America should always feature the theoretical informed by the practical, and vice-versa; additionally Coste proposes three regional medical schools and a national medical association; he further asks why Americans, though blessed with good air, food, and water, nonetheless do not often live past the age of forty.[434]

I

Remedia pauca numero suadebant et belli et maris et longinquae navigationis ancipites casus. Meis haec non mediocriter arridet votis necessitas, quae praestantiora in arte admittit tantum. Quo simplicior enim, eo melior, eo vere ditior medicina. Quae magis deceret viros, quibus libertatis genio duce et auspice, ut valentibus sola heroica tentanda et peragenda, sic sanitati et patriae et bellice amico foederi restituendis nulla nisi heroica profutura sunt auxilia!

II

Georgio Washington,
Libertatis et Patriae
Armis Parenti,
Pietate Filio;
Viro

Totius Vitae Integritate,
Tenacitate Propositi,
Constantia In Arduis,
Temperantia In Triumphis,
Famae
Vel Ipsis Hostibus
Intactae,
Suus Et Alter Orbis
Dum Plaudebant . . .
Hoc Tentamen
Quod Civium Incolumitati Iam Consecratum,
D.D.D.

III

Vestrum est, aut vestrum esse debet, Viri clarissimi, quidquid liberum, optimum et honestum. Libertatis ius orbi novo facitis, fecistis immo . . .[435] Liberam et facitote ipsi medicinam. Quae decet, haec proderit. Nulla homines vere liberos, nulla sapientissimos homines, nulla homines viros, nisi mascula, virilis, et philosophica decet medicina.

Non aliam, non extraneam exquiritote quam quae fuit divini Hippocratis. Haec praesertim experientiae doctrina coniunctae laude inclaruit.[436] Cuius, auditores, quo loci encomium opportunius, aptius, quam in hoc scientiarum optimarumque disciplinarum sanctuario; dum utile dulci miscere curiosi, cathedram arti saluberrimae erexerunt,[437] dum nosocomium hospes in academica, dum non aliis nisi academicis viris aegrotantes nostri utuntur hospitibus.[438] Quod certe dum singularis illorum humanitatis eximium prae se fert exemplar, non minus schema et quidem insigne praebet omnis illius commodi quo luxuriaretur scientia medica, si nosocomium semper in academia, aut potius si nulla esset unquam extra nosocomium medica academia.

O utinam sic ad rectae experientiae normam informaretur doctrina in medicis, semperque a doctrinae lumine experientia mutuaretur praesidium! Quo fieret ut nec toties manca, nec rudis toties experientia, nec toties inutilis, toties stulte superbiens scientia, principatum in alterutram vicissim usurparent . . . exule prorsus philosophia, divina illa philosophia, sine qua nec sublime, nec optimum, nec bonum, nec honestum quidquam, ab ullis unquam nec scientia, nec arte, nec hominibus expectandum esse videatur.

. . .

Omnem hanc medicinae docendae provinciam absolverent tres duntaxat scholae, omnibus foederatis Americae rebuspublicis dicatae; quarum prior Cantabridgiae, Novae quam vocant Angliae; altera Philadelphiae, mediis ditionibus; Gulielmopolitana Virginiae et Australibus magis competeret.[439]

Advocatis in conventum, hoc de negotio, quos quaeque respublica aptiores doctioresque artis magistros novit, penes ipsos sit, sic, non annuente solummodo, sed iubente supremo Senatu, quem Congressum vocant, qui totius reipublicae bono, commodis, honori invigilat, statuta de medicinae studio et praxi contrahere; libros temporibus et locis accommodatos scribere, aut iam scriptos et laudatos seligere, probare, commendare, sed nullos nisi dicto philosophiae medicinalis sigillo insignitos...

Penes ergo lectissimum medicorum illorum conventum, penes genuinos illos Apollinis filios et nepotes sit genuina artis statuta edicere, quae praeiudicia, quae pravas consuetudines abrogent; quae magistros artis suimet ipsorum iuris faciant . . . Penes ipsos sit quidquid parvum, vile, inconcinnum, prae-conceptae datum aut concessum opinioni visere denuo, corrigere, antiquare, damnare, rescindere. Ipsamet bona si affluant, ne effluant, intra suos et privatos coercere limites . . . Liberam liberi artem doceant, addiscant, imperent; non rudi superstitione stupratam exerceant.

Sed urget quis forsan: num parentes nostros occiderunt quos sic vocare amas aniles medici? Eheu! Civis bone! Monumenta adi . . . Lapides ipsi loquentur. A Bostoniensium scopulosis litoribus ad nicotianos usque Virginiae agros, brevitatem vitae testantur. *Ostendunt terris vos tantum fata.*[440] In regionibus sanis in quibus ex probatis, aër, cibus, potus a natura boni, unde brevitas illa vitae quae lustrum vix octavum superat?[441] Et a pessimo regimine et a prava medicinae praxi . . . Alio igitur modo tuenda, alio restituenda sanitas.

Num emendatio illa medicinae, libertatis limites circumscriptura ibit? Nulla, nec vos prorsus fugit, nulla potest esse nisi rationalis libertas. Alioquin licentia foret et damnanda. Quid civilis libertas, si praeiudiciis denuo serviant? Vilius est certe, Americani cives, vilius est praeiudicatae opinionis mancipium quam tyrannidis. Huius vinculis impotens et nolens premor . . . illius servitutem ni excutiam, liber esse nolo. Liber, liber sum, dic, age . . . Dicant et sint . . . indiscriminatim cuivis obvio sic vitas civium negotiari permittere delirium fuit cadentis imperii. Qui possent eadem culpa teneri Respublicae nascentes, Philosophia matre, Marte ipso parente?

Sources: I Jean-François Coste, *Compendium Pharmaceuticum* (Newport: Henry Barber, 1780).
II, III Jean-François Coste, *Oratio Habita in Capitolio Gulielmopolitano in Comitiis Universitatis Virginiae, Die XII Iunii M. DCC. LXXXII* (Leiden: 1783), 7–8, 89–90, 91–92, 103.

38 Unhappiness in the Heartland (1786)

The following is an excerpt from a 1786 letter of the Catholic priest Paul de Saint Pierre (1751–1826) written from Kaskaskia (see sections 29 and 30), a town with early missionary foundations located south of St. Louis on the Illinois side of the Mississippi River. Born Paul Heiligenstein in Germany, Saint Pierre entered the Carmelite order in France and by command of King Louis XVI emigrated to the American colonies where, probably, he served as chaplain to a German regiment in Count Rochambeau's army. He was present for the British surrender at Yorktown in 1781. Honorably discharged, he made his way to the far west of the newly independent colonies and served as pastor successively of three Mississippi River towns, Cahokia (just across the Mississippi from St. Louis), Kaskaskia, and St. Genevieve (on the western shore of the Mississippi and therefore in Spanish territory). He spent the last two decades of his life in Iberville, Louisiana.[442] The letter excerpted below was addressed to a priest in Detroit.

Plurimum Reverende ac Eximie Domine Confrater,[443]

. . . Nil novi his in partibus, quam quod Praefectus Apostolicus tredecim provinciarum[444] mihi adnuntiaverit iubilaeum a Summo Pontifice dictis provinciis nuperrime indultum.[445] De cetero patriam istam invenio adeo duram, ut vix hic permanere valeam. Nescio quo fato huc pervenerim. Fui bene in Gallia; iussus a rege christianissimo me transtuli in tredecim Provincias ubi fungebar munere Capellani campestris exercitus gallici. Finito bello Legatus Galliae residens Philadelphiae[446] tantum institit ut me huc transferrem, ut non possem renuere id quod petiit.

At vero cum invenio regionem totam quantam mutatam, pessimisque hominibus undequaque repletam, qui nec

Deum, nec legem timent,[447] omnino mentis sum illam data occasione prima derelinquere. Me transferrem quam lubentissime in Dioecesin canadensem accepto adnutu gratioso Illustrissimi Domini Episcopi,[448] quem ut desuper informet, instanter flagito, exspectans favorable [sic] responsum perenno ad cineres sum.

Reverende ac Eximie Domine confrater, humillimus servus, De Saint Pierre, Parochus Missionarius.

In parochia Immaculatae Conceptionis[449] 18 februarii 1786.

Source: Clarence Walworth Alvord, ed., *Kaskaskia Records, 1778–1790*, Collections of the Illinois State Historical Library, vol. 5 = Virginia Series, vol. 2 (Springfield, IL: Illinois State Historical Library, 1909), 532, 533–34.

39 How to Describe George Washington? (1786)

The most famous sculpture of George Washington, thought to capture his likeness better than any other, stands in the Rotunda of the Virginia State Capitol. It is the work of Jean-Antoine Houdon (1741–1828), one of the most accomplished sculptors of the Enlightenment era. Made of Carrara marble and completed in 1792 in France, Houdon's sculpture was erected in Richmond on May 14, 1796—three years before Washington's death—where, apart from two interludes, it has remained ever since. It depicts Washington as a modern Cincinnatus, retired from military service and not yet as President.[450] The pedestal of the sculpture bears an English inscription, the work of James Madison, composed when he was a member of the Virginia House of Delegates. Yet the pedestal could have borne a Latin inscription.

When the Virginia General Assembly authorized the statue in 1784, Governor (and later U.S. President) William Henry Harrison asked Thomas Jefferson and Benjamin Franklin, who were then in Europe, to locate a suitable sculptor to undertake this charge. Jefferson identified Houdon, who was already widely acclaimed for his sculptures of Voltaire, Diderot, St. John the Baptist, St. Bruno, and of Franklin himself. (Later Houdon would sculpt Jefferson, John Paul Jones and Robert Fulton.) As Jefferson explained to Washington, Houdon would "transmit you to posterity."[451]

Initially Houdon attempted to work from images brought over to him in France, but he soon decided that he would have to meet Washington in person. In the late summer of 1785 Houdon crossed the Atlantic—having first taken out a life-insurance policy on himself—and spent seventeen days with Washington at Mount Vernon, taking measurements and making casts. At some point during his time in America, Houdon was made aware of the text of Madison's English inscription, which had been approved by the Virginia General Assembly, but

Houdon waited until he was back in Paris to inform Jefferson that the proposed text was too long and therefore inappropriate.[452]

On February 8, 1786, Jefferson wrote Madison to inform him of Houdon's rejection of the already-approved-text and to suggest alternatives.[453] In fact, as Jefferson explained, the problem of what to put on the pedestal had been much discussed in social gatherings in Paris, and numerous proposals had emerged. Jefferson himself seems to have drawn up one proposal, which was in Latin. Yet he did not identify himself as the author; he merely indicated to Madison that this was his top choice.[454] The first passage below is this anonymous inscription.

But Jefferson also forwarded to Madison several other proposals that had been contributed by Europeans. More than half of these were in Latin. Three are presented below.

The first was the work of Jean-François Marmontel (1723–99), an author of tragedies and philosophical novels who for many years was secretary of the Académie Française. Marmontel submitted the proposal via Lafayette, who forwarded it to Jefferson.[455]

The second and third came from Paul-Henri Marron (1754–1832), a Leiden-educated Huguenot who had come to France as chaplain to the Dutch embassy and was serving as pastor of a Dutch Reformed congregation in Paris.

Madison, for his part, professed not to be attached to his own English composition, which he acknowledged was "in every respect inferior" to the inscription that Jefferson preferred,[456] but he doubted that the Virginia Legislature would revisit what they had already approved. In the end, the sculpture was installed without an inscription; only in 1814 was Madison's English text inscribed.

I

1st side: Behold, Reader, the form of George Washington. For his worth, ask History: that will tell it, when this stone shall have yielded to the decays of time. His country erects this monument: Houdon makes it.[457]

2nd side: Boston. Hostibus primum fugatis.

3rd side: Trenton. Hostibus iterum victis.[458]

4th side: York. Hostibus demum domitis.[459]

Creditis tot gentes eodem proelio domitas esse quae victae sunt? (Q. Curt., pa. 123, l.6 c.3)

II

Arma capit vindex, patria incolumi, exuit arma:
Nilque ducis retinet, comitum nisi, liber, amorem:
At decus invitum sequitur, celebratque latentem.

III

Hoc Cincinnati[460] Brutique[461] in marmore virtus,
　　Spirat in hoc Fabii[462] provida cura simul.
Exprimit Heroas tres Washingtonius unus
　　Depulit hoc felix Patria cive iugum.[463]

IV

Illa viri (aeternum fremat invidus Anglus) imago est,
　　Patria quo felix cive soluta iugo.
Mascula in heroë, Libertas, suspice vultu,
　　Ausonia eximium quidquid et Hellas habent.[464]

Sources: I, II, III Thomas Jefferson Papers, Library of Congress.[465]
IV *Journal encyclopédique ou universel* 2.1 (1788): 180.

40 Native Americans Write the Pope (1789)

The Oneida tribe of central New York was visited by French Jesuit missionaries since the 1660s, and in 1667 Jacques Bruyas (1635–1712) built a chapel for them. In 1789, six months before Baltimore was erected as the first Catholic diocese of the United States, nine members of the Oneida tribe signed a letter to Pope Pius VI (*r.* 1775–99) requesting that a bishop be appointed for them, who would also serve as primate for the entire Iroquois Confederacy. For this office they nominated Jean-Louis-Victor Le Tonnelier de Coulonge, a priest from Bourdeaux then living among the Oneida. Early historians suspected that the impetus for this request came from an enterprising French businessman and arms dealer, Peter Penet, who had gained influence with Oneida leaders.[466] A more recent historian surmises that the plan may have emerged from "Parisian aristocratic circles," but he is confident that "the Oneida signatories were fully aware of the proceedings."[467]

This letter was forwarded by Jean de la Mahotière, an agent for the Oneida, to the papal nuncio in Paris, who in turn forwarded it to the Propaganda Fide in Rome. Authorities in Rome were interested in this proposal, but they wanted more information regarding the jurisdiction under which the Oneida then resided.

Sanctissime Pater

Istam[468] habere veram religionem primum est hominis bonum, sicut fides est primum bonum supernaturale: donum caeleste ad quod nemo pervenire potest nisi per aditum ad Ecclesiam Catholicam, apostolicam romanam, cuius gubernacula tenet eius visibile Caput Summus Romanus Pontifex, Christi in terris Vicarius! Huius vestrae sanctae communionis gratiam ferventer appetunt, sanctissime pater, homines illi quos tam immerito europaei dixerunt agrestes ac feros; ii quippe ii in societates grandes, seu nationes, antiquitatis primas numeroque stupendas congregati, immensis americani continentis terris dominantur et imperant quae ab americanis finibus ad australia et occidentalia usque maria patent, easque hominibus liberis, familiis, villis, vicis atque pagis cum omnium inter omnes communitate summaque in parentes et seniores pietate frequentant.

Ardentissimo praesentim in fidem christianam studio flagrant, sanctissime pater, nationis illius indicae populi qui oneidaei dicti, gallice *les oneida*, proximi sunt septentrionales Americanarum ditionum fines numeranturque et sunt prima e quinque illis celeberrimis nationibus, ceterarum omnium debellatoribus, vulgo dictis *nationes quinque*; populi oneidaei statuta mente se ad officia civilia rite informandi, iam ratum habuerunt unum gubernationis modum aeque numeris omnibus absolutum ac sibi plene accomodatum, illud suae vitae, civilis grande consilium inniti voluerunt ac statuerunt firmo religionis christianae fundamento, quo ad felicem exitum properante, ceterae nationes indicae mox eamdem gubernationis formam in suam adoptaturae, eorum quoque bono exemplo simul ac verbi divini ministerio una pariter, uti firma proximaque spes est, convertentur ad religionem catholicam apostolicam romanam.

In quorum gratiam, pro propugnatione fidei et nostrarum salute animarum, nos supremi duces consilii, duces belli; bellatores, senes, mulieres et liberi totius oneideae nationis et nobis affinium nationum, sanctitati vestrae, supplicavimus et supplicamus providere, constituere, et confirmare Episcopum nostrae oneideae nationis et Primatem quinque nationum dilectum optimeque de nobis meritum Ioannem Ludovicum Victorem Le Tonnelier de Coulonges, equitem, origine gallum, unum vero e nobis nostra nationali adoptione, virum religione, moribus, bonis consiliis et exemplis maxime commendandum, iam selectum, nominatum et assumptum a nobis ad illas sacras functiones, illumque augere rogamus in hac prospera apud nos religionis facie quibuscumque iuribus, dignitate et praestantia in ordine ad conversionem nostrorum fratrum indorum, ad propagationem et conservationem fidei in nostris imperiis, et Deus totius auctor salutis vestram sanctitatem vestrumque pontificatum suis optimis cumulabit donis.

Datum in pleno oneideae nationis Concilio sub signo nostrorum supremorum ducum magnoque sigillo nostrae nationis, anno reparatae salutis millesimo septingentesimo octogesimo nono, et primo ab exercita nostra suprema potestate, die vero vigesima quinta Aprilis.

Tribus Lupi:
Ajestalate, Scanondoe, Hannah-Sodalh
Tribus Testudinis:
Shovonjhelego, Anthony, Sagoyowntha
Tribus Ursi:
Hagoyvownloga, Konwagalet, Agwilentengwas

(Interpretatum a nobis linguarum interprete apud sex famosas nationes indicas die et anno supradictis. De mandato supremi concilii. Nicholas Jourdain, indice Shakerad.)

Source: "A Bishop for the Indians in 1790," *Catholic Historical Review* 3 (1917): 79–89.

41 George Washington in Savannah: A Latin Greeting (1791)

In the early months of his first presidential term George Washington expressed a desire to visit each of the thirteen colonies in order to become better acquainted with the peoples and conditions of the new nation. To accomplish this end he made three separate tours. The last of these, in the spring of 1791, was an excursion of 1900 miles through the major southern cities from Delaware to Georgia. Washington kept a diary throughout this trip, which, augmented by surviving correspondence and local newspaper accounts, provides an exceptional view of the young country—its topography, history, business, and agriculture, as well as the manners and preoccupations of some of its inhabitants.[469]

The southernmost stop on this tour was Savannah, which Washington reached on May 12, and where he received, as he wrote in his diary, "every demonstration that could be given of joy and respect." Saturday, May 14 was an especially full day. He rose early to be conducted on a tour of sites related to the city's defense in 1779. Later that day, at Brown's Coffee House, he met with members of the Grand Lodge of Masons of Georgia, whose grand master, George Houstoun (1744–95), lauded Washington as the "Redeemer of his Country" and prayed that "the Great Architect of the Universe" would preserve him as "the brightest pillar of our temple." In the late afternoon Washington enjoyed an opulent outdoor feast under an elaborate arbor erected on the bank of the Savannah River. Thirteen after-dinner toasts were delivered, each accompanied not only by a blast from the Chatham Artillery Company, but also by a corresponding blast from an illuminated ship moored in the river. Later that evening guests were treated to a concert and "a tolerable good display of fireworks."

But between his meeting with the Masons and the outdoor dinner, Washington found time briefly to greet John Bergman (d. 1824), a Lutheran minister of a local German congregation. No details of Washington's conversation with Bergman are recorded, and Washington does not mention the meeting in his diary, but in at least one respect this brief encounter appears to have been unique among the other exchanges that characterized Washington's southern tour, for Bergman presented Washington with a laudatory letter written in Latin.

The Saxon-born Bergman, a graduate of the University of Leipzig, had arrived in Georgia in the spring of 1785 to minister to the Salzburgers, refugees from Austria who in 1734 had been welcomed by Gov. James Oglethorpe and directed to settle in the town of Ebenezer, about twenty-five miles upriver from Savannah. The Salzburgers had hoped to build a utopian colony, and for several decades they were regarded as model citizens by the Trustees of Georgia, but Ebenezer suffered greatly during the Revolutionary War. It was occupied nearly continuously from January 1779 to July 1783 by British troops, who appropriated the church as a hospital for their wounded and as a stable for their horses. Bergman's task, upon arrival in Georgia, was to revive the congregation in Ebenezer. But despite his efforts, the town never recovered; it remains uninhabited, although the Lutheran church constructed in 1769 is still standing.[470]

Characterized as a faithful servant and a man of "more than ordinary intellect," Bergman nevertheless "had *no knowledge of men and things*." He entrusted to his wife, a woman of "very remarkable business talents" all of his financial and professional affairs, and he himself preferred to spend time with his extensive library, some of which still survives.[471] Among the complaints that were registered against Bergman by contemporary parishioners as well as by later historians was his reluctance to consider the use of English rather than German in religious services. Apart from his religious objections to this practice, Bergman, it seems, never really learned English. It is unclear whether he expected a knowledge of Latin to be among the President's virtues. Yet Washington, though not averse to the classics—he supervised and for the most part supported his step-son's classical curriculum—did not know Latin. There is no record of Washington's response to this letter.

To the President of the United States of America.

Permittas, quaeso, Illustrissime Washington! ut devoti piique animi sensa tibi declarem, cui contigerit insignis illa felicitas, te Savannae adeundi, virum tot tantisque factis illustrem. Profecto admiratus sum tuam humanitatem et indulgentiam, qua me hominem ignotum excepisti, qui non ausus essem ad te accedere, nisi ab amico[472] optimo certior factus essem, tristem abs te discedere neminem. Georgia laetatur de tua splendidissima praesentia, qua eam exhilarare dignatus es. Diu vivas o Washington! deliciae americani populi, tuumque nomen et facta illustria sera posteritas celebrabit. Semper precabor Deum Optimum Maximum, qui te Praesidem harum civitatum constituit, ut omnibus rebus conatibusque tuis propitius adsit. Accipe hanc tenuiorem epistolam, nullo ornatu commendabilem, eadem indulgentia, qua me excipere dignatus es. Anglice quidem scripturus eram, si facultate pollerem eleganter scribendi, et ut dignum esse posset insignibus virtutibus et illustrissimis factis tuis. Peregrinus, in hanc provinciam missus sum benignissimam doctrinam Redemptoris nostri profitendi inter posteros colonorum Salisburgensium, quos inprimis quia curae meae concrediti sunt, cum omni gente germanica Georgiae Americanae tuo potentissimo patrocinio magnopere commendo. Ego vero nunquam desinam ardentissimas preces mittere ad Deum benignissimum, pro totius populi Americani salute.

Savannah. d. 14. May 1791.
John Earnst Bergman,
Minister of the German Congregation of Ebenezer

Source: George Washington Papers, Library of Congress.[473]

42 Eulogy for George Washington (1799)

The death of George Washington on December 14, 1799 elicited public expressions of grief throughout the United States and abroad. Memorial services were held in almost 200 American towns, and more than 400 eulogies were delivered in various venues—in churches of nearly every denomination, in state houses, Masonic lodges, town squares, and before various sorts of societies and groups. The Society of the Cincinnati, for example, sponsored several tributes. The Ciceronian Society of Philadelphia sponsored another. Many of these orations and sermons were printed in newspapers. Still others were printed separately and then distributed free of charge to local residents. Some, moreover, were delivered in, or were translated into, French, Dutch, and German.[474]

The brief Latin oration excerpted below was pronounced on December 28, 1799, at Harvard University, as the opening part of a program featuring prayer, music, "a solemn and pathetic discourse," an elegiac poem, and a funeral oration.[475] The orator, Joseph Willard (1738–1804), was Harvard's twelfth president. Willard's tenure saw the beginning of Harvard Medical School (1782) and a chapter of Phi Beta Kappa (1782) as well as the introduction of modern languages (French) into the curriculum (1787). Moreover, in 1799 Willard is said to have abandoned tradition and delivered his presidential commencement address in English rather than Latin, although the program for the day still featured the traditional Latin salutatory and valedictory orations and a Greek dialogue.[476]

Willard and Washington had interacted on several occasions. In 1781, during the Revolutionary War, Willard informed Washington that the General had been elected a member of the American Academy of Arts and Sciences. In the fall of 1789 Willard personally conducted Washington around Harvard's grounds during the latter's New England tour,[477] and a few months later Willard requested that Washington sit for a portrait that would adorn the university's "Philosophy chamber." Washington consented, as a demonstration of his "sincere regard and good wishes for the prosperity of the University of Cambridge."[478]

Willard, a Congregationalist minister, was born in (present-day) Maine and attended Harvard. Later he taught Greek, math, and astronomy at his alma mater—his notes for a proposed Greek Grammar still survive[479]—and he was a member of the Royal Society of England and of Göttingen.

A reviewer in the *Monthly Magazine* severely faulted the Latinity of Willard's eulogy: "On the whole, we have seldom seen a specimen of Latin composition which had so little claim to the character of purity and correctness, to say nothing of elegance."[480] A few of these criticisms are noted below.

Concio Brevis a Praeside[481]

Eheu causam lugubrem in hancce aedem conveniendi! Quid, nisi eventum acerbissimum,[482] omnibus publice deflendum, cordibus imis infligere vulnera potuisset! Video in haec atra funebria omnium vestrum ora luctuosissima oculosque humescentes, lacrimasque fere effusuros, silentio tristi conversos. Hac tacita maestitia, longe vocibus potentiore, mihi videmini dicere—"Nulla dies nobis maerorem e pectore demet; nam WASHINGTON venerandus dilectissimusque, quo nemo neque integrior esset, neque sanctior, neque spectatior, neque desiderabilior,—Ah! quomodo dicemus, praecordiis intimis non paene ruptis— WASHINGTON—vixit!" . . .

Talis fuisti, O WASHINGTON venerande et dilectissime, et sicui licitum mortem evitare, tibi fuisset: Te autem ad tempus modo divino munere donatum terrae—Te non tam diebus quam existimatione eximia longe lateque diffusa, fama insolita, gloriaque rarissima, quibus honoribus terrenis vero nihil amplius accedere potuisset, Deus poposcit, resumpsit, ad sidera revocavit—tibi ipsi quidem felicissimum, Reipublicae vero derelictae, Patre orbatae, Ah! quam acerbum. Dum autem hanc derelictionem tristissimam defleamus, quam animus intimis sensibus meminisse angitur, luctuque refugit, Deo luminum Patri, a quo descendit omnis donatio bona, et omne integrum donum,[483] qui vitam tuam, utilitate refertam, tamdiu Reipublicae foederatae protraxerit, gratias habendi ne simus negligentes;[484] nec ingrati te de lucis regnis ad hunc nostrum orbem tenebrosum redire optemus.

Beate WASHINGTON! vita nunc est tibi inter Caelicolas, nec tamen vita tua cessit ex terris; nam haec tua vita non dicenda fuit, quae corpore et spiritu contenta: Illa vero vita tua, quae civium animis inhaeret, quam posteritas alet atque tuebitur, et quae vigebit memoria saeculorum omnium. Ita civium pectora grata, cum praesentium, tum succedentium omnium tibi erunt monumenta, aereis vel marmoreis longe stabiliora, quae non innumerabilis annorum series, non fuga temporum poterit diruere, nec ferrum nec edax vetustas abolere;[485]—nomenque tuum, in cordibus imis penitus inscriptum, semper indelebile manebit.

Source: Joseph Willard, *An Address in Latin* (Cambridge, MA: Samuel Etheridge, 1800), 5, 7–8.

43 District of Columbia (1806)

In 1800, as a result of a compromise a decade earlier, the federal government relocated from Philadelphia to its present spot along the Potomac (or Potowmac) River, fifteen miles north of George Washington's Mount Vernon home. The diamond, ten-miles on a side, that comprised the District of Columbia encompassed the already-existing port towns of Georgetown and Alexandria (the latter was later retroceded to Virginia). Although George Washington conceived of a national university within the District of Columbia,[486] the region's first institution of higher learning, which in fact predates the legislative act establishing the District, was Georgetown College, which traces its roots to an academy founded by Bishop John Carroll in 1789. Since 1805 Georgetown has been administered by the Jesuits. In the following passage, the Alsatian-born Jesuit Anthony Kohlmann (1771–1836) describes the bucolic setting of Georgetown and the surrounding region, and he also remarks on the status of religious freedom in the region and the religious sensitivities of the American people.

Kohlmann was an important figure in the restoration of the Jesuits in the United States. Having fled to Switzerland during the French Revolution, he was ordained a priest for the Society of the Fathers of the Sacred Heart, an order that emerged in the wake of the suppression of the Jesuits. He worked in Austria, Padua, Pavia, Berlin, Amsterdam, and London. While in London he received word that he would be able to enter the Jesuits if he traveled to Russia, where they had never been completely suppressed. Sent to the United States to assist with the renewal of the Society, he ministered in Alexandria (Virginia) and to German congregations in Pennsylvania and New York City. He served as President of Georgetown (1817–20), and he was Vicar General of the Diocese of New York. His name adorns buildings at Gonzaga College High School (Washington, DC), which he founded, and at Fordham University. Kohlmann was also involved in a landmark court case in New York in 1813 that validated the seal of the confessional. He spent the last twelve years of his life in Rome, initially as professor at the Roman College.[487]

This letter was discovered in archives in Poland early last century and printed in the *Woodstock Letters*, an in-house journal published by the Jesuits at their seminary in Maryland.

Georgetown (Georgionopolis) Die 25 Nov. 1806
Reverendissime In Xto Pater Generalis,[488] P.C.[489]
Placuit demum Divinae Maiestati post varios casus variaque discrimina rerum[490] salvos nos, incolumesque plagis inferre Americanis . . .

Die 20 Aug. Hamburgo digressi Schotiam[491] circumlegimus ac vento fere nunquam non adverso utentes 4a demum Novembris Baltimorae tamdiu exoptatae illati sumus, ubi summa Illustrissimi Episcopi Caroll[492] laetitiae benignitatisque significatione excepti ad Collegium nostrum Georgiopolitanum secessimus finem tandem itineri imposituri. . . Ab isto Collegio exordium ducamus narrationis rerum, quas scire potissimum convenit Revdssmam Vram[493] Paternitatem.

Georgionopolis est civitas satis spectabilis, efficiens quasi partem Civitatis Vaschingthon,[494] utpote cui per pontem iuncta est.[495] Baltimora 12 fere leucis distat.[496] Collegium aedificium est regia Maiestate dignum,[497] in monte, loco omnium saluberrimo, omniumque, quae unquam viderim, amoenissimo situm. Eiusdem enim prospectus in totam civitatem Georgiopolitanam, Vaschingthon, vicinamque mira Insularum, fluminum, silvarum colliumque hinc inde assurgentium [corona] distinctam protenditur.[498] 200 ad minimum adulescentes una cum Magistris capere potest, licet in praesenti ultra 30 non complectatur. . .

Addo: videri mihi, hac aetate nullam sub sole reperiri regionem, ubi Societas faciliorem stabilioremque sedem invenire possit. Cum una ex primariis fundamentalibus Americae confoederatae legibus sit, plenissimam nullo non Religionis nomini concedere libertatem, haec sacratissima Regiminis civilis Religio, nulli se immiscere religioni.

Source: "Exemplar Litterarum P. Antonii Kohlmann ad A. R. P. N. Datarum ex America Foederata," *Woodstock Letters* 35 (1906): 1–2, 5.

44 Mission to the Cherokees (1806)

On January 10, 1806 Thomas Jefferson addressed a delegation of Cherokee chiefs who had journeyed to Washington, DC to conclude the second of two treaties with the United States. An earlier one had been signed in October 1805. One result of these treaties was the sale (at less than $0.02 per acre) of some 8.6 million acres of Cherokee hunting ground. For most Cherokees the consequences were devastating.[499]

In his address, Jefferson praised the chiefs for having taken steps to redirect resources from hunting and warring toward the promotion of agriculture and the raising of livestock. Soon, he counseled, the Cherokees should develop mills, and they should begin to work toward the establishment and proper enforcement of the rule of law. He also left them with an ominous warning not to interfere with the free flow of commerce on the Mississippi River, which, he declared, was now owned by the United States. Eventually Jefferson would offer the Cherokees the possibility of resettling west of the Mississippi, but following the Indian Removal Act of 1830, forced migration became official government policy.[500]

In the early 1800s Moravian and Presbyterian missionaries attempted to work among the Cherokees, but they had little success making converts. Another missionary attempt, very brief, was made by Frederick Caesar Reuter, a schismatic Catholic priest. Reuter had arrived in Baltimore in February 1798 and had been charged by Bishop John Carroll with ministering to German Catholics, yet he was soon suspended because, against the bishop's wishes, he encouraged the erection of a separate German Catholic parish within the city of Baltimore (St. John the Evangelist). Reuter appealed his case first to Rome (1799) and then to a Maryland court (1805), but he lost in both venues, and he resolved never again to attach himself to any denomination or congregation.[501]

In April 1806, not long after his case had been decided,

Reuter wrote President Jefferson a Latin letter proposing to undertake a mission to "civilize" the Cherokees.[502] Four months later he wrote another Latin letter, explaining that he had spent some time among the Cherokees but that he lacked the necessary resources to carry out a more permanent mission. The following is the second of these two letters.

Baltimore 30ma Augusti 1806.

Excellentissime Domine!

Quod ea, quae praeterlapso vernali tempore in litteris meis Excellentiae Vestrae a me oblatis, promittebam (de civilisatione scilicet Cherokiae Nationis) non impleverim, non in malum mihi vertat, quaeso, Excellentia Vestra, sed de omisso mihi ignoscat!

Hoc opus adgrediendi voluntas mihi non deerat, sed aliqua media tantum, hoc opus implendi, mihi deficiebant. Benevolentia Vestra, ut mihi a belli Secretario[503] litterae ad D^num^ Return Meigs[504] darentur, curabat, et eapropter debitum habeo eidem reditum meum ad urbem Baltimore insinuare; quin dictae Nationis culturae me adplicassem.

Quod promissa implere non valerem, quae tam libenter implevissem, re vera summopere dolebam. Variae circumstantiae mihi ad hoc impediebant. Illam ad cultivandam gentem necessariam litteraturam apud Cherokiam Nationem introducere mentis eram in propria eorum Cherokia lingua, optimum culturae medium, ast me ipsum ex propriis meis mediis sustentandi media necessaria mihi deerant. Iter ad illam Nationem propriis meis sumptibus perfeceram, ast tali modo mihi etiam pro futuro sustentando impar eram; et licet mihi summopere apud Cherokiam Nationem placeret, et tam libenter apud illam mansissem, tamen defectu necessariae sustentationis, Baltimore reverti, coactus eram.

Ex addita Copia Excellentia Vestra plura videbit.
Excellentiae Vestrae Servus Oboedientissimus
Fred[k] Caesar Reuter

Source: Thomas Jefferson Papers, Library of Congress.[505]

45 O Fontes Pennsylvaniae! (1809, 1810)

The United States is home to many mineral springs, which from an early date have attracted those in search of healing and, at times, a rich social life. Bedford Springs and Yellow Springs, both in Pennsylvania, were two such sites.

In 1803 John Anderson (1770–1839), a Philadelphia-trained medical doctor, constructed a 2 1/2-story, 12,000-square-foot resort with twenty-four guest rooms in order to accommodate those who desired to bathe in or to drink the waters of Bedford's four different springs, which early travelogues touted as diuretic and cathartic.[506] Anderson's resort was enormously popular. Bedford was situated along the stagecoach line linking Pittsburgh and Philadelphia, and the development of a turnpike and later the Pennsylvania Railroad only increased its accessibility.

Yellow Springs, located in southeastern Pennsylvania, had long been frequented by indigenous peoples, and they were prized by Europeans at least from the early 1700s. During the Revolutionary War George Washington established his headquarters in their vicinity, and the Continental Congress authorized the construction of a hospital there. Following the war they became a resort.[507]

In keeping with Roman models, the early American classical scholar James Ross (1743–1827) celebrated these springs in poetry.[508] The son of an Irish immigrant, Ross was educated at the College of New Jersey (Princeton), and he spent his professional career teaching in various schools and colleges in southeastern Pennsylvania. He was the first faculty member of what would become Dickinson College. Ross authored a widely-used *Latin Grammar* (Chambersburg, 1796) as well as a Greek grammar, and he produced several editions of the works of classical and humanistic authors, including Aesop, Caesar, Corderius, and Erasmus.

Ross is said to have written large quantities of Latin

verse, although only about ten poems have survived. The following Latin odes, which are not found in Kaiser's *Anthology* or in his "Census," were printed in an early medical journal. Ross dedicated the first to Dr. John Anderson "as a token of friendship." The second is dedicated to Ashbel Green (1762–1848), who two years later became Princeton's eighth president (1812–22).

J. Anderson, M.D. hos versiculos
symbolum amicitiae inscribit,
J.A. Ross

IN FONTEM BEDFORDIAE SALUTAREM

Monte decurrens, velut amnis, alto,
Fons loquax nunquam, tacitus recedis,
Abditus terris, latebrasque celans
 Fluminis unda.

Non alis campos virides vel agros;
Non greges pascis, vitulosque vaccas:
Non tuae ripae generant leones
 Dente furentes.

Sed tuas undas celebrant puellae,
Famulae et matres, puerique sponsi,
Has senes undas adamant anusque
 Ore bibentes.

Hisque gaudentes homines levabunt
Pectoris morbos, capitis dolores;
Aurium sensus, laterumque poenas
 Saepe lavando.

Has bibant isti quibus est podagra;
Has quibus tussis mala, nec fuganda
Artibus, cura aut medici periti;
Namque levabunt.

Quin et afflicti ac oculisque lumbis
Has bibant undas, stomacho dolentes:
Pauperes, dites, recreentque corpus
Saepe bibendo.

Has bibant undas vacui, salubres;
Nil nocent sanis[509] puerisve nymphis:
Pauperes multi haec, simul atque dites,
Dicere possunt.

Bedfordiae, (Pennsylvanorum) quarto Kal. Septemb. A.D. 1809.[510]

IN FONTEM FLAVULUM, PIKELIANUM, PENNSYLVANORUM.

Ad Ashbel Green, S.S.T.D.
Oden hanc
Cum plurima salute mittit Ja. Ross

Quaereret si quis, socios, amicos
Unde sanaret vacuos salute;
Flavulos fontes adeant salubres
Fontis ad undas.

Fons et hic mitis facilisque gustu,
Volvit ac undas liquidas bibenti;

Atque potando has, pariter lavando
Omnia cedunt.

Huius et fontis resident sodales
Lucus et pratum, nemora atque colles;
Rupibus[511] nec sunt scopulisve saxis,
Gramine culti.

Instar ac montis, domibus relictis,
Collis assurgens superas ad auras;
Destruat longas minitans et aedes,
Prospicit agros.

Fontis ac huius spatia atque culta
Frugibus pulchris, oculoque gratis:
Hic virent foetus, segetesque et Indi,
Tritica florent.

Arbores fructus variosque fundunt,
Hic iacent passim cerasa atque mala;
Hic vigent herbae, cucumisque melo,
Tempore quaeque.

Plurimae silvae viridesque circum,
Quae domos ornant, similes columnis;
Populi ingentes numerisque sertae,
Haec loca adumbrant.

Atque pascentes pecudes videndae hinc,
Et boves magni reboant canori,
Dum greges pingues ovium vagantes
Gramina carpunt.

Quisquis aut nervis debilis, laborat
Aut mala tussi, veniat citatus;
Quisquis aut vitet lateris dolorem;
        Has bibat undas.

Utilis hic fons capitisque poenis,
Mitigat valde stomachi dolores,
Excitat sensum, reficitque morsus
        Tempore edendi.

Fontis et vires aliae repertae,
Saepe et afflictis hominum medetur
Rheumatis morbo, medici nec ausis
        Artibus uti.

Si quis et morbi fugeret dolores,
Saepius fontes bibat ore hianti;
Quisquis hos potet liquidos habebit
        Fata morata.

Quisquis et vellet reparare corpus,
Adsit his, undae facient valentem:
Talis est virtus, recreatque membra
        Firmaque reddit.

Sentiat si quis, similis Catoni,
Viribus parci, bibere atque vellet
Nil aquae mixtae, velit atque puram,
        Hanc bibat undam.

Ergo (nec mirum) veniunt frequentes.
Coniuges carae, iuvenes, mariti,
Et senes, sponsae, pueri et puellae
        Dulce canentes.

Interim mites, hilaresque laeti
Accubant mensis; dapibusque pleni,
Quas Bonus struxit; redeunt refecti
        Viribus intus.

Aedibus J. Boni, Equitis.
Octavo Kal. Septembres, A.D. 1810.

Source: *New York Medical Repository* hex. 3, vol. 3 (1812): 34–37.

46 Latin Poetry Among Friends (1809, 1814)

St. George Tucker (1752–1827) was one of the most influential legal scholars in early America. He published a five-volume edition of Blackstone's *Commentaries* (1803). He was also a poet. In the words of his modern editor, throughout his eventful life Tucker sustained a "love affair with the Muse," although he is said to have had "the poet's passion if not the Muse's blessing."[512]

Born in Bermuda, Tucker moved to Williamsburg in 1771 in order to study law at the College of William & Mary. In 1774, following an apprenticeship under George Wythe, he was admitted to the Virginia bar. During the Revolutionary War Tucker utilized his contacts in Bermuda to oversee a smuggling operation, moving indigo, tobacco, rice, sugar, cotton, and arms between the colonies, Bermuda, and points in the Caribbean. Later, having enlisted in the Virginia militia, he was wounded at the battle of Guilford Court House, and he was present at Yorktown as a French interpreter on the staff of General Thomas Nelson. For the next four decades Tucker was at various times rector and professor at the College of William & Mary, delegate to the Annapolis Convention, and judge on three different Virginia courts. He also published numerous essays and tracts, including *A Dissertation on Slavery: With a Proposal for the Gradual Abolition of it, in the State of Virginia* (1796).[513]

Tucker's poems, mostly in English, are neo-classical. His corpus includes satire, narrative, and lyric, but he also intended to write a "Virginia version of *The Canterbury Tales*."[514] Not many of his poems were printed during his lifetime, and of those that were, few were printed with attribution.[515] Tucker also wrote at least two Latin poems. Neither of these was published; rather, they were included in personal letters.

One of these Latin poems was offered as a token of respect and friendship to Thomas Jefferson, who was seven months into his retirement from the presidency. In a cover letter, Tucker professed not to have thought of Latin composition for more than three decades. This poem bears the date "XX die Octobris. MDCCCIX," and according to an earlier draft, Tucker composed it in Fluvanna County, Virginia, "on seeing a fine print of Mr Jefferson in the Room in which I slept."[516]

Tucker wrote the second Latin poem for William Wirt (1772–1834), a Virginia lawyer and writer. Born in Bladensburg, Maryland, Wirt was orphaned at the age of eight but managed to receive a classical education. Eventually he served as Attorney General under three presidents (1817–29), and in 1832 he was the presidential candidate of the anti-Masonic party. He wrote *Letters of the British Spy* (1803) and a biography of Patrick Henry (1817), and he collaborated with Tucker on a series of essays, *The Old Bachelor* (1814), that were originally published in the *Richmond Enquirer*.[517] Wirt was said to have owned well-marked copies of Seneca, Quintilian, and Horace, and he was known for making classical allusions in court.[518] Tucker wrote this Latin poem immediately after Wirt lost an election to become a U.S. Senator from Virginia.[519] According to Tucker, the lines "were composed partly in Bed last night, & finished this morning, under the Expectation of receiving the pleasing Confirmation of those hopes which gave birth to them." As with the poem to Jefferson, Tucker offered them to Wirt as "a token of most sincere friendship & esteem."

I Ad Thomam Jefferson.

Inclyte civis! primus inter pares;
Patriae sortis impigerque custos.
Dudum, et salutis nostrae praesidium,
    Et dulce decus:

Dum Iovis ira terruit Europam,
Fulmina dum iam diruerunt urbes;

Dumque Bellona populos extinxit,
    Pax nobis risit:

Te nec ambitio (semper et iniqua,
Semperque fallax) maxima promittens,
Nec clamittantium civium caterva,
    Movit ad bella:

Te[520] neque ferox gentium tyrannus,[521]
Nutu qui reges tollitque, dimovet,
Nec qui Neptuni regnum usurpavit,
    Pollicit[522] tecum:

Socium belli sibi dum uterque
Iungere exoptat minisque insidiis,
Spectans utrumque, vultu non iniquo,
    Abnegas caedes.

Te duce, nobis quicquid est telluris
Fructus abundat. Laribus dilectis;
Iani bifrontis foribus occlusis,
    Dextera tua.

Tu libertatis dulcia munera, et
Gaudia, nunquam peritura, monstras:
Commoda pacis. Fideique purae,
    praemia doces.

Patriae carae stes consulentibus
Semper exemplar, resonentque laudes,
Inter faventis libertatis plausus,
    Dum volat aetas.

II

Ad amicum suum, Gulielmum Wirt.[523]

Paricidos ignes Catilina Romae
Magnae suppositos, ineunte flamma,
Patriae pater fortiter extinxit
In Capitolio.

Sic tu discordiae flammas, imitantes
Siculam Aetnae fulgura minantis,
Animi tui viribus extinguas,
Coetu Senatus.

Peregrinos ignes, arma peregrina,
Peregrinos dolos, spernere liceat,
Prava cum discordia, libertatis oris,
Exul effugit.

Sources: I Thomas Jefferson Papers, Library of Congress.[524]
II Letter from St. George Tucker to William Wirt, 16 November 1814, William Wirt Papers, 1784–1864, MS. 1011, H. Furlong Baldwin Library, Maryland Historical Society, Baltimore.

47 Friendly Advice on Foreign Affairs (1811)

The voluminous correspondence of James Madison contains a few letters in Latin, two of which were sent by the Presbyterian minister George Luckey (1751–1823), Madison's former classmate at The College of New Jersey (Princeton).[525]

Luckey was a staunch advocate of republican government, which, he believed, was "sent from heaven" and would soon "take place every where."[526] Though a minister, and therefore, he asserted, unable to take an active role in the deliberations of government, Luckey regarded himself and other Christians as the country's "unarmed guards."[527] Moreover, he considered it the duty and privilege of citizens, especially those with public roles, to voice their opinions to Congress and the President about matters that concerned the country's welfare.[528]

As President, Madison received at least ten letters from Luckey. Each contained particular advice on policy matters ranging from dueling to trade to foreign affairs. Luckey was emboldened to write not only by his Christianity and by his understanding of the duties of republican citizenship but also because, as he reminded Madison, he had once enjoyed a close association with Madison's family, even spending Christmas of 1773 and other vacations at the Madison estate in Orange, Virginia.[529]

It is not apparent why Luckey chose to write two of his letters to Madison in Latin. Luckey, to be sure, had been classically educated, and he was considered a "fine classical scholar."[530] Madison, for his part, received a classical education first at Donald Robertson's Latin school in Virginia and then at Princeton, and according to his biographer he "must have known Cicero and Virgil by heart." Late in life he was able to correct English translations of the works of Grotius, Pufendorf, and Vattel.[531]

The first of Luckey's Latin letters to President Madison is printed here.[532] The context is the rising tension between the United States and Great Britain that led to the outbreak of war later that year. Among other suggestions, Luckey encourages Madison to make use of privateers.

Chare Praeses Oct 17, 1811

Epistola tua ad me opportune veniebat et gaudeo te bene valere. Hodierne die tempora sunt difficillima per mundum et nos patimur dura, iniustitia, et crudelitate hominum repletorum invidia: sed melius nobiscum est quam cum multis aliis. Fruimur libertate quamquam nunc tam multi non delectantur libertate at quisque hominum eiusmodi sitant dominari orbem terrarum; o homines insani!!! Mutationes cito eveniunt? Quando scripsi tibi visum est nonnullis universum nostrum commercium ad rempublicam restringere, sed quotidie status rerum mutatur et quod esset hoc tempore optimum factu quis potest dicere?— Fortasse, debetur patriae nostrae permittere omnibus mercatoribus nostris et aliis armare et seipsos non solum defendere sed etiam ab hoste arripere in alto mari et per legem dare dimidium praedae captae captoribus. Multum lucri fecimus hoc modo in bello Americano; scis populos nostros esse avidos divitiarum— Fortasse possumus compactum negotiare cum Europeanis ut olim eos et nosmetipsos defendere a captu tyrannidis maris qui nunquam nisi necessitate iustitiam nobis faciet. Multum mali afferet permittere spiritum civium nostrorum frangi nimia patientia. Deus nobis multum boni dedit in causa nostra iampridem. Pugnavit pugnas, contulit libertatem pacem et salutem et adhuc haec vindicat—Nostra causa est optima quoniam est iustitiae et veritatis. Possumus adhuc debellare et patriam et libertatem et civium immunitatem defendere; sed videmus hostem nitentem dividere et nos debilitare. Deus bonus, iustus et misericors regit et est rex regum. O proceres nostri este bono animo, habetis vota et preces omnium bonorum, et quemadmodum Israelitae pugnabant ita pugnamus fortiter contra inimicos nostros, qui sunt inimici iustitiae et veritatis si nil aliud facit et nitamur deo et ille erit nobiscum et reddet nos prosperos. Vale.

Georgius Luckey

Source: James Madison Papers, Library of Congress.[533]

48 Northwest Territory (1815)

Throughout the nineteenth century Catholic clergy and prelates in the United States frequently wrote Latin letters to Rome. Many of these were addressed to the Propaganda Fide, the congregation that supervised the Catholic Church in the United States until 1908. Others were addressed directly to the Pope. The following are excerpts from a letter of April 10, 1815 written by Benedict Joseph Flaget (1763–1850), the first bishop of Bardstown (Kentucky), addressed to Pope Pius VII (*r.* 1800–23).[534]

Flaget, orphaned in France at the age of two, joined the Society of St. Sulpice (the Sulpicians), which was dedicated to reforming seminary instruction. Ordained in 1788 at Issy, he left France as a result of the Revolution and came to the United States. He taught at St. Mary's (Baltimore) and briefly at Georgetown, he attempted to found a college in Havana, and he was a missionary in Indiana Territory. He was consecrated Bishop of Bardstown in 1810.

In the following excerpts Flaget describes his vast diocese, which at the time comprised most of the Northwest Territory and included ten future states. The first paragraph provides details about two parishes in Michigan, and passing mention is made of a battle of the War of 1812 fought in Monroe, Michigan. The second paragraph contains an early reference to the city of Chicago. The final paragraph recounts information gleaned from William Clark (1770–1838), who along with Merriweather Lewis had explored the newly acquired Louisiana territory a decade earlier. Though a Protestant, Clark had asked Bishop Flaget to baptize his three children in St. Louis in August, 1814.[535]

In territorio Michigan est parochia quae dicitur Sanctae Annae in oppido vulgo dicto Detroit,[536] adeo numerosa ut necesse videatur illam in duas scindere; 1500 animas continet; alia est in loco vulgo dicto *la Rivière aux Raisins*, cuius nomen ignoro; 500 circiter animis consistens.[537] Utraque regitur a sacerdote Sancti Sulpitii.[538] Decimas ei solvunt parochiani. Has non potui visitare, propter bellum quod tempore meae visitationis in illis locis exardebat.

Praeterea, in mea excursione audivi de quattuor Gallorum congregationibus in medio Indianorum constitutis, quae ad meam dioecesim pertinent; unam in superioribus Mississippi partibus,[539] aliam in loco vulgo dicto Chicagou, aliam ad litus laci Michigan,[540] quartam denique versus originem fluminis Illiniensium, neque per tempus per bellum mihi licuit illos visitare . . .

Dominus Clark qui cum pluribus comitibus fluvium Missouri per spatium 3000 milliarium ascendit, montes ex quibus ducit originem, pertransivit, et per fluvium Columbiam ex altera parte montium, usque ad mare pacificum descendit, mihi asseruit innumeras se invenisse indianas nationes ex utraque parte montium, quae prius nunquam homines albos viderant, et quas testatur esse mansuetae atque humanissimae indolis, quae proinde haud difficile sub evangelii iugo colla flecterent. Quem mittam? et quis ibit nobis?[541]

Source: V. F. O'Daniel, "Bishop Flaget's Report of the Diocese of Bardstown to Pius VII, April 10, 1815," *Catholic Historical Review* 1 (1915): 305–19.

49 Harvard Oration (1816)

Jacob Bigelow (1787–1879), a descendant of one of the founding families of Massachusetts, was a prominent nineteenth-century physician and botanist. Born in Sudbury, Massachusetts, he received a B.A. (1806) and M.A. (1809) from Harvard and an M.D. from the University of Pennsylvania (1810). In addition to his private medical practice, Bigelow was on the staff of Massachusetts General Hospital, and for four decades he was a professor of *Materia Medica* at Harvard Medical School (1815–55). From 1816 to 1827 he held an endowed chair at Harvard—the Rumford Professor and Lecturer on the Application of Sciences to the Useful Arts.[542] Printed below is the text of the oration that Bigelow delivered on December 11, 1816, when he assumed this chair.

Bigelow was proficient in the classics throughout his life. He taught for a brief time at Boston Latin School, and as a young college graduate he belonged to a literary society whose weekly meeting minutes were kept in Latin. As an octogenarian he prepared a volume—privately circulated—containing translations into Greek and Latin of about two dozen Mother Goose rhymes. The classics, he wrote, were a "fountain of pleasure" which afforded him enjoyment throughout his life, and at one time he considered classical learning "the paramount object of human cultivation."[543] His published works abound with citations of the Latin poets.

Yet despite this lifelong Latin proficiency, later in life Bigelow was critical of the prominence of the classics in education, because he considered this pedagogy impractical. In a November 1865 address at the Massachusetts Institute of Technology Bigelow pronounced:

> "If, in a practical age and country, [a student] is expected to get a useful education, a competent-living, an enlarged power of serving others, or even of saving them from being burdened with his support, he can hardly afford to surrender

four of five years of the most susceptible part of life to acquiring a minute familiarity with tongues which are daily becoming more obsolete, and each of which is obtained at the sacrifice of some more important science or some more desirable language."[544]

Modern life, Bigelow was convinced, required knowledge of the sciences, modern languages, English literature, law, geography, economics, and "the great moving-springs and channels of modern industry and progress."[545]

Indeed, educational reforms in the post-bellum era would dramatically alter America's engagement with the classical tradition.[546]

Non animo ingrato, dignissime Praeses,[547] sed viribus parum fidenti, munera haec nova, vocatus, aggredior. Cum enim has sedes circumspicio,[548] hunc coetum doctissimorum virorum,[549] non me fugit, quantulum aut famae aut utilitatis corpori tam insigni possim afferre. Per multos annos floruit haec sedes philosophiae, dives opum, ingenii dives, nominibus praeclaris illustrata, et nunc demum *te* praesente et praesidente, malas supereminet omnes. Liceat mihi, academiae soboli ultimae et humillimae tantis auspiciis crescere, et me quoque parvum sub ingenti matris subicere umbra; felicem, si quando tam fausta cultura fructum vel exiguum dedero.

Vigeat in longe futurum nutrix communis nostra, ossibus medulla et uberibus laete repletis. Videat ingenuas artes, doctrinam humanam, moresque pios, his sedibus orientes, longe lateque diffundi. In singulis annis adaugeantur vires suae, in ultimis patriae oris audiatur fama suorum, domi circumsurgant filii, et beatam appellent, et dum haec aedes domicilium philosophiae atque arcem litterarum praebebunt, nomina illorum qui memores se nostri benefactis suis praestiterunt laudem promeritam ferant et memoria grata conserventur.

Source: George E. Ellis, *Memoir of Jacob Bigelow, M.D., LL.D.* (Cambridge, MA: John Wilson and Son, 1880), 47.

50 The Missouri Compromise: A View from Abroad (1820)

Early sections of this book featured several passages of Latin written in Europe about the Americas, yet this phenomenon is not confined to the colonial period. The following passage comes from the English classicist Henry Nettleship (1839–93), whom classicists know for his work on Latin lexicography and for his revision of John Conington's commentary on Vergil (1871). Nettleship's first publication, however, was a Latin treatise on the American Civil War, submitted for the Chancellor's Prize at Oxford University when he was a twenty-four-year-old fellow of Lincoln College. On June 17, 1863, two weeks prior to the Union victories at Gettysburg and Vicksburg, Nettleship read aloud a portion of his winning essay during the Encaenia, celebrated during the ninth week of Trinity Term.[550]

In his essay Nettleship probes nine decades of American history and identifies two causes of the War: the confusion embedded within the American founding concerning the relationship of states to the national government and the fatal flaw of slavery. Nettleship's impressive range of sources includes primary documents such as *The Federalist Papers* and the speeches of Daniel Webster (1782–1852), John Calhoun (1782–1850), and Henry Clay (1777–1852), as well as works by observers such as Alexis de Toqueville (1805–59) and Frederick Law Olmstead (1822–1903). But he also made use of histories and analyses by contemporary English and Irish scholars such as Harriet Martineau (1802–76), John Malcolm Forbes Ludlow (1821–1911), and John Elliott Cairnes (1823–75).

The following section describes the Compromise of 1820, when Missouri and Maine were admitted to the Union, the former as a slave state, the latter as a free state, thereby retaining an equal number of senators from slave and free states.[551]

Haec omnibus Reipublicae negotiis diu incumbebat quaestio, acri utrimque ira disceptata et ruinam discidiumque minans, dum delegatorum domus frustra pro libertate Senatui resistebat:[552] donec tandem rebus laborantibus remedium Clayii ingenio quaesitum esset, quod omnes nisi prudentissimi aeternum fore sperarent. Admissa in Missuriam servitus, cauto simul ne in futurum ultra certos fines unquam progrederetur.[553] Ita gravi discordiae libertatis ac servitii frustra medebantur, quam tum primum quanta esset sensisse primos in republica viros testatur optimi cuiusque[554] trepidatio ac terror nova pericula atque improbam Meridionalium ambitionem ominantis, praecipue vox illa quam supremos inter annos Jeffersonus quasi libertatis naeniam et inevitabilis ruinae augurium prodidit, "moram id esse mali, non effugium."[555] Pax sane fallax, quae fine servitium inter et libertatem fixo, novarum tantum omine discordiarum, malo mox rursus erupturo inania fomenta afferret.

Auctae inde Meridionalibus vires ac superbia, servitutique novus color datus, quae non iam pro malo vi Americanis imposito, sed pro iure nequaquam impediendo ac latius, si res ita ferret, extendendo haberetur. Pulchri mox spectabantur effectus, servitium in Floridam Arkansasque latum, iam civitates reipublicae futuras,[556] ac cum Indis Seminolensibus, quorum tutelam et connubia servi fugitivi petissent, bellum susceptum, servorumque venatio liberae Septentrionalium iuventuti imposita.

Source: Henry Nettleship, *Quibusnam Praecipue De Causis Exortum Sit Bellum Civile Americanum. Oratio Latina in theatro Sheldoniano habita, die Junii 17, 1863* (Oxford: Shrimpton, 1863), 23–24.

51 An Indigent Latin Scholar in Ohio (1821)

In the spring of 1824 American newspapers carried notices of an unusual book about to be published—a 300-page annotated biography of George Washington written in Latin.[557] The work, it was announced, was in "a state of considerable forwardness" and was likely to be available that summer. Students in colleges and seminaries as well as "classic gentlemen throughout the United States" were expected "with avidity" to purchase this volume, portions of which had already been reviewed by "enlightened professors" of esteemed institutions in Ohio and been pronounced exceptionally meritorious. The author was identified as Francis Glass, an indigent schoolteacher living in rural Ohio. Glass's *Vita Washingtonii* has long been heralded as one of the chief curiosities of American Latin literature, but much uncertainty surrounds both its publication and Glass's life.[558] The Latin letter printed below imparts new information on each of these questions.[559]

According to early biographical notices,[560] contemporary newspapers, and the editor's preface to the *Vita Washingtonii*, Glass was born in Londonderry, Ireland in 1790 and emigrated at the age of eight to Philadelphia. His father taught math and classical languages in Philadelphia schools (Lower Dublin Academy, Mount Airy Seminary). The younger Glass received a classical education—at some point he was associated with James Ross and is even said to have assisted Ross in the compilation of his Latin grammar (see section 45)—and he reportedly graduated from the University of Pennsylvania.[561] Like his father, he taught school in the Philadelphia area (Westchester Academy, Clermont College) until financial struggles compelled him in 1818 to move to Ohio, where he taught in various counties in the western part of the state.[562] In 1820 local newspapers announced Glass's intention to found a school in Lebanon, Ohio that would suppress "quackery," follow "a regular & systematic mode of education" principally in math and languages (ancient and modern), and feature a pedagogy superior to the "*needy, rambling, fair-faced* Imposters from the eastward."[563]

Glass was a proponent of what has come to be called the "direct method" of Latin pedagogy.[564] He maintained that students should hear only Latin in the classroom, that they should be compelled to speak and to write Ciceronian or Sallustian Latin, and that administrators should therefore hire faculty equipped to speak the Latin of Romans, not of foreigners. The land of Columbus, Glass believed, had no shortage of such men (*terra, enim, Columbi, talibus viris certissime abundat*).[565]

In the summer of 1823 J.N. Reynolds (1799–1858), whose studies at the University of Ohio had been interrupted and who was then editing a Wilmington (Ohio) newspaper, encountered the nearly destitute Glass in Lebanon, Ohio and began to receive instruction in the classics from him. In time Glass revealed to Reynolds his frustration at being unable to realize his long-standing ambition of writing a Latin life of George Washington. With Reynolds's encouragement and support, Glass relocated with his family to Dayton. In these more favorable conditions Glass managed to compose the *Vita Washingtonii* during the winter of 1823–24,[566] working solely from memory, without consulting any author or text ("me scriptorem aut librum nullum, inter scribendum, consuluisse"[567]), and he spent the summer of 1824 attempting to usher the work through press. Yet on August 24, 1824, before the work could be published, Glass died.[568]

Prior to Glass's death Reynolds had bought the copyright to the manuscript,[569] and in the fall of 1824 he attempted unsuccessfully to have it published. In September of that year newspapers around the country again carried notices of its impending arrival, and it was billed as "the first essay towards the production of an original work, in the Latin language, which has ever been made in the United States."[570] Yet again there was a delay, this time of more than a decade, during much of which time Reynolds was abroad.[571]

When it finally was published in 1835,[572] Glass's *Vita* received glowing tributes from professors and editors and even from former President John Quincy Adams.[573] Most reviewers were satisfied that Glass's Latin was pure, and was therefore fit to be studied by impressionable American youths. Edgar Allan Poe acknowledged initial skepticism, because he believed it "improbable" that "classical Latin . . . should emanate from the back woods of Ohio," but he declared himself convinced and pronounced that Glass's prose was "not one jot inferior to the Latin of Erasmus."[574] Several schools and colleges adopted Glass's text in their curricula, to be read prior to Caesar.

Yet not all critics looked favorably on the published work. James Luce Kingsley (1778–1852) of Yale allowed that Glass's "literary enterprise" did not deserve "censure" and "ought rather to be met with commendation," but he nonetheless assembled a large number of mistakes and infelicities that rendered it unfit to serve as a school text.[575] Even the title page engendered some controversy. It contained a lengthy epigraph prophesying (on the basis of the Sibylline books) the emergence of Washington, which was attributed as follows: "Ciceronis fragm. XV. ed. Maii, p. 52." This text was later revealed to have been written by Charles Anthon, who in fact had authored the first laudatory testimonial printed in the appendix to Glass's work.[576] (Cardinal Mai, for his part, disavowed having published such a fragment.[577])

The following Latin letter, which Glass addressed to former President James Madison, provides details not previously mentioned either in the introduction to Glass's *Vita Washingtonii* or in the biographical sketches or newspaper accounts referred to thus far. Not only does this letter offer new information about Glass's upbringing, financial plight, frustrated aspirations for a military commission, religion, and his intention to return to Philadelphia, but it also indicates—unless he is exaggerating—that Glass had completed the *Vita* three years earlier than was previously thought. It therefore prompts once again the question of why the *Vita* was not published earlier. Finally, the letter reveals that Glass intended to dedicate the work to former President Madison, whom he regarded as "a patron of every sort of literary activity."

Madison, however, tactfully and eloquently declined the honor. He responded one month later:

"If it were less foreign to my inclinations to be distinguished by a dedication, I should recommend, as more expedient, that you should bestow that mark of respect on some one who would find it more practicable to give value to his acceptance of it by a previous examination of the work, and whose known critical knowledge of the language would satisfy the public of the merit of its execution. This precaution is rendered particularly worthy of attention by the difficulty of giving to modern Latinity the classical purity requisite for a school book, and by the fewness of examples in which the undertaking has been regarded as successful."[578]

Glass is also said to have composed a Latin ode on the death of Lord Byron, which was printed in the *Dayton Watchman* (July 13, 1824), but efforts to obtain a copy have thus far been unsuccessful.[579]

Lebanon, Ohio, Tertio die Martii, A.D. 1821.

Vir Excellentissime.

Quamvis non sim de numero eorum, qui tui notitiam habent, tamen, quia compertum iamdiu habebam, te litterarum omnis generis patronum insignem semper fuisse: ideo ausus sum, vir inclyte, hasce epistolas ad te mittere, sperans te eodem, quo mittitur animo accepturum hanc epistolam. Scripsi, et in lucem iamiam daturus sum libellum, cui titulus, "Vita Georgii Washingtonii,[580] ducis nuperi harum Civitatum foederatarum Americae septentrionalis copiarum omnium, earundemque primi praesidis." In animo est mihi, istum librum tibi, vir clare, dicare dummodo id tibi bonum gratumque videbitur. Ideoque, valde scire laboro, utrum ausim illum tibi dicare, necne; Liber, de quo agitur, in usum scholarum a me exaratus est. Pauca de me ipso dicenda videntur. Oriundus de Republica Pennsylvaniensi sum, haud procul ab urbe Philadelphia. Duobus annis abhinc, migravi in hanc regionem, ubi in pueros erudiendo operam navavi; sed ingravescente valetudine, coactus fui, istud munus relinquere, et ad extremam pauperiem redactus sum, propterea quod, cum uxore, et sex parvulis liberis, nequaquam par fui, qui eos, in afflicta valetudine, (praesertim his temporibus,[581]) sustineam. Proinde inductus inopia, diraque necessitate, Vitam, Latine, illustrissimi Washingtonii, ad scribendum me contuli. Semper in votis meis fuit, assignationem aliquam in exercitu patriae adipisci; sed, nescio quomodo. Propter humilitatem amicorum, ab isto conatu depulsus fui. Sed, (ut vetus adagium prae se fert, "dum spiro, spero,") aliquem gradum in exercitu obtinendi spes me tenet. Nonnunquam aveo nonnihil agri coëmere; at pecunia mihi deest; et, vereor, ut semper deerit in hac regione, cum omnia collegia referta sunt clericis; nam, quod ad me spectat, laïcus sum; disciplinae ecclesiae anglicanae obnoxius. Linguas, et artes mathematicas, per decem fere annos, docui; sed docti et indocti praeceptores hac in regione, eodem in numero habentur. Sed, quia iuvenis sum, spero me aliquando ex hac aerumna miseriaque emersurum esse. Volo interdum reverti ad Philadelphiam, meum natale solum, sed paupertas, (durum telum, ut Erasmus facete ait,) me prohibet. Sed, quoniam valetudo mea habet sese melius nunc, quam dudum, spero me posse adhuc visere meliores regiones nostrae felicis Reipublicae; hanc licentiam mihi, Vir excellentissime, condonare et ignoscere te precor, bonique consulere, suppliciter peto, humillimeque rogo.

Sum, Vir Clarissime,
Tuae Celsitudinis Observantissimus,
Humillimusque Tuus servus,
Franciscus Glass

Ad virum excellentem, Iacobum Madison, Praesidem nuperum Sociarum Civitatum Americae Septentrionalis.[582]

Source: James Madison Papers, Library of Congress.[583]

52 Exiled from Hawaii (1831)

References in Latin to the Sandwich Islands (Hawaii) begin to appear shortly after they were visited by Captain James Cook (1728–79). For example, the beautifully illustrated *Novus Orbis Pictus* (1808) of Friedrich Justin Bertusch describes the *Certhia obscura*, whose splendid feathers were worn by inhabitants "in insulis Sandwichianis oceani pacifici," but this bird as well as others from Hawaii had been described as early as 1788 in the 13th edition of Carolus Linnaeus's *Systema Naturae*.[584]

Protestants from New England—seven married couples sponsored by the American Board of Commissioners for Foreign Missions—arrived in Hawaii in 1820 and began to establish missions throughout the islands. Several members of Hawaii's royal family were converted, including the Queen Regent Ka'ahumanu.

The first Catholic mission began in July 1827 with the arrival in Honolulu of the Congregation of the Sacred Hearts of Jesus and Mary (also known as the Picpus Fathers), led by Fr. Alexis Bachelot (1796–1837), a former seminary rector in France. The Catholic missionaries faced opposition from the beginning, from Hawaiian rulers as well as from Protestant missionaries. On August 8, 1829 Ka'ahumanu proclaimed that any Hawaiians who attended Catholic worship would be sentenced to hard labor, and a few months later she banned Bachelot and another priest, Patrick Short, from catechizing in the islands. In January of 1831 the priests were issued an ultimatum: they had three months to leave the islands; in the fourth month they would be imprisoned. On Christmas Eve 1831 Bachelot and Short were compelled to board the *Waverley* and depart for California.[585]

From his place of exile at Mission San Gabriel (Los Angeles), Bachelot addressed an eighteen-page Latin letter to the Cardinal Prefect of the Sacred Congregation Propaganda Fide in Rome, offering details about the political history of Hawaii, customs of the indigenous population, and his own forced departure. The following are excerpts from this letter, dated June 15, 1832 and titled "Missio Insularum Sandwichianorum in Oceanico—Vivat SS. Cor Jesu." The first portion recounts the political history of Hawaii, the latter portions recount the expulsion of the French priests.

In April 1837 Bachelot returned to Hawaii, but he was again compelled to leave, and on December 5 he died at sea a little north of the Marshall Islands. Despite the short amount of time he spent in Hawaii, Bachelot compiled a grammar and lexicon of the Hawaiian language as well as two catechisms in Hawaiian.

Hasce litteras scribo ad Eminentiam Vestram[586] ex alta California,[587] scilicet ex terra exilii nostri. Huc enim eiecerunt nos. Fiat et laudetur iustissima et ubique amabilissima voluntas Dei. Iniquitatem reperiit in suis, et invenit eos indignos se, propterea repulit eos ab opere suo. In eo tamen sperabimus. Non enim in aeternum irascetur, sed in aeternum misericordia eius.

Priusquam autem de iis omnibus referam, mihi pauca iterum dicenda de gente, de moribus eius, et de rebus inimicorum, quo facilius iudicet Eminentia Vestra de natura laborum nostrorum, quid timendum et quid sperandum sit.

Eo tempore quo detectae fuerunt insulae, anno scilicet 1778,[588] in quattuor dividebantur regna,[589] quae paulo post in tria, postea in duo, tandem sub una ditione redacta fuerunt, circiter a triginta annis.[590] Et nunc, qui Rex unicus habetur, alter filius est eius qui primus insulas omnes occupavit.[591] Ille, subiectos cupiens sibi devincere, quosdam equidem spoliavit; ceteros benigne suscepit. Consanguineos regum, qui et sibi proximi erant, praefecit insulis. Terras eis qui pro eo strenue militaverant dedit et quosdam ad dignitatem ducum provexit. Illo tempore, coeperunt insulae frequentari ab alienigenis, quos ille fovit, praeclare de illis sectibus.[592] Ad idololatriam summopere addictus fuit usque ad mortem suam. Kamehameha nomen eius. Mulierem habuit ex stirpe regia quae captiva primum, deinde uxor eius fuit et quidem inter primas. Keapaolani nomen eius.[593] Haec mater fuit Liholiho eius successoris qui Londini excessit a vita, anno 1824.[594] Huic successit germanus eius, Kanikeouli nomine, annos circiter decem natus.[595] Regens fuit dux qui praefectus fuerat insulae Oaha,[596] in qua degebamus nos simul cum alienigenis. Non enim permittitur alias habitare.

. . .

Mense Aprili 1831, ex commutatione publici status quae tunc accedit, omnino derelicti fuimus ducibus praedicatoribus addictis.[597] Hi in concilio congregati nos vocaverunt, nobisque mandaverunt ab insulis exire ad quaslibet alias terras.[598] Duos menses dederunt ut navem qui reciperet nos nancisceremur. Quibus elapsis diripienda erat nostra habitatio, et post tertium mensem in carcere detrudendi eramus. Cum autem natura violentiam abhorrent, multo magis contra alienigenas, cupere visi sunt ut libenter exiremus. Unde brevi a minis abstinentes, satagerunt a nobis consensum elicere, cum enim ut rem factam habuissent. Nos vero scientes tunc periculum esse violentiae, si directe et formaliter recusaremus, sperantesque procellam ab inimicis suscitatam momentaneam fore, nisi ut [?] accedit,[599] minus urgerentur duces nec promissum exeundi nec recusationem dedimus. Sed occasionem nobis datam quaedam de religione dicendi cum gaudio arripuimus.

. . .

Vigilia nativitatis Domini missus fuit qui eriperet nos et duceret ad navem quam extra portum tenebant iam vela dantem.[600] Nescientes ad quam terram translaturi essent nos. Dum enim interrogatus dicere noluit. Sic erepti fuimus ovibus nostris quae nunc absque pastore in medio luporum sunt. Speramus in misericordia divina. Ipsa gregi providebit, lumenque veritatis iniectum fructificare curabit.

Source and Owner: The General Archives of the Congregation of the Sacred Hearts SS.CC., Rome, used with permission.

53 Fire at Georgetown (1836)

On the evening of December 10, 1836 a fire broke out in the residence of the tailor and shoemaker at Georgetown College in the District of Columbia. The fire threatened other buildings on campus, but the action of faculty, staff, and students prevented its spread. The following hexameters commemorate this event. The author is Philip A. Sacchi (1791–1850), a Russian-born Jesuit who came to the United States in 1821. He worked in the mid-Atlantic and then in New England, where was a professor at the College of the Holy Cross. Sacchi was known as a gifted Latin poet, and he made a Latin translation of the *Star Spangled Banner* as well as of some of Moore's *Melodies*.[601] He wrote the poem below when he was a parish priest at St. Thomas Manor in southern Maryland.

Incendii Strages

Dira cano! rabiem vulcani ignisque furentis,
Exustasque domos McFadden[602] Leiferique;[603]
Horrendum ignis opus, multos memorabile in annos
Idque brevi factum spatio vix unius horae.
Quae volvebantur flammarum culmina tetra!
Sideribus bella ipsis intentata putares!
Tantane scintillis uni vis effera parvae?
Haec ennaranti linguis animisque favete.

Nox erat et somnus totum pervaserat orbem,
Et vigiles galli siluere, et odora canum vis,
Et fratres nostros passim sopor altus habebat,
McFadden rauco proflabat, gutture rhoncus,
Non tu, McFadden, tereres sic tempus inane
Si scires quae te maneant crudelia fata!

Heu surge infelix, torpentia discute membra,
Heu surge incaute, et pigro te proripe lectu!
Ni facias subito, ni qua fata aspera rumpas,
Tu McFadden eris claris ardentior astris!
Vana moror, dormitat iners, stertitque supinus.

Interea rumor per totam spargitur aulam;
Exciti somno pueri puerumque magistri,
Undam ferte viri, properate, extinguite flammas,
Ferte cito, clamant; eheu! iam proximus ardet
McFadden; ignisque consurgens occupat aures!
(Credebant aures, sed erat fratris *greasy night cap*)
Unus aqua magno cyatho tunc proluit ipsum:
Sic madefactus, inops mentis, perterritus, ultro
McFadden surgit, nec novit quo sit eundum—
McFadden frater, quo non solertior alter,
Seu veteres renovare coatas seu mendere breeches.

Hic ultra citraque viam remeare videres
Connolly, De Smettum, Liefer Cliffordque,
    Moorumque,
West cum McGuiro, Mullen, Hickeyque, Gavinque,
Sparks quoque Flant et Smith, magnum cum Stantone
    Clarkum,
Marbury, Fitzgerald (prior est dux ipse cohortis)
Et plures alios quos versu dicere non est.[604]
Rector adest: fratres nunc huc, nunc dirigit illuc,
Et quo ignis maior maiores exerit audax
His vires, fido Lopez comitante ministro.[605]

Tunc gemuit noster Logicae Sophiaeque magister,[606]
Solvere quod nullo valeat dilemmate casum;
Sed tamen instat acer, dextram tenditque labori,
Tandem McFadden sensus et reddita vox est.
Eheu me miserum (lacrimis sic fatur abortis)
Cur cessi somno? quae me dementia cepit?
Cur iacui stertens vel cur mea lumina clausi?
Perdita sunt nostri non parva peculia census;
Tres *segari* cum magno *quid*, pippaque tepenti;
Ut perii! ut cecidi! quis me malus abstulit error?
Ter conatus erat raros discerpere crines,
Ter cecidere manus, caput officiumque negarunt.
Talia iactabat, levibus suspiria ventis
McFadden plorans, nec quod speraret habebat.

At Frater Mead,[607] cui melior sententia mentis,
Ad ianuas adstat custos, ne forte latrones
Hoc nacti tempus, subeant penetralia patrum
Et rapiant libros, cartas, pilosve tricornes.

Haec inter secum tacito sic ore precatus,
"Do help our fathers and brothers Virgo benigna!"
Nec mora! Virgo suum visa est audire clientem
Nam pluviae magnam celso vim mittit Olympo,
Subsidere faces, extincti ignesque fatiscunt.

Source: John Gilmary Shea, *Memorial of the First Centenary of Georgetown College, D.C.* (New York: P. F. Collier, for the College, 1891), 114–15.

54 Sale of Slaves (1838)

In recent years some American institutions have been engaged in an excruciating effort to assess their former involvement with slavery.[608] At Georgetown University this has occasioned the formation of a Working Group on Slavery, Memory, and Reconciliation, the sponsorship of numerous public events, and the compilation of an extensive online archive of resources.[609] Of particular interest in the online archive are documents contextualizing and detailing the 1838 sale of 272 slaves in order to reduce the mounting debt incurred by the Jesuits's ambitious and rapidly-expanding school in Georgetown.[610] As a result of this sale, which earned the Jesuits more than $100,000, slaves who had worked on Jesuit farms in southern Maryland ended up on two sugar plantations in Louisiana.

The 1838 sale was not without critics and opponents at the time, including from within the Jesuit order, but it was supported by the two Jesuits who served alternatively as President of Georgetown and Provincial of the Maryland Jesuits, Thomas F. Mulledy (1794–1860) and William McSherry (1799–1839).[611] In April 2017 Georgetown University removed Mulledy's name from one of its campus buildings and replaced it with that of Isaac Hawkins, the first slave to be listed on the bill of the 1838 sale. Likewise McSherry Hall was renamed for Anne Marie Becraft (1805–33), who founded a school for free African American girls in Georgetown and later joined the Oblate Sisters of Providence.

The passage below is an excerpt from a letter dated December 27, 1836, in which the Jesuit General Johann Philipp Roothaan (1785–1853) stipulates conditions for the proposed sale of slaves.[612]

De nigris, iam P. Vespre,[613] qui nobis rem clare exposuit, rescripsit ad R^m^ V^m^, nobis persuasum esse, ut vendi possint et vendantur, ubi opportunitas sese offerat; id ego confirmo, et R^{ae} V^{ae} negotium hoc totum committo, sequentibus conditionibus.

1. ut conscientiae debito gravissimo satisfiat, omnis cura adhibeatur, ut ita vendantur, ut religionis catholicae exercitium liberum illis sit, eiusque exercendae opportunitatem habeant.—

Itaque

i. non vendantur nisi proprietariis fundorum, ne forte qui a nostris emit, postea emptos separet indistincte et aliis vendat.

ii. in venditione stipulandum, ut detur nigris commodum exercendae religionis, et assistentia sacerdotis.

iii. mariti et uxores, nullo modo separandi; immo nec parentes a filiis, quantum fieri potest.

iv. si quis servus vel serva nostrorum, uxorem vel maritum habeat in aliena possessione, hi omni cura coniungendi, alioqui nullo modo vendantur in regionem longinquam asportandi.

Circa ista oneratur conscientia R^{ae} V^{ae}, quod dico, non quod de R^{ae} V^{ae} in hac ipsa re sollicitudine dubium, sed ut ego meae conscientiae satisfaciam. Erit etiam charitatis et iustitiae, providere convenienter iis nigris, qui ob gravem aetatem vel ob morbos incurabiles vendi et alio transferri non possint.

2. Pecunia, quae ex ista venditione proveniet, nullo modo expendenda est in sumptus faciendos, neque in debitorum exstinctionem, sed est capitale, quod investiri debet ut fructificet. Optimus modus esset fortasse groundrent, in statibus

praesertim Pennsylvaniae et New York,—sed de hoc consilium ineundum cum viris probis et prudentibus rerumque huiusmodi peritis, tum nostris, tum externis.

Source: Archives of the Maryland Province of the Society of Jesus, Box 93, Folder 9, on deposit at the Booth Family Center for Special Collections, Georgetown University Library, Washington, DC.[614]

55 In Montes Saxosos (1839)

The origins of the Jesuit presence in the Pacific Northwest can be traced to the fall of 1831, when a delegation from the Flathead and Nez-Percé tribes, who inhabited the Columbia River plateau, arrived in St. Louis.[615] The delegation was comprised of four men: an approximately forty-four-year-old man named Tipyahlanah (Eagle), who was also known as Kipkip Pahlekin; Ka-ou-pu (Man of the Morning, or Man of the Dawn Light), the son of a Nez Percé tribal leader; an approximately twenty-year-old man named Hi-yuts-to-henin (Rabbit Skin Leggings); and another man of approximately twenty years old named Tawis Geejumnin (No Horns on His Head, or Horns Worn Down Like Those on an Old Buffalo). While in St. Louis the delegates visited with General William Clark (1770–1838), the Superintendent of Indian Affairs in the West, who along with Meriwether Lewis (1774–1809) had visited these tribes some two and half decades earlier during their expedition through the newly-acquired Louisiana Territory. The delegates were also taken to the Catholic cathedral of St. Louis, but the bishop, the Italian-born Joseph Rosati (1789–1843), was away from the city at the time. Two of the four members of the delegation (Tipyahlanah and Ka-ou-pu) died while in St. Louis, having first received baptism, and they were buried in the Cathedral cemetery. The other two departed for home in early 1832. Thanks to the American artist George Catlin, who encountered them on board a steamboat going up the Missouri River, we have portraits of them.

The purpose of the Native Americans's visit has been disputed, but according to Rosati it was to seek Catholic priests to minister among the Nez Percé and Flathead peoples, some of whom had heard of the Catholic faith from Iroquois who had migrated west two decades previously.[616] But initially there was no response from the Catholics of St. Louis to their request. It was not until

1840, after still other delegations had come to St. Louis (1835 and 1839), that the Jesuits sent the missionary priest Pierre-Jean DeSmet (1801–73) to begin what would be a lengthy missionary career in the Northwest.

The following is Bishop Rosati's diary entry that recounts the 1839 delegation. Rosati, a Vincentian priest, was not only "a most exact and painstaking recorder of contemporary events,"[617] but he was also a gifted Latinist, having been chosen by the First Provincial Council of Baltimore (1829) to compose the Latin letter to Pope Pius VIII on behalf of the American hierarchy.[618] Rosati was by no means unique in keeping a Latin diary (see section 32 and cf. section 72).

1839 Oct. 20. Dominica XXII post Pentecosten[619] . . . . Post Missam pontificalibus vestibus assumptis, et hymno *Veni Creator Spiritus* cantato, sermonem habui ad Confirmandos.[620] Confirmationis Sacramentum administravi duobus indigenis, Ignatio Ootstagleave, et Petro Okassaweita ex natione Iroquois. Hi in Canada ex Catholicis parentibus nati, et in Catholica Religione instructi, ante tres et viginti annos ad regiones quae intra oras pacifici Oceani et Montes petrosos continentur migrarunt, apud tribum quae *têtes plattes* (Flathead) dicuntur constiterunt, et ex illorum feminis uxores duxerunt, Religioni addicti illam nedum obliti fuerunt sed et infideles apud quos degebant docuerunt, nunc post trium mensium iter huc advenerunt, et petunt Sacerdotem Missionarium, qui apud gentes illas Evangelium praedicet.

Source: John Rothensteiner, "The Flat-head and Nez Perce Delegation to St. Louis 1831–1839," *St. Louis Catholic Historical Review* 2 (1920): 187–88.

56 The Republic of Texas (1840)

The establishment of the Republic of Texas on March 2, 1836 prompted efforts to minister to Catholics of this area, who had formerly been under the jurisdiction of the Mexican diocese of Monterrey. One initiative came from Count Charles de Farnesé, who proposed to Sam Houston (1793–1863), the Republic's first President, that a bishopric or archbishopric be established in Texas and that land grants be made throughout the state to accommodate future Catholic schools and churches. Houston was unable to guarantee land grants—these had to be done by the legislature—but he was in favor of an archbishopric, which he thought would contribute to "the snapping of the ties that still bind Texas to Mexico" and would "have none other than a salutary tendency to produce harmony among the Catholic citizens of Texas."[621] The Count forwarded the results of his exchange with Houston to ecclesiastical authorities in Rome, who were at the same time receiving information and recommendations about the condition of the Church in Texas from other sources as well.

Rome, however, was cautious in proceeding with the Texas mission, largely in order to avoid exacerbating already tense diplomatic relations with Mexico. Initially the Sacred Congregation Propaganda Fide asked Anthony Blanc (1792–1860), the Bishop of New Orleans, to arrange a fact-finding tour of Texas to determine how best to proceed. For this purpose Blanc selected John Timon (1797–1867), a Vincentian priest and Pennsylvania native who at the time was rector of a seminary in Missouri.[622] (Timon would later become the first Bishop of Buffalo.) Timon made an initial excursion into Texas in the winter of 1838–39, visiting Galveston and the new capital of Houston and even preaching for two hours before a diverse audience in the Capitol's Hall of Representatives. In April 1840 Timon learned that Pope Gregory XVI had established Texas as a Prefecture Apostolic and that he himself had been designated as the first prefect—not quite canonically equivalent to a bishop, but nonetheless with broad powers to care for the Catholic faithful in the region.

When Timon returned to Texas in December 1840 to assume his new position, he bore the following Latin letter. Dated July 18, 1840 and written by Cardinal Giacomo Filipo Fransoni (1775–1856), the Prefect of the Propaganda Fide, it was addressed to the President of the Republic of Texas, Mirabeau Bounaparte Lamar (1798–1859). Timon delivered the letter in person to Lamar, who was at his home in Independence, Texas on sick-leave and about to venture to New Orleans for medical care. Lamar, an accomplished poet and founding member of the Philosophical Society of Texas, did not know Latin, but when Timon translated the contents into English Lamar was gratified, and he regarded the letter as "not a personal communication but a state paper."[623] Lamar accordingly forwarded the letter to Austin, the site of the newly-relocated capital, to the attention of the Vice-President (and, in Lamar's absence, acting-President) David Burnet (1788–1870).

From the perspective of the Texas authorities, the major significance of this letter was the implicit acknowledgement by a foreign government of an independent Texas, which was a preoccupation of Lamar's administration. This acknowledgement, so it was thought, was demonstrated by the letter's salutation, which contemporary translations rendered: "To His Excellency the President of the Texian Republic."[624] The Papal States thus joined the United States and France on the growing list of foreign governments who recognized the Lone Star Republic.

The letter reveals that a chief concern of ecclesiastical authorities in Rome was the recovery of church property that had been appropriated by the Texas government during the struggle for independence. Among this property were numerous Franciscan missions, including the

Alamo, some of which dated back more than a century. In late December of 1840 and early January of 1841 this question was discussed in the Texas legislature, and despite some opposition particularly over the status of the Alamo, a bill eventually was passed confirming that such property was owned by "the chief pastor of the Roman Catholic Church in the Republic of Texas, and his successors in office, in trust forever."[625]

The original Latin letter has never been found. The following is a copy made by an official in Rome for the letterbook of the Congregation Propaganda Fide.

Celsissimo Reipublicae Mexicanae ad Texas Praesidi[626]
Die 18 Iulii 1840

Cum Sacra haec de Propaganda Fide Congregatio cognoverit permulta singulari[s] humanitatis ac benevolentiae argumenta ab excellentissima D.[627] tua et inclyto illo Consilio[628] erga probatos Christi ministros exhibita, qui semel et iterum ut religionis praesidia fidelibus istis populi adferrent missi fuerunt; maximas debitasque gratiarum actiones tibi refert, quas eiusdem S. C.[629] nomine exhibens benevolo etiam animo excipias rogo. Quoniam vero, prout compertum tibi est, Sacra ipsa Congregatio, ut spirituali Catholicorum istorum saluti ac necessitatibus firmius prospiceret, eximium virum ecclesiasticum Ioannem Timon in Praefectum Apostolicum seu Pastorem Catholicae istius Ecclesiae constituit, eique collaboratores alios presbyteros in sacro peragendo munera adsociavit, hinc D.[630] tuam etiam adprecor, ut ea qua praestas benignitate, et auctoritate memoratum Praefectum sociosque prosequaris ac faveas et quae sunt Catholicae Ecclesiae bona eidem tanquam legitimo Pastori resignari iubeas. Quamvis autem illum ob spectatas eius virtutes et egregias dotes vel maxime tibi acceptum futurum sacrumque eius ministerium rei quoque publicae cui tanta cum gloria praees profuturum summopere confidam; nihilominus ita eum tibi commendo, ut quae in eum contuleris beneficia, veluti mihimetipsi, et eminentissimis meis conlegis tributa me habiturum esse scias. Interea me tibi devinctissimum profiteor, ac D. O. M. precor, ut . . .[631]

Source: Archivio Storico "De Propaganda Fide," Rome, *Lettere e Decreti* 324 (1840, Part II): 660–61.

57 Thoreau Family Correspondence: Mother, Brother, Sisters (1840)

Five years before Henry David Thoreau went to the woods in order to live deliberately, he was a schoolteacher in the Concord Academy (founded 1822), giving instruction in Latin, Greek, French, natural philosophy, and advanced mathematics. Thoreau had assumed leadership of this school in the late summer of 1838, and he was soon joined by his brother John (1815–42) in what has been called "one of the most important of the nation's early educational experiments,"[632] inasmuch as it attempted to realize the primary aspirations of Transcendentalism. Thoreau was known as a gifted, conscientious, and exacting pedagogue. He is reported—although this stretches credulity—once to have kept a student after school for nearly an hour for failing to read an "et" in a Latin sentence,[633] yet one student recalled that even a brief conversation with him was capable of yielding immense "instruction and delight."[634]

Thoreau's proficiency in the classics derived from his education first at the Concord Academy and then at Harvard (class of 1837). Candidates for admission to Harvard in 1833 were examined on "the whole of Virgil, Cicero's Select Orations, and Sallust" as well as the ability to write Latin, and throughout their first three years at Harvard students were required to undertake "Exercises in writing Latin," and to progress through Livy, Horace's *Odes*, *Epistles*, and *Satires*, Cicero's *Brutus* and *De Officiis*, as well as Juvenal.[635] As a result, throughout his life Thoreau was able to read Latin "as readily as English," according to one who knew him.[636] His first publication was an essay on Perseus.[637] Moreover his journals show a desire, in the words of one author, to write an American *De Re Rustica*.[638]

Yet Thoreau's engagement with the classics was not limited to pedagogy or to essays in criticism; he also sustained a commitment to active Latin. He uses Latin in his journal.[639] He and his brother composed a Latin inscription for a Native American ruler, or sachem, which was placed on Fairhaven Hill in Massachusetts.[640] In conjunction with a rustic dinner he gave for a friend at Walden Pond, he drew up a menu in French, Latin, and Greek.[641] Moreover, Thoreau's extensive correspondence contains at least two Latin letters. They are presented below.

The first of these is dated Concord, Jan 23, 1840 (Concordiae, Dec. Kal. Feb. A.D. MDCCCXL) and postmarked two days later. It was addressed to Thoreau's older sister, Helen (1812–49), who, despite frequent bouts with sickness, was a schoolteacher in Roxbury, Massachusetts.[642] The motivation for the choice of Latin is nowhere stated. But according to one critic: "It gave him pleasure to use the language of Virgil and Cicero, for one of the many paradoxes in Thoreau's life was the union of true American contempt for tradition with an unaffected love of the classics."[643]

The second, much briefer, letter is addressed to "Cara Sophia," Thoreau's youngest sister (1819–76),[644] and the valediction indicates that it was written by Thoreau's mother, Cynthia (1787–1872), with Thoreau acting as amanuensis. It is likely that both Sophia and Helen learned Latin at the Concord Academy.[645]

It is unclear whether other Latin letters were exchanged by Thoreau family members. Sophia Thoreau, the last surviving member of the family, burned most of the family correspondence.[646]

I

Cara Soror,—

Est magnus acervus nivis ad limina, et frigus intolerabile intus. Caelum ipsum ruit, credo, et terram operit. Sero stratum linquo et mature repeto; in fenestris multa pruina prospectum absumit; et hic miser scribo, non currente calamo, nam digiti mentesque torpescunt. Canerem cum

Horatio, si vox non faucibus haeserit,[647]—

Vides ut alta stet nive candidum
Nawshawtuct, nec iam sustineant onus
Silvae laborantes, geluque
Flumina constiterint acuto?
Dissolve frigus, ligna super foco
Large reponens, etc.[648]

Sed olim, Musa mutata, et laetiore plectro,

Neque iam stabulis gaudet pecus, aut arator igne,
Nec prata canis albicant pruinis;
Iam Cytherea choros ducit Venus imminente luna.[649]

Quam turdus ferrugineus ver reduxerit, tu, spero, linques curas scholasticas, et, negotio religato, desipere in loco audebis; aut mecum inter silvas, aut super scopulos Pulchri-Portus,[650] aut in cymba super lacum Waldensem,[651] mulcens fluctus manu, aut speciem miratus sub undas.

Bulwerius[652] est mihi nomen incognitum,—unus ex ignobile vulgo, nec refutandus nec laudandus. Certe alicui nonnullam honorem habeo qui insanabili cacoethe scribendi[653] teneatur.

Specie flagrantis Lexingtonis non somnia deturbat?[654] At non Vulcanum Neptunumque culpemus, cum superstitioso grege. Natura curat animalculis aeque ac hominibus; cum serena, tum procellosa, amica est.

Si amas historiam et fortia facta heroum, non depone Rollin, precor; ne Clio offendas nunc, nec illa det veniam olim. Quos libros Latinos legis? legis, inquam, non studes. Beatus qui potest suos libellos tractare, et saepe perlegere, sine metu domini urgentis! ab otio iniurioso procul est: suos amicos et vocare et dimittere quandocunque velit, potest. Bonus liber opus nobilissimum hominis. Hinc ratio non modo cur legeres, sed cur tu quoque scriberes; nec lectores carent; ego sum. Si non librum meditaris, libellum certe. Nihil posteris proderit te spirasse, et vitam nunc leniter nunc aspere egisse; sed cogitasse praecipue et scripsisse. Vereor ne tibi pertaesum huius epistolae sit; necnon alma lux caret,

Maioresque cadunt altis de montibus umbrae.

Quamobrem vale,—immo valete, et requiescatis placide, Sorores.

H.D. Thoreaus.

Memento scribere!

II Cara Sophia,—

Samuel Niger[655] crebris aegrotationibus, quae agilitatem et aequum animum abstulere, obnoxius est; iis temporibus ad cellam descendit, et multas horas (ibi) manet.

Flores, ah crudelis pruina! parvo leti discrimine sunt. Cactus frigore ustus est, gerania vero adhuc vigent.

Conventus sociabiles hac hieme reinstituti fuere. Conveniunt[656] ad meum domum mense quarto vel quinto, ut tu hic esse possis. Matertera Sophia[657] cum nobis remanet; quando urbem revertet non scio. Gravedine etiamnum, sed non tam aegre, laboramus.

Adolescentula E. White apud pagum paulisper moratur. Memento scribere intra duas hebdomedas.

Te valere desiderium est

Tui Matris,

C. Thoreaus.

P.S. Epistolam die solis proxima expectamus. (Amanuense, H.D.T.)

Source: F.B. Sanborn, *Familiar Letters of Henry David Thoreau* (Boston: Houghton Mifflin, 1894), 30–33.[658]

58 A Presidential Vacation to New York (1840)

In a first for the nation, in the summer of 1839 Martin Van Buren, the sitting President, decided to campaign for reelection.[659] To this end he undertook a politician's vacation, traveling by train throughout the mid-Atlantic states to deliver speeches before enthusiastic crowds. On the morning of September 12, 1839 a special train brought him from Utica to Herkimer, a town with great political significance in New York politics of this era. After an initial welcome, he was conducted by carriage in a parade through the streets of the town, and he came to a halt in front of the meeting place of the Dutch Reformed congregation. John Peter Spinner (1768–1848), the local pastor, whose son, General Francis E. Spinner, was one of the marshals of the procession,[660] addressed the President in English, welcoming him with republican hospitality "toto ex corde" and commending his "public character" and the "distinguishing principles" of his administration. Spinner concluded his remarks with "Dixi! Ainsi soit-il." Following a brief response from the President, a military band played *Hail Columbia*, and the President received greetings from those in attendance for nearly one hour. According to a local newspaper, "party sycophancy" was absent from the gathering, and "no man worship" was in evidence.[661] A few months later Spinner wrote President Van Buren the Latin letter printed below.

The German-born Spinner had been ordained a Catholic priest in 1789, but he later married, left the Catholic Church, and became a Dutch Reformed minister.[662] Initially enthralled by the ideals of the French Revolution, Spinner looked with dismay as Napoleon, the "Corsican meteor," began to aspire to the position of consul for life, and in January 1801 he and his wife left his "miserably enslaved fatherland" and emigrated to the United States, which he deemed "the only true and genuine Republic on Earth (at least according to her heavenly constitution theoretically considered)."[663] He settled in Herkimer and became pastor, a position that he held until his death.

Spinner retained a command of Latin throughout his life. Even in his early seventies—when he wrote this letter—he was teaching Latin (in addition to French, German, and English). It is unclear whether he expected the President to be able to read this Latin letter. At any rate, Spinner did not presume to receive a Latin letter in response. Van Buren, for his part, had managed to learn a modest amount of Latin at Kinderhook Academy, a one-room wooden schoolhouse, but it is uncertain how much of this he retained later in life.

Domino illustri Martino Van Buren,
Presidenti dignissimo
Reipublicae americanae Septentrionalis, Washingtonii
Presidens mi peramande!
Pater Reipublicae nostrae americanae praestantissime!!

Iam diu incubuit mihi obligatio gravissima, apologiam meam praesentandi tibi, ea de causa, quando in offerendo tibi hospitalitatem concivium meorum herkemeriendium non potui intrudere amplius neque in ecclesia nostra neque in hospitio publico tunc temporis in turba multitudinis talis qualis confertae,[664] ad praebendam propriam invitationem meam—intra tectum mansionis familiae meae Presidenti summo nostro et meritissimo usque ad aram et focum familiae totae quantae democraticae et ab incunabilis constantis. Ast eheu! mansio mea tunc temporis erat nil nisi, quam hospitium febriens mentis et corporis inhabitantibus memetipso non excepto: detritus laboribus et vigiliis fatigatus die et nocte festinavi, peracta invitatione publica citius melius, ad danda medicamenta meis et mihimetipsi, iam diu suspensa, timendo, memetipsum redendi imparem ad functiones praestandas cordi meo totas quantas dilectissimas, in alloquendo Presidentem dignissimum reipublicae nostrae americanae unicae.[665]

Recepta tamen medicina obtinui una cum duabus filiabus meis totidem corporis virium, quot ad concomitandam unam filiam mentis aberratione laborantem, usque ad asylum hartfortense me non imparem probavi, quae nunc Dei benedictione sic valescit, ut doctori digno eius domino Fuller—, ad dandas instructiones in lingua teutonica imparem haud esse censeatur.

Scripsisse litteras has latinas, aegre non feres homini multiplicis doctrinae ab alma matre in Germania dotato:[666] mediante isthac lingua latina nimirum studui et perscrutatus sum omnia philosophiae brachia—Iurisprudentiam cum Iure canonico, scripsique dissertationes theologicas utpote magister pro me et aliis.—Utinam Patriae meae americanae iam diu adoptivae, qua cives democraticus totus quantus ab incunabilis, mutatione semper semperque obnoxius valuerim, dedicandi vires meas inquantum potuerim. Ast nunc senectute pressus, spiritus meus corpori adulto succumbens, non potest amplius peragere debita nisi in scribendo et docendo linguas idiomate approbo, scilicet latinam, gallicam, germanicam et anglicanam! Si humanitas et benevolentia tua vir illustrissime! me dignare valuerit ad locum unquam tutoris et professoris sive ad officium secretarii commendandi, paratum me invenies: ad persolvenda amplius officia parochialia excurrendo in longum latum et profundum diocoesis archiepiscopi ad instar latitudinis sed non valetudinis praesertim tempore hiemis, imparem me sentio et existimo.— Vale, et me ama aliqua saltem lineola linguae vernaculae tuae![667]

Deum maximum optimum valetudinis largitorem precor, ut te diu, diuque servet incolumen, in cuius tutelam et benedictionem te, tuosque ex animo depono

Excellentiae tuae observantissimus

Joannes Petrus Spinner
Ecclesiae reformatae germanicae Minister
per annos 39 in Germanflats et Herkimer et ts [?]:
Thelogiae Magister in Universitate
olim moguntina ad Rhenum in germania
dedi Herkimerii Status Novi-Eboraci
die 9na Januarii Anno Salutis 1840

Source: Martin Van Buren Papers, Library of Congress.[668]

59 Salmon Fishing in Washington State (1840s)

In the mid 1820s the Hudson's Bay Company established the important trading post of Fort Colville, located near Kettle Falls on the upper Columbia River in northeastern Washington.[669] In the summer of 1845 the Belgian-born Jesuit Pierre Jean de Smet (1801–73) established St. Paul's Mission at Kettle Falls, and he built a primitive chapel on a bluff amidst the huts of the Skoyelpi (or Kettle) tribe.[670] Each year from June to October Native American tribes gathered to fish at Kettle Falls, where as many as 2000 salmon could be caught daily by means of spears and massive baskets suspended from overhanging rocks.[671]

In the 1850s native tribes in the region were beset by several events: the outbreak of smallpox (1853–54), the construction of a nearby saloon (1854), the reservation policy proposed by the territorial Governor Isaac Stevens (1855), the influx of settlers following the discovery of gold (1855),[672] the Yakima War to the south (1855–58), and the emergence of a hostile nativist movement initiated by Smohalla, a Wanapum from British Columbia (c. 1860). The Jesuit mission was temporarily closed in 1859, and it was definitively abandoned in 1875. In 1939 the chapel was reconstructed to original specifications and is now owned by the National Park Service.[673]

The following excerpt, taken from *Historia missionis Sancti Francisci Regis, Colville (Wash.) exeunte anno 1889*, describes the early foundation of St. Paul's. It was regular practice for the Jesuits to compose histories of their foundations, and well into the twentieth century these were typically written in Latin.

This document indicates yet another reason for the abandonment of the mission: elaborate and highly successful net-fishing conducted below the falls and further downstream displaced these annual gatherings.

Primus e Patribus Societatis, Pater de Smedt iuxta Columbiam flumen, circa annum 1842, riparium Indianum baptizavit.[674] Existimavere tunc Superiores quod in Indianorum bonum plurimum conduceret si statio aliqua non longe a loco "Columbia Falls" nuncupato, erigeretur.[675] Etenim quum salmones, quotannis, aestivo tempore, praedictos aquarum lapsus transnatarent, aquis inter saxa diffluentibus, consuescebant Indiani pisces, mediante spiculo, expiscari. Inde frequens turba occasioque semen evangelicum seminandi eximia. Ecclesia hic sub titulo S[ti] Pauli tunc erecta in usu fuit usque ad annum 1885;[676] quo tempore nec pisces nec Indiani unquam visi fuerunt, piscatoribus in societates constitutis salmones retibus infra et prope oram fluminis includentibus.

Source: The Pacific Northwest Tribes Missions Collection of the Oregon Province Archives of the Society of Jesus, 1853–1960, microfilm reel 22, pp. 622–23 (original in Jesuit Archives and Research Center, St. Louis, Missouri).

60 Erie Canal (1842)

The Erie Canal, stretching 363 miles from Albany to Buffalo, is one of the engineering marvels of the nineteenth century. First proposed by a flour merchant, Jessee Hawley, it opened on October 26, 1825 after eight years of construction. It was 4' deep, 40' wide and had a 10' towpath on one side. It had an immediate impact not only on commerce but also on settlement. Between 1829 and 1841 shipments of wheat by canal from Buffalo increased from 3640 bushels to 1,000,000. Because of the canal, New York City became the largest port in the United States, surpassing New Orleans, Baltimore, Philadelphia, and Boston.[677]

Yet travel on the canal could be tedious and perilous. In the passage below, the Austrian-born Franciscan missionary, Otto Skolla (1805–79), recounts his trip in 1842. Motivated to work among Native American tribes by Frederic Baraga (1797–1868), who would later become the first Bishop of Marquette (Michigan), Skolla lived for fifteen years (1842–58) in the upper Great Lakes region, particularly among the Chippewa and Menominee.[678] Other selections from Skolla are presented in section 62.

Initio vero mensis Maii cum praevie petita licentia ab Episcopo Neo-Eboracensi[679] ad novum iter me accinxi versus Michigan. Itaque navem conscendi, quae ex litore ab equis tractim et lento passu progredientibus, ope funium trahebatur, quam aquam angusti spatii, quiete fluentem et undique clausam, Canalem vocant: vectura haec certe fastidiosa, 15 diebus durabat: quae alias ope navigii vaporistici duabus noctibus perficitur. Trahitur autem ista navis per canalem sub trabibus frequentium et valde demissorum pontium, et proinde non paucorum, minus cautorum hominum capita, contra trabem transversam allidebantur et in deliquium vertebantur; alii saeve vulnerati sunt vel subita morte perierunt, quinimmo etiam per truncum prominentem capite truncati sunt. Ego ipse vidi tunc nonnulla funesta et tristia eiusmodi accidentia. Et propterea nauclerus (capitano) saepe defendit, gentem ascendere superiorem partem navis; ne, inquit, caput perdant. Hodie[680] tamen apud Americanos eiusmodi vasa navalia non amplius in usu habentur, sed potius vaporistica. Postquam autem traiectum hunc periculosum per Lacum Huron et Erie complevissem, appulsus sum Detroitum, civitatem capitalem in Statu Michigan anno 1842,[681] medio Maio.

Source: "America Septentrionalis," *La Palestina e le Rimanenti missioni Francescane in Tutta la Terra* (1891): 74–75.

61 Transatlantic Steamship Travel (1842)

The 1840s were not a propitious time to be collecting money in Ireland. Yet this was the task assigned to Rev. Charles Constantine Pise (1801–66), who was commissioned in the fall of 1842 by Bishop John Hughes (1797–1864) to collect money for the debt-ridden parish of St. Peter's, New York's first Catholic church, located on Barclay Street in lower Manhattan. The following Latin poem commemorates Pise's transatlantic steamship journey on the *Great Western*, and it pays tribute to its commander, James Hosken (1798–1885).

Pise, born in Annapolis to an Italian father (Luigi, or Lewis) and a Philadelphia-born mother (Margaret Gamble), was one of the leading Catholic literary figures in the United States in the mid-nineteenth-century. Educated at Georgetown, he entered the Jesuit order and in 1820 was sent to Rome for further education, his superiors intending that he and his American classmates, among whom were Thomas Mulledy and William McSherry (see section 54), would supervise the restoration of the Jesuits within the United States and in particular would inculcate the famous *Ratio Studiorum* within American Jesuit schools and colleges.[682] After only a brief time in Italy he withdrew from the Jesuits and returned home—according to some biographers this was occasioned by the death of his father—and having finished his seminary formation at Mount St. Mary's in Emmitsburg, he was ordained in Baltimore in March 1825. Over the next four decades he taught at Mount St. Mary's and was pastor in Washington, Annapolis, New York, and Brooklyn. He was awarded an M.A. by Georgetown (1830), and in 1832 he was granted a doctorate in Rome. In December 1832, by virtue of his association with Henry Clay, he was appointed chaplain to the United States Senate, the first and only Catholic to hold this position.

In the midst of his pastoral responsibilities, Pise published extensively, notably a five-volume *History of the Church* (1827–30) and *Saint Ignatius and his First*

Companions (1844) as well as *Father Rowland: a North American Tale* (1829) and *The Indian Cottage: A Unitarian Story* (1831), these last two being some of the first novels written by a Catholic within the United States.[683] With the exiled Cuban priest Félix Varela (1788–1853), he edited *The Catholic Expositor and Literary Magazine* (1841–43). A prolific poet, Pise published *The Pleasures of Religion and Other Poems* (1833), which was dedicated to Washington Irving, as well as an English blank-verse translation of the Acts of the Apostles (1844). His most famous poem, often anthologized, is a tribute to the American flag, written to counteract charges that Catholics were insufficiently patriotic.[684]

Among his poems are several in Latin. Thus far searches have turned up the following:

1) "In mortem Pii Pontificis VII Elegia." One historian prints the first six lines of this poem, which is said to have been sixty-eight lines long, but no indication is given of the location of the manuscript or the date of its composition, although presumably it was not long after the pope's death on August 20, 1823.[685]

2) "In S. Mariae ad Montes Novi Seminarii Incendium Elegia" (1824), written to commemorate a fire on June 6, 1824 that destroyed the recently-completed main building at Mount St. Mary's, where Pise was completing seminary studies as well as teaching. The printed version of this poem, found in a history of Mount St. Mary's, contains 41 lines of elegiac couplets, so presumably at least one is missing.[686]

3) "Ad Venerabilem virum Carolum Carroll Diem natalem celebrantem, Elegia," (1827). This twenty-line poem, which begins "Do tibi natalem, (nunquam est peritura) corrollam," was originally published in a Baltimore newspaper where it was attributed to Polyhymnia; an appended note requested an English translation.[687] Pise enjoyed a close relationship with Carroll, the last surviving signer of the Declaration of Independence, and he delivered a much-admired eulogy when Carroll died in 1832.

4) "In mortem Ambrosii Marechal, Archiepiscop. Balt. Terti. Elegeia," (1828). This twenty-two-line poem was published in a Baltimore newspaper, where it was attributed to Polyhymnia and where again an English translation was requested.[688] Mareschal had ordained Pise to the priesthood on March 19, 1825.

5) "Lines Written on Board the Great Western, October 5, 1842." Printed below.

6) "Glanmirae Vallis," a poem of twenty-six hexameters, the first line of which is "Quamvis per totam hanc contingeret Insulam amoenam," written in the fall of 1842 when Pise went sightseeing in the countryside near Cork during his collecting tour to Ireland.[689] In his travelogue, "Horae Vagabundae," Pise describes the Vale of Glanmire as perhaps the most beautiful spot in all of Ireland.

7) "Ad Alumnos, in memoriam Joannis Dubois, et Simonis G. Bruté, collegii Sanctae Mariae ad Montes Fundatorum," consisting of 21 alcaic stanzas, whose first line is "Non usitato congredimur modo." This was recited in October 1858 on the occasion of the fiftieth anniversary of Mount St. Mary's.[690] Pise professed trepidation at delivering this ode, composed "in the language of the Church," in the presence of his distinguished audience, because he suspected that the lines were "more fraught with thrilling reminiscences than classic inspiration."

Pise's Latin poems, some of which likely remain to be discovered, would be a fitting subject for a study.[691] Moreover Pise himself is yet to be the subject of a full-length biography; to date there is only one M.A. thesis devoted to him.[692] As Gilbert Gigliotti has noted, any true appreciation of American Literature must take into account the presence of the rich corpus of Neo-Latin literature.[693] So too the realistic appreciation of Pise, among other authors, would require an investigation into his Latin poems.

The following poem, which was originally published in *The New World* (November 12, 1842) and later reprinted with an English translation in *The Catholic Expositor and Literary Magazine* (1843), commemorates

Pise's voyage on the *Great Western*, which was the first passenger steamboat constructed to make regular transatlantic crossings.[694] Launched in July 1837, its maiden voyage to New York took place in April 1838, and it quickly developed a reputation for speedy and reliable transport.

Although the poem's title indicates that it was written "on board" ship on October 5, 1842, in his travelogue Pise relates that he departed New York on August 11 and sighted the coast of Ireland on August 23, at which point he was transferred to a fishing boat that took him into Cork.[695] October 5 must therefore be the date he finalized or submitted the poem.

Bishop Hughes, it has been suggested, chose Pise to undertake this mission to Ireland because Pise enjoyed a high reputation in European circles.[696] He was, for example, the first American priest to have been designated a Knight of the Sacred Palace and Count Palatine, an honor which he received from Pope Gregory XVI in 1832.[697] Moreover, due to his role as Senate Chaplain, Pise was able to carry to Ireland a letter of recommendation from President John Tyler.[698] Pise's mission, however, was not successful enough to resolve the financial difficulties under which St. Peter's labored throughout the 1840s and 1850s.

Lines Written on Board the Great Western, October 5, 1842

Tu discedenti[699] redientique arca[700] fuisti
Navis, fausta mihi—tu mea vota meres.
In Maris aestivis, nec non hiemalibus undis,[701]
Persequeris cursum prospera rite tuum.
Nulla tibi cura est ventorum; namque secundis
Tollis vela, aliter ponere vela potes.[702]
Et tamen adversum rapido motu mare findis
Aequoris immensum nil reputans spatium.[703]
Et tempestatem spernis pigremque quietem:

Victrices superant has celeresque rotae.[704]
Interea sublime tenens iter aequore in alto
Vis manifesta mihi magna vaporis adest
Rideat et Fortuna tibi quocumque meabis,
Favoremque Duci[705] det Deus usque tuo;
Quum fuerit vita hac a tempestate revulsus,
Tunc statio in caelis sit—benefida quies.[706]

Source: *The New World* 5 (November 12, 1842): 309.

62 Midwestern Adventures (1843–45)

The passages below recount the adventures of the Franciscan missionary Otto Skolla (see section 60) on and around Mackinac Island in the mid-1840s. The first selection describes the topography of the island as well as its fort and populace, and it notes how Skolla's work was affected by the outbreak of the Mexican-American War. Subsequent excerpts relate Skolla's perilous ice-crossing from Mackinac Island to St. Ignace, on the upper peninsula, and his precarious journey in a birch canoe across Lake Superior with Frederick Baraga (see section 60) in the fall of 1845.

These passages are taken from a much longer account, written at the request of Very Rev. Bernardino Trionfetti de Montefranco, the Minister-General of the Franciscans from 1856–62, after Skolla had returned to Europe. They were published many years after Skolla's death in a Franciscan missionary journal. This account, which stands in the tradition of the earlier Jesuit *Relations* as well as the missionary reports published in the *Annales de la propagation de la foi*, indicates that stories from the American frontier, even when written in Latin, continued to enjoy a welcome readership in Europe.

Mackinac, seu Michilli-Mackinaw, est oppidum, non quidem amplum ambitu, sed valde gracile aspectu, situatum in una pulcherrima insula ad Lacum Michigan, quae insula in suo diametro est vix duorum milliariorum et in circumferentia tantum sex, cuiusque superficies modico elevata, cedrorum, aliorumque arbustorum viriditate consita, in collem valde deliciosum exurgit. Habet in loco elevatiori Arcem munitionis militarem,[707] quae prospectum valde amoenum preabet finitimis oris Lacus Michigan. Incolae huius insulae, quorum numerus ad 2000 se extendit, sunt advenae Canadiani et Semi-Canadiani, i.e., Metifs, ex Canadiorum connubio, mixto cum Indianis. Eorum vitae ratio consistit in captura piscium, quos illi sale sat conspersos mercatoribus venditant; porro in vendendis pellibus caprearum, ursorum, vulpium, cervorum, et aliorum animalium silvestrium: in vendendis rebus ab indica industria ex betulinis corticibus confectis, uti, corbibus, sportulis, crumenis, situlis et eiusmodi paribus, quas mulieres indianae ope hystricum spinarum diverso colore tinctarum floribus aliisque figuris intextis, valde artificiose exornant; denique in vendendo sacharo indico flavi coloris, quod singulis annis ex certae arboris succo productum, ab indianis conficitur.

Finaliter autem quoad milites supra-dictae Arcis munitionis, restat mihi paucis verbis commemorare, quod confidenter usi sint mea conversatione, in omnibus bonis et honestis, et libenter intrarunt in domum meam ad invisendum me, et colloquendum; hincque facilius potui corda eorum pro frequentanda ecclesia sollicitare. Ast revera, omni Dominica venerunt missi a centurionibus suis turmatim in ecclesiam,[708] et non solum Catholici sed etiam ipsi Americani. Itaque statim post sermonem gallicum, praelegi meae perdilectae copiae militari diebus Dominicis Epistolam et Evangelium in lingua anglica, et feci eis in eadem lingua brevem discursum spiritualem ad promptiores reddendos ad terendam viam salutis et pacis.

Erat autem anno sequenti 1845 ab Americanis bellum declaratum adversus Mexicanos.[709] Hinc isti boni milites, antequam Mackinac pone reliquissent, unus post alterum venientes ad me, valedixerunt mihi, dum iam nigrum navigium bellicum ingens, supra fretum Lacus stabat, ad eos recipiendos.

Praeter modo dictam, etiam aliam missionem habui, nempe la Pointe de S. Ignace, sex milliariis distantem a Mackinac; ibi erat ecclesia cum sibi cohaerenti presbyterio.[710] Traiectus autem aquarum per lacum Michigan erat nonnunquam sat periculosus . . . Etenim toto tempore hiemali, usque ad mensem Aprilem, omnes Lacus Amer. Septent. superiorum regionum glacie tam spissa obducti sunt, ut media hieme (Ian. et Feb.) plaustri onera ponderosissima, absque ullo periculo supra glaciem lacuum vehi et transportari possint. Accidit autem semel, cum essem in missione in Pointe de S. Ignace, ut quidam homo, cum equo et traha a civibus Mackinacensibus missus, veniens accersisset me, ut revertar in Mackinac. Consensi quidem, sed cum quadam apprehensione mali. Resedi ergo in traha. Cumque medium iter supra Lacum Michigan confecissemus, ecce de repente isti equi albi militares, toto corpore submersi sunt aquis, capitibus duntaxat prominentibus, et in tali conditione permanserunt per spatium quinque minutorum horae trementes, et oribus hiantibus spumantes. Egomet protinus ex traha exiliebam, quae sola tunc supra glaciem semiruptam stabat. Ad bonam tamen sortem, quidam vir Canadius, ex sua vicinitate ab elonginquo per conductoris mei clamorem accitus, festinantissime prosiliens, adiuvit infelicem meum conductorem, et sic ambo feliciter equos demersos salvarunt. Interim forti animo continuavi et residuam itineris medietatem, et sic Deo propitio, sospes et bene servatus Mackinac reversus sum.

Denuo tentavi transmissionem meam per magnum et profluum fretum Lacus Superioris, ope navicularum indicarum ex corticibus confectarum, in consortio cum D.

Baraga et sex Indianis remigibus, unde non raro perculsi fuimus magno terrore ob manifestum periculum pereundi.[711] Ast quis sibi ideam fingere queat, quam imperterriti sint a natura ipsa Indiani, quamque apti sint ad remigandum et remigium dirigendum? quippe immergi iam fluctibus incipiente navicula (cuius fundum sola simplex cortex ab aquarum voragine defendit) atque aquis prope ad summum onusta, ipsi tamen nil mali pertimescentes, capiebant animum, assidue haurientes aquam ex carinula, exultabant, ridebant, canebant, et quasi ipsi Lacui insultantes, ramis undas intumescentes in profundum prosternebant, ut propemodum cuiquam appareret, ac si cum ipsis aquae fluctibus inanimatis dimicare et luctare vellent. Atque timorosissimus quisque ex eiusmodi generosis facetiis Indianorum, animo resumpto, mox ab omni timore liberari debuit.

Source: "America Septentrionalis," *La Palestina e le Rimanenti missioni Francescane in Tutta la Terra* (1891): 78–79, 80–81.[712]

63 A Chaplain in the Mexican-American War (1846)

Almericus Zappone (b. 1822), born in Naples, came to Georgetown in 1845 as a Jesuit scholastic (seminarian). After one year he left the Jesuits and moved across the Potomac to Alexandria, Virginia where he married a much older widow. His wife died in their second year of marriage. For the next decade he taught guitar and languages and he offered translation services in Alexandria and Washington. He later remarried, and with his wife he administered a girls' school, The Circle Institute, in Washington. In 1860 he graduated from Georgetown's Medical School, and he practiced medicine and dentistry in Washington throughout the Civil War years. His name falls out of local newspapers in the mid-1860s.[713]

In the late 1840s and early 1850s Zappone published Latin poems, some of which initially appeared in Washington-area newspapers. The following alcaic ode, printed in the January 5, 1847 edition of the *Alexandria Gazette*, commemorates the departure of Rev. Anthony Rey (1807–47) to serve as a chaplain during the Mexican-American War. Born in Lyons, France and educated in Switzerland, Rey came to the United States in 1840 and taught philosophy and served as Vice-President at Georgetown—where he would have met Zappone—and he ministered in parishes in Washington and Philadelphia. Rey, along with fellow Georgetown Jesuit John McElroy, was appointed unofficial chaplain by President James K. Polk (whose nephew was a student at Georgetown) as part of an effort to neutralize a perception both at home and abroad that the Mexican-American War was a religious war, waged by United States Protestants against Mexican Catholics.[714] While in Mexico Rey ministered to Catholics both within the United States army as well as among the Mexican populace. Said to have enjoyed a close relationship with General Zachary Taylor, Rey distinguished himself in the siege of Monterrey, and he died while en route to Matamoros, exactly two weeks after this poem was published. He was the first Catholic chaplain to be killed while serving in the United States military.[715]

Zappone later published a 73-stanza Carmen Panegyricum for General Taylor, whose merits he likened to Cato's and Agrippa's. Taylor alone, Zappone gushed, "kindle[d] up some sparks of my declining Muse;" Zappone therefore "willingly . . . [took] refuge in the resources of a tongue to which Virgil and Horace have lent a grace and vigor which cannot be altogether dissociated from it by the most unskillful hand."[716]

It is likely that other poems by Zappone will yet be located. In addition to the ones mentioned here and in section 65, his "De Iesu Natu," appeared in the *Alexandria Gazette* on Janaury 27, 1847.

ODE—ALCAICA.
REV. P. ANTONIO RAY
in bellum contra Mexicos profecturo.[717]

Deducta belli carmina tempore
Si Musa promit, si valet intimis
Dum fluctuat curis, sereno
Laetitiam simulasse cantu:

Heu! flos virorum, Loiolidum[718] decus,
Ne rere nostro te cito pectore
Obliviis lapsum, utque vultus
Ferre animos pariter remotos.

Videre multas iam videor virum
Oras fluenti sanguine squalidas,
Taboque concreto rubere
Flumina, spumiferosque Nerei

Campos; cruenta cum metit undique
Mors falce vitas, aether et instrepit
        Clamore bellantum, fragorque
                Increpat horrisonus per aera

Martis furentis. Discere at expetam
Quid clara virtus, quid valeat Ray[719]
        Devota vis, lapsisque rebus
                Impavidi bene prompta verba.

Qualisque noctes lacrimulis agit
Insomnis osas, dissitum et intimo
        Haerens cubili inauspicatus
                Mente puer memorat parentem,

Et ceu remotam pullus hirundinem
Avet volatu, aut anxius irritis
        Plorat querelis, quam paterno
                Subripuit manus atro nido:

Grati sinus sic tu usque fidelibus
Urgere votis, nec mihi Phosphoro
        Cedente decedent amores
                Nec tereti pereunte Luna.

Ac tempus extet quo fera mitibus
Mutentur, et ver purpureum plagas
        Has rursus invisat, volatu
                Praepetis huc Zephyri revectum.

Voces morentur—Vivito, sed memor
Vatis—Ministrum Numinis alitem
Te spectet orbis, nulla tantum
Plectra virum cecinisse parcant.

Source: *Alexandria Gazette*, January 5, 1847.

64 Classical and Romantic Poetry in South Carolina (1848)

The following poem, like those of Almericus Zappone (sections 63 and 65), indicates that Latin poetry in nineteenth-century America was not exclusively prompted by academic or religious events. The author, James M. Legaré (1823–59), although little known today, was an accomplished writer and inventor in the antebellum south.

Born in Charleston, Legaré received a classical education first at home, then at the College of Charleston, and finally at St. Mary's College in Baltimore. Due to poor health he was unable to sustain a job for an extended period of time, and he held a series of positions: law clerk, schoolteacher, painter, poet, and postmaster. He was also an inventor, and toward the end of his life he was awarded two patents, including one for "plastic cotton." His poems, all but one of which were in English, have been described as both romantic and classical.[720] In reviewing his work, the *Boston Evening Transcript* discerned a "true sense of the poetical in sentiment if not in expression." Nonetheless, they hailed Legaré's "remarkably composite style," and saw in his poems "tokens of scholarship."[721] Henry Wadsworth Longfellow, with whom Legaré corresponded on several occasions, claimed to have "highly prized" Legaré's compositions, which were "so full of tenderness and 'the dew of youth.'"[722]

Legaré gave Greek or Latin titles to several of his poems,[723] but the last poem in his published volume, "Orta-undis," was entirely in Latin. This poem is reproduced below. A twentieth-century translator muses that the choice of Latin may have been due to Legaré's "reluctan[ce] to put the old topos of unrequited love into English." Yet the Latin, this same translator notes, appears "rather forced and at times faulty," and he concludes: "I am at a loss to account for the poem's place in the book save on grounds of personal attachment."[724]

Orta-Undis
Strophe

Orta virgo resonantem
        Vocem auribus undis,
Mihi animo praedulcem
        Umbra solitudinis
Audio. Calentes agri
        Nemoraque muta sunt:
Greges gratam coryleti
        Umbram lassi conquirunt;
Umbram cantus insectorum
        Sopientes[725] qua sonant,
Aquae gelidae saxorum
        Fissurisque murmurant.
Mihi fervidis sed horis
        Deest quies nemore
Solo: Aestus nam amoris
        Oritur in pectore
Vestibus cor palpitare
        Solet laetum niveis.
Id tunc speras tu servare
        Quod ab omnibus capis?
Felix qui cor (evax!) tuum
        Palpitare audiat;
Caput cirrisque[726] iampronum
        Pectore ut sentiat.
Tuos risus, palpebrasque
        Iam demissas video—
Cur me pacem spoliasque
        Cur me sequeris, Virgo?

Source: James M. Legaré, *Orta-Undis, and Other Poems* (Boston: Ticknor, 1848), 101–2.

65 The Death of an "excellent and Universally Respected Consort" (1851)

Congressional Cemetery in Washington, DC is home to the impressive James H. Causten Family Vault, named after a once-prominent Baltimore-born lawyer and ambassador (1788–1874). On the vault's brick façade, flanking an imposing door leading to a partially underground chamber, stand two massive stone tablets inscribed "Inexorable Death's Doings," which bear the names of the vault's occupants.[727] One of the twenty-one Caustens interred there is Mary Elizabeth Carvallo Causten (1815–51), James Causten's daughter and the wife of the Chilean ambassador to the United States, Manuel Carvallo (1806–67). Mary Elizabeth was highly regarded in Washington—"excellent and universally respected" according to the *Washington Union*.[728] Among the large crowd in St. Patrick's Church for her funeral on March 25, 1851 were President Millard Fillmore, several cabinet members and their wives, members of the diplomatic corps, Major General Winfield Scott, and Mayor Walter Lenox.[729] The following Latin poem by Almericus Zappone (see section 63) commemorates her death. It was published in a Washington newspaper. Mary Elizabeth's infant son, James Causten Carvallo, died the day after her funeral.[730]

In mortem D. Mariae de Carvallo, illustris uxoris Ministri Chilensis—Cubiculi Prosopopoeia[731]

Illa ego quae poteram fortunatissima dici
        Una omnes inter conspicua aula domus:
Illa eadem nunc orba querelas, te inde remota,
        Effundo, inferiis ultima pompa tuis.
Mi decus interiit, sim quamvis nobilis aula,
        Et tua me decorent, nulli habitanda vaco.

O quoties hic quum sederis socialis amante
    Audivi dulces ore rubente sonos!
Omnibus ipsa placebas plus quam filia matri,
    Et plus quam puero mater amata suo—
Qualis in immenso iactatur marmore navis
    Undique quam saevi verberat ira noti;
Sic consors Emmanuel anxio adactus amore
    Nutat et huc illuc fluctuat ambiguus;
Nox abit in precibus, suspiria pectore fundit
    More nivis lacrimae sole madentis eunt.
Ah! redeas, precor, atque domus miserere dolentis,
    Vel semel et vultu nos sine dulce frui.

Source: *Washington American Telegraph*, August 2, 1851.

66 Catholic Council in Baltimore (1852)

In May 1880 the Catholic hierarchy of Pennsylvania gathered in Philadelphia for a Provincial Council. At the same time American Presbyterians were gathering in Wisconsin for their annual Assembly. The *New York Tribune* painted a stark contrast between the two meetings. The latter convened "in a plain building" and their proceedings were "plain, logical, and bare of any similitude of imaginative drapery," with discussions that were "simple and business-like." The Catholic council, by contrast, was replete with music, ceremony, incense, flowers, and "a throne on which sat a dignitary addressed as 'My Lord,'" i.e., with "all the pomp and dramatic effect which that hierarchy have learned so well through centuries of practice to use." Additionally, the *Tribune* noted, the discussions at the Catholic council took place in Latin; but, they qualified, "as they were secret, if they slipped into the vulgar tongue nobody was the wiser."[732]

The first Catholic council (or synod) in the United States took place in Baltimore in 1791, but beginning in 1829 they were held somewhat regularly, not only in Baltimore but also, as dioceses and archdioceses were formed, in Oregon City, St. Louis, Cincinnati, New York, New Orleans, and elsewhere. At times these councils involved only the clergy from a particular diocese, at other times they involved prelates from an ecclesiastical province, and on three occasions the entire hierarchy gathered in Baltimore for a Plenary Council. These larger councils consisted of public and private sessions, at which prelates discussed various administrative matters, notably the erection of new dioceses.

As the *Tribune* article suggests, the use of Latin at ecclesiastical councils required justification. Before the Second Plenary Council (1866), Baltimore Archbishop Martin J. Spalding explained that Latin was "the official language of the Church" and that it was "the usage from the very beginning of the Church" for official acts to be composed in Latin. Moreover, he noted, Latin was a bond bringing the assembled prelates into "immediate relations with all other portions of the Church." Therefore, Latin was not only "a striking evidence of antiquity," but it was also "a striking bond of communion." Far from being a fossil, Latin was capable of expressing "living thoughts."[733] Spalding does not mention another, more practical consideration: many of the bishops present at these councils were born in non-English speaking countries, and often they had achieved fluency in Latin before they had begun to learn English.

Following these councils the official minutes (*acta*) and the text of any approved decrees (*decreta*) were sent to Rome for approval by the Propaganda Fide. The submission to Rome also included a formal Latin letter addressed to the Pope on behalf of the entire assembled American hierarchy.

The following is taken from the *Acta* of the First Plenary Council of Baltimore (1852). It describes the procession of prelates and theologians through the streets of Baltimore on the Council's opening day. According to the *Baltimore Sun*, "so imposing an array of ecclesiastical and official dignity in connection with this church, or so brilliant and extensive a display of its rich and symbolical insignia, ha[d] scarcely ever before been seen in this country."[734]

Sessio Prima Solemnis

Die 9 Maii, qui erat tertia Dominica post Paschatis festum,[735] A.S.[736] MDCCCLII, hora 10 A. M. conveniunt Patres omnes cum suis theologis, Ordinumque Religiosorum, Congregationumque proceres,[737] necnon et alii permulti sacerdotes, in aedibus Archiepiscopalibus, unde ordinata processione, per vias frequentissimas[738] Metropolitanam ecclesiam S. Mariae[739] petunt Archiepiscopi et Episcopi[740] pluvialibus[741] induti ac mitris;[742] Abbas autem S. Mariae de Trappa,[743] pluviali et mitra; Ordinum Religiosorum ac Congregationum Superiores vel pluvialibus, vel Ordinis habitu, ac biretis;[744] Sacerdotes tandem indumentis sacerdotalibus, stolis nempe et planetis.[745]

Ut processioni via pateret inter turbas densissimas tum fidelium, tum acatholicorum, curavit egregia Societas iuventuti catholicae amica,[746] quae hoc munus, tum hodie, tum quandocumque processio facienda erat, eo decore, ea erga omnes morum suavitate persolvit, ut omnium laudes plaususque merito exciperet.

Ubi vero ad ecclesiam perventum est, omnibus sedes iuxta ordinem adsignantur, Archiepiscopis quidem et Episcopis scamna ornata hinc inde a dextris et a sinistris altaris maioris; ceteris vero scamna tum intra, tum extra cancellos chori, necnon et apud altaria S. Josephi et Boni Pastoris: non enim omnibus intra chorum sedendi copiam permisit sacerdotum, aliorumque multitudo.

Missam de Spiritu sancto celebravit ipsemet Revmus et Illmus D. Archiepiscopus Baltimorensis,[747] Sedis Apostolicae Delegatus, cui adstiterunt archidiaconus, Adm. Rev. D. F. Lhomme;[748] diaconus, Rev. Alexius J. Elder;[749] subdiaconus, Rev. D. Carolus M. E. Voirdye;[750] diaconi vero iuxta thronum adsistentes, Adm. Rev. D. Henricus B. Coskery[751] et Rev. D. Thomas Foley.[752]

Absoluto sacro, concionem ad populum habuit Revmus et Illmus D. Archiepiscopus Neo-Eboracensis:[753] qua finita, Sessio prima solemnis huius plenarii Concilii habita est.

Source: *Concilium Plenarium Totius Americae Septentrionalis Foederatae Baltimori Habitum Anno 1852* (Baltimore: John Murphy, 1853), 12–14.

67 A Pope Writes a President (1853)

In late March 1853 the American Chargé d'affaires to the Holy See, Lewis Cass, Jr. (1814–78), wrote Washington to inform authorities of the impending arrival in the United States of Archbishop Gaetano Bedini (1806–64). Ostensibly Bedini was stopping in the United States to pay his respects to the President of the United States before continuing on to Rio de Janeiro, where he was to serve as nuncio to the imperial court of Pedro II of Brazil. Cass looked favorably upon Bedini's proposed stopover as "a new and additional testimonial of the highly friendly and favorable sentiments entertained by Pius IX towards the Government and Institutions of the United States." As far as Cass knew, Bedini would remain within the United States "but a few days."[754] Yet Bedini's visit to the United States lasted a full six months, and he did not journey on to Brazil. As some American prelates suspected, the real purpose of Bedini's visit was to investigate the Catholic Church in the United States, where, if prudent, Rome hoped to establish a nunciature.[755]

Bedini landed in New York on June 30, 1853 and proceeded to Washington, where on July 7 he was graciously received by President Franklin Pierce. During this meeting Bedini handed the President the following Latin letter from Pope Pius IX. Pierce perhaps was able to read the letter unassisted, for he had received a classical education. Still extant is his Oratio Salutatoria, entitled "De Seculo Augusti," which he delivered at Bowdoin's Commencement on May 20, 1824, nearly three decades earlier.[756]

Yet Bedini's extended tour of the United States was marked by conflict. In certain cities his presence elicited protests, which at times became violent. Criticized sharply in editorials, he was several times burned in effigy, and he was the target of an assassination attempt. Much of this animosity arose from German and Italian immigrants who had fled the failed 1848 revolutions in

Europe and who saw Pope Pius IX as a major obstacle to liberal reform. Prominent among the Italian exiles was the former Catholic priest Alessandro Gavazzi (1809–89), who shadowed Bedini throughout his visit. But Bedini's visit also coincided with a crescendo of nativism, much of which was embodied in the rise of the Know-Nothing party, and it evoked anxiety concerning the role of the Catholic Church within American society and specifically the Church's potential threat to liberal institutions. Bedini had to leave the country clandestinely, for fear of further riots. On the morning of February 4, 1854 he and his secretary slipped out of Staten Island and were conveyed by a special deputy of the United States Marshals to the England-bound *Atlantic* waiting in New York Harbor.

One consequence of Bedini's visit was the establishment in 1859 of the North American College in Rome, which is still extant as a seminary for Catholic students from American dioceses. It would be nearly four decades until the Holy See sent another papal delegate to the United States.

A month before Bedini's departure, at the request of Senator Lewis Cass, Sr. of Michigan (1782–1866), the father of the American Ambassador to the Holy See, the United States Senate discussed Bedini's treatment and sought to ascertain whether the federal government ought to have secured better protection for him. As part of these proceedings, the Pope's Latin letter and an English translation were submitted to the Senate. The letter was read aloud (it is unclear whether the Latin as well as the English was read), placed conspicuously upon a table within the Senate chamber, and later printed.

Pierce met Bedini once again, when traveling in Europe after his presidency.

Illustris et Honorabilis Vir, Salutem:

Cum venerabilis Frater, Caietanus, Archiepiscopus Thebarum,[757] ad ordinarii nostri et Apostolicae Sedis Nuncii munus apud Imperialem Braziliensem aulam[758] obeundum a nobis destinatus per istas transeat regiones, eidem in praecipuis mandatis dedimus, ut nostro nomine nobilitatem tuam conveniat, tibique has nostras reddat litteras, plurimam salutem dicat, ac simul nostri in te animi sensus luculentis verbis exprimat, atque testetur.

Procerto habemus, haec nostra in te studia pergrata tibi fore, ac minime dubitamus, quin eumdem venerabilem fratrem egregiis animi, ingeniique dotibus ornatum pro eximia tua humanitate benignissime sis excepturus. Et quoniam universi dominici gregis cura nobis divinitus est commissa, idcirco haud possumus, quin hac quoque occasione libentissime utentes, a te totis viribus enixe efflagitemus, ut Catholicos in istis regionibus degentes valido tuo patrocinio et auctoritate tegere ac tueri semper velis. Dum autem confidimus, nobilitatem tuam nostris hisce desideriis, ac postulationibus perlibenter esse satisfacturam, haud omittimus a Deo optimo Maximo humiliter exposcere, ut te, illustris et honorabilis vir, caelestis suae gratiae donis, omnique verae felicitatis genere cumulet, ac perfecta nobiscum caritate coniungat.

Datum Romae, apud S. Petrum, die 31 Martii, anno 1853, Pontificatus nostri anno septimo.[759]

Pius P.P.[760] IX.

Source: *Index to Executive Documents Printed by Order of The Senate of the United States, First Session, Thirty-Third Congress, 1853–'54* (Washington: Beverley Tucker, 1854), Ex. Doc. No. 23.[761]

68 Bleeding Kansas (1854)

The Jesuit priest William Stack Murphy (1803–75) was an eyewitness to the tumultuous aftermath of the Kansas-Nebraska Act, which Congress passed and President Franklin Pierce signed into law on May 30, 1854. Kansas and Nebraska thereby were admitted into the Union. But contrary to the stipulations of the Missouri Compromise (1820) each state was left to decide on its own the question of whether or not to allow slavery (see section 50). Kansas was immediately overrun by partisans on both sides of the slavery question, each intending to outdo the other at an upcoming referendum. Violence ensued, "a miniature civil war of Kansas' own,"[762] which involved, among others, John Brown and his four sons. Native Americans especially suffered.

Murphy, a native of Cork, Ireland, had entered the Jesuits in France and had held positions in Kentucky and New York before being appointed Superior of the Missouri Province. He was renowned for his knowledge of the classics as well as of French and English literature. A mid-20th-century historian cites the following excerpt from one of Murphy's letters, dated Sept 14, 1854 and addressed to the Jesuit General Peter Jan Beckx, as testimony of his fine Latin style.[763]

Vicariatus[764] Rev^{mi} Miège[765] in terram frequenter habitatam celerrime excrescit. Scilicet tota Indica regio in duas provincias[766] nuper est divisa. Singulis colonis 150 iugera publice assignantur. Infinita hominum multitudo in dies eo immigrat; iam conventus agunt; iam sub ipsis arboribus edunt Diaria.[767] Motus vero ac tumultus mox futuri. Scilicet plane contra pacta conventa anni 1820, inter Status omnes in quibus servitus aethiopica exsistit et reliquos, res geritur. Quippe lege cautum erat, ne ultra lineam quandam geographicam novae provinciae deinceps constituendae mancipia admitterent.[768] Nuper vero ea lex eatenus mutata est, ut singulis Statibus rite administratis liceat ex colonorum suffragiis istiusmodi servos habendos vel prohibendos intra fines suos statuere. Inde fit ut qui legem ita mutatam esse indignantur nullum non moveant lapidem quo maior evadat mancipia respuentium numerus, cum ad suffragia ventum fuerit. Quin etiam, data pecunia, in dies efficiunt ut coloni mox suffragia ex sententia laturi creberrimi adventent.[769] Missouriani vero Kentuckiani aliique, qui secum servos adduxerunt arma ac vim parant, negantque se mancipia eici passuros. Interea Indi miserrimi, irruentibus Americanis, sibi abeundum esse perspiciunt, nec tamen quo se conferant satis sciunt, cum omnia undique ab iisdem occupentur.[770]

Source: Archivum Romanum Societatis Iesu, Rome, Miss. 1005–II, Epistolarum communium pars II.[771]

69 American Rubicon: Superfluvium Mississippi (1856)

In the 1950s Walter Agard (1894–1978), a longtime professor of Classics at the University of Wisconsin, took issue with the famous thesis of Frederick Jackson Turner (1861–1932), which held inter alia that Americans on the frontier were savvy, practical, but uncultured individualists, little concerned with the past. Agard responded that the American frontier was imbued with a robust culture by virtue of its many classically-educated teachers, ministers, writers, lawyers, and doctors.[772] The first passage below supports Agard's argument. It is an elegant Latin letter of apology written by Joseph Salzmann (1819–74), a Milwaukee priest, addressed to Mathias Loras (1792–1858), the founding Bishop of Dubuque.

The Austrian-born Salzmann is considered the fundator of St. Francis de Sales Seminary in Milwaukee, which opened its doors in January 1856 to educate priests for emerging German-speaking congregations in the upper Midwest.[773] Salzmann served at times as professor (of Latin and Greek, among other subjects), procurator, rector, and fund-raiser for the seminary. In the latter capacity he undertook several lengthy collecting tours that took him not only throughout Wisconsin but also to the mid-Atlantic states, New England, St. Louis, and New Orleans. It has been estimated that between 1854 and 1874 Salzmann collected about $100,000.

Salzmann's modus operandi on these journeys was to preach in a German parish on Sunday and then go door-to-door early in the week soliciting contributions. These collections, when they took place outside the Diocese of Milwaukee, required the consent of the local bishop. Usually this was secured in advance, but in Iowa in the fall of 1856 Salzmann's eagerness outstripped his prudence. He crossed the Mississippi River into the Diocese of Dubuque and took up a collection in the German-speaking parish of New Vienna. He therefore found himself in the unpleasant position of having to tender an apology to Loras.[774] The first passage below is this letter of apology. The structure of the letter replicates the sacrament of penance: Salzmann succinctly (but eloquently) confesses his misdeed, offers his *mea culpa*, commits to undertake penance (albeit self-imposed), expresses his firm purpose of amendment, and makes a hasty exit.

Why did Salzmann write his apology to Loras in Latin?[775] He does not specify, but it seems likely that he would have heard from clergy in New Vienna or elsewhere that Loras was capable of, but not altogether comfortable, handling German correspondence.[776] Had Salzmann used German, he would have risked alienating Loras by placing him in a position of disadvantage. On the other hand, any attempt to write in French would have frustrated the sort of eloquence with which Salzmann wanted to invest his letter. Latin, however, was the native language of neither man, but it had been studied and used in varying degrees by both; Loras and Salzmann could equally claim a share in its inheritance. Of course, the same could be said about English, but Latin had a distinct advantage: it enabled Salzmann to make terse but recognizable allusions to Scripture and Catholic doctrine as well as to cite passages of classical literature. Moreover, Salzmann's urbane Latin was a compliment to Loras because it presumed a high degree of fluency on Loras's part.[777] Indeed, of Loras's surviving Latin correspondence, which consists of thirty outgoing and about fifteen incoming letters, the latter mostly from German speakers, Salzmann's is by far the most artful.

For all its rhetoric, however, Salzmann's letter did not achieve its desired outcome. Loras was not mollified, and Salzmann's aspirations in New Vienna were somewhat frustrated by Loras's intervention. In one of his last surviving letters, Loras instructed James Orth, the pastor in New Vienna, that the parishioners in New Vienna were not bound to pay Salzmann anything. He further stipulated:

> "He has no authority from me to collect in my diocese, nor has he any right or authority to establish any fraternity within the limits of this diocese. If I hear any more such interference, I shall be compelled to write to the Bishop of Milwaukee regarding his improper conduct. Let your good congregation hold no communication with him."[778]

The second passage below is a sapphic poem written in 1897 to commemorate both the dedication of a ten-foot gilded statue of St. Francis de Sales at the Milwaukee seminary as well as the fiftieth anniversary of Salzmann's arrival in the United States.[779] The author was Rev. Joseph Rainer (1845–1927), the Rector of the Seminary, who wrote a biography of Salzmann.[780] Rainer also published *Greek and English Exercise-Book,* and he is said to have written Latin poems on Columbus and George Washington.[781] This poem was printed in a Milwaukee newspaper.

I

Reverendissime[782] Episcope! Illustrissime Praesul![783]

"Quid non mortalia pectora cogis · · auri sacra fames!" ait quondam Horatius,[784] scrutator cordium;[785] sicque ego, esuriens & sitiens[786] complementum Seminarii nostri,/: instituti prae caeteris cunctis longe praecellentissimi;/ postquam peragraveram totam nostram diocesin per tres abhinc annos, rediens a LaCrosse domum superfluvium Missisippi, hunc non reputans Rubicon hostile, transgressus non hostis Romae sed visurus amicum Rev. Schneider,[787] quem Guttenbergae antea fuisse commoratum compereram; sed quum parochus Rev. Orth[788] profectus fuisset in missionem New-Viennam,[789] ego, qui Viennae in Austria per tres annos qua sacerdos pro rigorosis studui,[790] partim ex curiosa novitate nominis, partim attractus dulci spe, visendi Neo-Mystam,[791] partim & praesertim abreptus sancta auri fame, prosecutus sum usque New-Viennam, ibique (non quidem inscio, sed fors invito parocho) collectionem pro Seminario nostro colligere ausus sum. Etenim Rev. Galtier at Prairie du Chien,[792] et Rev. De Kayelle[793] consignarunt mihi Insignem Praesulis Benevolentiam, ut ego nonnisi ὑστερον προτερον commiserim, istud Placetum Episcopale post factum repetierim. Erravi - & errare humanum; - "peccavi" & Davidi hoc verbum professo statim apparuit Nathan condonans,[794] talisque mihi hoc mane confesso apparuit Revdus McCabe[795] dicens: "all right now". Modo revertor placatus & reconciliatus Praesuli, Cui: numquam tale quid heîc a me aut nostris eventurum esse, manu & ore sacerdotali promitto. Placeat Gratiae Vestrae Episcopali, mittere juvenem bonae indolis in Salesianum nostrum quem rite informatum & egregie disciplinatum, remittemus ad manus Episcopales imponendas.[796] Miserere, Illst.me Praesul! miserere[797] conditionis nostrae, $20000 debitorum aggravant—onus humeris Croesi tremendum[798]—ego solus contuli $1000,[799] & anno seq. $4000 ultra reliqua cuncta & singula sunt colligenda. Quapropter ignoscas—ignoscere est res divina; necessitas extrema[800] consuetum saepe transit modum. —Singulis feriis Vtis missa offertur pro benefactoribus Seminarii,[801] ergo et pro Gratia Vestra Ep.spli;—Gratias agens maximas, majores adhuc mente tenens, Congregationem istam New-Viennam,/:quae declaravit una voce dicens: se Episcopo Ipsi non tantum, quantum mihi, sed plus adhuc esse praestituram;/ Cordi Paterno enixe commendans, perseverare dicere audet

Gratiae Vestrae Episcopali addictissimus,
devinctissimus cliens
Jos. Salzmann Procurator Sem. Milw.
Dubuique in festo s. Dionysii 1856.[802]

Festinantem excusatum sexcenties habere dignemini!

II

Divo Patrono S. Francisco Salesio,[803]
recurrente quinquagesimo anniversario die
Josephi Salzmann, Seminarii fundatoris[804]
in Americam adventus
quo die Sti Francisci statua sollemniter dedicata est
d.d.d. Salesiani

Dive, festivo celebrande plectro
Cui Sales ortum dedit atque nomen
Te celso gaudens titulo coruscum
Iubilat orbis,

Gestiens plaudit iuvenum caterva
Tuta sub tali supero Patrono,
Hoc die fausto sine concinamus
Optime Doctor![805]

Nam diem festo renovamus oestro
Quo vir advenit pietate fortis
Qui domum fidens tibi consecrandam
Condidit almam;

Cuius ex tecto rutilans imago[806]
Reddit insignis speciem Patroni
Sacra mitrati benedictione
Metropolitae.[807]

Supplices te nunc famuli precamur:
Devios vitae rege, Dive, calles
Ut viam semper Domini parantes[808]
Astra petamus.

Sources: I Archives of the Archdiocese of Dubuque[809] (with permission).
II Joseph Salzmann Papers, 1847–1898, Box 1, Folder 11, Archdiocese of Milwaukee Archives, Milwaukee, Wisconsin; also printed in *Milwaukee Journal*, September 30, 1897.

70 A Cathedral and a Cable (1858)

In 1844 the painter and inventor Samuel F. B. Morse (1791–1872) transmitted the brief telegraph message, "What hath God wrought?" between Washington and Baltimore, a distance of 38 miles. Fourteen years later, on August 5, 1858, after three failed attempts, a 1950-mile long cable was successfully laid on the floor of the Atlantic Ocean between Valentia Harbor, Ireland and Trinity Bay, Newfoundland, thereby enabling telegraph communication between Europe and the Americas. The first transatlantic message was sent by Queen Victoria (*r.* 1837–1901) to President James Buchanan on August 14. In his reply—which required more than one hour to transmit—Buchanan noted that the cable was a triumph greater than any "won by conquerer on the field of battle," and he prayed that it would be "a bond of perpetual peace and friendship between the kindred nations, and an instrument, destined by Divine Providence, to diffuse religion, civilization, liberty and law throughout the world."

This cable lasted only three weeks, and a more permanent one was not laid until 1866, but the immediate reaction in the summer of 1858 was exuberant.[810] The *New York Herald* acclaimed the cable as "the great event of the age" and a "triumph of science," and the editors pronounced: "never on any occasion was there so universal a burst of joyous excitement created in New York by any event."[811]

The day after President Buchanan replied to Queen Victoria, John Hughes (1797–1864), the Archbishop of New York, laid the cornerstone of St. Patrick's Cathedral, which still stands on Fifth Avenue, ensconced in skyscrapers.[812] Due to the Civil War, the cathedral would not be dedicated until 1879, but the laying of the cornerstone was a momentous religious and civic event for New York City. The *Herald* remarked that this was "one of the grandest ceremonies that was ever witnessed on this continent," and they judged that the crowd, which may have numbered as many as 100,000, was "the largest assemblage our reporter ever saw in this city."[813] The original cornerstone of the cathedral has never been found.[814] But contemporary accounts report that Hughes placed within a cavity of the cornerstone a copper box that contained a parchment bearing the following Latin inscription, which mentions the recent laying of the transatlantic cable.

A. M. D. G.[815]
Hac die,
Decimo Octavo Kalendas Septembris,
A. D.
Millesimo Octingentesimo Quinquagesimo Octavo,
Festo Assumptionis Semper Beatae Et Immaculatae Virginis,[816]
Dei Et Domini Nostri Iesu Christi,
Matris, Mariae,
Lapis Hic Primarius
Novae Ecclesiae Cathedralis Sancti Patricii,
Ritu Pontificali[817] Solemniter Positus Est,
Novi Eboraci;
A Reverendissimo Domino Iohanne Hughes,
Episcopo Quarto Et Archiepiscopo Primo
Huiusce Sedis;[818]
Assistentibus Omnibus Episcopis Provinciae,[819]
Necnon Numero Pergrandi Presbyterorum Ex Diversis
Et Dissitis Locis, Et Cum Concursu Immenso
Piorum Fidelium Astantium Et Admirantium:
Sanctitate Sua Pio Nono, Pontifice Maximo,[820]
Successore Beati Petri,
Feliciter Gubernante Auctoritate Suprema

Universam Christi Ecclesiam;
Iacobo Buchanan,
Statuum Horum Foederatorum Praeside;[821]
Iohanne A. King,
Statum Neo Eboraci Regente;[822]
Et Daniele F. Tiemann,
Huius Civitatis
Summo Magistratu Fungente;—[823]
Iacobo Renwick Et Gulielmo Rodrigue,
Architectis.[824]

P. S.—Hoc Contigit Lapsis Paucis Diebus a re gesta, vere miranda scilicet, depositione funis electri, in profundo maris, Trans Oceanum Atlanticum, a litore ad litus, Sicque instituitur momentanea relatio intelligentiae Americam inter et Europam foederatorum statuum imperia et Britanniarum. Huic operi quidem large faverunt quod autem ad finem felicem perductum, sit maxime debetur invictae fortitudini concivis nostri insignissimi, CYRI. W. FIELD.[825]

Source: *The Metropolitan: A Monthly Magazine, devoted to Religion, Education, Literature, and General Information*, n.s. 1 (1858): 516–17.

71 Latin Writing: The Custom of Learned Germans (1858)

Carl Friedrich Wilhelm Walther (1811–87) is considered the founder of the Missouri Synod of Lutherans. Born in Saxony, Walther attended the Latin School in Schneeberg and the University of Leipzig, and he was a pastor for a brief time in Germany before he emigrated to the United States and settled in St. Louis. In addition to twice serving as President of the Missouri Synod, he was instrumental in 1839 in founding the gymnasium that grew into Concordia College and Seminary in St. Louis, and he served as Concordia's president and professor of theology for four decades. The following is a Latin letter that he sent to Charles Porterfield Krauth (1823–83), a Lutheran pastor in Pittsburgh. The prompting for this letter was a sermon that Krauth delivered on Thanksgiving Day in 1858.

Born in Martinsburg (then in Virginia), Krauth received a classical education first at a gymnasium in Gettysburg and then at Pennsylvania (now Gettysburg) College. But in a restrospect written for a Baltimore journal five years after his college graduation, he derided this kind of education as entirely unsatisfying for boys: "To attempt to satisfy his wants *exclusively* in this way, is as tantalizing as for a famished man to sit down with a hammer, a pointed nail, a flat-iron, and a basket of hard-shelled hickory nuts to make his dinner." Krauth acknowledged the value of classics for "mental discipline and cultivation of taste," but he protested that English authors provided a superior all-round training: "We are not expected to believe that Tacitus can supply the place of Hume's 'History of England.' Sophocles did not write 'Macbeth,' nor Euripides 'Hamlet,' . . . Burke is our Cicero and Pitt our Demosthenes . . . Milton is Hesiod, Homer and Virgil in one—nay more than all, he is MILTON."[826]

Krauth pastored Lutheran congregations in the Shenandoah Valley, Baltimore, the Virgin Islands, and

Pittsburgh before settling permanently in Philadelphia in 1859, where he edited the *Lutheran and Missionary* and headed the Lutheran Theological Seminary, devoted to a stricter reading of the Augsburg Confession than was prevalent in American Lutheranism. Additionally, he was a professor of philosophy at the University of Pennsylvania for fifteen years, and for part of this time he served as Provost. Krauth, in Walther's estimation, was the most outstanding English (non-German) Lutheran in America, "a man of unusual learning."[827]

Walther, for his part, retained an active facility with Latin throughout his life.[828] Among his papers is a bound volume of commentaries handwritten in Latin.[829] The gymnasium that he founded in Missouri was intended to inclulcate on the American frontier the high aspirations of mid-nineteenth-century German scholarship, which included the advanced study of Latin. As one biographer notes, "true to Leipzig tradition" Walther marked the dedication of a new building at the Concordia gymnasium by delivering a Latin oration.[830] And Walther, like other Lutheran theologians in America, at times published his works in Latin.[831] Yet a larger question for Lutherans in the United States at this time was the role not of Latin but of the German language in worship, culture, and education.

Donum mihi gratissimum accepi, sermonem tuum: "The Altar on the Threshing-floor," in ecclesia tua die gratiarum habitum;[832] et gratias quam maximas tibi ago. Donatio enim honorificum non solum benevolentiae tuae erga me documentum est, sed opus ipsum tum idearum copia tum elocutionis vigore et splendore magnam vim in meam animam exercuit. Verba verissima eademque gravissima recto tempore pronunciata hic audita et nunc legenda sunt. Arma firmissima contra errores et vitia nostri aevi, nostrae nationis gessisti fortissime; imprimis contra egoismum, illum daemonem, qui regnum divinum devastare maxime conatus est, et haud exiguam partem agri divini et seminis puri adeo devastavit. Ubi τὸ Ego, studium sui ipsius, ardor propri lucri, propriae voluptatis causa, praevalet, quasi sceptrum tenet et omnia negotia gubernat; ibi fugit caritas, sensusque christianus et Salvator noster ipse flere coactus est; immo deest omnis iustitia, virtus, δικαιοσύνη, quae placet Deo. Sed morbos non solum conspicuos nobis fecisti sed remedia quoque contra eos—et quidem rem acu—detegisti. Attamen solamen lugentibus! Dominus pater noster in caelis qui est per Iesum Christum nostra firma arx, recto tempore mittit fideles, peritos ac strenue certantes ministros in vineam suam! Ignoscas, quaeso, mihi Latina lingua utenti et veniam des mori Germanorum eruditorum hominum. Vale faveque.

Pittsburgiae, Ian. 11, A.D. 1858

Source: Adolph Spaeth, *Charles Porterfield Krauth, D.D., LL.D.*, 2 vols (New York: Christian Literature, 1898), 1:300.

72 Theology in Latin in America (1860)

As noted in the previous section, in addition to poems, letters, diaries, inscriptions, and orations, Americans have also written monographs in Latin. Leo M. Kaiser's census of American Latin Prose lists many of these, beginning with John Norton's treatise on the government of New England (London 1648).[833] Particularly numerous in Kaiser's census are inaugural dissertations published by American students graduating from medical schools in Edinburgh and Leiden and later in Philadelphia and Cambridge (MA).

Despite increasing opposition, Latin monographs continued to be written in America throughout the nineteenth century.[834] Many, but not all, of these were theological and philosophical treatises, written for the benefit of seminarians or clergymen. The 1870s were a particularly productive era in this regard. The Jesuits at Woodstock Seminary in Maryland published several massive Latin tomes on their in-house press, including Camillus Mazzella's 935-page *De Deo Creante* (1877) and his 811-page *De Gratia Christi* (1878) as well as Aemilius DeAugustinis's 755-page *De re sacramentaria* (1878).[835] But it was not only Jesuits who wrote such works. In 1876 the Dutch-born Redemptorist priest Anthony Konings (1821–84), who was sent to Baltimore in 1870, published two volumes of Moral Theology that together came to more than nine hundred pages.[836] Such works were intended not only for students. One reviewer of Mazzella's *De Deo Creante* commented: "it will prove invaluable to the clergy who desire to revise their theological course, and bring to perfection that knowledge of which the seminary or college provided only the elements." This same reviewer noted that Mazzella's style was appropriately "clear, lucid, and intelligible."[837]

Two of the most influential Latin theological treatises to emerge from nineteenth-century America are the four-volume *Theologia Dogmatica* (1839–40) and the three-volume *Theologia Moralis* (1841–43) by Francis Patrick Kenrick (1797–1863). A native of Ireland, Kenrick received his seminary formation in Rome but then opted to undertake missionary work in the United States. Initially he taught Greek, history, and theology at St. Joseph's College and Seminary in Bardstown, Kentucky. Eventually he was consecrated Bishop of Philadelphia and then Archbishop of Baltimore.

Kenrick sustained a robust scholarly regimen in the midst of his episcopal duties. In addition to theological works, he produced an annotated English translation of the Bible as well as various apologetic tracts. He was also highly adept with Latin. He kept multiple diaries in Latin, and for more than three decades he corresponded in Latin with his brother, Peter Richard Kenrick (see section 78), who eventually was consecrated Archbishop of St. Louis. He was resolute, even in the face of criticism from his brother, that the Latin of his theological treatises be classical and elevated. As he explained, he did not wish to heap up "verborum barbariem" but rather to provide "ratiocinii formas exercitationi studiosorum."[838]

The following is the preface to the second edition of his *Theologia Moralis.*

Tractatus de christiana ethice universa iterum in lucem damus, quae tradiderunt principia insignes theologi nostratium usibus idonea aptantes. Quum ius commune Anglicum, a caesareo diversum,[839] nostrarum legum basis sit, et singulorum Statuum instituta concordia varietate quadam distinguantur, oportuit plurima tractare quae antecessores nostri iuris civilis cultores alia prorsus ratione investigarunt. Servitus etiam in nonnullis provinciis vigens quaestionum segetem praebet, quas praetermiserunt qui per saecula proxime elapsa floruerunt in Europae regnis.[840] Difficultates aliae enatae ex societate coalescente, civibus nullo religionis vinculo coniunctis, unicuique permissa facultate suo utendi arbitrio, salva pace publica, solvendae erant, ut omnium iura servarentur, morum regula illaesa. Non igitur inutile vel supervacaneum fuit opus quod suscepimus, ut doctorum hominum insistentes vestigiis, et rerum experientia edocti, semitam tutam theologiae candidatis et animarum rectoribus, quibus non licet patria ignorare instituta, indicaremus. Placuit ad calcem paginae legum civilium dare excerpta, vel etiam quae scripserunt plerique ab Ecclesia alieni, testes veluti inviti veritatis.[841] Haec Anglico plerumque idiomate conscripta nostratibus subsidio esse possunt, quae tamen aliis praetermittere licet. Novam hanc operis editionem studio ampliori, consilio eruditorum, et rerum experientia, emendatam, ex prelo Europaeo dandam curavimus,[842] quum pleraque iis qui iure Anglico utuntur possint haud esse ingrata, aliis etiam qui nosse cupiunt quo successu morum principia in scholis recepta rerumpublicarum nostrarum conditioni attemperentur.

Baltimori, Festo die Nativitatis B. M. V.[843] 1859

Source: Francis Patrick Kenrick, *Theologia Moralis*, 2nd ed. (Mechelen: Dessain, 1860), vii–viii.

73 The Death of Football (1860)

Long before the first Harvard-Yale football game (1875) or the formation of the Harvard University Foot-Ball Club (1872), Harvard students were playing intensely competitive football games on campus. At least as early as the 1820s the culmination of the first Monday of the fall term featured a spirited contest pitting freshmen against sophomores. Football, in those days, was a "manly, straightforward game, rough and vigorous," in which players attempted to kick a leather ball across the opposing side's goal line, but much of the game consisted of attempting to "hack" or trip the "rushers," those players who were trying to advance the ball.[844]

The annual competition between freshmen and sophomores grew increasingly violent. A journal from 1855 described the contest as marked by "great spirit, and some violence and brutality."[845] Critics of these contests complained of frequent injuries and rampant drunkenness. Supporters countered that attendance was optional, that participants were well aware of what they were getting into, that only rash players incurred injuries, and that drinking was not a problem. But on July 2, 1860 the faculty of Harvard decided to ban the annual first-Monday game.

When the fall term began that year students staged a mock funeral for the now-lost game. A solemn procession wound its way towards the Delta, the triangular plot of land between Quincy, Kirkland, and Cambridge Streets, where Memorial Hall now stands. Mourners carried a coffin, which they deposited in a grave dug for the occasion. A dirge was sung. There was an elegy. And there was a tombstone, inscribed with Latin. One enterprising scholar even composed a Latin inscription as an obituary, which was published in the *Harvard Magazine*.[846] The epitaph and obituary are printed here.

I

HIC IACET
FOOTBALL FIGHTUM,
OBIIT JULY 2, 1860,
AET. LX YEARS[847]
RESURGAT.

II

MORTEM · OBIIT
III · NON · SEPT · A · D · M DCCC LX
SENECTVTE · PROVECTA
THE FOOTBALL GAME
COLLEGII · HARVARDIENSIS ·
IGNOTIS · E · PARENTIBVS · GENITVS
INCERTO · AEVO
HONESTA · TAMEN · FAMA · DIV · VSVS · EST
VEL · TVRPITVDINE · DETECTA · CORROBORA-
TAQVE · TEMPORE ·
PRAECIPVE · ILLVSTRIS
INIQVITATE · AVDACIA · OPPRESSIONE · SAEVITIA
PRAVITATE · DENIQVE · TOTA
EO · DECORO · CAREBAT · VT · MORTEM · SIBI ·
CONSCISCERET ·
AMATVS · A · NVLLO · A · MVLTIS · SVSTENTATVS
IIS · EGEBIT
QVI · EXITIVM · PROPERATVM · LVGEANT
AD · QVOD · TANDEM · DVCTVS · SIT ·
SED · INNVMERABILES · VICTIMAE
QVAE · FVERUNT · QVAE · NONDVM
GRATES · DIIS · AGENT
QVOD · MALVM · NON · AETERNVM · ESSE ·

POTEST ·
EXSECRATIONES · EORVM · QVIBVS · NOCVIT
EI · LINTEO · FERALI · ERVNT ·
OBLIVIORVM · ABYSSVS · EI · SEPVLCRO ·
CVIVS · HAEC · INSCRIPTIO :
monstrvm · nvlla · virtvte · redemptvm
a · vitiis ·[848]

Sources: I *Washington Evening Star*, November 28, 1909.
II *Harvard Magazine* 7 (1861): 18.

74 War: Baltimore and Pittsburgh (1861)

Members of the Redemptorists, a Catholic order founded by St. Alphonsus Liguori in Naples in 1732, came to the United States in 1832 to work among immigrants and Native Americans. Eventually they established houses in the major eastern cities (Philadelphia, Rochester, Buffalo, New York, Pittsburgh, and Baltimore) as well as in New Orleans. The Redemptorists, like the Jesuits, required seminarians to undergo a lengthy formation, which included acquiring proficiency in Latin.[849]

The first of the following two passages is an account of how the Redemptorist community in Baltimore (established 1840) was affected by the outbreak of the Civil War. Particular reference is made to what has come to be known as the Pratt Street Riot,[850] when twelve persons were killed—soldiers and civilians—and many more were wounded as secessionists disrupted the transfer of the 6th Massachusetts Infantry between Baltimore's President Street Station and Camden Station on April 19, 1861.

The second passage describes the raising of the United States flag atop Pittsburgh's St. Paul's Cathedral on April 20, 1861—the day after the Baltimore riot—in an effort to counter suspicions that Catholics in Pittsburgh, particularly priests, were secessionists. According to a local newspaper, in a "daring feat" that was "witnessed by thousands of people," the Stars and Stripes was fastened to the cross atop the cathedral by a Navy veteran.[851]

These passages are taken from the *Annales*, which were compiled on the basis of the diaries that individual Redemptorist houses kept.

Res Baltimorenses S. Alphonsi[852]

De bello civili, quo per quadriennium respublica Americana dire vexabatur, plura referre extra finem Annalium foret. Passim autem pauca notanda sunt quae historiam nostram aliquatenus attingunt.

Die 12 Aprilis castro Sumter per "Confoederatos" occupato, hora serotina, nuntio electrico accepto, tota civitas Baltimorensis commota est. Multi ex civibus Confoederatorum causae favebant, alii vero conservandae Unionis partes sequebantur. Omnium autem animi vel timoribus vel indignatione et odio agitabantur. Nemo iam de bello civili impendente dubitabat. Paucis post diebus nuntiatum est, milites e statibus septentrionalibus mox expectari, qui urbem transeuntes adversus "rebelles"—ita vocabantur Confoederati—essent profecturi. Tali nuntio exasperati decreverunt cives causae illorum consentientes quod omni quo fieri posset modo transitum militum impedirent. Die 19 Aprilis per viam ferratam 1200 milites Baltimoram pervenerunt. Qua re cognita tota fere civitas perturbata et mox tumultus exortus est, in quo non pauci laesi, nonnulli occisi sunt. Nemini tamen ex nostris iniuria facta est, quippe qui domi manerent donec quies et pax esset restituta. Summopere autem etiam nostris erat cavendum, ne ullo modo sive verbis sive signis mentem reipublicae integritati adversantem exhiberent.

Res Pittsburgenses

Exorto bello civili fere omnium animi per totam rempublicam acerrimo partium studio flagrabant, alii causae Unionis integrae servandae, alii separationis firmandae favebant. Cultiores ius gentium advocabant, vulgus vero plerumque aliquorum principum conclamationes sequebatur. Odium autem rei Catholicae et speciatim sacerdotum, quod in multorum animis adhuc gliscebat, suspicionem fovebat, clerum Catholicum Unioni adversari et clam separationem iuvare. Tales suspiciones Pittsburgi tunc potissimum, saltem inter rudiores homines, praevalebant. Ad avertenda igitur quaecunque gravia pericula quae inde facile oriri potuissent, Episcopus mandavit,[853] ut in summa turri ecclesiae vexillum reipublicae suspenderetur et preces publicae singulis Dominicis post sacra solemnia fierent. Tali agendi ratione animi omnium etiam malevolorum sedabantur. In aliis urbibus similia mandata ab Ordinariis promulgata sunt.[854]

Source: Joseph Wuest, *Annales Congregationis SS. Redemptoris, Provinciae Americanae*, vol. 4, part 1 (Boston: Typis Congregationis Sanctissimi Redemptoris, 1914), 230, 237.

75 Wartime Correspondence: Father to Son (1863)

At times, as we have seen, Latin has been a language of communication in America even within the family. The following is a portion of a Latin letter from Friedrich Muench (1799–1881) to his eleven-year-old son Hugo (1851–1936), written during the Civil War.[855]

Muench was a leading member of a group of German immigrants known as the Latin Farmers, due to their high level of education. Disenchanted with the political climate in Germany in the 1830s and attracted by the report of more favorable conditions in Missouri, Muench, a Lutheran minister, co-founded the Giessen Emigration Society, and in 1834 he led 500 immigrants across the Atlantic.[856] Most of them settled along the Missouri River between St. Louis and Jefferson City in an area that came to be called New Rhineland. Muench was a prolific author, especially on the subjects of viticulture and rationalist religion. Although he had once been a slaveowner, he eventually became a staunch abolitionist. He was elected to the Missouri state Senate in 1862. When the Senate was in session Muench wrote letters home to his son using multiple languages—German, English, and Latin—and as a school exercise he often asked his son to translate these letters from one language to another.

The following is an excerpt from a letter dated Jefferson City, January 24, 1863. In the earlier part of the letter, written in English, he critiques the translations that his son had previously submitted, and then he indulges in sentiment:

> "It is a pleasing idea to me to imagine that I see you sit to the side of your good mother, telling to her your lessons & gathering your thoughts for a communication to your far distant father. Remember always that I am from you not for my own pleasure, but on account of solemn duties, which I desire to perform as faithfully as it is

within my abilities. 'Salus publica suprema lex esto'; not in vain do I see this inscription on the door of the Capitol so often as I enter by it; that excellent sentence was my guide through all my life."

Frequently in the Latin portion of the letter Muench inserts parenthetical notes, in English and German, prompting his son on issues of vocabulary, morphology, and syntax, and at times he indicates quantities. A few, but not all, of these notations are retained in the text printed here.

In a later session of the Senate Hugo accompanied his father and worked as a page. Later he became a lawyer and served as consul in Germany and then as judge in Missouri.

Additurus sum (*addo*) pauca verba in lingua latina, ut habeas aliquid quo exerceas mentem tuam atque diligentiam. Valde gaudeo adventu parvae puellae, cui etiam dedistis nomen pulchrum ac mihi carum; est nomen matris tuae et matris meae, et idoneum esse videtur, ut conservetur in familia nostra.[857] Quando haec puella habebit duos annos et potens erit ambulandi (*gerund*), capies (*f. fassen*) eam manu et duces in hortum et vineam, decerpens flores pro ea atque offerens ei bacas dulces. Quum habebit quinque aut sex annos, tu eris magister eius et docebis eam legere atque scribere.

Laudo te, quod curam gessisti (*gero*) herbae nostrae Nicotianae. Hic habeo unum tantum fumisugium, nec ullum qui referciat id aut expurget. — Nuper die amoena putavi vites, quas Doctor Brunsius[858] habet in horto suo prope domum. Plures amicorum meorum aderant (*adsum*) videndi (*ger.*) causa, quomodo faciendum est. Rectum est pro omnibus, ut discant quod adhuc ignorent, debemusque esse parati communicandi (*ger.*) cum aliis nostram scientiam et experientiam.

Habeo bellum cubiculum et bonum lectum, nec non victum meliorem et largiorem quam necesse est.

Da operam transferendi has literas, et reminiscere (*imper. dep.*) patris tui amantissimi (*superl. partic.*).

Frederici Munchii

Source: Letter of Friedrich Muench to his son, 24 January 1863, Muench Family Papers, 1776–2013, Missouri Historical Society Archives, St. Louis.[859]

76 Between Two Armies: West Virginia (1863)

Beginning in the 1830s Catholic bishops in the United States sent promising seminarians to study in Rome at the Urbaniana, a college founded in 1627 by Pope Urban VIII to train missionary priests. Latin was the common language at the Urbaniana. Classes were in Latin, textbooks were in Latin, and students, who came from dozens of countries worldwide, were required to speak either Latin or Italian. Students also took an oath that bound them, inter alia, regularly to write their alma mater following graduation with updates on their labors. Many alumni chose to write these letters in Latin, and these are intriguing because they showcase the classical idiom applied to various features or events of modern life.

A good example of one such Latin letter is presented below. The author, Thomas Andrew Becker (1832–99), a native of Pennsylvania, converted to Catholicism after studies at Western University of Pennsylvania (now the University of Pittsburgh), the Allegheny Institute, and perhaps Saint Xavier College (Cincinatti) and the University of Virginia.[860] After attending the Urbaniana he was ordained a priest in June 1859 in the Basilica of St. John Lateran, and a month later he was awarded a doctorate following his public defense of theses (in Latin). Upon his return to the United States, Becker was assigned first to a church in Richmond and later, on the eve of the Civil War, to various churches in the upper Shenandoah Valley, his home parish being St. Joseph's in Martinsburg.[861]

Martinsburg changed hands numerous times during the War, and the churches that Becker pastored were used at times as hospitals, prisons, and stables. One of Becker's brothers, a Union soldier, was captured at Gettysburg and eventually died in Andersonville, but Becker's loyalties were with the South. He was arrested on Monday, March 9, 1863 and briefly imprisoned because he refused to insert prescribed prayers for the Union in the previous day's Mass.[862] He was later released from custody through the intervention of Francis Patrick Kenrick, the Archbishop of Baltimore (see section 72), and he spent a year teaching at Mount St. Mary's Seminary in Emmitsburg before becoming secretary to Martin John Spalding, Kenrick's successor as Archbishop of Baltimore.

Becker developed a reputation not only for theological competence and administration—he was secretary to the Second and Third Plenary Councils of Baltimore, and he was consecrated the first Bishop of Wilmington (Delaware) and later the sixth Bishop of Savannah—but also for his Latin abilities. In an influential 1876 essay he lamented the post-bellum decline of the classics in the United States. For Becker and others, classical scholarship was to be gauged by one's active facility with Latin. Yet, as Becker alleged, a typical graduate from even the best American college "knows so little of Latin and Greek, that even his own gross ignorance thereof, though backed by the presumption engendered by the possession of a diploma, would shame to attempt, we will not say making himself orally intelligible in tolerably correct Latinity, but even to write a Latin letter with any assurance of correctness."[863] This and two subsequent articles are believed by some to have laid an important foundation for the establishment of The Catholic University of America in the following decade.[864]

Becker wrote the following Latin letter to the Propaganda Fide a few days after his arrest in March 1863.[865]

Martinsbg. Va. 12° Martii 1863
Eminentissime Cardinale Praefecte
S. C. De Propaganda.[866]

Ex eo quo Eminentiam tuam certiorem feci de conditione mea, nil nisi horrida cernimus bella.[867] Ab Episcopo Reverendissimo quoque meo[868] ferme nihil audivi, nisi quod oretenus ab iis colligere potui, qui limites belligerentium transgredi quoquomodo potuerint, quos, quam pauci sint periculo subituros, tuo iudicio relinquendos duco.

Forsitan Eminentia tua haud bene intelligit quaenam sit positio mea; namque cum ita pro peccatis meis sors mihi ceciderit, ut nunc sub una, nunc vero sub altera potestate constitutus sim, res nostrae per milites propemodum omnes ablatae sunt; nec facile est dictu, quisnam rei totius exitus futurus sit.

Unam ex ecclesiis meae curae commissis a militibus esse combustam maximopere doleo,[869] utrum necne remunerationem accepturus sim nescio; ea tamen praeliminaria posui ut, si qua pax sit futura, quicunque erit hic sacerdos pro rata accipiat. Ego vero credo impossibile futurum esse mihi, amplius vivere in loco quo usque adhuc, bello flagrante, vitam degere conatus sum. Licetque Illustrissimo ac Reverendissimo Archiepiscopo litteras misi (de Archipraesule-Baltimorensi loquor[870]) cumque eodem loquutus sim, nil tamen districtim ab eo accepi quod faciam; is quippe est ille, cui videtur iureiurando me obligari Virginiae Statui, ac presse quidem Dioecesi Richmondiensi; ast totam provinciam intellexi esse "Archiepiscopatum cum suffraganeis suis."[871]

Quanto meliori sint loco, qui vel intra unam vel aliam potestatem duarum contendentium domum habeant suam, nemo est qui non intelligat. Attamen, precibus effusis, cum Dei sit voluntas ut aliquid patiar, libenter oneri subibo. Ut nobis det Deus O. M. pacem, Eminentiae tuae vitam ad caelum ducentem, humillime orat ac deprecatur

Alumnus Coll. Urb. De Prop.
Eminentiae Tuae Ill^{mae} ac Rev^{ssmae}

obsequentiss. servus
Thomas A. Becker.
Sacerdos Romanus

Source: Archivio Storico "de Propaganda Fide," Rome, *America Centrale*, vol. 20, 149rv.

77 Abraham Lincoln and Servius Tullius (1865)

The assassination of President Abraham Lincoln elicited expressions of sympathy worldwide. One of the most unusual tokens of condolence was a 300-pound block of tufa (27.5" x 19" x 8.75") sent from Italy, which was inscribed with a Latin tribute. The donors were members of the Roman National Committee (*Il Comitato Nazionale Romano*), an unofficial revolutionary organization whose members sought to free Rome from papal control or, in the words of the American consul, "to direct that liberal sentiment which is in Rome more than anything else in the world denied the quality of expression and development."[872]

The tufa block was taken from the Servian Wall, and the inscription associates Lincoln and Servius Tullius (*r.* 578–535 B.C.) as fellow defenders or vindicators of liberty. In fact, the inscription had been composed after Lincoln's second inauguration, but following his assassination the donors drafted a letter dated June 22, 1865 and addressed to President Andrew Johnson, casting the gift as a tribute to the now-fallen President. In this letter the Roman National Committee drew further comparisons between the two leaders: both rose from humble beginnings, both were benefactors of the disenfranchised, both were cut down by those who opposed their liberalizing policies, both are rightfully considered the second founders of their nations. The letter also claimed that contemporary Romans, stymied in their quest for freedom by the Pope, admired the Americans for having successfully attained what they themselves still sought.[873]

The stone underwent a labyrinthine and subterranean odyssey before reaching its present location in the Lincoln tomb in Springfield, Illinois. The ship that was conveying it from Italy was wrecked off the coast of Bermuda, and the stone sat on a beach for some time before it was auctioned off. When it eventually reached America in January 1867, the box containing the stone stood unopened on the White House porch before being relegated to the cellar. By an Act of Congress (July 19, 1867) the stone was rescued, only to be placed in the cellar of the U.S. Capitol. Three years later another Congressional Act (June 17, 1870) transferred the stone to the Lincoln Monument Association, and it was brought to Springfield and eventually displayed in Memorial Hall of the Lincoln National Monument (dedicated 1874) in Oak Ridge Cemetery. When Lincoln's tomb was renovated in 1930, the stone ended up in yet another cellar, this time of the Illinois state Capitol. It was extracted five years later for the benefit of the visiting Italian ambassador, who had inquired as to its whereabouts. Finally, on October 11, 1936, in the presence of various dignitaries,[874] the stone was permanently placed in the Lincoln tomb, where it blocks an old entrance to the stairwell of the obelisk.[875]

ABRAHAMO LINCOLNIO
REGION FOEDERAT • AMERIC.[876] PRESIDI II.[877]
HVNC EX SERVI TVLLI AGGERE[878] LAPIDEM
QVO VTRIVSQVE
LIBERTATIS ADSERTORIS[879] FORTISS
MEMORIA CONIVNGATVR
CIVES ROMANI
D.
A. MDCCCLXV.

Source: *Harper's Weekly* 13 (February 6, 1869): 84.

78 The Drake Constitution (1865)

The divisions among residents of Missouri did not cease with the conclusion of the Civil War. Article 2, Section 3 of the Missouri Constitution of 1865, known as the Drake Constitution, required all lawyers and religious ministers within the state to take an "Oath of Loyalty" or "Test Oath," affirming, on eighty-six counts, that they had supported the government of the United States at all times. A challenge to the Test Oath was brought before the court by the Catholic priest John A. Cummings (1840–73), the pastor of St. Joseph Church in Louisiana, Missouri, who had been indicted and then incarcerated—because he did not pay the $500 fine—for preaching on September 3, 1865 without having taken this oath.[880] This sentence was upheld unanimously by the Missouri Supreme Court, but eventually his case came before the initially reluctant Supreme Court of the United States, which handed down a 5 to 4 decision in his favor. Despite this verdict, the Test Oath did not cease to be administered,[881] and this provision of the Drake Constitution was not repealed until 1871.[882]

The following is a letter from the Archbishop of St. Louis, Peter Richard Kenrick (1806–96), directing his clergy not to take the oath. In the late summer and fall of 1865 Kenrick's letter was widely mentioned in newspapers in the United States and abroad,[883] with some even printing the Latin text,[884] and it elicited divergent reactions. The *San Francisco Pacific* paraphrased Kenrick's action: "in other words, the Archbishop ordains that loyalty and Romanism are inconsistent terms."[885] The *New York Tribune* faulted Kenrick for emboldening Protestant clergymen to act similarly, and it further anticipated that "the ignorant Irish" would riot when police arrested any clergymen who did not take the oath, thereby provoking a "reign of terror."[886] Yet other papers voiced objections to the oath itself.[887]

The following is taken from the *Missouri Republican*.

Sti Ludovici, 28 Julii, 1865

Revde. Dne:

Cum iuxta Novum Statutum Iusiurandum quoddam a sacerdotibus exigendum sit ut iis liceat verbum Dei annuntiare et matrimoniis assistere, id quod nullo modo praestare possent absque dispendio libertatis ecclesiasticae, meam ea de re sententiam tibi significandam duxi, ut prae oculis habeas normam in hac difficili materia sequendam. Spero fore ut civilis potestas ab huius modi Iuramento exigendo sese abstentura sit. Si quid autem aliter eveniat, volo ut me certiorem facias rerum adiunctarum in quibus verseris ut consilium et auxilium, tibi praebere possim.

Sum, Revde. Dne.,

tuus in Dno. famulus,

†Petrus Ricardus,

Archiepiscopus S.L.

Source: *Missouri Republican* (St. Louis), August 28, 1865.[888]

79 Cicero and the Second Plenary Council of Baltimore (1866)

The Second Plenary Council of Baltimore assembled in October 1866 with four ends in mind: a) to shore up ecclesiastical discipline in the United States; b) to make recommendations about new dioceses to be erected; c) to demonstrate that the unity of the Catholic Church had not been damaged by the Civil War, which had rent other Christian denominations; d) to address the pastoral care and evengelization of newly emancipated slaves. This Council, the largest Catholic gathering in the United States to date, met for two weeks, and like the First Plenary Council (see section 66) it afforded a curious spectacle for onlookers: on the one hand prelates in magnificent attire, the Apostolic Delegate seated on a throne, and the conspicuous use of Latin, and on the other hand the use of the parliamentary procedure of the United States Senate, crowds thronging the Baltimore streets to witness the opening procession, and a beleaguered President Johnson present to witness the closing ceremony.

The following two passages appear in the published *Acta et Decreta* of the Council. They were written by the lead secretary of the council, James Andrew Corcoran (1820–89). A native of Charleston, Corcoran studied at the Urbaniana and spent several years as parish priest, seminary professor, and editor in his home city, but during the Civil War he was sent to Wilmington, North Carolina to assist during an outbreak of yellow fever. Later in life he was professor and briefly rector of St. Charles Borromeo Seminary in Philadelphia. Widely regarded as one of the most learned theologians and finest Latinists of his era, he was the first (or one of the first) to be offered a position at the newly-established Catholic University of America, which he declined. He was secretary to many ecclesiastical councils, and he was the lone American theologian selected to undertake preparatory work in Rome for the First Vatican Council. Corcoran left no monograph, but he published more than two dozen lengthy review essays as editor of the *American Catholic Quarterly Review*. Additionally, he composed at least six highly-regarded commemorative Latin inscriptions and one Latin poem.[889]

The first selection below, taken from the published *Acta*, concerns a proposal made early at the council to send a message of greeting to Pope Pius IX by means of the newly-laid transatlantic cable (see section 70). Surprisingly, a bid to use Latin or French was defeated, and English was chosen. The message took five hours to reach Rome.[890]

The second selection below is the opening paragraph of the formal letter sent by the council prelates to the Pope. Ordinarily a bishop authored these letters, but in this instance Corcoran himself was selected to compose the letter. The opening sentence is based on the beginning of Cicero's Third Philippic.

I

Congregatio Prima Privata.

Die octava Octobris, in aedibus Archiepiscopalibus habita.

Decretum de nuntio telegraphico (despatch) ad Summum Pontificem mittendo oblatum est ab Archiepiscopo S. Ludovici,[891] cui accessit Metropolita Cincinnatensis,[892] et voce unanimi receptum est a Patribus. Decretum his verbis conceptum est: "Patres huius Concilii censent nuntium telegraphicum ad Summum Pontificem mitti oportere, ut sensus nostros erga Sanctam Sedem Pontificem exprimamus."

Archiepiscopus Cincinnatensis suggessit ut nuntius telegraphicus Anglice scriberetur; cui accessit Episcopus Velingensis.[893]

Episcopus S. Pauli[894] proponebat ut lingua Gallica aut Latina, potiusquam Anglica, in nuntio conficiendo adhiberetur, cui tamen Patres minime assenserunt.

Episcopus Buffalensis[895] votum emisit, ut in nuntio aliquid haberetur quod Patres velle iura omnia Pontificis sarta tectaque servari debere declararet. Episcopus Montereyensis[896] accessit Buffalensi.

De hac propositione inter Patres hinc inde disceptatum est. Patres deinde in eam sententiam iverunt. Archiepiscopus Neo-Eboracenus suggessit, ut Revmus Delegatus Apostolicus nonnullos praesules designaret, quibus nuntii scribendi munus committeret: id quod omnibus placuit.

Designavit deinde Rev^mus Delegatus Apostolicus[897] Archiepiscopum Neo-Eboracenum[898] et Ep^um Buffalensem sibi assessores in hoc nuntio conficiendo; nam ipsi unanimi voce praesulum in primis id muneris commissum est. . .

Qui nuntii telegraphici conficiendi munus in se susceperant, formam his conceptam verbis retulere:

"Seven Archbishops and forty Bishops, in Council, unanimously greet your Holiness, wishing long life, with preservation of all ancient and sacred rights of the Holy See."

II

Serius omnino, Beatissime Pater, quam nostrum omnium vota flagitabant, aliquando tamen, quam primum nobis id per tempora licuit, in Concilium Plenarium convocati sumus.[899] Quo enim tempore illud ex proposito et instituto cogendum erat, ea iam rerum publicarum conversio facta fuerat, ut nobis oves nostras relinquere, et in unum locum omnes ad deliberandum nos conferre, nullo modo liceret. Vix autem e mediis procellis dissidiisque civilis belli luctuosis emerseramus, quum in hac veteri atque Catholica urbe convenimus, ut disciplinae, si forte opus esset, resarciendae operam daremus; atque ut charitatem, amorem, necessitudinem, sacrorum denique communionem, quam neque studia civium divisa, neque diuturni belli calamitates tollere aut minuere potuerant, iterum inter nos, redintegrata societate atque animorum coniunctione, foveremus ac tueremur.

Source: *Concilii Plenarii Baltimorensis II . . . Acta et Decreta* (Baltimore: John Murphy, 1868), lx–lxi, cxxviii.

80 A Condemnation of Racism (1870)

Latin was the official language at the First Vatican Council, which formally opened in Rome on December 8, 1869 and was attended by more than seven hundred bishops from around the world. According to James Gibbons (1834–1921), the Vicar Apostolic of North Carolina and the youngest prelate in attendance, French was the vernacular of the largest number of participating bishops, but Latin alone was used in the debates of the council, a practice which he deemed not only useful but necessary.[900]

At the time some critics complained that Latin was ineffective as a means of communication. They charged that it rendered mute those prelates who were not in the habit of speaking it or rendered unintelligible those who spoke it poorly or with unfamiliar accents. Moreover, the poor acoustics of St. Peter's were not ameliorated by the construction of a large awning over the meeting area. Yet according to Léon Dehon (1843–1925), one of the council's stenographers, the use of Latin enabled participants "very easily to exchange their ideas." Without it, he adds, the council would have degenerated into "a Babel of languages."[901]

Some prelates gained notoriety for eloquence. Bishop Joseph George Strossmayer of Bosnia (1815–1905) was said to utter periodic sentences that "flowed with the grace and majesty and musical rhythm of a Cicero."[902] Archbishop Peter Richard Kenrick (see section 78) of St. Louis, spoke Latin "with admirable ease and elegance." According to Gibbons, "I observed [Kenrick] day after day reclining in his seat with half-closed eyes, listening attentively to the debates, without taking any notes. And yet so tenacious was his memory that, when his turn came to ascend the rostrum, he reviewed the speeches of his colleagues with remarkable fidelity and precision without the aid of manuscript or memoranda."[903]

One of the Americans participating in the Council

was the French-born Bishop of Savannah, Augustin Verot (1805–76).[904] Dubbed "L'Enfant Terrible" of the Council, Verot was singled out for his perceived impertinence as well as for his barbaric or "kitchen" Latin.[905] Verot's speeches were "sensational,"[906] eliciting laughter and protest from fellow prelates as well as censure from the Council's officials, who sharply rebuked him for uttering buffooneries (*scurras*) and witticisms (*facetias*). On one occasion he was advised to speak more respectfully about patristic authors (he had been discussing a homily of St. Augustine), to which he responded: "quandoque bonus dormitat Homerus."[907]

Verot, a Sulpician priest, had come to the United States in 1830, and for twenty-three years he taught mathematics and science (minerology, zoology, and geology) at St. Mary's College (Baltimore) and briefly at St. Charles College (Baltimore). Following a five-year stint as pastor of a parish in Ellicot City, Maryland, in 1857 he was appointed Vicar Apostolic of Florida. Three months after shots were fired at Ft. Sumter, he was appointed Bishop of Savannah. Verot supported the Confederacy, and in a widely-published tract (1861) he attempted both to defend and to delimit the institution and practice of slavery,[908] yet before and after the war he distinguished himself for his efforts to minister to African Americans. He was, according to one recent study, "the only American bishop to implement a diocesan program for the freed Blacks in the southern United States."[909]

Between December 28, 1869 and January 10, 1870 the Council discussed the draft of the *Dogmatic Constitution on the Catholic Faith against the Manifold Errors of Rationalism*. The revised version of this would be known as *Dei Filius*, which was approved unanimously on April 24, 1870. The following passage, an excerpt from Verot's initial speech before the Council on January 3, 1870, pertains to chapter 15 of this schema, which concerned the unity of the human species and the origin of the different races. Dehon, the above-mentioned stenographer, remarked that Verot was "very concerned about the lot of the American slaves" and that he sought to affirm the equality of blacks and whites.

Venio ad aliud punctum nempe unitatem speciei humanae et generis humani, quae impugnatur, lacessitur a quibusdam patronis falsi nominis scientiae, et quam opportunum, omnino opportunum est condemnare illos falsi nominis scientiae doctores, nempe agitur de unitate speciei humanae. Illa materia est maximi momenti . . . Nam venio de dioecesi, in qua multi nigri, plusquam dimidia pars millionis nigrorum hominum. Nunc nigri non generantur ex albis, nec albi ex nigris, et forsitan sunt quidam hic, qui putant, quod homines quando vitam degunt in calida regione fiant nigri, et quod nigri si vivant in frigida regione deveniant albi. Illud, eminentissimi praesides, est error, qui tantum risum movebat in regionibus ubi res cognoscitur. Itaque si Adamus erat albus, quomodo fit ut sint nigri, quia nigredo non est in superficiali parte pellis, sed est interior. Itaque ratio propter quam dicendum est, esse tantum unam speciem humanam, est quod ita invenimus in Scriptura. Sed praeterea, reverendissimi patres, non sufficit condemnare illos qui dicunt plures esse species humanas: non curant de nostris condemnationibus et anathematibus, sed dandae sunt rationes propter quas illorum assertio reiici debet. Itaque volo dicere quod in America liber quidam editus fuerit cum titulo *Ariel*, in quo libro dicitur quod duplex creatio hominis fuerit in principio; una creatio hominis albi in persona Adami, et altera creatio pro hominibus nigris, qui nigri, dicebat ille liber, sunt gradus inter bestiam et hominem.[910] Hae sunt assertiones, quae inveniuntur in hoc libro. Et praeterea in mea dioecesi venit aliquis methodista praedicator, minister protestantium, qui ex professo docuit, et multi ad eum veniebant, ex professo docuit nigros non habere animas rationales. . . . Itaque illud inseri deberet in schemate, ideoque propono additionem sequentem huic capiti XV, ut illa materia de unitate generis humani decenter et adaequate tractetur a concilio. . . . *Specialiter autem condemnamus errorem ineptum eorum, qui asserere ausi sunt, nigros ad familiam humanam non pertinere, nec anima spirituali et immortali praeditos esse.*

Text: J.D. Mansi, ed., *Sacrorum Conciliorum Nova et Amplissima Collectio*, vol. 50 (Arnhem: H. Welter, 1924), 165–66.

81 A Pope Writes the Coeur d'Alenes (1871)

In early 1871, Vincent (of the Stellam family) and Andrew Seltis, two leaders of the Coeur d'Alenes, who for the most part inhabited present-day Idaho and Washington, sent an encouraging letter to Pope Pius IX (*r.* 1846–78).[911] Not only did they express sympathy and prayers for the pontiff's struggle against Italian nationalists, but they also enclosed a donation of $110 and offered to despatch militia from their tribe to assist him.

The following is the Pope's Latin letter of response, dated July 31, 1871. It was transmitted to Idaho by means of the Jesuit General Peter Jan Beckx and Fr. Pierre-Jean De Smet. At a tribal assembly on August 15, 1872 this letter was read aloud in Latin and then translated into native dialects.

Dilecti Filii, salutem et apostolicam benedictionem!

Iis devotionis sensibus, quos in simplicitate cordis vestri Nobis significastis, Dilecti Filii, non mediocriter delectati sumus, cum in dolore a vobis concepto ob insectationes Ecclesiae, non minus quam in filiali erga hanc Sanctam Sedem obsequio et amore, splendescere viderimus fidem illam et caritatem, quae diffusa est in cordibus vestris, quaeque, vos huic Unitatis centro arctius obstringit. Quocirca, sicuti non dubitamus quin orationes et obsecrationes vestrae, fidenter et instanter elatae ad Deum, suffragaturae sint Ecclesiae et Nobis, sic stipem a vobis tanto corrogatam amore pretiosissimam ducimus. Et quoniam manus Domini est super omnes quaerentes eum in bonitate, confidimus pia opera vestra conciliatura quoque vobis esse, cum auxilium adversus corruptionis, pericula quae timetis, tum spiritualia subsidia quae pro filiabus vestris concupiscitis. Nos certe Deum rogamus ut gratiae suae opus in vobis plenius semper perficiat, vosque suis omnibus ditet muneribus. Horum autem auspicem, et grati animi Nostri ac paternae benevolentiae pignus, apostolicam benedictionem vobis peramanter impertimus.

Datum Romae apud S. Petrum die 31 julii, anno 1871, Pontificatus Nostri anno vicesimo sexto.

Pius P. P. IX

Source: E. Laveille, *The Life of Father De Smet, S.J. (1801–1873)*, trans. Marian Lindsay (New York: P.J. Kenedy & Sons, 1915), 370.

82 Cuba and the History of La Florida (1871)

Some of the oldest surviving documents written by Europeans within the continental United States are the 1340 pages of parish registers of the cathedral of the Diocese of St. Augustine. Although these records (which are in Spanish) do not survive from the first twenty-nine years of the parish's existence (1565–94), perhaps because they were destroyed when St. Augustine was attacked and burned in 1586 by Sir Francis Drake (see section 12), they date back to the year 1594. The first entry records the marriage of the Spanish soldier Gabriel Hernández to Catalina de Valdes on January 24 of that year.

That these records are in Florida today is due to Augustin Verot (see section 80), the first Bishop of St. Augustine, who manifested great interest in the Catholic history of Florida. In his quest to uncover and promote this unique history, Verot contacted the Bishop of Havana to see whether the parish registers had been transferred to Cuba after Florida was ceded to England in 1763. In the summer of 1871—in the midst of Cuba's first War for Independence—Verot journeyed to Havana to search personally for these records. He was successful—he wrote in his Episcopal Acts, "I found the old records of St. Augustine for three hundred years"—although it was not until 1906, after considerable negotiation, that they were brought to Florida.[912]

The brief Latin letter printed below grants Verot permission to research in Havana and to preach and celebrate the sacraments while there.

Havanae, die 10 Maii 1871

Illustrissime Domine.

Quantum ad me est, potestis ad publica Scrinia libere accedere, si forte inveniatis vetera documenta circa historiam religiosam Floridae, prout Exmus ac Illustrissimus Habanensis Episcopus[913] vobis indulsit dum Romae degeretis; simulque Missae Sacrificium celebrare, confessiones audire, verbum Dei praedicare, necnon Pontificalia exercere in tota Dioecesi valetis—

Vestrae Reverentiae
humillimus et adictissimus servus
Benignus Merino et Mendi[914]

Source: Archives of the Catholic Diocese of St. Augustine, Florida (with permission).

83 Wedding Poetry (1875)

The following witty poems were written to commemorate the marriage of Mary A. Angle to Selden Jennings Coffin, a long-serving professor at Lafayette College in Easton, Pennsylvania, which occurred on December 22, 1875. The son of a prominent meteorologist, Coffin (1838–1915) studied at Lafayette as well as Princeton Theological Seminary, and he was ordained a Presbyterian minister in 1874. Two years later he was granted a Ph.D. by Hanover College (Indiana). He taught mathematics and astronomy at Lafayette until 1886 when, having lost his voice due to a throat ailment, he was appointed Registrar. Six years later his voice returned, and he was granted a chair of astronomy, which he held until his retirement in 1904.[915]

The author of these poems, the Delaware-born Nathaniel B. Smithers (1818–96), was in the first graduating class at Lafayette (1836).[916] A precocious student, Smithers began to study Latin at the age of five. After earning a law degree at Dickinson, he maintained a private practice in Dover for many years, and he became known as "the Nestor of the Delaware bar." As a member of the U.S. House of Representatives during the latter years of the Civil War (1863–65), Smithers advocated the gradual abolition of slavery within Delaware. In his retirement Smithers returned to the classics, and he published a well-regarded book of translations of medieval hymns,[917] and he made a Latin version of Bret Harte's satirical poem, "Plain Language from Truthful James/The Heathen Chinee," which became the basis of a spoof alleging that Harte was a plagiarist.[918]

The Coffin-Angle wedding reception was attended by most of the Lafayette professors and their wives as well as by many students. Before guests sat down for the meal, the President of Lafayette announced that Latin poems had been written in honor of the occasion. Smithers himself was not present, so the poems were recited by

Rev. Lyman Coleman (1796–1882), Lafayette's professor of Latin, Hebrew, and Biblical Geography. Coleman also recited English translations that he himself had made.

Coffin, for his part, was well equipped to understand these poems. At the time he attended Lafayette (mid-1850s) the study of the ancient languages occupied nearly 40% of a student's time, although this was down from 50% in the early 1840s. As a freshman, Coffin would have studied Livy, Xenophon's *Anabasis*, the *Odes* of Horace, Homer's *Odyssey*, Latin and Greek Prose Composition, and the Greek New Testament.[919]

N.B.S.[920]
Amico S.[921] Selen.[922]
in Nuptias
gratulans dat Odem
et Salutem.

In Nuptias

Lucidae stellae, viduae decore,
Nunc parum oblectant oculos Seleni,
Namque terrestris cupiens amoris
        Despicit astra.[923]

Euge, ter felix! nimium beatus,
Cui dies offert cupide quid optas;
Tuque salvebis, peramoena virgo,
        Digna marito.

Munera auri argenti eborisve ecquis
Offert?[924] Est munus melius precari
Ut daret vobis Pater affluenter
        Cuncta benigna.

Ad Mariam.
Dans Nugas et Salutem.

Non Angulus[925] sed Angelus
Esses nominata,
Quae recta semper Angulus
Sponso care amata.

Quo gaudet ille ab Angulo, in
Illum ut vertereris,
Dum triste stant in angulos
Belli Belvideris.[926]

Ut tu beare in Angelis
Votum corde mitto,
Quae sola non es Angulus,
Quadrans cum marito.

Et, care Mensor, anxie
Cures ut futurus
Circlus, datis tibi Angulis,
Aequus sitque purus.

Source: *The Lafayette College Journal* 1.5 (January 1876): 86–87; available at Lafayette Digital Repository.

84 Latin Epigraphy in Modern America (1880)

Caroline Winterer has memorably characterized the transformation of classical studies in mid-nineteenth-century America as a movement from words to worlds.[927] Classics professors and their students increasingly sought to contextualize the works they were parsing, and by the end of the century the influence of *Altertumswissenschaft* had permeated most institutions of higher learning within the United States. Eventually these changes had repercussions for the curricula of American schools and colleges.

For some communities, however, the ends espoused by the older approach to classics remained paramount. Many Jesuits, in particular, well into the twentieth century remained committed to the study of the classics as models of eloquence. For example, in Jesuit schools Cicero was read not in order to learn about the late Roman Republic but to learn how to speak and to write in Latin as well as English. Cicero's speeches were not an "occasion of exacting high-school accuracy in translation" nor, one reviewer argued, should they furnish "an introduction to graduate studies in archaeology;" rather, Cicero's rhetoric "should positively help the student to write as Cicero wrote."[928]

This continued preference for words, in the face of the increasing emphasis on worlds, animates the text presented below, which is an excerpt from a series of notes for a course in Latin epigraphy given at Woodstock College in 1880–81. The author, Fr. Charles Piccirillo (1821–88), was one of the many exiled Italian Jesuits who taught at Woodstock in the latter 1800s.[929] For several years Piccirillo was a professor of mathematics and physics, and his interest in natural science led him to acquire for Woodstock exotic biological specimens,[930] but Piccirillo was also an extraordinary Latinist, to judge from the many anecdotes that have been handed down concerning him. As a seminarian, having been assigned to write a Latin oration modeled on one of Cicero's,

Piccirillo submitted twenty-five pages, well beyond the four or five submitted by other students.[931] During the 1876 World's Fair in Philadelphia, Piccirillo delighted his fellow Jesuits with an account, in Ciceronian Latin, of the splendid inventions on display in Machinery Hall: "there were no pauses, no hesitations, but one continued flow of perfect word painting in idiomatic Latin."[932] Called upon "informally" to give an opinion at the Third Plenary Council of Baltimore in 1884, Piccirillo delivered "a splendid address in handsomely rounded Ciceronian periods, full of solid thought, and convincing all who heard."[933] His Golden Jubilee was celebrated in May 1884 with a linguistic cornucopia: prose, oratory, poetry, and a lavish inscription all in Latin, as well as English prose, an Italian sonnet, a Spanish poem, a French address, and a classical Greek poem.[934]

According to Piccirillo, the study of epigraphy yielded valuable historical knowledge, but as he candidly admits towards the end of this introduction, the real attraction for the Jesuit scholastic was the benefit that epigraphy imparted to Latin style. *Non res sed verba*: more than access to historical realities, epigraphy offered training in the eloquentia perfecta to which Jesuits aspired.

Pro Academia Linguae Latinae habenda anno schol. 1880–81. Introductio

Magna sunt aemolumenta quae ex studio Epigraphiae latinae derivari possunt et solent. Alia ad eruditionem spectant, alia ad usum.

A. Eruditioni plura conferunt quotidie tituli monumentis inscripti:

1. Temporum rationes probe conficiunt. . .

2. Historiam novis factis, vel gravibus factorum adiunctis augent. . .

3. Geographia vetus non nisi ex inscriptionibus determinatur. . .

4. Plurimum locis Romanorum meribus addunt.

5. Clarissimorum virorum intermortuam memoriam renovant.

6. Romanae venustatis et elegantiae gemmas nobis servant. . .

B. Usui deserviunt: saepe enim contingit nostris temporibus vel eas invenire, vel inscriptiones scribere. Primae non intelligerentur, secundae non scriberentur sine hoc studio.

Hinc eruitis quare a doctis viris ultimis hisce temporibus tantum studii positum fuerit in colligendis titulis, in illis illustrandis.

Sed fateor me hisce motivis motum non fuisse ut hanc materiam huic nostro litterario exercitio praefigerem.

Omnia enim ista eruditioni faciunt, et humaniori culturae, sed parum scopo huius Accademiae.

Nos enim non historiam, sed latinas litteras, non monumenta sed stylum latinum, non res sed verba tractare debemus. Iuvabuntur ista ex inscriptionum studio?

Quam maxime.

1° Thesaurus latinorum verborum in titulis continetur.

2° Gemmas latinae venustatis.

Hisce tamen limitibus non me continebo. Artem ipsam Epigraphicam exponere satagam. Hisce rationibus:

1° Haec ars tota quanta nunc est a viris Societatis inventa et evoluta fuit . . .[935]

2° Quia frequentes occurrunt occasiones scribendi titulos: occasiones variae. (Univ. Harvard Cantabrigii prope Bostonium)

Nisi ars haec agnoscatur inconcinnue inscript.

Obiectio: Quis scribit latine?

1° Christiani in templis, in sepulchris, in sacro supellectile etc.

2° Culti et eruditi homines in solemnioribus monumentis

3° Qui latine noscit eas scribere; anglice noscet

Source: Archives of the Maryland Province of the Society of Jesus, Charles Piccirillo, S.J. – Papers, Woodstock College Archives, IIA-4.1, Box 46, Folder 1021, on deposit at the Booth Family Center for Special Collections, Georgetown University Library, Washington, DC.[936]

85 An American in Hungary (1881)

Joseph Henry Allen (1820–98) is well known to classicists as the co-author with J.B. Greenough of *A Latin Grammar for Schools and Colleges* (1872).[937] Born in Massachusetts and educated at Harvard (class of 1840; Divinity School 1843), Allen was a Unitarian minister, responsible at different times for congregations in Massachusetts, Washington, DC, and Maine. He also traveled widely to address congregations from Ithaca to Ann Arbor to San Diego. In the midst of his pastoral activities he remained committed to robust scholarship, publishing and editing works on theology and ecclesiastical history as well as classics.[938] In 1878 he was appointed Lecturer on Ecclesiastical History at Harvard, and the following year Harvard awarded him a Doctorate in Divinity.

In August 1881 Allen attended the Supreme Consistory of Unitarians in Kolozsvar (Klausenburg) Hungary. He had been appointed a delegate of the British and Foreign Unitarian Association as well as of the American Unitarian Association. While in Hungary, Allen delivered the following Latin speech, which, according to his later description, his audience "could all follow without difficulty."[939]

Hungary retained a robust tradition of Latin as a means of communication well into the nineteenth century.[940] Only in 1840 did Hungarian, rather than Latin, become the language of Parliament.

Viri spectatissimi ac reverendissimi!—Cum mihi apud vos breviter loqui liceat, utar (pace vestra) non lingua mea, quae paucioribus fortasse cognita sit; nec vestra, quod non possum: sed illa, quam vernaculam paene dixerim Ecclesiae occidentalis, lingua Romana, tam diu tamque recenter in publicis regni Hungarici consiliis usitata.

Salvete igitur omnes, fratres in Domino dilectissimi!

Novimus enim labores vestros, patientiam, fidem, amorem veritatis. Itaque ex partibus terrae tam longinquis, e civitate, ex universitate remotissima, trans oceanum, fere trans continentem, hanc salutationem a fratribus vestris, cum Anglicis tum Americanis, vobis adfero.

Nec prorsus vobis ignotus vel alienus, neque omnino rerum vestrarum ignarus, huc venio. Calamitatibus patriae vestrae nos quoque illacrimavimus; his rebus melioribus magnopere gavisi sumus et gaudemus. De quibus nimis pauca, confiteor, cognovimus; plura audire valde cupimus. Nunc autem in mera benevolentia, hospitio, fide communi, convenimus. Haec enim duo maxima communiter tenemus, fidem atque libertatem: in fide libertatem, in libertate fidem. In his igitur plena sint gaudia nostra.

Quam unitatem profitemur—ut pro mea parte dicere ausim—haec non est mera opinio, sed (ut ait Paullus) *unitas Spiritus in vinculo fidei.*[941] Reconciliatio quam praedicamus non est, quam quidam fingunt, pacatio Dei irae, ut quodammodo amor eius cum iustitia concilietur; sed foedus illud dignissimum inter Deum et homines, quod efficitur nostram vitam conciliando, nostros mores et amores, cum voluntate, legibus, mandatis Dei semper omnipotentis, semper amantis.

Sed hanc fidem nostram obtinere oportet inter magnas mutationes rerum et sententiarum diversitates. "Tempora mutantur, nos et mutamur in illis." Gloria transit, imperia cadunt, instituta pereunt, maximae civitates dilabuntur, veteris Ecclesiae vires attenuantur; immo, ipsa ingenia humana, cogitationes, sententiae de die in diem in novum quiddam transmutantur. Inter omnes has vicissitudines rerum humanarum Verbum Dei solum stat. Verbum, inquam, quod non in monumentis modo fidei Christianae inscriptum est—quae ego plurima et nobilissima interpretari conor—verum etiam in volvendis caelis, in rerum terrestrium ordine, in iis quae recte nominantur Naturae legibus, quas in cursum et (ut ita dicam) in *evolutionem* omnium vitae formarum, porro in successum rerum humanarum et eventus historiae humanae Deus ipse quasi sigillum suum impressit.

Hic est noster labor, hoc opus nostrum, ut has leges discamus, his pareamus, secundum has vitam nostram in spiritu Christi ordinemus. Sic enim, neque aliter, fidem nostram tam caram, tam sanctam, tam per tot saecula inter tot errores omni veneratione retentam et transmissam, nos quoque—studio quidem omnium bonarum artium et litterarum, sed maxime oboedientia animorum vitarumque castitate—honorabimus ac tuebimur. Valete.

Source: J.H. Allen, *A Visit to Transylvania and the Consistory of Kalozsvar* (Boston: George H. Ellis, 1881), 11.

86 Laetare! (1883)

John Dawson Gilmary Shea (1824–92) is considered the founder of Catholic historical studies in the United States.[942] Born in New York to an Irish father and an American mother, Shea abandoned formal schooling when he was on the verge of entering Columbia, and he went to work in a New York trading firm headed by a Spanish merchant known as Don Tomas. Through this experience he learned Spanish, which gave him access to the rich archival material concerning the southern part of the United States. Later, after practicing law for two years, he entered the Jesuit novitiate, recently relocated to Montreal, which enabled him not only to learn French but also to meet the prolific Jesuit archivist Felix Martin (1804–86), who introduced him to the study of manuscripts and to historical scholarship in general. Eventually Shea left the Jesuit novitiate and devoted his professional life to writing and editing volumes about the history of the Catholic Church in the United States. Among his notable publications were *History of the Catholic Missions Among the Indian Tribes of the United States* (1854) and *History of the Catholic Church in the United States* (1886–92). The John Gilmary Shea Prize is awarded annually by the American Catholic Historical Association.

Shea's professional achievements were acknowledged in 1883 when the University of Notre Dame bestowed on him its first Laetare medal. This gold medal, still awarded on Laetare Sunday (the fourth Sunday of Lent), was established in order to recognize a Catholic "whose genius has ennobled the arts and sciences, illustrated the ideals of the Church and enriched the heritage of humanity." A Latin inscription on the medal reads: *Magna est veritas et praevalebit.* Accompanying the medal was a Latin address (consisting of an inscription and poem) composed by Rev. Stanislaus Fitte, C.S.C. (1842–1907), a philosophy professor at Notre Dame, and illustrated by Luigi Gregori

(1819–96), a professor and artist at Notre Dame.

In response to this award Shea wrote a letter of gratitude to the faculty of Notre Dame, and he sent a collection of his own writings, a 1582 version of the Rhemish Testament, and the Latin composition printed below. The Latin text was written on parchment with an arabesque and an initial letter illuminated by one of his daughters, and it was framed by gold and maroon velvet. In this composition Shea protests that he is unworthy to receive this medal and he suggests more worthy candidates, four of whom eventually did receive the award.

Nostrae Dominae Universitatis Facultati et Alumnis

Num donis me vultis, amici viventes, opprimere vestris,
Qui mortuos inter perdulci memoria gradior amicos?
Ut quid relinquere charas vultis me cogere umbras,
In lucem acturi, ac Magnum, invitum? Magnos habetis:
NEWTONUM[943] habetis, et virum scientia factisque praeclarum,
Ac medicos inter est EMMET,[944] qui celeber eminet certe,
Ecquid de CAROLO, legum perito, edicam O'CONOR?[945]
Post leges sunt bella,—ita! bellorum ac nobiles duces:
Nobilem ROSECRANS[946] bene ornetis commeritis signis!
Vel etiam artis insigni, LAFARGIO,[947] honorem donate,
Aut CORCORAN[948] illi, theologo, digno merito, laude!
Nostrumque denique EGAN,[949] qui dulciter canit ornate!
En viri! En magni! quos iuxta, videte, quam tenuis ego!
Iam donum, amici, perenni manebit pro monito mihi:
Quam longe ab eo consisto, quem me esse putastis.

Ioannes Mariae Shea (1883)

Source: *The Ave Maria* 19 (1883): 496.[950]

87 The Brooklyn Bridge (1883)

As classicists in the late nineteenth century examined their pedagogy, a particular issue was whether Latin should be spoken in the classroom. This era saw the emergence in the United States and abroad of the so-called Natural or Direct Method.

To be sure, this method had always been practiced in some quarters, notably by the Jesuits. When challenged on this notorious aspect of Jesuit pedagogy, which was increasingly seen as impractical, A.J. Elder Mullan (1865–1926) of Woodstock College pronounced: "There can be no doubt of the possibility of having American boys speak Latin: it is a thing that has been done before this often enough, and is now being done in certain of our colleges, at least in some classes." To the objection that Latin was good for mental discipline but need not be spoken, Mullan maintained: "our course of instruction is impossible in the higher classes, quite impossible, if Latin has not been taught the boys earlier as a living language."[951]

Strong and practical support for the natural method came from the classicist Edgar Solomon Shumway (1856–1928), who founded and edited *Latine* (later *Latine et Graece*), a monthly Latin newspaper that ran for four volumes (1882–86). Shumway, according to his obituary, "believed in Latin as a living, not as a dead language."[952] The epigraph to the first volume of *Latine* indicates the creed of the natural method: "Iter est longum per praecepta, breve et efficax per exempla" (Seneca). Shumway designed *Latine* as a aid to the many classics teachers who were, he believed, desirous of improved Latin pedagogy. A typical issue contained classical readings accompanied by numerous questions in Latin designed to foster the ability to think in Latin. It also offered Latin translations of well-known English hymns, exercises in prose composition, a Kalendarium of monthly events, philological or lexical notes, and correspondence, often in Latin, from classics teachers and professors. Occasionally *Latine* printed original Latin poetry. Additionally, Shumway encouraged the formation of Latin clubs (*catenae*), whose members (*anuli*) would gather to work through some of the exercises and readings found in his journal. *Latine* won acclaim from classicists at home and abroad, to judge from the letters of approbation regularly printed in its pages. Even the United States Secretary of Education wrote a letter of commendation.

Shumway, who earned a B.A. and M.A. at Amherst (1879, 1882) and a Ph.D. at Rutgers (1893), taught at a number of schools and universities in the mid-Atlantic. After he was dismissed from Rutgers in 1899 following a conflict with the university president, he taught briefly at the University of Pennsylvania and then for many years at the Manual Training High School in Brooklyn. He published *A Handbook of Latin Synonymes* (1884) and *A Day in Ancient Rome* (1885).

The following sapphic poem, found in volume 1 of *Latine* and reprinted with annotations in volume 3, is a commemoration of the Brooklyn Bridge, which opened on May 24, 1883. The author, Constantine Stauder (born Luigi Felice Leonardo Stauder, 1841–1913), a native of Italy, entered the Franciscan order and came to the United States in 1866.[953] After briefly serving as professor of moral theology at St. Aloysius Seminary (Columbus, Ohio), he left the Franciscans and the Catholic Church and became an Episcopalian minister, attending to a community of Italian Protestant immigrants in New York City. He married and had six children. Later in life he moved to London, and eventually he ceased to function as a minister. A gifted linguist, Stauder published *Post Prandium: Pleasantries in Colloquial Latin* (1891), and he contributed several original Latin compositions to *Latine*, including an elegy for Heinrich Schliemann (3:61–63).

In laudem pontis pensilis Neo-Eboracensis
IX Kal. Iun. MDCCCLXXXIII[954]

Iam satis[955] Rivi tumidis Eoi[956]
Credidit lymphis Pater has marinas
Nobiles urbes,[957] nebulisque, ventis,
    Grandine pressit.

Iam satis vexit geminas ad oras
Horrida cymba sitiens avarus
Impigros cives Moderator, actus
    Nummuli amore.[958]

Pons enim, pendens solidis colossis,
Praegravans uncis retinaculisque
Ferreis, pini trabibus politis
    Contabulatus,

Pondus immensum, Rhodium antecellens!
Iure "Romanus labor" elocutus,[959]
Nesciis fati resonante linguis
    Dignus honore,

Conditus nunc est. Properate, cives . . .
Terra telluri sociata . . . ! En dant
Murmur orchestrae. Tuba tympanumque
    Perstrepit Euoe!

Fulminans rauco catapulta bombo
Detonat celsis solidisque castris:
Bellicus non est crepitus; triumphi
    Nuncia defert.[960]

Echo Eboraco reboat Novello;
Corda pervadit stimulatque vulgi.
Insulae Longae stygiis cavernis
    Penetrat orcum.

Liber incedit populus—magister
Arte, naturae domitor, creator,
Insulas iungens, freta ponte sternens,
    Aethera scandens.

Liberae incedunt animae silentum,
Lintre semoto, domito Charonte,
Saeculi mores cupidae celebres
    Visere nostri.

Prout semel Troiae stupuit sub arces
Terra, dum muros init "Ars Minervae;"
Sive dum celsae Babylonis hortus
    Pensilis halat;

Os ita intentum teneat: prehendat
Quod valet liber populus creare,
Viribus iunctis opibusque; quaeque
    Gignere monstra.

Hinc Alexander, Pharao, Philippus,
Cyrus, Atridae, Cythereius dux,
Caesar, Henricus, Bonapars cohorsque
    Martia cuncta,

Socrates magnus, Xenophon, Platoque
Et Stagirites, Megaraeque prudens,

Tullius, Paulus venit, ac sophorum
        Densa corona.

Prodeant. Locis spatietur altis
Qui, stylo promptus gladiove, mundo
Profuit, fas est: regat Archimedes
        Dummodo passus.

Hincque doctorum subit et caterva
Quae extudit nobis operosa et usus
Et bonas artes, hominem trahentes
        Altius arvo.

Auctor hic pulvis pyrii, hic typorum,
Hic modi cantus, vitreaeque lamnae hic,
Machinae hic filo duplici suentis,
        Proflui hic ignis;[961]

Hic levem mutat rigida vaporem
Vi: iubet plaustrum vehere et carinam;
Hic rapit fulmen, radiare, fari,
        Pellere mandat.[962]

Sub iugum aut pontum caveas per imas
Ferreum hic sternit bivium,[963] metalli
Hic loquens stamen. Spatium nec extat!
        Ardua nec sunt!

Inclyti heroes! Simulacra grandis
Vestra Pons gestet; basibusque docta
Turba quae prelo nova promit acta

Publice et affert—

"Nuncius" (vulgo vocitatus "Herald")
"Tempora" ac "Sol" ac "Aquila" ac "Tribunus,"
"Mundus" aut "Censor," "Graphicus" vel "Argus"—
Rite ea ponet.[964]

Dum puer vernans tenera et puella
Ter rosis sternunt viridique lauro
Tramitem, ne quid subeat sinistri
Forte viator;

Candidis stellis roseisque pulchrum
Fasciis dum almae fluitat Rei huius
Publicae signum gemina serenam
Turre per aethram;

Insulae Longae venerande Praesul,[965]
Fausta ab excelsis chalybi precare
Pensili. Adstantes, manibus supinis,
Iungite voces:

O potens Numen, sapiente cuius
Hactenus cura Phariis stat oris
Pyramis, surgunt tumulique prisci,
Stantque obelisci,

Laetus intersis populo Columbi!
Atque votivum decus hoc paterni
Fluminis surgens opulente ripis,
Foedus et arcus,

(Iris ut quondam decorata coelo
Mansit in signum placiti fidelis),
Te tuente, almae stet hic universum
        Pacis in aevum.

Dulce sic possit "gelidis" Britannis
Et Scythis, Scotis Alemannicisque,
Africae nudis profugis, Ebraeis
        Undique oberrent,

Atque Romanis aquilis, cruore
Ebriis olim, populisque cunctis
Libera haec Tellus, data nuper orbi,
        Praebere[966] asylum.

Source: *Latine* 1 (June 1883): 2–4.[967]

88 Isolation in South Dakota (1883)

The author of the following Latin letter, Ephraim M. Epstein (1829–1913), was a Russian Jew, born in Babruysk, who came to the United States in 1850, shortly after his first child was born. He converted to Christianity and graduated from Andover Theological Seminary (1856). Having earned a medical degree from the College of Physicians and Surgeons of the University of the State of New York, Epstein practiced medicine in diverse places within the United States and abroad, including Turkey, Syria, Austria, Kansas, and Ohio. Following the tragic death of his five-year-old son due to a pharmacist's error, he abandoned medicine and taught briefly at Heidelberg College in Tiffin, Ohio before moving to Dakota Territory and becoming a Baptist preacher. In 1882 he became the first president of Dakota University (later the University of South Dakota) located in Vermillion, but he was removed after only a short tenure, due to "sectarian and political chicanery," as he put it in an autobiographical notice. After a few years teaching in West Virginia, Epstein returned to the field of medicine and spent the remainder of his life in Chicago, contributing articles and translations to the *American Journal of Clinical Medicine.*[968]

This letter was written during the time that Epstein was in Vermillion, teaching most of the classes and serving as registrar and bookseller for the nascent university. It appears to have been prompted by a letter he received from Edgar Shumway, the editor of *Latine* (see section 87).

Vermillione, Dakotianorum,
die quinto mensis October,
Anno MDCCCLXXXIII
Professori Edgaro S. Shumuuayo,
Potsdami, Novi Eboraci.

Doctissime Domine! Recepta hodie epistula tua de primo die mense currente non parvo me in stupore redditum sentiebam. Num fieri posse exclamavi, ut quis orientis solis in locis, quo fulgore lucis praeclarae gaudent, ab uno illorum in longe qui occasu fere perditi scintillulam etiam levem petisset? Nos vero, qui quamquam pratis in vastis ut aequore nautae gaudiamus [sic] (et si cuiusvisque non sint), at his paribus multis de rebus cultus, socialisque amoenitate, et, omnium pessime, conversatione viris cum doctis egentes, quid nos, quid ego vobis, viris fortuna fautis, in augendum rerum literarum dare possimus, vel possim? Iam satis sit, si tantum literas vestras tacentes legere possimus.—Et hac in re dicendi memor, quod ephemeridem tuam, "Latine," iam per aliquos menses non recepi. Estne solutio in antecessum a me facta iam delapsa? Si ita sit rursus solvere futurus sum.

Velis me in bona retinere memoria ut amicum et servum tuum,

Eph. M. Hederolapis,[969] M.D.

Source: *Latine* 2 (1883): 50–51.

89 Maryland Commemoration (1884)

Throughout the nineteenth century Latin was employed on solemn occasions and for commemorations within academic and religious communities, but at times it was also heard in more public settings. This was the case at Maryland Day in the year 1884, which marked the 250th anniversary of the landing of the *Ark* and the *Dove* (see section 18).

The first large-scale commemoration of this event had occurred in May 1842, the result of an initiative by the Philodemic Society of Georgetown College, and it had featured a procession, speeches, the singing of a celebratory ode, a High Mass celebrated by the Archbishop of Baltimore, and a steamboat ride between St. Inigoes and St. Mary's City (the site of Maryland's first Jesuit mission and first capital, respectively).

The 1884 commemoration was largely a Baltimore initiative, with a sizable contingent known as the Maryland Pilgrims' Association taking an overnight steamer down the Chesapeake Bay to reach the event. Following a Solemn High Mass celebrated by Rev. E.A. McGurk (1841–96), the president of Loyola College, the program offered music, a Latin ode as well as an English ode, an address by McGurk, and a formal oration by Richard T. Merrick (*c.* 1828–85), a prominent Washington lawyer and a major benefactor of Georgetown's Philodemic Society.[970]

The author of the Latin ode was J. Francis Coad (1866–1938), a sophomore at Loyola College. Following his graduation in 1886, at which he delivered the commencement address, Coad spent fifty-one years as professor and Vice-Principal of Charlotte Hall Military Academy in Southern Maryland. An English translation of Coad's ode appeared in the *Baltimore Sun* on May 16, 1884.

The following Latin text, said to be "an advanced copy" of this ode, was printed in the May 1884 *George-*

town College Journal. Yet the Latin does not match the English translation given in the *Baltimore Sun.* Indeed, the June number of the *College Journal* issued a correction, clarifying that this "fine Latin ode" had not been composed for the recent Maryland Day celebration, but the *College Journal* provided no further information about its authorship or the occasion that prompted its composition. Moreover, the *College Journal* did not print the correct text of Coad's ode.

At this point, then, the authorship of and the occasion for the following ode have not been determined, nor has the Latin text of Coad's ode been located.

Appulsus ad Terram Mariae

Cum Leonardus[971] freta transiisset
Saeva, servatus miserante caelo
Regna prospectans nova, gestiente
  Corde canebat.

Iam diu nostris precibus negata,
Terra de duris revocata fatis,
Tristibus tandem data, multa nostris
  Debita votis!

Terra iam matris decorata dulci
Nomine,[972] Oh! cordi bona plura spondens,
Gentibus pressis melius datura
  Terra Mariae!

Saepe dum noctis tenebrosus horror
Abdidit caelum et Boreas furebat
Efferam in mortem, tua stella nobis
  Spem renovavit![973]

Heu! nimis mentes timor occupavit,
Luridus dum Sol pelago renascens
Undique ostendit nova monstra genti
Plena minarum!

Dura sors pressit! socii viarum
Fluctibus ponti cecidere nigris
Atque direpti graviore luctu
Corda replerunt![974]

At suis parcens benedictus usque
Reddidit vitae Deus atque terram
Denuo laeti petimus reducta
Mente fugacem.

Dulce solamen! miseros revisis[975]
Alter et fesso Paradisus ultro
Exuli spondes requiem laboris
Atque salutem.

Ecce quam laetos aperit revolvens
Saeculum visus, licet et molestos
Misceat casus, quibus ampla nobis
Res nova crescat.

Quid valent armis populi futuri,
Bis duo dicunt bene gesta bella;
Pace quid possunt, tua, Baltimora
Clara revelant.

Quid maris pugnas celebrabo notas?
Quid canam belli meritas coronas?
Quando concurrunt inimica signa
        Patria vincet!

Haec tamen non est animo procaci
Magna tam parvo tenuare cantu;
Debiles vires, superant, rogantque
        Digna poetam.

Gaudeant multi celebrare tanta;
Sit mihi ratum potius tuorum
Nomina, Oh! Loyola, meo sacrare
        Carmine fausta.

Hi canent plectro—tibi, Baltimora
Hi dabunt famam velut inter urbes
Maximae et grandem repetent quota
        Carmine laudem!

Cresce, Oh! quantum patriae venustas,
Crescet et nomen studiis perenne et
Vivet aeternum pietas novumque
        Proteget orbem!

Ergo nunc sacras faciamus, usque
Victimas grati, neque tempore ullo
Absque odoratis maneat verenda
        Ara coronis!

Sit Tibi semper, Deus O benigne!
Gloria et laus, qui profugos misertus,
Hanc domum mutas patriae quietam
        Asperiori.

Gratias iustas dabimus redempti
Gratias vere Tibi sempiternas
Corde devoto, Deus, offeremus
        Nocte dieque.

Source: "The Maryland Anniversary," *Georgetown College Journal* 12.8 (May 1884): 113; available at DigitalGeorgetown.[976]

90 "The Italian Problem" (1888)

Between 1880 and 1920 an estimated 4.5 million Italian immigrants arrived in the United States, most of whom were Catholic peasants from the Mezzogiorno (southern Italy) fleeing escalating land and housing costs, depressed wages, and poor harvests. As one economist tersely noted at the time: "the main cause of the great emigration from South Italy can only be expressed by the word '*misery*.'"[977]

Once in the United States these immigrants largely settled in cities, but the transition to industrial life and tenement living was often excruciating, and it has been estimated that as many as one half of all Italian immigrants eventually returned home. With low levels of literacy (compared to other immigrant groups), an initial reluctance to enroll in schools, a language barrier, and a brand of piety not often seen in the United States, Italians were regarded with suspicion by many Americans, even by many Catholics. From an early date the term "Italian Problem" was coined to describe the challenge of incorporating Italian immigrants within Catholic parishes in the United States.[978]

In 1888 Gennaro De Concilio (1836–98), a Neapolitan-born priest who had been a pastor in Jersey City and a professor at Seton Hall, wrote a pamphlet on the religious condition of Italian immigrants (*Su lo stato religioso degli italiani negli Stati Uniti d'America*), which was excerpted in a leading Catholic journal in Rome and much discussed by Catholic prelates, including Pope Leo XIII (*r.* 1878–1903).[979] In December of the same year, the pontiff issued an encyclical letter, *Quam aerumnosa*, devoted to the plight of Italian immigrants. The following are the opening paragraphs of this letter.

Leo XIII was an accomplished and acclaimed Latinist. As a student at the Roman College he won a contest for writing without assistance the most Latin hexameters on a prescribed topic within a span of six hours—

he composed 120.[980] Today he is perhaps best known for his brief poem "Ars Photographica" (1867),[981] but during his lengthy pontificate the American press regularly carried reports, for the most part favorable, of his new poems, particularly his 85-line hexameter "Tenui Victu Contentus Ingluviem Fuge" (1897), which was the subject of a front-page Sunday exclusive in the *New York World*.[982] Moreover, he regularly contributed riddles, anonymously, to the Latin-language journal *Vox Urbis* (see section 105). He continued to write Latin poetry until his death at the age of ninety-three.[983] A study of his poetry remains to be written.[984]

Venerabiles Fratres,
salutem et apostolicam benedictionem.

Quam aerumnosa et calamitosa sit eorum conditio, qui ex Italia quotannis in Americae regiones ad vitae subsidia quaerenda turmatim commigrant, tam compertum Vobis est, ut nihil attineat id fuse per Nos explicari. Immo vero mala, quibus illi premuntur, vos quidem ex propinquo intuemini, eaque, datis non semel ad nos litteris, commemorata dolenter sunt a plerisque vestrum. Deflendum sane, quot tot miseri Italiae cives, solum mutare inopia coacti, in mala plerumque graviora incurrant, quam quae effugere voluerunt. Ac persaepe ad labores varii generis, quibus vita corporis absumitur, longe miserior adiungitur animarum pernicies. Prima ipsa demigrantium transvectio periculis plena ac detrimentis est: incidunt enim plerique in cupidos homines, quorum quasi mancipia fiunt, et gregatim in naves coniecti, atque inhumane habiti, ad depravationem naturae sensim impelluntur. Ubi vero ad destinatas oras appulerunt, linguae et locorum ignari, quotidianis operis addicti, improborum insidiis, et potentiorum, quibus sese manciparint, patent insidiis. Qui autem industria sua satis sibi parare potuerunt unde vitam tueantur, versantes tamen assidue inter eos, qui omnia ad quaestum et utilitatem suam referunt, nobiles humanae naturae sensus paullatim exuentes, eorum vitam vivere discunt qui omnes spes et cogitationes suas in terra defixerunt. Huc accedunt obvia passim irritamenta cupiditatum, fraudesque sectarum, quae istic late grassantur, religioni infensae, et plerosque in viam trahunt quae ducit ad interitum.

In his autem malis illud longe luctuosius est, quod in tanta multitudine hominum, amplitudine regionum, difficultate locorum, haud facile praesto esse iis potest ea, quae par esset, salutaris cura ministrorum Dei, qui, Italicae compotes linguae, ipsis verbum vitae tradant, sacramenta administrent, et opportuno subsidia impertiant, quibus eorum erigatur animus in spem bonorum caelestium, et vita spiritus sustentetur ac vigeat. Hinc multis locis rari admodum sunt ii, quibus sacerdos adsit morituris, non rari quibus nascentibus minister deest ad regenerationis lavacrum: plurimi sunt quibus nuptiae nulla habita Ecclesiae legum ratione ineuntur, unde similis patribus propagatur proles, atque ita passim apud hoc genus hominum oblivione delentur christiani mores, pessimi quique inolescunt.

Source: *American Ecclesiastical Review* 1 (1889): 45–46.

91 Latin between Sister and Brother (1890)

The following is a pair of letters exchanged between a brother and sister in late-nineteenth-century Iowa. The siblings were the children of Evarts Bradford Kent (1843–1924), a Vermont native and graduate of Middlebury College who was a Congregationalist pastor in various places around the country. Kent's oldest son, Ernest (1873–1952), earned a Ph.D. in Education from Columbia and worked at schools in Indianapolis, New York, and Philadelphia before settling in Jersey City, where he was director of manual training and industrial teaching in the public schools for thirty-two years.[985] Kent's daughter Grace (1875–1973) earned a Ph.D. in Psychology from George Washington University and worked in hospitals and clinics in South Carolina and Massachusetts and later taught briefly at the University of Miami. She developed the widely-used Kent-Rosanoff Association Test.[986]

Fifteen-year old Grace wrote the first letter printed below to Ernest while he was in college at Grinnell (then known as Iowa College). The second is Ernest's response.[987]

At the time, the requirements for admission into the Classical course at Grinnell (which Ernest was pursuing) included four books of Caesar, seven orations of Cicero, the *Eclogues* of Vergil and six books of the *Aeneid*, one book of the *Anabasis*, and the ability to read the Greek Gospels at sight. In the fall of 1890 Ernest was studying Livy, Tacitus, and Cicero's *Brutus*, and he was learning how to read Latin at sight and from dictation.[988] Yet during the 1890s Grinnell's curriculum would shift from the classics in favor of the sciences.[989]

Eldora, Iowa, Novem 6th 1890

Care frater Diligens—

Laetissima eram tuam epistulam accipere. Si tu habes impuram quattuor-in-manu,[990] mihi id mittas, et id lavabo.

Catulus bonus, Leo nomine, tibi amorem mittit.

Magis te quam oculus amo meos.

Gratia.

Post Scriptum. Placet excusare omnia errata.

Grinnell, Ia., Kal. Nov. IX 1890

Gratia carissima —

Magnum gaudium mihi, cum epistolam tuam classicalissimam acciperem, fuit.

Nec mirabile erat; quattuor in manu enim, cujus scripsisti impurum et impurior per quemque diem, γέγονεν, ut non licet, id quattuor in manu dicari, sed quattuor in pede.

Gaudiens maxime itaque, matri nostrae id dabo, cum illa ad castigandum me venit; expectans id iterum recipere, tam clarum, ut ego, potius quam quattuor in pede, quattuor in ore dicem.

Doctor nonne te hanc epistolam recipiet pro Latino studio?

Carissime, Ernestus.

Source: Evarts Kent Family Papers, 1790–1928, Manuscripts Division, William L. Clements Library, University of Michigan.

92 The Golden Age of Latin Drama in the United States (1890s)

The distinction of being the first college or university within the United States to stage a large-scale Latin drama probably belongs to Boston College, whose students performed the *Philodenus*, a comedy written by the Jesuit Charles Porée (1675–1741), during Commencement Week in 1877.[991]

The last two decades of the nineteenth century and the first two decades of the twentieth might be called the Golden Age of Latin Drama in the United States. From New York to California, from Wisconsin to Alabama, in sectarian as well as public schools, male as well as female students staged plays not only by Plautus and Terence but also by authors of a much later date. In addition to notices in classical journals, major newspapers lavishly detailed the casts, touted the historical accuracy of stages and costumes, and triumphantly recorded the dignitaries regularly in attendance at these productions.

On June 17, 1882 eleven sophomores at the University of Michigan staged Terence's *Adelphoe*.[992] Evidently unaware of Boston College's earlier production, the *Chronicle* of the University of Michigan confidently asserted that this was "the first Latin play ever produced in this country."[993] In May 1884 female students at Washington University in St. Louis performed Plautus's *Rudens*, which prompted the *St. Louis Post-Dispatch* to boast that "beyond doubt" there would be a "renaissance" of Latin drama and that St. Louis would be "its chief theater." The article predicted: "The talent is here, the culture is here, and the interest is here, and nothing more is necessary to an assurance that hereafter the Latin drama will be a principal among the many forms of intellectual recreation which the more scholarly of St. Louisians indulge in."[994]

The following years abounded with Latin productions, including at least three in 1890. In that year students at the University of Michigan performed Plautus's *Menaechmi* twice, first on campus and then in Chicago. That same year students at St. Francis Xavier College in New York performed Plautus's *Captivi*, which the *New York Herald* deemed "a thorough success."[995] The *Woodstock Letters*, an in-house Jesuit journal, boasted that the audience at the *Captivi* was "probably the most cultured ever gathered together in New York City." The classical speech of the actors, according to this same article, "would have delighted old Plautus himself, if his shade could have returned to this world of steam and electricity."[996] In June 1890 the students of Boston's Girls Latin School staged *The Feast of Dido* as a fundraiser for their school newspaper. Papers around the country carried the following assessment, which compared the girls's performance to that of the students from St. Francis Xavier: the latter students had "all the advantages of the training and historical research of the scholarly Jesuit fathers," while the girls of Boston Latin "had only their bright intellects and their Yankee mother wit."[997] Other productions of this decade include: Plautus's *Trinummus* at Syracuse (1895) and at Stanford (1899), the music and scenery of the former being "as near historically correct as possible,"[998] while the latter was "the first time that any western institution [had] attempted anything in this line;"[999] Plautus's *Captivi*, "staged in a remarkably complete and realistic manner" at Boston University (1896);[1000] Plautus's *Mostellaria* at the commencement exercises of St. Lawrence College (1897), which afforded attendees "a correct conception of the Roman drama and theater;"[1001] and Terence's *Phormio*, staged with "archaeological correctness" at Bailey Springs University (Alabama), which was thought to be the first such production in the South.[1002]

The first decades of the twentieth century saw an increase in the staging of Latin drama in schools and colleges within the United States and at times a branching out beyond Plautus and Terence. *The Classical Weekly* noted productions of the *Captivi* and *Aulularia* at Hamilton College, the *Captivi* at Wilson College, the *Adelphoe* at Smith College, *Pan Soter* at Union College, *Herodes sive Adoratio Magorum* at Jamaica High School (NY), *Aeneas of Troy* at Western High School (Baltimore), *Sponsus* at the University of Chicago, *Dido* at Hollywood High School (Los Angeles), at Catskill High School (NY), and at Wadleigh High School (NY), *A Roman School* at Oakwood Seminary (NY), and *A Roman Wedding* at Canajoharie High School (NY).[1003] These last two plays were the original compositions of Susan Paxton, a Latin teacher at Omaha High School.[1004]

Latin plays, it was widely held, were an important way to invigorate the study of Latin.[1005] The classicist H.R. Fairclough, whose house had been the setting for Stanford's initial presentation of the above-mentioned *Trinummus*, observed that the introduction of Terentian dialogue into the curriculum of California secondary schools had led to a "reawakened interest in Latin studies," because students now grasped that Latin was "the living speech of a living people" rather than "a purely artificial language, used only for literary purposes, but never employed as the speech of daily life."[1006]

The Jesuits, for their part, frequently staged Latin drama of a later era, in part because few unexpurgated classical plays were deemed morally acceptable. In December 1893 the College of the Holy Cross staged *Sibylla*, written by the college's professor of rhetoric. The following year the Jesuit school in Prairie du Chien, Wisconsin staged *John Damascene*, a five-act Latin play written by the German Jesuit Caspar Harzheim (1838-1910), and Loyola College (Baltimore) staged *'ΑΠΑΤΩΝΤΑΠΑΤΩΜΕΝΟΙ, seu, Deceptores Decepti*, a three-act play written by the nineteenth-century Italian bishop Carlo Maria Rossini.[1007]

The inscriptions below refer to two of the most consequential productions of this era: St. Francis Xavier's multiple performances of *Captivi* in 1893 and Harvard's performance of the *Phormio* in 1894.

In October 1893 the students of St. Francis Xavier staged the *Captivi* at their College Theatre on Sixteenth Street in New York City before an audience that included the Archbishop of New York, Michael Corrigan (1839–1902), as well as the Apostolic Delegate to the United States, Francesco Satolli (1839–1910). The first inscription below commemorates this production. It was printed in the *New York World*.

A week later the troupe from St. Francis Xavier took the train to Chicago where they twice staged the *Captivi* for the World's Columbian Exposition. The production in Chicago received lavish publicity. The *Chicago Record* commented: "many entered the hall expecting to see an amateurish performance, but they were disappointed."[1008] The *Woodstock Letters* predicted that one consequence of the play would be to incite the "old universities" in the United States to rival St. Francis Xavier.[1009] The Jesuits, indeed, viewed these highly-acclaimed Latin productions as vindications of their pedagogy, which was under increasing criticism in the 1890s.[1010] They also viewed this performance as a sign of the progress in classical studies in the United States and particularly in New York City, where they took pride in having established an early Latin school (*c.* 1684). The second inscription below pertains to this Chicago performance of *Captivi*.

The third inscription below refers to Harvard's April 1894 production of the *Phormio*. This production, too, was highly acclaimed—"an unqualified success," according to the *New York Tribune*[1011]—and its audience included President Eliot and his wife, the President of the Board of Overseers, several Harvard deans and professors, the presidents of several prominent New England colleges and universities, the Governor of Massachusetts and his wife, and the Hindu monk Swami Vivekanauda (1863–1902). According to the *Boston Globe*, perhaps never before had there been such an assembly of culturally prominent persons. The *Boston Herald* remarked that many theatergoers no doubt had expected "a mere archeological curiosity" but instead found themselves "entertained and amused" for hours.[1012] Preparations for this play had begun a full eleven months prior to the event, and rehearsals spanned seven months. Tickets for the event were in Latin, and a Latin advertisement was prepared with large red letters, in imitation of posters used in Pompeii.[1013] The libretto for the performance contained reproductions, never before made, of the famous miniatures from the tenth-century Vatican MS of Terence.[1014] Professor J.B. Greenough composed a new Latin verse prologue for the play. Following the production the audience applauded for several minutes, and invited guests enjoyed a reception at President Eliot's home. The inscription below, printed in the *Boston Globe* on Friday, April 20, 1894, was taken from the program for the play.

The fourth passage below, a brief poem, also commemorates Harvard's production of the *Phormio*. It was composed by Arthur W. Hodgman (1869–1948), a winner of several prizes in Latin and Greek composition during his time at Harvard. In 1896 he earned a Ph.D. from Harvard, and he taught Classics at The Ohio State University.

I

T. Macci Plauti Captivi
In Lycaeo Sancti Francisci Xaveri Neo Eboraci
ad IV. Idus Octobres MDCCCXCIII.
Latine agetur.

Cives Americani plaudite[1015] vestrum Eboracum gestiens sinu suo excipit duos fama inclitos Umbriae viros[1016] alterum Musarum alumnum T. Maccium Plautum suam edisserentem fabulam de Duobus captivis, alterum dignitate, litteris, scientia, legationibus rebus gestis longe clariorem Franciscum Satolli Pontificem naupactensem[1017] summae Christiani gentis patris ac legiferi rite in America vices gerentem.[1018]

II

Q · B · F · F · Q · S ·
QVOI · FABVLAI · NOMEN
CAPTEIVEI · DVO
AVCTORE · T · MACCIO · PLAVTO · POETA
A · D · FRANCISCI · XAVERII · CONLEGII
IN · AVL · COETVS · ORBIS · VNIVERSI
A · D · XIV · ET · XIII · KALENDAS · NOVEMBRES ·
AGETVR
MODOS · FACIET · RENATVS · HOLAIND · E · S · I ·[1019]
TIBIIS · FIDIBVSQ · RECENTIORIBVS[1020]
MITTETVR · AVLAEVM · HORA · VIII · VESPERI
SINGVLI · X · III[1021] · ADMITTVNTOR
M · DCCC · XCIII

III

P · TERENTI · AFRI
PHORMIONEM
FABVLAM · PALLIATAM · IN · V · ACTVS · DIVISAM
CVM · MODIS · NOVIS · FACTIS
A · FREDERICO · DE FOREST · ALLEN[1022]
AGET · GREX · HARVARDIANVS
IN · THEATRO · ACADEMICO[1023]
DIE · CONCORDIENSI[1024] · DVOBVSQVE · INSEQVENTIBVS
A · CONL · HARV · CC · LVIII

PERSONAE	ACTORES
...	
...	

DISSIGNATORES · SVNT · SOCIETATIS · PHILOLOGAE · SODALES

Statim post spectaculum carri aderunt qui ui seminum fulmineorum spectatores in urbem uicinam abripiant.[1025]

IV

Ad curatores Ludorum

Fabula viginti post saecla relata Terenti
Acta est hic festo perplacuitque die;
Curavere viri docti spectaculum agendum—
Hi laudis meritae praemia larga ferunt.

Sources:
I *New York World*, October 11, 1893.
II *The Latin Play, the Two Captives of Plautus, by the Students of the College of St. Francis Xavier New York* (n.p., n.d.).
III J.B. Greenough, "The Latin Play at Harvard," *The New England Magazine*, n.s. 10 (1894): 494.
IV *The Harvard Graduates' Magazine* 2 (1894): 524.

93 Columbus Anniversary (1892)

Christopher Columbus has elicited numerous neo-Latin compositions. He has been the subject of at least six epics, dating from Lorenzo Gambara's *De navigatione Christophori Columbi libri IV* (Rome 1581), and including the recently-identified *De invento Novo Orbe inductoque illuc Christi sacrificio* of José Manuel Peramás (Faenza 1777).[1026] American poets too have commemorated Columbus, notably the precocious fourteen-year old Edmund Griffin (1804–30), who made him the subject of a 103-line hexameter poem.[1027] The year 1892, the fourth centennial of Columbus's initial voyage, prompted multiple commemorative Latin poems, including the following sapphic ode by the Vincentian priest Joseph Alizeri (1822–93).[1028]

Alizeri, born in Genoa, emigrated to the United States and was ordained a priest in 1849 by Archbishop Peter Richard Kenrick (see section 78). For four decades he taught theology and languages and occasionally held administrative posts at seminaries in Missouri (St. Mary's at the Barrens, St Vincent's in Carondolet and later in Cape Girardeau), Pennsylvania (Mount St. Vincent's in Germantown), and New York (Our Lady of the Angels in Niagara). Renowned as a skilled teacher and theologian, late in life he resumed an earlier interest in Latin verse composition, and several of his efforts were published and lauded in newspapers and journals in the 1880s and early 1890s. In addition to the poem below, which he wrote at the age of seventy, Alizeri composed an 82-line elegiac poem to commemorate the Silver Jubilee of Our Lady of the Angels Seminary (1881, revised and reprinted 1891), a 31-line hendecasyllabic poem in honor of the Virgin Mary (1890), and a series of poems addressed to Pope Leo XIII (*Carmen Leoninum*, 1893).[1029]

CONCIVI • CHRISTOPHORO • COLUMBO
TRIUMPHALI • DIE • XII • OCTOBRIS • A • D •
MDCCCXCII
QUARTO • EXEUNTE • INVENTAE • AMERICAE •
SAECULO
CARMEN • DICAT
IOSEPHUS • A • ALIZERI • C • M[1030]

Salve, Concivis,[1031] Genuae "Superbae"
Nobilis proles, decus atque summum,
Hoc melos, quaeso, patrii Poetae
Sume benigne.

Dulce enim est prorsus mihi tum decorum
Principem Nautam decorare laude,
Quamquam iners Musam impediat morosa
Saepe senectus.[1032]

En tibi texunt roseas coronas
"Virgines castae, puerique puri,"[1033]
Dum simul te mellifluis honorant
Dulciter hymnis.

Nam die hoc fausto meritos libenter
Quattuor reddunt tibi saecla honores;
Maximus grati resonat tibi orbis
Plausus ubique.

Sed tuum imprimis celebrat triumphum
Urbs vetus regnans Ligurina in ora,[1034]
Quae suam te vult, titulo Parentis,
Dicere prolem.

Ast et Hispanus repetit triumphum,
Quem piget tarde, ac pudet heu ! laboris
Praemium tanto tribuisse nautae
    Ferrea vincla![1035]

Teque collaudat generosa tellus
—Quam novam Europae veteri dedisti—
Splendidis gestis, cito proditura
    Splendidiora.

Hinc tui nunquam immemor, hos benigno
Excipit corde Ausonios, avita
Quos reluctantes patria exulare
    Cogit egestas.[1036]

Nec tuum urget cor perituri honoris
Splendide mendax,[1037] vehemens cupido,
Sed neque auri sacra fames[1038] frequenter
    Pectora cogens.

Et tibi sceptrum haud cupis obtinere
Barbaras gentes avidus domare,
Nec tuum tentant animum procacis
    Gaudia vitae.

Sed vis ad lucem fidei vocare
Nescium Christi populum benigne,
Quem premit dire tenebrosi Averni
    Perfidus hostis.

Atque vis sacram revocare terram
Turcico immanique iugo et Sepulchrum
Quo novo Christi iacuere ternis
Membra diebus.[1039]

Hinc iter tutat dubium, atque fluctus
Frenat, ac iras Boreae coercet
Qui lacum verbo domuit furentem
Gennezarethi.[1040]

Fervide unaquaque die invocata
Protegit te Stella Maris potenter,
Et ratem optatas fragilem remotas
Ducit ad oras.

Mira res prorsus! pavidum COLUMBUM
Esse te terris tua sors volebat;
Sed novam reddunt te aquilam peracta
Splendida gesta.

Interim terris probat hos honores
Sponsa Christi nobilis, immo et auget,[1041]
Quae tibi Romae aureolam est datura
Caelicolarum.

Maior at Caelis agitur triumphus,
Dum tuam frontem aethereo serenam
Ipsamet gaudet redimire serto
Magna Isabella.

Salve, Concivis, patriae vetustae
Gloria haud saeclis peritura mille,
Tu decus nostrae assidue futurus
Urbis et orbis!

Source: *American Ecclesiastical Review* 7 (1892): 296–98.

94 Native Americans Lose Land in the Northwest (1895)

Throughout the middle and late nineteenth century the United States government bought vast tracts of land from Native American tribes and subsequently opened them up to white settlement. The following excerpt, from an Annual Letter of the Jesuit mission of St. Joseph in Idaho, describes the aftermath of one such agreement with the Nez Percé tribe.

In the year 1800 the Nez Percé inhabited about 13 million acres in Idaho, Montana, Washington, and Oregon, and according to an estimate by Lewis and Clark their population numbered about 7600.[1042] As a result of treaties in 1855 and 1863, Nez Percé lands were reduced to about 750,000 acres,[1043] and Chief Joseph's War of 1877 led to the defeat and forced removal to Oklahoma of many tribal members who resisted governmental demands to move to a reservation. On May 1, 1893 American agents concluded yet another agreement with tribal leaders by which they purchased additional lands in Idaho in exchange for $1,626,222. According to a proclamation issued by President Grover Cleveland, these lands were to be opened for settlement at noon (Pacific time) on November 18, 1895. Repeated attempts were made by the United States government to induce the Nez Percé, who numbered about 2000 at this time,[1044] to comply with the terms of this settlement.

The Nez Percé had been visited by Fr. Pierre Jean de Smet in 1840, and a permanent Jesuit mission, St. Joseph's, was established in 1867. A chapel, still standing and now incorporated into the Nez Perce National Historic Park, was constructed in 1874.[1045] At the time of this letter, the Jesuit missionary in residence was the Dutch-born Aloysius Soer (1853–1931).

A die vigesima secunda Novembris A.D. millesimi octingentesimi nonagesimi quinti, reservatio nostra alborum occupationi relicta fuit, id est: terra non occupata ab Indis illisque mensurata individuis.[1046] Praeerat dissentio maxima inter Indos, quando Commissarii a gubernio missi terram emendi advenere. Monetum oblatum arridebat multis, terram ubi usque adhuc quasi caeli aves liberi equis suis quasi volabant, in proximo futuro alborum sepibus obstructam, sibique infantibusque pro semper ereptam videre, deterrebat pluriores. Ex decem deputatis ex variis Indorum pagis, duo tantum initio tractatum accipere voluere. Quum autem albi intellexerunt, tali modo non proficere, alium iniere modum: a pago in pagum circumierunt, pecunia et promissionibus aliquos inter magnatos et ministrum Protestantem emerunt et non requieverunt usque sufficientem votorum numerum obtinuerunt.

Erat patri Missionis positio difficilis. Contraire legibus gubernii aperte declarantibus, suam esse mentem omnes et singulas reservationes annihilare, erat huius intentioni aperte contraire, frustum ut putabat, opus conari et indignationem incurrere gubernii et alborum. Inducere Indos ut suo nomine signarent tractatum propositum erat adiuvare eorum destructioni. Neutri parti favere erat ergo patri praestandum. Huic incumbebat. Ideo obligationis memor, fuit primum eius verbum, quando Commissarii Missionem visitarunt: non est meum Indos inducere ut tractatum signent, ipsissimi videant quid facere expediat. Ad quod responderunt: non est nostra intentio inducere te ut hoc facias, sed ut scias, velimus, legas tractatum et explices. Legit tractatum propositum et ad quaestionem quid existimet de summa oblata, tria scrutata pro agro, respondit in praesentia duorum Indorum, considerans quod multa terra erat lapidosa et non bona, satis ut occuparetur, puto satis esse. Erat in provisionibus et sequens, omnis Societas religiosa vel alia organizatio usque nunc occupans propria auctoritate, religionis sive educationis causa inter Indos, terras illis concessas, habebunt duos annos, quo tempore suam hanc facere possunt, solvendo tria scrutata pro agro.[1047] Explicavit pater Indis hanc provisionem bonam esse, quia ex hac certi erunt, Missionem ab aliis occupari non posse in futuro. Pro ceteris quando illum quandoque interrogaverunt non solum Catholici, set et Infideles et protestantes quid putas: Estne bonum vendere terram necne, semper respondit: Indos prope Missionem dicere solere: timor est ne pecunia causa futura sit inebrietatis, ludorum et vitiorum multorum; numquam, ne uni quidem Indo persuasit, quamquam pauperrimo, ut signaret tractatum, quamquam certe pro pauperibus erat acceptabilis. Inculpabant Indi, praecipue prope Missionem supra allata et dixerunt: esset Missionarii directe opposuisse tractatui, debuisset non accepisse Commissarios in domo, debuisset praedicasse: nolite auscultari eos, nolite eorum optioni indulgere; ex quo non hostilis te manifestasti, multi putaverunt, est bonum tractatum inire et es tu vera causa cur signaverint.

Source: The Pacific Northwest Tribes Missions Collection of the Oregon Province Archives of the Society of Jesus, 1853–1960, microfilm reel 21, pp. 302–4 (original in Jesuit Archives and Research Center, St. Louis, Missouri).

95 Postprandial Eloquence in New York City (1895)

The three hundred guests at Delmonico's, New York's oldest and grandest restaurant, had just finished a lavish meal and lighted their cigars when they were surprised to hear their toastmaster declaiming the Latin speech printed below. The occasion was the thirty-first annual dinner of the Dartmouth College Association of New York, held on Friday, Feburary 1, 1895. The toastmaster was Charles L. Dana (1852–1935), a New York physician. Dana reportedly joked that he had decided to speak in Latin because his friends told him he was incapable of delivering a good speech in English.

Dana, a Vermont native, graduated from Dartmouth in 1872.[1048] He moved to Washington, DC and served as secretary to Senator Justin Smith Morrill of Vermont and then to Spencer Baird, the head of the Smithsonian Institute. He earned medical degrees from the National Medical College (1876) and the College of Physicians and Surgeons in New York (1877), and he devoted much of his professional career to the young field of neurology, serving as president of the New York Neurological Society, the American Neurological Association, and the Academy of Medicine of New York. He published extensively, including *A Textbook of Nervous Diseases* (1892), which went through ten editions.

Dana also nurtured a life-long interest in the arts and literature, particularly poetry, as well as in the classical world. In 1898 he and four other physicians founded the Medico-Historical Club (later known as the Charaka Club, after the early Indian physician), devoted to the "literary, artistic and historical aspects of medicine,"[1049] and Dana published several articles in the society's *Proceedings* on the role of medicine in antiquity.[1050] The epigraph to these *Proceedings* proclaimed: "Post multa virtus opera laxare solet." Later in life he published *Poetry and the Doctors* (1916) and *Poems and Songs of Patriotism and War* (1918).

Newspaper reports on the Dartmouth dinner at Delmonico's engendered a minor but apparently friendly controversy. The *New York Times* claimed that Dana's speech, far from being crude Latin, was rather "the simon-pure article" and was understood by most of those in attendance.[1051] This claim was disputed by the *Boston Herald*, whose editors countered: "not one college graduate in a hundred can either talk or understand colloquial Latin . . . it is an accomplishment that is confined almost exclusively nowadays to the Catholic priesthood."[1052] One week later the *Times*, unwilling to concede this point, furnished proof: "The alumni of the college who were present at the dinner when asked about the matter declare positively that, whether he descended to playful caninity in his Latin, or rose to classic diction, the diners appeared to follow the remarks of the President with perfect ease, full understanding, and frequent appreciative applause."[1053] The *Boston Herald* seemed to acquiesce: "Let us hope that the alumni of the other colleges will appreciate this sort of postprandial eloquence."[1054]

Fratres Sociique!
Audite, si vobis placet.

Cena finita, vobis omnibus repletis cibo,[1055] vino, conversationibus, aqua pura, Apollinarique,[1056] nunc demum hora est audire orationes, carmina, historias novas atque antiquissimas, iocos, castaneas, et cetera facete dicta.

Poeta dixit: Dulce et decorum est desipere in loco[1057] Delmonicono.[1058] Ergo, dum possumus desipiamus, gloriae Almae matris nostrae Dartmuthensis causa.

Me indignum, medicum miserabilem, fecistis praesidem vestrum.[1059] Vobisque Dartmuthensibus immortalibus maximas ago gratias, et faciam meum optimum.

Post prandium quotidianum, digestio et requies; post autem prandium qualia habent Darthmuthenses, post coffeam cigarrosque, audietis vocem mei clamantis in Delmonico,[1060] et introducentis hospites nostros illustrissimos, praeclarissimos, qui dicent verba calida eloquentiaeque plenissima, in lingua Anglica.[1061] Vos autem fratres plaudite!

Source: *Spirit of the Age* (Woodstock, VT), February 16, 1895.

96 Questionable Latin in Boston (1897)

By the last decade of the nineteenth century the increasing marginalization of classics in culture as well as the profound reorientation of classical studies towards *Altertumswissenschaft* had produced widespread uncertainty about the end, or ends, of the study of the classical languages. This was no abstract question. The choice of a Latin textbook, for example, might be determined by the answer. One reviewer in the Jesuit periodical *America* stated this succinctly: "We can never decide on the merits of this system or of any other, until we make up our minds what precisely our purpose is in teaching Latin at all."[1062] He then identified four possible ends of Latin study: to speak Latin, to appreciate excellent Latin literature, to gain access to Roman culture, to train the mind. According to this same review, if the end of classical studies is to speak Latin, the approach advocated by Arcadius Avellanus (born Arkád Mogyorossy, 1851–1935) has much to recommend it.

It was the conviction of the Hungarian-born Avellanus, a prolific and ambitious proponent of what he called the Tusculan, or direct, method of Latin instruction, that classical teaching by the 1890s had been reduced to administering a sort of "mental gymnastics" that were not conducive to fluency. Avellanus, a former Franciscan friar who had come to the United States to teach at St. Bonaventure College, advocated doing away with speculative grammars and instead teaching the languages colloquially from the beginning. In his prognosis, once a student gained "an instinct of idioms and phraseology," he could begin to read "indifferent," i.e., everyday Latin, and only later would he encounter the classics.[1063] To this end he composed a textbook, *Palaestra*, which, it has been argued, was an influence on Hans Ørberg's *Lingua Latina per se illustrata*.[1064] He also founded and edited a Latin newspaper, *Praeco Latinus*, which appeared first bi-weekly and then monthly from 1894–1902, which might be regarded as the successor to Edgar Shumway's *Latine* (see sections 87 and 88).

A typical issue of *Praeco Latinus*, eight pages in length, offered news and commentary on national and international events, original poetry, correspondence (mostly in Latin), a running alphabetized Florilegium of original Latin proverbs, small treatises on Latin pedagogy (in Latin or English), and serialized editions of narrative Latin texts to be used in schools (e.g., *Robinson Crusoeus* or *Thomae Vallaurii Epitome Historiae Romanae ab urbe condita ad Odoacrem*). The editors of *The Classical Review* regarded the appearance of this journal as a sign of "the vigour of classics in America;" though leery of the "tall talk and that ignorant abuse of established methods which appears to be inseparable from propagandism," they nonetheless urged classics teachers to pay attention to "the Philadelphia solution."[1065]

The June 1897 number of *Praeco Latinus* began with a tendentious comment on the Latinity of a recently-dedicated monument on Boston Common. The questionable Latin was an inscription on Augustus St. Gaudens's bronze relief monument to Col. Robert G. Shaw and the African American soldiers of the Massachusetts 54th Volunteer Infantry, which was unveiled on May 31, 1897 in the presence of sixty-five veterans of Shaw's regiment. Above the head of Col. Shaw's horse are inscribed the Latin words:

OMNIA·RELINQVIT
SERVARE·REMPVBLICAM.

The Latin text was the motto of the Society of the Cincinnati, of which Shaw was a member, but critics lambasted its correctness and its propriety. One writer to the *Boston Herald* charged that the Latin was "open to the gravest criticism as to its correctness and purity of expression." It was not true Latin, but rather English in Latin dress, and it constituted "a public scandal and a disgrace." It was not so much a problem of vocabulary—although some had faulted the use of *rempublicam* rather than *patriam* and *servare* rather than *servire* (!)—but rather with the "grammar and syntax" as well as the appropriateness of the words for the image. As for the grammar—the present tense (*relinquit*), the word order (not ending the sentence with a verb), and the use of the infinitive (*servare*) to express purpose were all problematic. But this same letter writer—who apparently was a veteran—also faulted the inscription for using the singular verb (*relinquit*), thereby exalting "one brave white man" and neglecting "those negroes whose souls were heroic, even if they had black skins, who fell beside him in that fatal charge."[1066]

Avellanus, for his part, saw in this questionable Latinity a justification for his Tusculan method.

BOSTONIUM, Athenae Americanae,[1067] novissime specimen edidit suae Latinitatis eximium. Simulacrum vidl. aeneum heroi cuidam Shaw, Caucasio duci Aethiopum Americanorum, in bello civili caeso erigendum curarunt, cui Latinitate "classica" hunc titulum inscripserunt:

"OMNIA RELINQUIT
SALVARE[1068] REMPUBLICAM."

Critici sero rem animadverterunt, adeoque animi Bostoniensium ira pudoreque fervent. Derisionem & cachinnum orbis terrarum merentur. Ex alio obtutu exemplum hoc es[t] saluberrimum, quod principia nostra luculenter vindicat, vidl. *versiones* pestem esse atque foveam. Auctor enim *Anglice* cogitabat, non Latine. Remedium est *Methodus Tusculana*,[1069] h.e. institutio *viva voce*.

Source: *Praeco Latinus* 3.9 (June 1897): 1.

97 Yale Bicentennial (1901)

In October 1901 Yale University, the third oldest institution of higher learning in the United States, celebrated its bicentennial. The four-day celebration began on a Sunday morning in Battell Chapel with public worship: President Arthur Twining Hadley (1856–1930) read the Scriptures, the Rev. Joseph Hopkins Twichell (1838–1918) preached a sermon, and former President Rev. Timothy Dwight V (1828–1916) pronounced benediction. Subsequent days featured orations, artistic performances, a torchlight procession, and a football game, as well as some Latin.

The event was attended by representatives from other universities as well as by national and international dignitaries or their representatives. For example, Bishop Knut Henning Gezelius von Schéele, a professor of theology at Uppsala University and a member of the Swedish Parliament, delivered the congratulations of King Oscar of Sweden, to which President Hadley replied ex tempore in Latin.[1070] Additionally, numerous institutions at home and abroad sent congratulatory letters and telegrams, 105 of which were printed in a commemorative volume. Of these letters, 48 were in English. The second most prominent language was Latin, which was used in 28 instances (or about one fourth of the total) followed by German (21) and French (5).[1071] Of the letters in Latin, 8 came from universities in the United States and Canada (The Catholic University of America, Lafayette, Luther, Princeton, Rutgers, Wesleyan, Trinity University [Toronto], and the University of Toronto), while the remaining ones came from Europe.[1072]

The letters received by Yale were often ornate, not only linguistically but also materially. The Latin letter from Wesleyan, for example, was written "on hand embossed, illuminated parchment scroll, the scroll being inclosed in a roll lined with cardinal silk."[1073] Typically these letters identified points of connection between the congratulating institution and either the history of Yale or some other episode in American history. For example, the letter from the University of Klausenburg drew attention to the Hungarian Stephen Parmenius's role in the 1583 English expedition to New England (see section 14) and to Captain John Smith's military service for Hungary prior to his role at Jamestown, and it also acknowledged that America had graciously received numerous Hungarian immigrants.

The following is the letter sent by Princeton University, whose first three presidents were Yale graduates. Princeton's delegation consisted of seven members—the President, two deans (one of whom was the eminent classicist Andrew Fleming West), and the future President of the United States, Woodrow Wilson, who was a Professor of Jurisprudence and Politics. It was the largest delegation in attendance. (Harvard appointed eight delegates, but two were unable to attend; likewise Glasgow appointed seven, but one was unable to attend.) Princeton's President, moreover, was one of eight attendees upon whom Yale conferred an honorary Doctor of Laws. Princeton also sent a delegation of twenty-five students from the Senior class, dressed as tigers, who were undoubtedly conspicuous in the proceedings.

Universitati Yalensi Matri Dilectae Honore Distinctae Devinctae Amore Fausta Felicia Fortunata Pientissime Exoptat Filiarum Primigenia Universitas Princetoniensis

Haud facile exprimere possumus, viri doctissimi Yalenses, quantis afficiamur gaudiis quod Universitas vestra per annos ducentos paulatim ex minimis crescens hodie ad apicem honorum eminere longe lateque conspicitur. Quis in illo fidei virgulto parvulo iampridem in agro vestro posito eodemque fortunis tempestatum adhuc dubiis obnoxio hanc arborem scientiae magnam cuius in ramis requieverunt omnes artes et disciplinae liberales tunc providere potuisset? Parvi sane illi dies. Quis autem dispexit dies parvos? Profecto ea non sunt parva censenda sine quibus magna constare non possunt.

Quod optanti divum promittere nemo
Auderet volvenda dies en attulit ultro,

olim cecinit vates Mantuanus.[1074] Vos autem meliora in schola Christi didicistis. Non enim volvenda dies sed Deus Ipse qui maiores vestros transtulit eorumque posteros sustinet haec quoque attulit.

Ut pervenire ad summa nisi ex principiis non potest ita nihil rerum Deus voluit magnum effici cito. Longa utique porrigitur annorum series quae vestram academiam in immensum crescentem comitatur. Quoniam insuper accedit quod in ratione rerum congruenter naturae crescentium summa in principiis latent principia autem in summis patent, vetera vestra praeconia sunt novorum. Diu ergo vigeant illae fidei radices pristinae ex quibus pullulaverunt in vestra Universitate tot rami scientiae nobiles quorum sub tegmine grato requiescentes, velut in umbraculis ulmorum vestrarum pulcherimarum, habitent filii vestri et filiorum filii multum studiis incumbentes multa hominibus profutura sibi proponentes multa secum volventes de veritate aeterna quae velut sol alia et eadem iterum iterumque nascetur.

Franciscus L. Patten,[1075] Praeses

Datum in Aula Nassovica[1076]
Idibus Octobribus, MCMI

Source: *The Record of the Celebration of the Two Hundredth Anniversary of the Founding of Yale College* (New Haven: Yale University, 1902), 547–48. See also *Princeton University Bulletin* 13 (1901): 2–3.

98 African Americans and Latin (1902)

Recent scholarship has drawn attention to the achievements of nineteenth and twentieth century African American classicists.[1077] Still to be explored, however, is the experience with the classics by African Americans of these eras who were not professional classicists. Typically this experience resulted from having taken a classical course of studies at one of the numerous colleges and universities emerging in the post-bellum era that were dedicated to the education of African Americans, later known as HBCUs (Historically Black Colleges and Universities).

In the late 1860s the requirements to matriculate in the Collegiate Department at Howard University were comparable to those at Harvard, and the curriculum was more stringent than Harvard's.[1078] A student seeking admission to Howard for the academic year 1868–69 was examined on Latin Grammar, two books of Caesar, six orations of Cicero, Vergil's *Eclogues*, *Georgics*, and six books of the *Aeneid*, Sallust's *Catiline*, and Harkness's *Prose Composition*, in addition to Greek grammar, three books of Xenophon's *Anabasis*, and the first two books of the *Iliad*. (These readings would have been covered by a student enrolled in Howard's Preparatory Department.) Similarly, a student seeking admission to Harvard for that same academic year was examined on Latin grammar, Latin composition, all of Vergil, all of Caesar, and select orations of Cicero, in addition to Felton's *Greek Reader*, the entire *Anabasis*, three books of the *Iliad* (except for the catalogue of ships), Greek grammar, and Greek composition.

Once enrolled in Howard's Collegiate Department, a student in 1868–69 would have pursued the following Latin curriculum: Freshman Year: Livy, Horace's *Odes*, Arnold's Prose Composition; Sophomore Year: Horace's *Epistles* and *Satires*, Cicero's *De Officiis*, or *De Senectute* and *De Amicitia*, Tacitus's *Germania* and *Agricola*; Junior

Year: Juvenal's *Satires*, plays by Terence and Plautus, Quintilian. This student's Harvard counterpart similarly spent Freshman year studying Livy, Horace's *Odes* and *Epodes*, Cicero's *Epistles* and *Tusculan Disputations* and composition, but in sophomore year Latin was no longer required, although it was available as an elective.

Howard was not alone in its embrace of the classics. Lincoln University (founded in 1854 as the Ashmun Institute) required a knowledge of Latin and Greek Grammar for those seeking admission to its Collegiate Department, and once enrolled students studied Latin and Greek every semester, progressing through Caesar, Sallust, Cicero, Vergil, Arnold's Prose Composition, Tacitus, and Horace.[1079] Lincoln's administrators protested against those who, preferring to emphasize industrial courses, wanted to deny African Americans a classical and humanistic education.[1080]

Those HBCUs that operated primarily as Normal Schools, i.e., to train teachers, occasionally required students in the Academic track to undertake the study of Latin during freshman year, and to proceed through a sequence of classical authors for three or four years. This was the case, for example, at Storer College, founded in Harpers Ferry in 1867.[1081] At Shaw University in Raleigh, founded in 1865, during the academic year 1878–79, 192 students were pursuing the Normal Course, 27 the Scientific Course, and 48 the Classical Course, while 60 students were studying for the ministry. Those in the Classical (or College) course at Shaw took Latin throughout their first three years and began Greek during the second term of their third year.[1082]

A particular desideratum is to locate original Latin compositions by African Americans. A starting point for such an inquiry would be a search through the archives of those HBCUs that featured Latin salutatory addresses on class days or at commencement exercises. At Lincoln University, for example, a Latin salutatory was a staple of such occasions. Not surprisingly, students delivering these orations often went on to have distinguished careers. Archibald Henry Grimké (1849–1930), the future Vice-President of the NAACP, gave the 1870 Latin oration at Lincoln. Thomas Heath Slater (1865–1952), later a doctor in Atlanta, delivered the 1887 address. (He is also said to have delivered a Greek salutatory on Class Day.[1083]) Francis Cecil Sumner (1895–1954), later a pathbreaking psychologist, delivered Lincoln's 1915 salutatory, which was considered "one of the best of recent years."[1084] Theodore Milton Selden (1897–1922), recently commemorated by the University of Pennsylvania Law School, gave the 1919 speech.[1085]

Additional material will likely be found in the archives of those Catholic religious orders that cultivated African American clergy. For example, in 1893 Joseph Griffin, an African American seminarian at Epiphany Apostolic College in Baltimore, was selected to give the Latin address of welcome to the visiting Apostolic Delegate, Archbishop Francisco Satolli.[1086]

The following is a valedictory Latin poem written by James Kwegyir Aggrey (1875–1927), a student at Livingstone College in Salisbury, North Carolina.[1087] Aggrey, the oldest of eight children, was born in Anamabu on the British Gold Coast (present-day Ghana). Baptized at the age of eight and educated in a Wesleyan Methodist school in Cape Coast, Aggrey matriculated at Livingstone, which had been founded in 1879 by A.M.E. Zion ministers to train African Americans to undertake missionary work in the South and in Africa. By the time of Aggrey's arrival, the school had expanded its focus to include the education of African students who would then return home to evangelize.

Aggrey won two gold medals at Livingstone—the S.C. Fuller Prize for English composition and the Bishop C.R. Harris prize for general scholarship and deportment. He gave the third Latin Salutatory address and the first Greek oration in the history of the college, and he is said to have been the first Livingstone student to write a Latin poem.[1088] Following his 1902 graduation, Aggrey earned a master's degree from Livingstone (1912) and pastored two congregations in North Carolina. During the summers he took graduate coursework in sociology at Columbia University. Eventually he earned an M.A. from Columbia and completed the coursework necessary for a Ph.D.

Aggrey was a popular preacher and lecturer not only in the United States but also abroad, and he twice traveled to Africa as a delegate of the Phelps-Stokes fund. In 1924 he returned to Africa and became Vice-Principal of Achimota College. It has been suggested that Aggrey represented a synthesis between two competing educational visions for African Americans (and for Africans): he continued to advocate the scholastic path that he himself had traveled, but he also embraced the industrial and agricultural initiatives of Booker T. Washington and George Washington Carver. Moreover, he was insistent that Christianity, more than scholastic achievement or agricultural development, was essential for any solution of the race problem and for any authentic emergence from colonialism. Aggrey died suddenly on a visit to Columbia in 1927 while he was attempting to complete his doctoral dissertation. He is buried in Salisbury, North Carolina.

Aggrey sustained an interest in the classics throughout his life. He studied Latin and Greek with his wife, and he is reported to have read Horace's *Odes* and *Epistles* to his child in utero. While at Columbia's summer school in 1914 Aggrey wrote a Latin valedictory ode entitled "Bene Valete," which so impressed his sociology professor that Aggrey was asked to read it aloud to the class on the final day of the term.[1089]

CLASSIS CARMEN (MCMII)

Quattuor annos hilaritatis et laetitiae hos
Per lucos vagati sumus. Hoc loco manus almae nos

Duxerunt ad aetatem. Sed nunc, Alma Mater, nos iubes
Decedere. Hac occasione congregamus multis
Lacrimis et pectoribus maestis; habentesque corda
Amantia salutamus vos, nos salutamus omnes.

Scimus pro patria mori dulce et decorum, atque
Vivere pro eadem dulcius. Abituri sumus
Auxilium ut feramus—quanquam viae sint diversae
Tamen finis unus—ius obtinere, pravum fugare,
Lucem dare et noctem expellere auxilio Dei.
Tandem praeceptores atque amici, bene valete!

Source: William Frank Fonvielle, *Reminiscences of College Days* (printed for the author by Edwards & Broughton, 1904), 102.

99 Tobacco (1903)

As soon as it was imported into Europe, tobacco began to elicit strong reactions.[1090] Perhaps its first appearance in Latin verse was an ode by the Scottish poet George Buchanan, "Doctus ab Hesperiis rediens Nicotius oris."[1091] The Dutch-born physician Raphael Thorius (d. 1625), who studied at Oxford and practiced medicine in London, wrote a lengthy *Hymnus Tabaci*, which according to one scholar of British Neo-Latin was the most popular Latin poem in seventeenth-century England, printed in at least four editions and translated three times into English.[1092]

The following ode to tobacco was composed by Robert J. Bonner (1868–1946), who at the time was a professor of Latin and Instructor of Law at Stetson University in Deland, Florida.[1093] A native of Ontario, Bonner studied classics at the University of Toronto before completing Law School and being admitted to the Bar in Ontario. He soon opted to undertake graduate studies in classics at the University of Chicago, working under the lawyer-turned-classicist Paul Shorey. Bonner taught for three years at Stetson, during which time he authored *Greek Composition* (1903), and then spent four decades at Chicago, publishing frequently in Greek law and history and sponsoring a research group that came to be known as the Bonner School of Greek Law.

The catalogues of Stetson in the early 1900s stipulate that sub-collegiate students under the age of twenty-one were strictly prohibited from using tobacco, although the 1903 catalogue makes an exception if written permission were obtained from parents or guardians.[1094]

Quam divam potius te, Nicotina era,
Collaudare decet, quae colis insulam
Praeoptatam aliis Hesperii maris,
Seu poscas fidibus, carmine seu velis?

Tu curas misero pectore dimoves;
Spes et tu revocas mentibus anxiis.
Terrarum domini membraque barbari
Picti te pariter sollicitant prece.

Quem non mirifice post epulas tuo
Adventu recreas? Ingenio admoves
Tormentum leviter, dux sapientiae
Dulcis. Quid sine te non gravius pati?

Tandem, oro, statuas ducere naribus
Tus fumans penitus, nam foliis tibi
Flavis ara calet plurima fictilis;
Nec fragrant violae nec rosa suavius.

Semper virginibus vel pueris nefas
Ritus scire deae, nec veniat licet
Si quis caeruleum palluit[1095] halitum.
Coetu verba procul tristia pellite.

Large pone, puer, ligna super foco.
Nunc sermone iuvat noctis amabilis
Horas nos vario degere posteri
Securos quia nos, alma dea, aspicis.

Source: *University of Toronto Monthly* 3 (1903): 156.

100 The Miseries of African Americans (1903)

In the late summer of 1903 a slender red 46-page volume marked "Confidentiale" and bearing the title *De miserabili conditione Catholicorum nigrorum in America* arrived in Rome at the offices of the Sacred Congregation Propaganda Fide. An epitaph on the title page read "Et ait Dominus ad Caïn: Ubi est Abel frater tuus? Qui respondit: Nescio. Num custos fratris mei sum ego?" (Genesis 4:9). The author was Ferdinand Joseph Marie Ghislain Anciaux (1858–1931), a Belgian priest who had labored for nine years among Native Americans and African Americans in Oklahoma (known then as Indian Territory) and Virginia. With "language of white-hot passion,"[1096] Anciaux detailed the plight of African American Catholics in the United States ("pessima conditio Nigrorum"). Not only citing his personal observations, experiences, and conversations, but also mentioning by name high-ranking prelates, Anciaux methodically described in Latin the inferior status that African Americans held in every aspect of life: political, civil, juridical, social, and religious. He concluded by recommending the establishment of a prelature (somewhat akin to a diocese) devoted solely to the evangelization of the 10,000,000 African Americans within the United States.

Anciaux's report reached the highest circles in Rome, including Pope Pius X (*r.* 1903–14). In the following year Cardinal Girolamo Maria Gotti, the prefect of the Propaganda Fide, sent a blunt letter to the Apostolic Delegate in the United States instructing him to inform the American bishops that they should eradicate the humiliating, unchristian treatment of African Americans. In 1907 the United States bishops established the Catholic Board for Work among Colored People, which took up several initiatives over the next two decades, such as the admission of African Americans to Catholic colleges and universities and the ordination of African Americans to the priesthood.

Anciaux himself evidently was motivated to write his Latin missive by a homily that had been delivered by Rev. Joseph Slattery in Baltimore in June 1902. Preaching on the occasion of the priestly ordination of the African American John Henry Dorsey, Slattery proclaimed "a scathing sermon" that he later dubbed "his farewell to the Church," in which he indicted white Catholics for their prejudice against African Americans and castigated some of the misguided approaches towards their evangelization.[1097] Slattery's homily elicited strong reaction. The critical response of one Baltimore priest, who apparently represented other clergy of the archdiocese, was published in the *Baltimore Sun*.[1098] But Anciaux, who at the time was establishing a mission to African Americans in Lynchburg, Virginia, offered his support. In response to Slattery's homily Anciaux penned "Plain Facts for Fair Minds" (August 27, 1902), in which he sharply criticized what he deemed to be the segregationist, prejudiced, and timid mentality of many American Catholics, including members of the clergy and hierarchy.

One consequence of "Plain Facts for Fair Minds," was that Anciaux was forced by his bishop (a fellow Belgian) to leave the Diocese of Richmond. He returned to Oklahoma where he supervised the integrated Holy Family School in Langston.[1099] But he also found time to retreat to a house owned by the Christian Brothers in the small community of Gray Horse, where he wrote his impassioned Latin treatise.

In 1904 Anciaux joined the Josephites, a community of priests and brothers devoted to evangelizing African Americans. Amidst chronic health problems and the fallout from his fiery writings, he worked in Mobile, Baltimore, Houston, St. Louis, and New Orleans. He returned to Belgium in 1920.[1100]

The following are extracts from Anciaux's Latin missive to Rome, dated "Pawhuska, Territorii Indorum, die 21[a] Junii, 1903."

Pessima conditio Nigrorum

Multi dicunt omnia bene procedere, nigros bene tractari et nihil deesse eorum felicitati et spirituali instructioni, dummodo bonam voluntatem prae se ferant.

Hoc plane nego. Hoc dico esse mendacium, aut, ut mitius loquar, *maximum errorem*. A novem fere annis sum missionarius nigrorum Americae,[1101] et eorum conditionem esse lugendam dico. Existunt decreta Concilii Baltimorensis et synodales regulae prescribentes maximam pro nigris caritatem,[1102] sed *praeiudicii americani causa* saepe fit ut decreta ista *vi careant*. Ianua Ecclesiae Catholicae nondum *vere ac plene* nigris aperta est.

Video eos sicut canes foras stare. Video, sicut in parabola Evangelii, sacerdotes et levitas transeuntes et de paupere vulnerato Samaritano non curantes:[1103] "Parvuli petierunt panem, et non erat qui frangeret eis."[1104]

Status politicus nigrorum

In meridionali parte Foederatorum Statuum Americae nigri neque *eligi* neque *eligere* possunt, exceptis paucis privilegiatis. Hoc aperte contrarium est Constitutioni Foederatorum Statuum proclamanti *aequalitatem in iuribus* sine distinctione coloris.[1105] Sed *nuperrime* particulares leges variis in locis ita confectae sunt ut nigris ius eligendi auferatur, praetextu ignorantiae aut incapacitatis, dum cives albi coloris etiam ignorantes aut incapaces *eligere* et *eligi* possunt. Sed in hoc puncto non immoror cum mere politicum sit. Utinam *hoc tantum* genus iniustitiae adesset in America!

Status civilis-socialis-iuridicus

Conditio Iuridica

Dum in Virginia morarer, (anno 1901), herus famulum de gravi crimine "*suspectum*" propria manu occidit; deinde coram iudice secundum legem comparuit. Iudex **sine ulla poena** eum dimisit, quamvis *privata auctoritate* et *sine ulla necessitate* hominem occiderit. Immo istius heri advocatus coram tribunali verba Evangelii profanans dixit: "*Euge, serve bone et fidelis!*[1106] Hoc fecisti ad tuam familiam protegendam."

Status Socialis

Nigri ab omni aequalitate sociali prorsus excluduntur. Neque eis fas est in curribus viae ferreae, sive in publicis cauponibus, vel in hortis, vel alibi cum albis sedere.

Unum tantum exemplum adducam: frigente hieme in Oklohoma publicum cauponem ingrediens cafeum petivi, quod mihi alboque amico meo cito allatum est, sed *nigro* cuidam iuveni mecum degenti prorsus denegatum est. Nequidem *cafeum bibere stando* ei concessum est; unice quia nigri coloris erat. Et ita tractantur non soli nigri veri, sed ii omnes qui aliquid, licet minimum nigri coloris habent; ita ut omnis qui guttulam africani sanguinis indicium praebeat ab omni prorsus sociali contactu excludatur.

Ab omnibus fere publicis officiis, nisi infimis, nigri excluduntur. Praesidens Roosevelt magnam invidiam et acerbissimas increpationes in se excitavit eo quod quandoque aliquos *nigros* merito dignos ad altiora quaedam publica officia *promovere* ausus fuerit.[1107]

Sed forsan mihi dicent adversarii: "Numquid nigros famulos nostros non bene tractamus, eis tribuentes cibum potumque et de eorum valetudine curantes?

Respondeam: "Utique! Bene eos tractatis in quantum eorum labore indigetis. Immo, dummodo velint esse quasi equi et pecudes, de eis curam habetis; eis autem si *homines* esse clamant, cito "*Raca*" dicitis."[1108]

Status Religiosus Nigrorum

Supradicta quasi praeliminaria sint! Veniam ad gravissimam et moestissimam quaestionem, nempe: *statum americanorum nigrorum in Ecclesia...*

Omnis spes certe reponi debet in zelo *missionariorum* et in *maxima facilitate nigris procuranda ecclesias catholicas cum albis adeundi.*

Sed heu, quid video?

Sacerdotes fere omnes (etiam piissimi) adeo alborum civium reprehensionem timent ut pro nigris *minimum conatum* adhibere vix audeant; immo alii tanto praeiudicio imbuti sunt ut dicant: "*De nigris cura non est mihi, nec ad meum ovile pertinent isti.*"

Sacerdos quidam de me loquendo dicebat: "*De nigris curando tempus et pecunias in vanum dissipat;*" et alius me alloquendo dicebat "*Quaenam tibi ratio esse potest ut de nigris tantopere sollicitus sis?*"

In multis ecclesiis nigri angustum despectumve locum habent, qui anglice vocatur: "back-side" aut "gallery"; suam ecclesiam adire nequeunt, nisi humiliationem subeundo.[1109]

Source: Joseph Anciaux, *De miserabili conditione Catholicorum nigrorum in America* (Namur: James Godenne, 1903), 7–9, 10–13, 14–15.

101 Winter (1905)

The rise of modern universities and the rapid development of scientific research in the post-bellum era dislodged the study of the classical languages from their position of prominence in American higher education.[1110] For example, in the 1850s a Harvard student devoted 40% of his coursework over the first three years to the classics, but by 1900, after the reorganization of Harvard's curriculum by President Charles W. Eliot, only a third of Harvard's first-year students opted to study Latin at all.[1111] According to one historian, "to be modern and American in the early twentieth century meant doing science,"[1112] and for many educators Latin was increasingly deemed incompatible with, and even detrimental to, this imperative.

Catholic colleges were not immune to these changes. Eventually even the Jesuits, though often reluctantly, made adjustments to their curriculum, first by introducing a commercial course as an alternative to their traditional classical course and then by reducing requirements in the classical course itself.[1113] But in the late nineteenth and early twentieth centuries, Jesuit colleges resisted the disintegration of a core curriculum based on classical literature, even as they sought to incorporate the sciences. For many years they were successful. When Daniel Coit Gilman, the first President of Johns Hopkins University, visited the Jesuit seminary in Woodstock, Maryland, he was struck by the "fluency in Latin" he encountered as well as by "the amount of time given to science."[1114] Similarly, in 1919 the Golden Jubilee of Woodstock Seminary was celebrated not only with a Latin disputation, a Latin poem, and Latin letters of congratulation, but also with a lecture on subatomic structure.[1115] It was not uncommon in the late nineteenth and early twentieth centuries to find Jesuit professors who taught or researched in the sciences but were also renowned for their Ciceronian Latin compositions (see section 84).[1116]

Francis A. Tondorf (1870–1929), a native of Boston, exemplifies this dual commitment to the classics and to science.[1117] Tondorf, who studied for a time at Johns Hopkins (1897–99) and earned a Ph.D. at Georgetown (1914), spent twenty-seven years at Georgetown as assistant in the astronomical observatory, professor of physics, professor of geology, head of the Medical School's Department of Physiology, and for many years director of the Seismological Observatory. In this last role he worked closely with the United States Weather Bureau.[1118] He won acclaim for being the first American seismographer to alert the American press about the calamitous Tokyo earthquake of 1923. It was Tondorf's aspiration to develop a method for predicting earthquakes, although he acknowledged that this was many years away.[1119] In 1929, the year of his death, Tondorf acquired for Georgetown—the only place in the United States to have one—a Galitzin horizontal seismograph, the most advanced measuring device available.[1120]

Tondorf also maintained a life-long interest in Latin. The archives at Georgetown University contain three notebooks of Latin verse from his seminary days in the early 1890s.[1121] An obituary mentions his "proficiency" in Latin prose and verse as well as his valuable skill as a "lapidarist."[1122]

The following Latin poem by Tondorf was printed in the January 1905 edition of the *Georgetown College Journal*, a literary magazine that first appeared in 1872 and sought to provide "encouragement of literature among the students and maintenance in Georgetown College of a paper worthy of the institution" (see section 89).[1123] Subsequent issues of the journal contained poetic responses to Tondorf's poem, one of which was in Greek.[1124]

Querela hiemalis

Frigidus en! saeva Boreas incedit ab Arcto,
    Solem captivum dum Capricornus habet.
Pascitur ac nullo Zephyri nunc flamine campus,
    Tectaque brumali sub nive terra silet.
Turdus nec patulis celatur frondibus ulmi,
    Et niveo quercus pondere triste gemit.
Rivus ubi, nuper crepitans per laeta virecta,
    Concrevit, radios duplicat ecce iubar.
Et rosa, miraris? teneris viduata labellis
    Dormitat tectis, somnia veris alens.
Lilia dum dubitant calycem reserare modestum,
    Ne rigeat ventis aurea lingua sua;
Cur viola exiguum, quaeras, haud spirat odorem?
    Frustra tentaret, dum riget aura gelu.
Sic Capitolini prati dolet angulus omnis
    Tristitia et marcens tempora verna cupit:
Queis reditis campus noster resonabit alumnis;
    Floribus hortus ovans iam paradisus erit.

Source: *Georgetown College Journal* 33 (1905): 153, available at DigitalGeorgetown.

102 A Presidential Nomination in Latin (1907)

On the evening of March 18, 1907 the Phi Beta Kappa chapter at Yale held its 127th annual banquet, with some 150 persons in attendance, including most members of the faculty, several Phi Beta Kappa alumni, and distinguished speakers, notably the U.S. Secretary of War, William Howard Taft (1857–1930). The celebration was, in the estimate of one Yale professor, "the greatest gathering at any Yale dinner."[1125] A New Haven newspaper judged that this banquet marked the "renaissance" of the Yale chapter of Phi Beta Kappa, membership in which was no longer "an empty honor" but was now becoming "one of the most coveted college prizes a man can win."[1126] Prior to the initiation of members of the class of 1908, Tracy Peck (1838–1921), Emeritus Professor of Latin at Yale, rose to deliver the following tribute to Secretary Taft. This brief speech caused a minor sensation at the time—newspapers around the country carried reports of it—and it was regarded as the "first formal nomination" of Taft for the U.S. Presidency.[1127]

Peck, born in Bristol, Connecticut, graduated from Yale in 1861, having received the Berkeley Prize for Latin composition and having given the Latin oration during his Junior year.[1128] Deterred by poor health from fighting in the Civil War, he studied classics in Germany (Berlin, Jena, Bonn) before returning to the United States to teach, eventually at Cornell (1871–80) and then at Yale. Highly regarded as a scholar, he served as President of the APA (1885–86) and director of the American School of Classical Studies in Rome (1898–1900). Peck did not publish extensively, but he was co-editor of the College Series of Latin Authors, to which he contributed a text of Livy XXI–XXII (1893, co-authored with J.B. Greenough). He is buried in the Protestant cemetery in Rome, where he lived for the last thirteen years of his life, enjoying close connections to the American expatriate community, giving lectures before learned societies, and socializing with members of the Catholic hierarchy.

Several examples of Peck's engagement with active Latin survive. According to Yale President Arthur Twining Hadley, "What Tracy Peck was as a Latin scholar you cannot understand, unless you had the pleasure of hearing him stand on the platform and speak Latin."[1129] In addition to his speech for Taft—no doubt delivered in the restored pronunciation, which he staunchly advocated[1130]—Peck also delivered an Oratio Gratulatoria at the 1886 Yale inauguration of Rev. Timothy Dwight[1131] and a Latin address at the Darwin Centennial in Cambridge, England (1909),[1132] and he composed a Latin address to celebrate the birthday of the American painter Elihu Vedder (1836–1923), who like Peck was a long-time resident of Rome.[1133] Additionally Peck translated into Latin the concluding portion of Tennyson's "Ulysses"[1134] as well as four stanzas of Tennyson's "Enid,"[1135] and in the fall of 1904 he spoke Latin with Pope Pius X when he was received in private audience.[1136]

During the academic year 1883–84 Peck was a member of a faculty committee charged with making a final recommendation to the Yale Corporation concerning curricular changes,[1137] which included an overall reduction (temporary, it was argued) in Greek and Latin in order to allow for the study of French or German. Whatever his personal opinions, Peck defended the changes in print, arguing that although culture and civilization were ineluctably based on the classical world, "in the long run, any study which is cosseted and forced by hot-house methods can have but a sickly vitality."[1138]

Taft, for his part, had delivered the Latin oration as salutatorian at Yale (class of 1878), and later in life—following his Presidency—he contributed a statement of support in connection with Andrew Fleming West's 1917 Princeton conference on the classics.[1139] A long-time member of the Yale Corporation—in 1899 he turned down an offer to become Yale's President—Taft opposed a 1923 initiative to remove the Latin requirement from admission to B.A. programs, reportedly declaring "Over my dead body."[1140] By means of what one scholar dubs "devious parliamentary procedures," Yale dropped the requirement in 1931, one year after Taft's death.[1141]

Te, rei nostratis militaris Praefecte,[1142] grati laetique salutamus. Te non Martem solum, sed etiam Minervam colere gaudemus, precamurque ut tuo auspicio imperioque templum Iani sit perpetuo clausum.[1143]

Mater Yalensis filios quoscunque apud Lares familiares vultu benigno videt, sed animo laetissimo illos excipit qui, e ministeriis pro patria, vel potius pro genere humano factis, coronas triumphosque reportant.[1144] Tu quidem, quidnam est quod his paucis annis non feceris? Et omnia quae tangis ita perficis et exornas ut quod Romani, de Catone prisco iudicabant, idem nos de te iudicemus: "tibi versatile ingenium sic pariter ad omnia est ut natus ad id unum videaris quodcunque agas."[1145] Si igitur vox populi te ad munera ampliora,—etiam ad summum Reipublicae magistratum vocabit, hanc populi vocem credimus fore vocem Dei.

Source: James M. Lamberton, ed., *Tricennial Supplement to Quarter-Centenary Record of the Class of 1878 Yale University* (privately published, 1909), 19.[1146]

103 Spring (1907)

In April 1907, at the first meeting of the Classical Association of the Atlantic States (then called the Classical Association of the Middle States and Maryland), Harry Thurston Peck (1856–1914), the Anthon Professor of Latin at Columbia, presented arguments in favor of resuming the practice of Latin Verse Composition in American colleges. Latin poetry, Peck claimed, was not fully intelligible apart from a consideration of form, and the best way to appreciate form is to attempt to replicate it. He allowed that verse composition should not become an end in itself (as, he argued, had happened in England), but he advocated that it ought to be seen as a valuable means. In his experience, students who were new to this exercise could learn to write "quite respectable" verse after spending one hour per week over the course of a year.[1147]

After summarizing Peck's talk, the editors of *The Classical Weekly* printed examples of contemporary Latin poetry. One of these was "Birota Velocissima" by the Italian priest Maurus Ricci, which had been published in the Latin newspaper *Vox Urbis* (see section 105). Another consisted of four elegiac couplets by William Hamilton Kirk (1857–1947) of Rutgers. A third (the first selection presented below) was the poem "Ver Pulchrum" that had been printed in the *Milwaukee Journal.*

Some controversy surrounded the authorship of this last poem. Initially it was said to have been the work of Edward W. Hawley, a Minnesota lawyer, who had written it while he was a student at Harvard, but a correspondent to the *Milwaukee Journal* challenged this claim. When the editors of *The Classical Weekly* attempted to verify the authorship by contacting Hawley directly, they received by way of response, in two separate installments, the three sapphic stanzas printed below. The editors could not resist identifying a few errors of quantity in Hawley's verses, but they remarked: "It is most refreshing to find a man immersed in the cares of a large practice and deeply engaged in municipal politics still keeping up his interest in the writing of Latin verses."[1148] Nonetheless, prior to their printing, Hawley's verses were "slightly modified" by Princeton Professor George D. Kellogg.

Hawley (1867–1952), a native of Red Wing, Minnesota, gave the valedictory speech upon his graduation from Hobart College (1888), and he earned a B.A. at Harvard, with honors in Classics. He is said to have studied Latin verse composition under Frederic De Forest Allen at Harvard (cf. section 92). After briefly teaching math in Illinois, he earned two law degrees from the University of Minnesota (LL.B. 1893, LL.M. 1894) and then practiced law in Minneapolis for over fifty years. A man of diverse interests, he is said to have taken notes in Greek during meetings of the Minneapolis City Council.[1149]

I

Ver pulchrum atque nitens prope adest nunc sero reductum;
Aura Noti lenis Boreae flatus superavit.
Vincula frigida nunc amnes celeres modo frangunt,
Turbate in mare se evolvunt fugiuntque loquaces.
Sub tecto aedificat nidum iam sedula hirundo;
In montes pecudes, armenta in prata profecta;
Questibus implentur saltus silvaeque columbae;
Dulce onus ab campis domum apes iam vespere portant.
Vitis claviculis "ulmo coniuncta marito"[1150]
Robusto truncoque haerens gemmas pedetentim
Trudit. Ver reddit laeta omnia amoenaque praesens.
Cur semel aetatis ver solo homini modo venit?

II

Si rogaris me faceremne versus
quos super nomen mihi pervideres,
haud velim captare senex dolose:
sum reus ipse.

Si tamen captes aliud poema
ex eodem, me piget hoc referre,
"Quam senem temptare tenella facta
stultius est nil."

Heu! nihil possum tibi me roganti
de poesi reddere praeter hoce,
"His labor" certe, "est opus hoc, Latine
versificare."

Sources: *Classical Weekly* 1 (1907): 59; 3 (1910): 238.

104 Harvard without Eliot: Oratio Salutatoria (1909)

Harvard and Princeton retain the tradition of a Latin speech during commencement exercises, a practice that dates back to their foundations. Numerous colleges and schools throughout the United States once had similar traditions, and at times Greek and even Hebrew have been incorporated into these proceedings. In the latter nineteenth century this custom faced increasing opposition. For example, in June 1888 the *Columbia Spectator* lamented the persistence of these outworn traditions, especially in an era "when humbug is at a discount." The editors exclaimed that it was "almost farcical" to feature languages that "nobody speaks and very few understand," and they expressed the hope that only English would be used at the next Commencement.[1151]

Yet Commencement Day at Harvard in June 1909 was "carried out in all its ancient formality."[1152] The sheriffs of Middlesex and Suffolk counties walked in the academic procession. Numerous dignitaries were present, including the Secretary of the Navy, Princeton's Woodrow Wilson, and the Governor and Lieutenant Governor of Massachusetts. Those in attendance also heard much Latin.

Harvard's 1909 commencement exercises were especially notable because they marked the first time in forty years that diplomas were not conferred by Charles William Eliot, who had retired as President a little over one month earlier. Instead, the new President, A. Lawrence Lowell (1856–1943), who would be formally installed that coming fall, presided over the exercises. Yet contemporary newspaper accounts—which, it seems, were focused rather on the Harvard-Yale rowing competition—leave no doubt that commencement day belonged to Eliot. In a first for Harvard, Eliot was made President Emeritus, and he was granted two honorary degrees, a Doctor of Laws and a Doctor of Medicine.[1153] These announcements elicited sustained applause from those in attendance. According to the headline in the *Boston Herald*, this was the "greatest demonstration Sanders Theatre ever saw."[1154]

Following the opening prayer, the Latin oration was the first event of the formal exercises. The 1909 address was delivered by Fletcher Nichols Robinson. Originally from Southern Pines, North Carolina, Robinson had graduated from Reading High School in Massachusetts. A scholarship student at Harvard, Robinson graduated summa cum laude in Classics. Following graduation he taught Latin at Philips Exeter Academy.

In Omni Re Vincit Imitationem Veritas[1155]

Vobis omnibus, amici, qui ita frequentes ad hanc diem celebrandam convenistis, et singulis et universis multam dico salutem.

Atque omnium primum te, praeses,[1156] qui es nuper huic Americanarum universitatum vetustissimae clarissimaeque praefectus, qui iam diu in omni recto studio versaris, qui es artium humanarum doctissimus fautor adiutorque, te ante omnes iubeo salvere. Harvardianis cunctis de te gratulamur, neque minime gaudemus quod universitatem extollens collegium haud negleges.[1157] Te duce aetatem novam inimus, quae nomen Harvardianum doctrinae liberalis studio imbutum et ad fastigium gloriae videbit elatum.

Vos etiam salvete, consocii et curatores,[1158] per quos academia nostra, maxima illa veritatis origo, magna cum scientia propagatur.

Tu quoque, gubernator honestissime,[1159] salutem accipe et gratulationes nostras. Tibi enim contigit ut huius civitatis cursum accurate et praeclare dirigas. Quae in hac academia instituenda interfuit atque etiam nunc cum ea quasi habet coniunctionem. Itaque te ut amicum sociumque accipimus.

Tibi autem, O illustrissime,[1160] qui per annos quadraginta nostram universitatem maiore laude administravisti quam alii terras regnaverunt, qui plura effecisti quam ceteri cogitaverunt; quem in populo Americano civem principem habemus, tibi pro sodalibus meis omnibus plurimam dico salutem. Ubi tandem gentium melius praecepti mei exemplum inveniam? Nam semper veritatem fovisti, semper fraudi restitisti.

Decani,[1161] qui nos per hos quattuor annos tanta prudentia accepistis, tanta patientia habuistis, vos quoque iubeo salvere. Ducibus vobis et auctoribus veritatem secuti sumus, salvique ad hunc gradum pervenimus.

Et vos, professores eruditi,[1162] qui hominibus per annos tam multa clara inventa profertis, qui magis veritatem petitis quam famam, quibus tamen ne fama quidem deest, vos omnes salutamus. Nos enim et diligentia docuistis et eloquentia accendistis, neque quemquam hodie libentius spectamus.

Et alumni, quorum nonnulli artium fitis magistri vel etiam philosophiae doctores, nolite nos contemnere, sed mementote et vos olim baccalaureos fuisse. Atque vobis sincere de scientia vestra gratulamur, quae non solum veritatem invenit sed etiam hominibus prodest. In vobis autem positum est matris nostrae famam et servare et dilatare.

Et puellae, quibus, ut opinor, pulchriores vel hilariores neque ullae adhuc in hoc theatrum convenerunt neque umquam posthac convenient, vos ex animo vereque saluto. Etiam vos praeceptum meum confirmatis, nam in pulchritudine velut ceteris in rebus "vincit imitationem veritas."[1163] Nolite autem admirari nos his togis esse amictos; nam nisi ita insignes simus, quis credat nos esse baccalaureos?

Parentes ac familiares nostri, vos libenter salutamus; iam enim videre potestis quanta industria in studiis nostris laboraverimus. Haud opus est vos verba mea intellegere; satis erit si vos intellegere simulabitis. Quod Anglica verba intellexistis cum pecuniam quaesivimus, vobis magnas agimus gratias.

Et nunc ad vos, fratres, me converto, vos saluto ipsos. Vos hodie animadvertere volo quantum valeat veritas: quam in huius academiae sigillo ideo inscriptam videtis, quod in studiis persequendis ea omnibus est praeferenda. Haud aliter in vita tota, quoniam veritas optima est virtutum omnium, nihil diligentius expetere debemus. Neque consistit illa omnis in verbis veris dicendis, sed praesertim oportet ut erga ceteros animum praebeamus simplicem et verum. Si harum rerum memores et verbo et facto vitam sinceram degemus, tum demum erimus, ut ait litteratus ille, "veritatis cultores, fraudis inimici."[1164] Itaque hanc aetatem novam praecipue salutamus, quo veritas summa valitudine florebit. Hac spe, hac fide vos omnes iubemus salvere.

Source: *Secretary's First Report, Harvard College Class of 1909* (Cambridge, MA: Crimson, 1910), 229–30.

105 Nuntii Latini de America (1912)

The Italian architect Aristides Leonori (1856–1928) founded the Latin journal *Vox Urbis*, which aspired to offer commentary "de litteris et bonis artibus."[1165] Based in Rome, it had offices in Russia, England, and Canada. A typical issue had sixteen pages and consisted of a theological article, original poetry (much of it by the Redemptorist priest Francis Xavier Reuss, 1842–1926), original drama, news of the Pope's doings and those of the Sacred Roman Congregations, jokes, riddles, and a chronicle of world events. In general this journal was favorably received, and it was seen as an attempt to reestablish Latin as an international language of scientific or scholarly communication. Yet some had concerns about the subjects to be treated and about the Latinity employed. The *Classical Review* admonished: "If however the *Vox Urbis* is to become the *Vox Orbis*, it must spell Catholic with a small c. *Verb. sap*;" a decade later this same journal lamented that "the editor's ideas of Latin verse are not those of Terence."[1166]

Vox Urbis attracted an American readership, and in turn it regularly chronicled events in the United States.[1167] For example, the 1912 volume began by announcing that a Latin treatise by Theodore T. Chave of the United States, "De studiis quibus eget res latina," which had appeared in the previous year's volume, had merited one of the three silver papal medallions awarded annually. This same volume contained an illustrated article on the inhospitable climate of Alaska, "Induratae Nives in Alaska Peninsula."[1168]

The following excerpts, which pertain to the United States, are drawn from the *Annales* section for the year 1912. These news items are precursors to more recent initiatives, such as the *Nuntii Latini* produced by Radiophoniae Finnicae Generalis, Radio Bremen, Western Washington University, Vatican Radio, and others, or the Warsaw-based Latin newspaper *Ephemeris*.

die X. [mens. Ianuarii MCMXII] Neo Eboraco in urbe aedes Societatis parsimoniae provehendae, cui nomen *Equitable*, improviso incendio diruuntur. Humanae victimae duodecim lugentur, quarum quinque ex impavida vigilum cohorte.[1169]

d. XXII [mens. Februarii MCMXII] Houston, in urbe septemtrionalis Americae, septem domorum insulae, per longitudinem passuum mille, furente incendio absumuntur.[1170]

d. XXI [mens. Martii MCMXII] Sambois, in oppido Foederatarum Civitatum Americae Septentrionalis, dum cunicularii in fodinis operi intendunt, improvisum fit incendium, in quo miseri opifices fere omnes horrendam inveniunt mortem.[1171]

d. XXVI [mens. Martii MCMXII] Neo-Eboraco ex urbe notum fit in fodinis ad Bluseld [sic], ob praerupta nec opinato loca, cunicularios nonaginta calamitose sepultos esse.[1172]

d. VI [mens. Aprilis MCMXII] Mississipi [sic] flumen in Nordica America, oppositis hinc inde molibus abruptis, campos et oppida per aquarum cursus inundat magna tum rerum tum hominum ruina.[1173]

d. XVI [mens. Aprilis MCMXII] maxima quae huc usque vectoriarum navium exstructa fuerit nomine *Titan* ab Anglia ad civitates foederatas Americae septentrionalis primum profecta, noctu, in immensam glaciei molem ab arctico polo procedentem occurrens, disiicitur atque submergitur. Mille et sexcentae circiter humanae victimae inde heu lugentur![1174]

d. XXII [mens. Aprilis MCMXII] venti vis in Colorado Americana regione furens, quinquaginta et ultra domus civitatis Hennessey solo aequat.[1175]

d. VII [mens. Maii MCMXII] novae eaeque gravissimae inundationes Luisianam, septentrionalis Americae provinciam, late pessumdant.[1176]

d. XXX [mens. Maii MCMXII] Vilbour ille Wright, studiis atque machinis suis maximus aviationis impulsor, Deyton, Septentrionalis Americae in oppido, febri, curis omnibus rebelli, viridi adhuc aetate interit.[1177]

d. IX [mens. Iunii MCMXII] coram immensa populi multitudine Washingtonia in urbe monumentum, Christophoro Columbo dicatum, sollemni ritu inauguratur.[1178]

d. V [mens. Iulii MCMXII] Corming, in ferriviarum statione Neo-Eboracensis civitatis Septentrionalis Americae, ex curruum serie vapore actorum in aliam occursu, quadraginta viatorum victimae lugentur.[1179]

d. XII [mens. Iulii MCMXII] autem, in fodinis apud Moundsville, in civitate Virginia occidentali, operarii ad centum numero crudeli eidem fato immolantur.[1180]

d. XV [mens. Septemrbis MCMXII] Milwaukee in urbe Civitatum Foederatarum Americae Septemtrionalis, vita

Rooseveltii illius, earumdem civitatum quondam praesidis, scelesta insani cuiusdam manu petitur. Quamquam manuballistulae pila vulneratus Rooseveltius orationem per integram horam productam populo, ea die illic congregato, habet.[1181]

d. XI [mens. Novembris MCMXII] curruum series mercibus onustorum vapore actus in viatorum alteram, Iazoo, prope Novam Aurelianensem Americanam urbem, misere occurrit. Triginta viatorum mors horribilis, quinquaginta et ultra lugentur vulnera.[1182]

Source: *Vox Urbis* 15 (1912): 30, 47, 63, 78, 79, 95, 110, 126, 175, 191.

106 Storm in Alaska (1916)

The Jesuits arrived in Alaska in 1887, two decades after Andrew Johnson's Secretary of State William Seward negotiated its purchase from Russia for $7,200,000 and nine years before the discovery of gold in the Klondike. Eventually the Jesuits established missions throughout Alaska, including north of the Arctic Circle.

The following passage is from the *Historia Domus* of the mission of St. Mary, which at the time of writing (1916) was located in a remote southwestern village on the western bank of the Akulurak River, where the Jesuits maintained a boarding school.[1183]

All Jesuit residences kept house histories, which were typically written in Latin and followed a prescribed format: a listing of the Jesuits in residence, details concerning the condition and furnishings of the mission, a financial report, a description of dealings with local civic officials, and mention of any difficulties encountered. The following section concerns the difficulties occasioned by Alaska's short growing season and the effects of a major storm in January 1916. It was signed by Philip Delon, one of the two priests in residence. A native of France, Delon (1876–1930) had only arrived in Alaska the previous year.[1184]

Residentia Akulurakensis S^{ae} Mariae
St. Michael, P.O., Alaska

Historia Domus a 1^{a} Julii 1915 ad 30^{m} Junii 1916

Tota haec missio, si templum tres ante annos exstructum excipiatur, non est nisi congeries, ne dicam acervus, aedificiorum variis temporibus hac atque illac quomodocumque exstructorum, prout necessitas cogeret. Ventus et pluvia, glacies et nives ab eis plane vix arceri possunt: eis enim aditus patet per rimas quibus muri lignei ubicumque fere dehiscunt, stuppa utcumque referciantur.[1185]

Pro expensis victus et vestitus tum NN.[1186] tum etiam scholae puerorum puellarumque omnium, dependet haec nostra domus a fundo generali totius Alaskae Missionis. Excepta enim mercede menstrua octoginta dollariorum (\$80.[00]) quae, septies in anno, moniali a S[a] Ursula in schola missionis docenti a Gubernio Statuum Foederatorum tribuitur, (nostra enim schola quasi "publica" a Gubernio recensetur) reditus quivis hic prorsus desunt.[1187] Nec ulla omnino spes adest hortum seu agrum sic coli posse ut fructus sufficiant etiam pro paucis personis. Tempus enim quo tempestas aliquo modo propitia fieri posset ad hortum excolendum brevissimum est. Hoc anno, rivus Akulurak glacie desuper per totum solidatus est die 15 Octobris, 1915, nec tandem mare versus defluit confracta glacies nisi 2[a] Iunii 1916. Quattuor isti menses ab hieme ad hiemem, ob pluviam frequentem, aerisque frigiditatem, nullo modo propitii sunt ad fructus quosvis nutriendos et educendos. Tentamine pluries facto per viginti fere annos, rapa tantum (turnips) aliquo modo excolere potuimus.

Ineunte mense Ianuario 1916, nocte tertiam inter et quartam mensis diem, tempestas subito invaluit, ventusque tam validus crevit ut tecta quattuor ab nostris domibus prorsus tollerentur, aliaque plura partim destruerentur.[1188] Cumque magis magisque ingravesceret tempestas, magnus in nos eruit timor ne domus ipsa in qua degebamus funditus subverteretur, quam tamen calamitatem Dei benignitas a nobis avertit. Tectorum maxima pars vento trans flumen coniecta est, vepres inter et virgulta, ibique nive fere obruta, nec iterum transferri potuit absque arduo labore, dum thermometrum viginti quinque circiter gradus Fahrenheit infra zero notaret.

Eadem ista procella maxima intulit damna plurimis in vicis huius districtus. Cum ab occidente flaret ventus, glacies maris Beringensis confracta ingenti cum impetu in terram proiecta est, undaeque vento propulsae maxima glaciei fragmenta in terram ad plura millia passuum usque convexerunt. Quodam in pago, familia quaedam quinque personarum tota exstincta est, in propria domo fluctibus oppressa. Alio in pago, cum undae glaciem e mari vehentes per ianuam fenestrasque in domos irruerent, summo mane diei 4ae Ianuarii, inhabitantes omnes per fenestram quae in medio tecto, more regionis, sita est, egredi coacti sunt; ibique, supra tectum, propriae domus conferti, per horas quasi duodecim algentes iacuerunt, usque dum denuo recedente mari, sub tectum descendere potuerint.

Non multos post dies, Pater Delon cum per varios pagos excurreret, propriis intuens oculis vastationem procella illatam, ab indigenis nonnullis rogatus est ut apud Gubernium Statuum Foederatorum miseriam gentis eorum exponeret, levamenti auxiliique impetrandi causa. Nam pluribus in locis, cibaria ipsa piscis fumo exsiccati, ut mos est Eskimorum, vento aut glacie aut undis fere omnino destructa fuerant.

Source: Oregon Province Archives of the Society of Jesus, Alaska Mission Collection, Microfilm 772, reel 3, Akulurak Collection, Historia Domus et Annuae Litterae, pages 293–96 (original in Jesuit Archives and Research Center, St. Louis, Missouri).

107 Icarus and the U.S. Mail (1918)

Since airplanes had proven to be sufficiently safe and reliable during the First World War, the United States began regular air-mail service in 1918, at first between Washington, Philadelphia, and New York. The aircraft, which were initially supplied and staffed by the Army Air Service, flew a mininum of 90 mph at an elevation of 5000 feet. The 250-mile trip between Washington and New York, including the stop in Philadelphia to change planes, took three hours. As the *Brooklyn Times Union* noted, this was a significant improvement from the thirty-six hours that it had taken a stage-coach/railroad/steamboat team to make the trip in 1832.[1189]

On the morning of Wednesday, May 15 large crowds, including President Woodrow Wilson and the First Lady, gathered to watch Lieut. George L. Boyle take off in a Curtiss biplane from the Polo Grounds near the Washington Monument. His plane was carrying four pouches of letters, and he himself carried a map of his route strapped to his right leg. At the same time Lieut. Torrey Webb, an alumnus of Columbia University, took off from Belmont Park outside of New York City carrying several thousand letters. Webb reached Philadelphia exactly 90 minutes later and was relieved by Lieut J.C. Edgerton, who brought the mail the remaining 140 miles to Washington in another aircraft.[1190] Boyle, however, got lost shortly after takeoff, and was forced to land on a state highway in Waldorf, Maryland, about twenty-five miles southeast of Washington, and another aircraft had to be despatched to complete the run.[1191] But in the three months that the Army Air Service handled these runs—in August the United States Post Office Department assumed this route—ninety-six percent of the 270 flights were successful.[1192]

The following Latin poem commemorates the inauguration of this service. The author, Jesuit priest John C. Reville (1867–1929), born to Irish immigrants in

Brooklyn, was for many years the associate editor of *America*, where this poem was initially published.[1193] He was one of the initial faculty members of Fordham's Graduate School of Arts and Sciences, and for the last four years of his life he taught English literature and drama at Loyola University in New Orleans. The editors of *America* sent this poem by the initial airmail flight from New York to Washington. It was to be delivered to the faculty at Georgetown.

Icarus Alter

Daedalus ecce novus mirandas suscitat artes,
Ocior ac ventis Icarus alter adest.
Remigio alarum densas evectus in auras,
Fratribus ille geret munera grata meis.
Murmurat en currus, ductorque repagula scandens
Adspernit terras, caeruleasque petit
Sedes, atque audax gaudet volitare per astra.
Caelipotens Rector, te vehat ipse Deus!
Quumque petes cursu Capitoli immobile saxum
Coelo delapsus, navita, siste pedem.
Icariam vinces sortem, felicior arte:
Laudes et nomen, postera fama canet.

Source: *America: A Catholic Review of the Week* 19 (May 25, 1918): 170, cf. 175.[1194]

108 World War I and a Pandemic: Oregon (1919)

Catholic misssionaries were active in northeast Oregon since the 1830s, and the Jesuits initiated a permanent mission there in the late 1880s. With financial assistance from (now-canonized) Katharine Drexel, St. Andrew's Industrial School opened in February 1890 on the Umatilla Reservation, which had been established by treaty in 1855 for three tribes—the Cayuse, Umatilla, and Walla Walla. The following is the *Litterae Annuae* from July 1918 to July 1919 from St. Andrew's, which at the time was under the charge of the Jesuit priest Thomas M. Neate (1861–1934).[1195] Particular mention is made of the ravages of the Spanish Influenza on the surrounding region. Indeed, headlines in the *East Oregonian* (Pendleton) in the fall and winter of 1918—announcements of cancellations and quarantines, a statement from the Surgeon General, reports of multiple waves of the pandemic, as well as death notices—are evocative of the spring of 2020. At the same time, newspapers also carried reports of the War in Europe.

Egyptiorum plagis similes, afflictiones et miserias in nos bellorum ferocitas multas intulit. Pestilentia et fames nec non hominum paucitas cum frumenti pecuniaeque inopia dire in nostra plaga contigerunt. Digitum Dei autem in omnibus cernimus et Providentia Divina singulariter nos sublevavit. Nam etsi Pestilentia, "The Spanish Influenza," praevalebat; in nostram scholam ipsam tamen, non invasit, et omnes convicti omnino morbi expertes manserunt. Extra domum, autem, multi catholici afflicti sunt et non pauci obierunt. In hac penuria bellicosa, valde difficile est auxilium obtinendum. Magister noster et etiam Morum Prefectus, ad arma vocati, conscripti sunt, et trans mare abierunt. Omnes adulti pueri igitur, ad Sororum scholam frequentandi sunt.[1196]

Operarii etiam valde pauci sunt et non nisi magna pecunia ad agros colendos conducti sunt. Post annum, tamen, mense Maii, Magister noster ex Gallia, ad nos reversus est incolumis, et forte iam advenit novus morum prefectus, et adulti pueri, qui necessitate, apud sorores instructi sunt, nunc iam iterum in nostram domum recepti sunt, et annus qui propter pessimum bellum lugubre incepit, nunc iucunditer finem duxit. Hieme propter operariorum inopiam, fratres Coadiutores, Ios. Giraudi, Hort. et Aloyso Varaldi arment. et agr. custos,[1197] ipsi soli omnia opera, magno labore fideliter executi sunt. Sed, tametsi, magna diligentia et industria adhibita, propter terrae ariditatem valde pauci segites collecti sunt. In schola pueri et puellae duo et septuaginta numerantur. In Corporis Christi solemnitate Rev[mus] noster Episcopus Ios. F. McGrath praefuit,[1198] eodem die festo quattuor et triginta sacramentum Confirmationis acceperunt et duo et triginta prima vice Communiomem accesserunt. Speramus, ut, Ille qui, 'maris fluctus mandavit,'[1199] tranquilitatem nostro tempore concedat.

Source: The Pacific Northwest Tribes Missions Collection of the Oregon Province Archives of the Society of Jesus, reel 27, pp. 415–16 (original in Jesuit Archives and Research Center, St. Louis, Missouri).

109 Prohibition (1920)

In the late nineteenth century Latin Clubs took shape around the United States in an effort to vivify instruction in the ancient languages in the face of increasing apathy or opposition. Some clubs were connected with a particular school, college, or seminary, while others drew their members from an entire city.

The Classical Club of Philadelphia, founded in 1895 by Alfred Gudeman (1862–1942), who would later die in a concentration camp,[1200] was comprised of teachers, scholars, professionals, and businessmen who convened six times each year to listen to papers on classical themes. On February 9, 1912, this club celebrated its one-hundredth meeting with an elaborate banquet. The exquisite menu, printed in *The Classical Journal*, was entirely in Latin, and the listing of each item was glossed by a citation from classical literature. Thus the first *ferculum*, which was *ostrea ex sinu Lynnoportu*, was amplified by Juvenal's "ostrea callebat primo deprendere morsu" (4.142). Similarly, Vergil's "omnis humi [sic] fumat Neptunia Troia" (*Aen.* 3.3), gave a classical context to the after-dinner *fumisugia* or *fumisugiuncula*. Again, following the mention of *vinum Burdigalense*, guests were encouraged by Horace: "Siccis omnia nam dura deus proposuit, neque/ Mordaces aliter diffugiunt sollicitudines" (*C* 1.18.3–4).[1201]

Eight years later, on April 16, 1920, the Classical Club of Philadelphia celebrated its 150th meeting with the reading of a scholarly paper, the election of officers for the coming year, and a luxurious banquet attended by forty-eight members and guests. Once again the sumptuous menu was printed in Latin, but noticeably absent was any alcoholic beverage. Instead banqueters were served *vinum Bryanicum Zingiberale*,[1202] and Horace's exhortation was now replaced by Solomon's counsel: "Ne intuearis vinum quando flavescit, cum splenduerit in vitro color eius: ingreditur blande; sed in novissimo mordebit ut coluber et sicut regulus venena diffundet" (Prv. 23:31–32). Three months earlier, at midnight on January 17, 1920, the Eighteenth Amendment had taken effect, and the United States had entered the era of Prohibition.

The following Latin ode was read at the 1920 anniversary dinner. It was composed by John Rolfe (1859–1943). Well known today for his Loeb translations (Sallust, Suetonius, Nepos, Gellius, Ammianus Marcellinus, Quintus Curtius). Rolfe was professor of Latin Language and Literature at the University of Pennsylvania for nearly three decades, and he published widely on philological matters.[1203] Later in life he took up writing Latin poetry, largely of a celebratory nature.[1204]

Praeteriere citi, comites, feliciter anni:
noctibus accedunt centum bene quinquaginta.
Tempora laeta vocant sollemnia concelebrare,
volventes animis veterum monumenta virorum.
Vidimus interea tristis certamina Martis,
vidimus et comites terris altoque merentes.
Conditor ille hostes inter numeratur, ineptus
qui populo externo posset mutare penates.[1205]
Nunc iterum pax arva colit, restante Senatu,
at belli factis multo asperiora videmus.
Stulti nam vinum prohibent, et, volvere fumum
quamvis concedant, tamen id pro crimine ducunt.
Improbus, a! pereat, qui se insinuans pede felis,
virtutis simulator et effusissimus auri,
corrupitque senatores populumque fefellit.
Mox in Tartareo demersus gurgite, frustra
imploret liquidi cyathum, circumdatus igni!
Di meliora duint! Et aquam nunc ducite, amici,
doctrina et sicca cunctantes fallite noctes.

Durum; at nos etiam "Haec olim meminisse
iuvabit"[1206]
pocula siccantes per umida tempora laetos.
Ne sit perpetuo nobis patria arida nutrix.

Source: *Classical Weekly* 13 (1920): 216.

110 Celebratory Ode At Mount Holyoke (1921)

The steady erosion of Greek and Latin requirements in American colleges and universities that began after the Civil War reached somewhat of a crisis in the second decade of the twentieth century.

In 1916 Abraham Flexner published *A Modern School*, in which he called for a complete overhaul of the curriculum of American schools and a drastic diminishment of the classics. Flexner (1866–1959), the founder of Princeton's Institute for Advanced Study, had earned a B.A. in Classics from Johns Hopkins and had taught Latin and Greek in his hometown of Louisville, but he had become convinced that traditional educational methods as well as traditional subjects were ill-suited to modern America. His essay baldly proclaimed: "neither Latin nor Greek would be contained in the curriculum of the Modern School." His indictment was severe and unequivocal: "Instead of getting orderly training by solving difficulties in Latin translation or composition, pupils guess, fumble, receive surreptitious assistance or accept on faith the injunctions of teacher and grammar. The only discipline that most students could get from their classical studies is a discipline in doing things as they should not be done."[1207]

Classicists responded to Flexner's challenge. Princeton's Andrew Fleming West (1853–1943) rallied a seminal conference in June 1917—"The Second Battle of Princeton," as one observer styled it[1208]—in which academics, businessmen, journalists, and a United States Senator robustly argued for the perdurance of the classics within American schools. In the following year, classicists meeting in Pittsburgh for the National Education Association voted to establish an American Classical League. Support continued to be solicited from the highest levels.[1209] In July 1921 Vice-President Calvin Coolidge addressed the second annual meeting of the American Classical League.[1210] But the case for Classics had to be made above all in classrooms around the country.

Margaret Coleman Waites (1883–1923) offers an instructive example of labor on behalf of the classics. Waites earned three degrees from Radcliffe—B.A. summa cum laude (1905), M.A. summa cum laude (1906), and a Ph.D. (1910) with a dissertation on Greek rhetoric.[1211] She taught for three years at Rockford College (1910–12, 1913–14) surrounding a year at the American Academy in Rome (1912–13) and was then hired at Mount Holyoke. A diligent scholar, she was a member of numerous societies (AIA, APA, CANE, AAUP), and she published regularly in academic journals.[1212] She was also devoted to demonstrating that Classics could compete on a level footing with the disciplines emerging in American higher education. As head of the Latin and Greek Department at Rockford she delivered lectures to the general public on classical themes, and she organized a Classical Club that sponsored activities such as Latin plays or Greek games.[1213] At Mount Holyoke she staged Terence's *Phormio,*[1214] not to showcase dramatic talent but rather "to obtain the educational stimulus and the curiously vivid impression that Latin is after all a real language."[1215]

In May 1921 Mount Holyoke celebrated the twentieth anniversary of the inauguration of Mary E. Woolley (1863–1947), its eleventh president (1900–37). The festivities were attended by 3000 current and former students as well as friends and benefactors, and they included a performance of Euripides's *Electra*, the presentation of a pageant based on Book I of Spenser's *Faerie Queene*, and an academic procession and convocation featuring tributes from professors within and outside of Mount Holyoke.[1216] According to Woolley, this two-day celebration was "one of the most delightful experiences of my life at Mount Holyoke."[1217] The following Latin ode, composed by Waites and set to music by Mount Holyoke professor Albert Moody Tucker, was sung during this convocation.

The ode is preserved in the archives of Mount

Holyoke, but it was published in an early issue of the *Phi Beta Kappa Key*, which also contained an article about Woolley's recent trip to China as a member of the China Educational Commission, tasked with studying the possibilities for Christian education in China.[1218] In 1907 Woolley had become the first woman to be elected a member of the Phi Beta Kappa senate.

Waites died of pneumonia on March 14, 1923, two days before the Board of Trustees was to elect her full professor.[1219] She left her estate and library to Radcliffe.

Clara Musarum domus et deorum,
Quattuor lustris placide peractis
Praesidis nostrae imperio sub aequo
        Te veneramur.[1220]

Prorogent divi tibi in omne tempus
Gloriam dulcem, nitidaeque proli
Dent tuae mores dociles valenti
        "Spernere volgus."[1221]

O vale! nobis stabilem benigne
Fausta quae donas fidem et, alma mater,
Filias omnes cole ter beatas
        Praeside cara.

Source: *The Phi Beta Kappa Key* 4 (1921): 537–38.

111 Flight: *Los Angeles* Across the Atlantic (1925)

One of the most prolific Latin poets in the United States in the early twentieth century was the Jesuit Anthony F. Geyser (1870–1952). Born in the Rhineland, Geyser taught at Jesuit schools in the Midwest, including many years at Campion College in Prairie du Chien, Wisconsin. He published original Latin poetry and Latin translations in college magazines and classics journals (especially *The Classical Weekly*), and he also published five volumes of *Musa Americana* (Chicago: Loyola University Press, 1919–22), the last of which was a Latin version of Shakespeare's *Julius Caesar*. In reviewing Geyser's third volume, Professor George Dwight Kellogg (1873–1955) of Union College remarked: "Father Geyser . . . to whom Latin is the living language of the Church, is steeped in the ecclesiastical and liturgical literature; while he does not wander far from the classic fold, nevertheless he worships no Latinity fetish." Kellogg offered several criticisms, yet he concluded by encouraging Geyser to compete for the prestigious Praemium Hoeufftianum.[1222] Geyser also published *Orator Latinus: Popular Selections for Public Delivery* (Boston: Allyn & Bacon, 1924), and he was associate editor of *Auxilium Latinum*, a Latin newspaper founded in Brooklyn in 1931.

The following is an excerpt from a poem, "Aer Perdomitus," which commemorates the conquest of the skies by aircraft, particularly by the ZR-3, which arrived in Lakehurst, New Jersey on October 15, 1925 after a three-day transatlantic flight. (This was a year and a half before Charles Lindbergh's flight in the *Spirit of St. Louis*.) The ZR-3 was built for the U.S. Navy in Friedrichshafen, Germany, as part of reparations for American losses in the First World War. Capable of traveling upwards of 70 miles per hour, this dirigible featured five passenger compartments, each of which had fold-out sofas. Flight attendants served hot food cooked on electric stoves.[1223]

In Washington on November 19, First Lady Grace Coolidge rechristened the ZR-3 "Los Angeles," a name chosen by Secretary of the Navy Curtis Dwight Wilbur to evoke tidings of peace (Luke 2:14) in the aftermath of the First World War.[1224]

Terque quaterque mihi salveto, clara triumpho
Aeris, O Navis, quae nuper vecta per altos
Europae tractus, freta trans Atlantica, victrix,
Continuo volitans cursu, feliciter oras
Ad nostras veniens, iam gloria nostra manebis!
"Angelicum" nomen fauste impositum tibi, Navis,
O celebris, felix omen pignusque fidele
Pacis sit verae, violet quam nulla cupido,
Non calcet pedibus vis insidiosa tyranni,
Non rapiat populi rabies odiumque cruentum![1225]

Source: *The Classical Bulletin* 2 (1926): 115.

112 Horace Bimillennium (1935)

Only two months after the completion of the successful celebration of the Vergil Bimillennium (1930), Roy C. Flickinger (1876–1942), a professor of Classics at the University of Iowa and the editor-in-chief of *The Classical Journal*, proposed a similar celebration for Horace.[1226] Despite certain factors militating against his initiative—a small budget, the absence of Horace from many high school curricula, and potential weariness over a second bimillennial celebration within five years—Flickinger's goal was that some sort of celebration occur in every American school, college, or university where either Latin or Greek was taught.[1227]

As part of this celebration, undergraduates in the United States and Canada were invited to submit entries for an Essay and Ode Contest, which entailed a metrical translation of fifty to seventy-five lines of Horace's *Odes* or *Epodes*, a 5000-word essay concerning Horace and Augustus, and an original Latin ode or satire (20 to 30 lines in length) written upon a Horatian theme and in a Horatian meter.[1228] The entries were judged by Charles E. Bennett of Amherst College, Roy J. Deferrari of The Catholic University of America, and Mary A. Grant of the University of Kansas.

The unanimous winner of this prize, announced at the December 26 meeting of the American Philological Association in New York City, was Jean Holzworth (1915–2007),[1229] a senior at Bryn Mawr College, whose work had, per contest stipulation, been submitted under a false name, viz., John Michael. Judges were impressed by the originality and philosophical bent of her ode. Holzworth, a native of Port Chester, New York and a graduate of Greenwich Academy, used her $1000 prize money to spend a year at the American Academy in Rome. Eventually she earned an M.A. and a Ph.D.[1230] in Latin from Bryn Mawr and then took a position at Mount Holyoke, but in 1943, following the death of a cherished cat, she left the field of Classics to enroll in Veterinary School at Cornell. She graduated in 1950 and spent thirty-six years at Angell Memorial Animal Hospital in Boston, where she gained an international reputation for her work on feline diseases.[1231]

The text of her winning ode was included in an issue of the *Bryn Mawr Alumnae Magazine*, whose editors remarked that the Latin poem was "by far the most difficult feature of the contest, for, except in certain Catholic colleges, there is little or no training in the writing of Latin verse in American colleges and universities."[1232]

At the time the ode was written (August 1935), Mussolini was preparing to invade Ethiopia.

Iam novo surgit duce Roma rursus
E ruinis, regna petente prisca;
Iam viris telisque onerata solvit
    Trans mare navis.

Caesarem se credit et Africani et
Caesaris vestigia ad Africam ardet
Dux sequi, decreta novans Elissae
    Ab prece bella.

Roma cum Poenam superaret urbem,
Victorem sedum cineres tuentem
Roma ne fato simili periret
    Perculit horror.

Nescius non augur erat futuri:
Urbs ruit demum domitos tenere
Romuli quondam cata, barbaris et
    Ignibus arsit.

Quis prius Romae revocare fatum
Audet augentemque ducem monere
Terminos: "Romam domuit domandi
        Saeva libido,

Et sua dextra urbs cecidit Quirini.
Cuique pollendi spatium vicissim
Dat deus; iam Roma diu peregit
        Saucia cursum,

Gentibus cedens liberis. Novari
Ilion Iuno vetuit superbum;
Cur deo adversante iterum laboras
        Surgere, Roma?"

Source: *Bryn Mawr Alumnae Bulletin* 16.3 (March 1936): 7–8.

113 Eisenhower at Oxford (1945)

In October 1945, five and a half months after V-E day, General Dwight David Eisenhower (1890–1969) was awarded an honorary doctorate of civil law from the University of Oxford. General Mark W. Clark and Ambassador John G. Winant were similarly honored during the ceremony, as were high-ranking British military officers including Field Marshal Sir Bernard L. Montgomery, Field Marshal Lord Alan Brooke, and Air Marshal Sir Arthur Tedder. During this same year Eisenhower received honorary doctorates from Queen's University Belfast and the University of Louvain, and in the following year he was similarly honored by eleven institutions, including Cambridge, Edinburgh, Harvard, Toronto, and Lafayette. During the Oxford ceremony, which took place in Sheldonian Theater on St. Crispin's Day (October 25), Thomas Farrant Higham (1890–1975), Oxford's public orator from 1939 to 1958, presented Eisenhower to the Chancellor of Oxford with the following Latin address.

Higham, a fellow of Trinity College, had won the Gaisford Prize for Greek verse in 1912 for his translation into Theocritean hexameters of the first nine stanzas of George Meredith's "Love in the Valley" (Oxford: B.H. Blackwell, 1912). Later he was co-editor of *The Oxford Book of Greek Verse* (1930) and *The Oxford Book of Greek Verse in Translation* (1938). During the First World War he served in Salonika, and he was one of the many academics who performed "difficult" and "vitally important" intelligence work at Bletchley Park during the Second World War.[1233] In November 1923 Higham and six other Oxford tutors formed an informal club dedicated to Latin and Greek composition. When some of the clubmembers's pieces were published,[1234] one reviewer remarked that Higham deserved a "special prize for all-round excellence."[1235]

Dubbed the "prince of Public Orators," by classicist James Diggle,[1236] Higham also published fifty of his Oxford orations.[1237] In addition to the oration for Eisenhower, selections in this published volume honor President Harry S. Truman, former First Lady Eleanor Roosevelt, Secretary of State George C. Marshall, Secretary of State Dean Acheson, and Professor and Nobel Prizewinner Harold Clayton Urey of the University of Chicago. Speaking about the speeches that honored Americans, one reviever commented: "in each instance Mr. Higham's *oratio* says just the right thing in the right way."[1238]

At the time of the ceremony Eisenhower was head of the American Occupation in Germany. A few months later he would return to the United States to become Chief of Staff of the Army.

Virum videtis morum modestia, animi aequitate, Cincinnatum alterum: cuius tamen res tantae exstiterunt, ut viri primores maximarum civitatium eius unius voluntatibus assenserint; ut plus minus quinquagiens centena milia hominum, ad societatem belli diversis ex gentibus evocati, incredibili quadam conspiratione atque consensu eius unius imperium acceperint; denique ut bello difficillimo, quod ductu eius tractandum erat, neque maius ullum commemorari possit neque maiore consilio et felicitate confectum. quis unquam fuit in omni bellandi genere scientior? quis in bello praesertim triformi inferendo, cum simul 'caelo, mari, terra' cum hoste contenditur? quid loquar Mauretaniam, Numidiam, Zeugitanam regionem triformi impetu ex improviso occupatas? quid versam ex illo die in melius fortunam? quid illum diem, sempiternae hominum memoriae commendatum, quo summam rerum in aleam dando optatam fecit in Franco-Galliam escensionem? quid loquar artes imperatorias, quibus singulos hostium exercitus distinuit, interclusit, ad internecionem redegit? verum ex omnibus diebus quos celebres vidimus et laetos, nonne ille nobis dies optatissimus, ille clarissimus fuit, quo reluxisse Europaeis libertatem audivimus,[1239] actum esse de tot innocentium cruciatibus, tot captivorum miseriis,

'teque, rebellatrix, tandem, Germania, magni
triste caput pedibus subposuisse ducis'?[1240]

praesento vobis imperatorem et re et titulo summum, Dwight David Eisenhower, honoratissimo Ordini de Balneo Magnae Crucis Equitem adscriptum,[1241] ut admittatur honoris causa ad gradum Doctoris in Iure Civili.

Source: Thomas Farrant Higham, *Orationes Oxonienses Selectae* (Oxford: Clarendon Press, 1960), 45–46. By permission of Oxford University Press.

114 Immigration (1950)

The post-WWII era saw an enormous spike in migration. Between 1945 and 1954 about five million persons left Europe, a third of whom settled in the United States, while the remaining two thirds settled for the most part in Canada, Australia, and Argentina.[1242] Emigration occurred from non-European countries as well, especially Mexico, Colombia, Algeria, India, China, and Korea.[1243] Migration also occurred within the United States. Beginning in the 1940s large numbers of African Americans relocated from the South to northern cities in a movement that has come to be termed the Second Great Migration (1940–70).

In the following excerpt from an Apostolic Brief, Pope Pius XII declares St. Frances Xavier Cabrini the patron saint of immigrants. Cabrini (1850–1917), born in Lombardy, founded the Missionary Sisters of the Sacred Heart of Jesus in 1880, whose initial seven members were former orphans, and in 1889, at the request of Pope Leo XIII, she came to the United States to undertake missionary work among Italian immigrants (see section 90). She became a citizen of the United States in 1909. In a span of thirty-five years she traveled extensively throughout the United States (especially New York, Chicago, and New Orleans) as well as in Europe and South America—she is said to have crossed the ocean thirty times—and she founded sixty-seven orphanages, hospitals, schools, and convents. In 1946 she became the first United States citizen to be canonized.[1244]

Superiore iam aetate, sed praesertim hac, qua degimus, perturbata et iniqua, plurimos ad quaeritandum victum atque ad hominum nequam insectationes et laqueos declinandos a patriis avelli focis novimus et in transmarinas regiones commigrare. Quodsi hi eo modo fortunam interdum valent amplificare, saepe tamen in sat magnum discrimen spirituale veniunt, quin nonnulli, Fidei patrimonio naufragi, sancta maiorum instituta plane dediscunt. Atque exstitit mulier, virtutis et probitatis lumen spectabile, Francisca Xaveria Cabrini, quae gloriosum exsudavit laborem demigrantes et animo et corpore relevandi.

Multis ergo in locis Americae Septentrionalis, Mediae, Australis, ludos infantiae pro patria extorrium subole condidit, aperuit scholas pro eadem, publica instituit hospitia pupillorum. Ex ea ipsa gente, quae alibi sedes collocaverat, adversa valetudine affectos saepe invisebat, in carceribus detentos solabatur, capitis damnatos flexanimo sermone componebat ad pianda facinora et ad supplicium christiana cum moderatione subeundum. Pelago pluries se credens, tumescentes tempestates fusis precibus compescuit animosque demigrantium erexit atque confirmavit; quae vecturam interdum obstruebant, difficultates easque graves, ipsa sustulit cum modestia et fide. Ita vivens et post mortem, Sanctorum gloria circumfluens, nobilis haec Ecclesiae alumna praesidio erat et est miseris eius generis hominibus ea quidem caritate, quae, ut ait Sanctus Augustinus, "ad alios se inclinat, ad alios se erigit, aliis blanda, aliis severa, nulli inimica, omnibus mater" (*De cath. rud.* XV).

Quapropter merito appellata est Sancta Francisca Xaveria Cabrini "Mater Emigrantium" et, hoc nomine praestabilis, in vota solet vocari. Quare Institutum Missionariarum a Sacratissimo Corde, quod ipsa condidit, omnesque emigrantes per Venerabiles Fratres Archiepiscopos et Episcopos Civitatum Foederatarum Americae Septentrionalis et Canadensis Dicionis Nobis supplicaverunt, ut Sanctam Franciscam Xaveriam Cabrini omnium Emigrantium Caelestem apud Deum Patronam renuntiare dignaremur. Nos autem, antiquissimum rati saluti consulere eorum qui, de finibus suis exeuntes, alias quaerunt sedes, precibus huiusmodi libenti animo statuimus obsecundare. Idcirco, e Sacrae Rituum Congregationis consulto, omnibus rei momentis attente perpensis, certa scientia ac matura deliberatione Nostra deque Apostolicae potestatis plenitudine, harum Litterarum vi perpetuumque in modum Sanctam Franciscam Xaveriam Cabrini, Virginem, omnium Emigrantium Caelestem apud Deum Patronam constituimus et declaramus, omnibus adiectis honoribus ac privilegiis liturgicis quae praecipuis coetuum Patronis rite competunt . . .

Datum ex Arce Gandulphi,[1245]
sub anulo Piscatoris,
die VII mensis Septembris,
anno MCML,
Pontificatus Nostri duodecimo.

Source: *Discorsi e Radiomessaggi di Sua Santità Pio XII*, vol. 13 (1951–1952): 575–76 (by permission of Libreria Editrice Vaticana).[1246]

115 Gettysburg Address (1959)

On June 17, 1959 some seventy guests gathered in the State Reception Room of the Apostolic Delegation in Washington, DC.[1247] Among those in attendance were several members of the diplomatic corps as well as Senator John S. Cooper of Kentucky, the chair of the Abraham Lincoln Sesquicentennial Commission, designed to commemorate the 150th anniversary of Lincoln's birth. During the reception Cooper presented the Apostolic Delegate, Cardinal Egidio Vagnozzi, with a Latin translation of the Gettysburg Address, "Abraham Lincoln Apud Gettysburg Pronuntiata Contio." The Latin text, which had been engrossed on parchment and framed in black and gold, was to be given to Pope John XXIII for exhibition in the Vatican Library. The translation—196 Latin words rendering the 272 of the famously terse and poignant English speech—was the work of Msgr. Edwin Ryan (d. 1960), a priest of the Archdiocese of New York.

In his remarks at the reception, Senator Cooper drew attention to Lincoln's "humanity," "humor," and "humility," and he highlighted the Gettysburg Address's commitment to "government by the people."[1248] Msgr. Ryan, in his remarks, focused on the significance of the Address's language of freedom and equality. Lincoln, Ryan argued, "expressed succinctly the truth that human freedom is based upon human equality," and that equality is "an essential concomitant of human nature." The presence of the Address in Rome, he averred, would be "a testimony to the fundamental harmony between "what Abraham Lincoln proclaims in the order of nature" and "what St. Paul proclaims in the order of grace." In accepting the Latin translation, Cardinal Vagnozzi paid tribute to the Address as "a great American document . . . a great human document . . . and . . . a great Christian document." Three months later on the floor of the Senate Cooper requested that the speeches at the reception as well as the Latin translation be entered into the Congressional Record.[1249]

At the time of the ceremony Ryan was teaching at Stepanic High School in White Plains, New York. A graduate of St. Francis Xavier (New York City) and of St. Joseph's Seminary (New York City), Ryan was ordained a priest in 1906 and then pursued graduate work at The Catholic University of America and in Rome. He taught at St. Joseph's Seminary, St. Mary's College (Baltimore), and The Catholic University of America. His scholarly specialty was the history of Latin America,[1250] but he also published on Cardinal John Henry Newman, the sacred liturgy, and the role of medieval Latin in classics pedagogy.[1251] According to some reports, an initial draft of the Latin version was made by Ryan's students in White Plains as part of a class project, and Ryan spent two years revising it.[1252]

Ryan's version, to be sure, was not the first Latin rendering of the Gettysburg Address. Included here by way of comparison is an earlier version authored by James A. Kleist (1873–1949), a Silesian-born Jesuit who at the time of composition was on the faculty of Campion College in Prairie du Chien, Wisconsin.[1253] Kleist's version, with 247 words, is about 25% longer than Ryan's, but still shorter than the English. Ryan's version is presented first below, Kleist's follows.[1254]

I

Abraham Lincoln Apud Gettysburg Pronuntiata Contio

Octoginta et septem ahhinc iam annos rempublicam novam, libertate inceptam atque hominibus natura paribus dedicatam, maiores his in regionibus ediderunt. Nunc bello intestino ac tremendo illaqueatis oritur nobis percontatio num civitas aliqua tali spiritu informata diutina perdurare valebit. Loco insigni luctationis, ad partem campi consecrandam in sepulcrum eorum qui animas ad patriae vitam conservandam hic posuerunt, confluximus. Congruit omnino decetque peragere haec, sensu tamen altiore hanc terram dedicare, consecrare, sanctificare, nobis non competit, quoniam fortes qui hic proeliati sunt, sive superstites manent sive interfecti iacent, facultatem exiguam nostram aut amplificandi consecrationem aut imminuendi magnopere superaverunt. Effata nostra haec paululum animadvertentur homines atque ea brevi obliviscentur, id tamen quod hice confecerunt nullo pacto de memoria dilabetur. Nobis adhuc in vita versantibus immo vero potius incumbit operi incompleto dedicari quod in hac pugna fortissimi hactenus tam praeclare provexere. Remanet ut huic penso nos conferamus, nempe, ex his defunctis coronatis studium corroboratum haurire muneri fungendo cui illi ex imo corde sese obtulerunt, hic mentibus elatis statuere necem his observatis illatam non fore irritam. Quo fiet ut civitas haec Deo adiuvante libertati renascetur, et ditio in populo fundata, a populo gesta, ad populi salutem directa, nequaquam de mundo tabescens interibit.

II
Abrahami Lincoln Oratio Gettysburgensis

Octavus iam et octogesimus annus est hic, cum maiores nostri novam in hac terrae parte rem publicam pepererunt, quam libertatis in condicione conceptam in illam consecrarunt sententiam: aequo nasci iure homines universos. Nunc vero ingenti bello civili inito nos experimur, haecne res publica vel alia, sic nata sic consecrata, per longum temporis spatium possit stare. Convenimus in eum ipsum locum, ubi acerrime in hoc bello pugnatum est; convenimus autem huc, ut huius campi partem aliquam ad supremam quietem eorum consecraremus, qui ut viveret haec res publica, vitam hoc loco profuderunt. Quibus id nos merito ac iure praestamus. Verum hunc locum, si altius rem spectaverimus, neque inaugurare neque dedicare neque consecrare nos posse videbimur; quem illi ipsi viri fortissimi, qui hic dimicarunt, sive mortui sunt sive superstites, tanta consecrarunt sanctitate, ut nos neque addere quicquam neque demere possimus. Nos enim, quae hic dixerimus, neque multum attendent homines neque diu recordabuntur: illi quae hic fecerunt, oblivioni dabitur nunquam. Nos potius, qui in vita sumus, hoc loco consecrari oportet ad opus illud perficiendum, quod illi tam praeclare propagarunt; nos, inquam, consecrari ad hoc tantum opus, quod reliquum nobis videmus; ut ab illis, quos hic honoramus mortuos, maiore in dies pietate eam discamus amplecti causam, qua in defendenda illi hic morientes pietatem praestiterunt summam; ut magno hic animo id statuamus, ne animas illi frustra devoverint; ut huic civitati nova, Deo volente, nascatur libertas; denique ut imperium populare, quod et a populo et pro populo administretur, ne pereat unquam in orbe terrarum.

Sources: I *Congressional Record, Proceedings and Debates of the 86th Congress, First Session*, vol. 105, part 15 (Washington, DC: United States Government Printing Office, 1959), 19600 (September 14, 1959).
II *Classical Journal* 7 (1912): 306–8.

116 Nuclear Weapons (1964)

The Second Vatican Council (1962–65) has been described as the largest meeting in world history.[1255] On a typical day the central nave of St. Peter's Basilica was filled with 2400 council fathers, who came from 116 different countries. Also present were theologians and secretaries as well as non-participating observers, some representing other religions.

Although the Second Vatican Council is often seen as a watershed event in the decline of the Latin language, Latin nonetheless remained the official language of the Council itself. At times other languages were heard—the Melkite Patriarch Maximos IV Saigh, for example, chose to speak in French, and he was insistent that Latin not be seen as the exclusive language of the universal Church—but most council fathers addressed the assembly in Latin, and the official documents were in Latin. Indeed, eight months before the Council's opening Pope John XXIII had issued the Apostolic Constitution *Veterum Sapientia* (February 22, 1962), in which he identified Latin as "lingua Ecclesiae viva" and prescribed its promotion and employment, particularly in priestly formation. A few months later the Father General of the Jesuits, Jean-Baptiste Janssens (1889–1964) issued a strong defence of the active use of Latin, dismissing claims that the Jesuits were "clinging intransigently to an outmoded notion of humanism."[1256]

Unlike the situation at the First Vatican Council, acoustics were not a problem at the later Council, and speakers had ready access to one of thirty-seven microphones positioned throughout the Basilica. Although at times the council fathers struggled with the various accents given to Latin, and some, to be sure, struggled with Latin itself,[1257] the use of a simultaneous translation system such as the one employed at the United Nations was rejected, not for financial or technical reasons, but because some fathers, fearing that their words would be incorrectly translated and thereby misinterpreted, preferred to be heard in Latin.[1258] Proceedings were recorded by a team of stenographers—originally forty-two but then only fifteen—who had taken a special course in Latin shorthand prior to the Council's opening.[1259]

Perhaps the most famous of the sixteen documents to emerge from the Council is the Pastoral Constitution on the Church in the Modern World, commonly known as *Gaudium et Spes*, which was promulgated by Pope Paul VI on December 7, 1965 just before the Council's conclusion. In its second part this wide-ranging document, which is addressed not only *ad intra* ("ad Ecclesiae filios") but also *ad extra*, i.e., to all Christians and in fact to all human beings ("ad universos homines"), treats issues such as marriage and family, the economy, international relations, and war. As a recent historian remarks, "no council had ever attempted anything like it."[1260] Debate on this document, originally known as Schema 13, took place between October 20 and November 10, 1964, and it featured more than 150 speeches.

The following Latin text, which concerns nuclear weapons (chapter 25 of the original schema), is from a speech given on November 10, 1964—the last day of discussion—by Philip Hannan (1913–2011), auxiliary Bishop of Washington and later Archbishop of New Orleans, who one year earlier had delivered the eulogy at the funeral of President John F. Kennedy. Hannan, a former paratroop chaplain with the 82nd Airborne Division during the Second World War, had concerns that the pacifist language of *Gaudium et Spes* contradicted traditional Catholic teaching on the legitimacy of a "just war," and he also feared that the document unwisely offered a blanket condemnation of nuclear weapons.[1261] In his speech Hannan affirmed the necessity of war in certain instances, the licitness of using nuclear weapons in a targeted strike, and the legitimate role of nuclear weapons in deterrence. Yet as he recalled much later in his memoirs, his primary objective on November 10 "was simply to knock out that one sentence that weapons would lead to war."[1262]

The approved version of *Gaudium et Spes* stopped short of an outright condemnation of nuclear weapons, yet Hannan was not satisfied, and during the last week of the Council (December 1965) he led an unsuccessful effort to secure a negative vote on the paragraph in question.[1263]

The text below is taken from the *Acta Synodalia*, published a decade after the close of the Council.

Haec sane in memorata paragrapho reprehendenda videntur. . .

3. In sectione II, gravis error facti quod attinet ad nuclearia arma, et falso inde conclusio, inducitur. In secunda sententia huius sectionis ita enim legitur: "usus tamen armorum, praesertim nuclearium, quorum effectus maiores sunt quam qui aestimari possint ac proinde ab hominibus rationabiliter temperari nequeunt, excedit omnem iustam proportionem ac propterea scelestissimus coram Deo et hominibus iudicandus est." Sed non recte affirmatur, quia non desunt hodie nuclearia arma quorum vis destructiva angusto limite circumscribitur. Sunt quaedam id genus arma mobilia. Ut apparet, nisi vis delendi horum armorum esset valde circumscripta, iidem milites mortem non effugerent ex effectibus explosionis. Tenuiora arma quae nunc adhibentur ictum inferre possunt spatio inter tria et quinque "kilometri" et eorum missile vim dirumpendi possidet quae attingit 40 "tonnellate" explosivi.[1264]

Quamvis omnia huius generis arma, etiam quae parva sint, grave damnum inferant, non potest tamen dici ut in citato textu legimus: "effectus maiores sunt quam qui aestimari possint." Nam eorum effectus sunt intra certos limites sat praefiniti et ideo omnino praevideri possunt. Insuper, licitum sit his armis cum effectu limitato uti contra obiecta militaria in bello iusto iuxta principia theologica.

Tota paragraphus igitur ignorare videtur communem doctrinam Ecclesiae eiusque normas quae iusto bello gerendo applicari debent.

4. Videretur etiam innui, tali paragrapho, omnes nationes pariter neglexisse munus consulendi paci communi universali. Id vero iniuste asseritur et plures offendit nationes et moderatores qui haud parvam impenderunt curam ad pacem procurandam et tuendam. Sed id praesertim iniuriosum est nationibus quae nunc incursiones militares patiuntur. Omnes populi probe sciunt unde hae aggressiones oriantur.

Quaestio maximi momenti, hodie et pro futuro, est evitare bellum et defendere libertatem, tum nationis tum personae. Ut dialogus prosequatur cum atheisticis militantibus oportet nos gaudere libertate plena et actuosa. Nullus dialogus possibilis est si in servitutem cadimus. Quia libertas est fundamentum humanae vitae, ii qui libertatem defendunt laudandi sunt. Ergo, cum hoc schema agat de rebus practicis, debet verbum saltem dicere de libertate defendenda et in laudem eorum qui libertatem defendunt, etiam eorum qui vitam libenter obtulerunt ut nos libertate plena filiorum Dei gaudeamus.

Itaque tota paragraphus, mea humili sententia, penitus emendanda est. Gratias. Dixi.

Source: *Acta Synodalia Sacrosancti Concilii Oecumenici Vaticani Secundi*, vol. 3.7 (Rome: Typis Polyglottis Vaticanis, 1975), 54–56 (by permission of Libreria Editrice Vaticana).

Endnotes

1 Albert Cook Myers, *Narratives of Early Pennsylvania, West New Jersey, and Delaware, 1630–1707* (New York: Charles Scribner's Sons, 1912), 94.

2 Myers, *Narratives of Early Pennsylvania*, 105–6, 127.

3 Georg H. von Langsdorff, *Voyages and Travels in Various Parts of the World*, part 2 (London: Henry Colburn, 1814), 150–51.

4 George O. Schanzer, "A Russian Visit to the Spanish Franciscans in California, 1836," *The Americas* 9 (1953): 456.

5 Translations are in *Records of the American Catholic Historical Society of Philadelphia* 27 (1916): 133–44.

6 *The American Catholic Historical Researches* 12 (1895): 28.

7 Bartlett B. James and J. Franklin Jameson, *Journal of Jasper Danckaerts 1679–1680* (New York: Charles Scribner's Sons, 1913), 264.

8 Philip Rappagliosi, *Letters from the Rocky Mountain Indian Missions*, ed. Robert Bigart, trans. Anthony Mattina and Lisa Moore Nardini (Lincoln: University of Nebraska Press, 2003), 10.

9 This was the subject of a paper, "Latin as a language of communication within the family in early America," that I delivered at the Fifth International Neo-Latin Symposium in Cork in April 2017, which I hope to publish.

10 Robert C. Winthrop, *Proceedings of the Massachusetts Historical Society*, ser. 2, vol. 7 (1891/92): 11–17.

11 *Winthrop Papers*, vol. 1, *1498–1628* (Boston: The Massachusetts Historical Society, 1929), 368, 392–93, 415.

12 See James Daybell, *The Material Letter in Early Modern England: Manuscript Letters and the Culture and Practices of Letter-Writing, 1512–1635* (New York: Palgrave Macmillan, 2012), 55–58.

13 Luis Garesché, *Biography of Lieut. Col. Julius P. Garesché, Assistant Adjutant-General, U.S. Army* (Philadelphia: Lippincott, 1887), 38–43.

14 Joseph T. Durkin, *General Sherman's Son* (New York: Farrar, Straus & Cudahy, 1959), 16.

15 Timothy Alden Taylor, *Memoir of the Rev. Oliver Alden Taylor of Manchester Massachusetts*, 2nd ed. (Boston: John P. Jewett, 1854), 77, 251, 324–28, 331–33, 342.

16 An image of a page from one of these letters can be seen in Traveling Summer Republic and City Archives of Giessen, eds., *Utopia: Revisiting a German State in America* (Bremen: Edition Falkenberg, distributed by University of Chicago Press, 2013), 228.

17 *Christian Advocate* 2 (1824): 397–400.

18 *A Jesuit Missionary in Eighteenth-Century Sonora: The Family Correspondence of Philipp Segesser*, ed. Raymond H. Thompson, trans. Werner S. Zimmt and Robert E. Dahlquist (Albuquerque: University of

New Mexico Press, 2014), letters 18, 19, 22, 25, 28, 30, 57. All but one of these were written before Segesser left Europe. The last was written from Tecoripa (in Sonora).

19 Those from Francis to Peter have been translated by Francis E. Tourscher, *The Kenrick-Frenaye Correspondence* (Philadelphia: Wickersham, 1920). I am working on an annotated translation of those from Peter to Francis.

20 *The Letters of Jacob Baegert 1749-1761, Jesuit Missionary in Baja California*, ed. Doyce B. Nunis, trans. Elsbeth Schulz-Bischof (Los Angeles: Dawson's Book Shop, 1982), 236–37.

21 Robert C. Winthrop, *Proceedings of the Massachusetts Historical Society*, ser. 2, vol. 8 (1892): 6.

22 The Papers of John R. Guerrant and the Guerrant Family, 1881–1927, Special Collection, The University of Virginia Library: http://ead.lib.virginia.edu/vivaxtf/view?query=john+guerrant&docId=uva-sc%2Fviu00835.xml&chunk.id=. I have not seen these diaries.

23 *Acta et Dicta* 1 (1907): 39–43.

24 *St Louis Catholic Historical Review* 3 (1921): 185-86.

25 Robert I. Burns, "A Jesuit at the Hell Gate Treaty of 1855," *Mid-America* 34 (1952): 89.

26 Richard M. Gummere, *The American Colonial Mind and the Classical Tradition* (Cambridge, MA: Harvard University Press, 1963); Meyer Reinhold, *Classica Americana: The Greek and Roman Heritage in the United States* (Detroit: Wayne State University Press, 1984); Wolfgang Haase and Meyer Reinhold, eds., *The Classical Tradition and the Americas*, vol. 1, *European Images of the Americas and the Classical Tradition* (Berlin: Walter de Gruyter, 1994); Carl J. Richard, *The Founders and the Classics: Greece, Rome, and the American Enlightenment* (Cambridge, MA: Harvard University Press, 1994); Caroline Winterer, *The Culture of Classicism: Ancient Greece and Rome in American Intellectual Life, 1780–1910* (Baltimore: Johns Hopkins University Press, 2002); Lee T. Pearcy, *The Grammar of Our Civility: Classical Education in America* (Waco: Baylor University Press, 2005); Carl J. Richard, *The Golden Age of the Classics in America: Greece, Rome, and the Antebellum United States* (Cambridge, MA: Harvard University Press, 2009); James Turner, *Philology: The Forgotten Origins of the Modern Humanities* (Princeton: Princeton University Press, 2014). See also the work of Ward W. Briggs, especially *Biographical Dictionary of North American Classicists* (Westport, CT: Greenwood Press, 1994), and *Database of Classical Scholars*, which he edits.

27 *The North American Review* 43 (1836): 28–52 (p. 43).

28 "A Census of American Latin Verse, 1625–1825," *Proceedings of the*

American Antiquarian Society 91 (1982): 197–299; "Contributions to a Census of American Latin Prose, 1634–1800," *Humanistica Lovaniensia* 31 (1982): 164–89. An example of Kaiser's numerous studies of individual poets and their works is "John Beveridge: Latin Poet of Two Worlds," *Classical Journal* 58 (1963): 215–25. For his work on inscriptions see "Latin Epitaphs for CIGLA," *Classical Journal* 51 (1955-56): 69–80, 141–44, 294–301, 342–44. His anthology is *Early American Latin Verse, 1625–1825, An Anthology* (Chicago: Bolchazy-Carducci, 1984).
29 Josef IJsewijn, *Companion to Neo-Latin Studies*, vol. 1, 2nd ed. (Leuven: Leuven University Press, 1990), 289–94; Ann M. Blair, "Neo-Latin in North America," in Philip Ford, Jan Bloemendal, Charles Fantazzi, eds., *Brill's Encyclopedia of the Neo-Latin World* (Leiden: Brill, 2014), 833–43; John Gallucci, "North America," in Sarah Knight and Stefan Tilg, eds., *The Oxford Handbook of Neo-Latin* (Oxford: Oxford University Press, 2015), 547–54.
30 Stuart M. McManus, "*Classica Americana*. An Addendum to the Censuses of Pre-1800 Latin Texts from British North America," *Humanistica Lovaniensia* 67 (2018): 427–67. Among the contributions of McManus's work is the attention given to the Latin of the Moravians and of Ezra Stiles (1727–95).
31 See the many publications of Andrew Laird, notably his surveys in *Brill's Encyclopedia of the Neo-Latin World*, 821–32 and *Oxford Handbook of Neo-Latin*, 525–40 and see also Rose Williams, *Latin of New Spain* (Mundelein, IL: Bolchazy-Carducci, 2015).
32 Regarding the integration of Latin literature within the American literary tradition, see especially Gilbert L. Gigliotti, "*Musae Americanae*: The Neo-Latin Poetry of Colonial and Revolutionary America" (PhD diss., The Catholic University of America, 1992).
33 Joseph Fischer, *The Discoveries of the Norsemen in America*, trans. Basil H. Soulsby (St. Louis: Herder, 1903), 1.
34 Carl F. Hallencreutz, *Adam Bremensis and Sueonia: A Fresh Look at Gesta Hammaburgensis Ecclesiae Pontificum* (Uppsala: Uppsala University Press, 1984), 5.
35 Arthur F. J. Remy, "Adam of Bremen," in *Catholic Encyclopedia* (available at newadvent.org). On medieval historiogaphy in general, see Roger Ray, "Historiography," in F.A.C. Mantello and A.G. Rigg, eds., *Medieval Latin: An Introduction and Bibliographical Guide* (Washington, DC: Catholic University of America Press, 1996), 639–49.
36 For discussion of this passage in particular, see Fischer, *Discoveries of the Norsemen in America*, 1–4; Julius E. Olson, *The Voyages of the Northmen* in *The Northmen; Columbus, and Cabot, 985–1503* (New York: Charles Scribner's Sons, 1906), 67–68; Kirsten A. Seaver, *Maps, Myths,*

and Men: The Story of the Vinland Map (Stanford: Stanford University Press, 2004), 213–19.

37 For speculation on the location(s) of Vinland, see David B. Quinn, *North America from Earliest Discovery to First Settlements* (New York: Harper & Row, 1977), 31–40 and Birgitta Wallace, "The Norse in Newfoundland: L'Anse aux Meadows and Vinland," *Newfoundland and Labrador Studies* 19 (2003): 5–43, esp. 27–32.

38 recitavit : the subject is Sven Estridsen, the King of Denmark.

39 Today the furthest north that grapes grow is 44° latitude, but some have speculated that at the time of the Norse settlements the Newfoundland climate was milder, and others have suggested that what is meant are wild grapes, which do grow in Newfoundland. See Quinn, *North America from Earliest Discovery*, 32 and Wallace, "The Norse in Newfoundland," 26–27.

40 The text from "post" to the end of the passage is printed in brackets by Schmeidler because it is not found in the principal manuscript.

41 ait : the subject again is Sven Estridsen

42 Martianus Capella, *De nuptiis*, 6.666.

43 Cf. the note in *Martianus Capella and the Seven Liberal Arts*, vol. 2, trans. William H. Stahl and Richard W. Johnson, with E.L. Burge (New York: Columbia University Press, 1977), 249: "The location of Ultima Thule—identified, among other suggestions, as Iceland, Norway, the Faroes, the Shetland Islands, or the Orkneys—is one of the most controversial subjects of ancient geography."

44 See also Adam of Bremen, *History of the Archbishops of Hamburg-Bremen*, trans. Francis Tschan, intro. Timothy Reuter (New York: Columbia University Press, 2002).

45 Quinn, *North America from Earliest Discovery* (note 37 above), 22–23.

46 On the Capitulations, see Samuel Eliot Morison, *Journals and Other Documents on the Life and Voyages of Christopher Columbus* (New York: Heritage, 1963), 26–36. On Columbus in general, see J.T. Milanich and S. Milbrath, eds., *First Encounters: Spanish Explorations in the Caribbean and the United States, 1492–1570* (Gainesville: University of Florida Press, 1989); Valerie I.J. Flint, *The Imaginative Landscape of Christopher Columbus* (Princeton: Princeton University Press, 1992).

47 Examples of Latin works in Columbus's library include Aeneas Silvius Piccolomini's [Pope Pius II] *Historia Rerum Ubique Gestarum*, Pierre d'Ailly's *Imago Mundi*, and Marco Polo's *De Consuetudinibus et Conditionibus Orientalium Regionum*.

48 Kirkpatrick Sale, *Christopher Columbus and the Conquest of Paradise*, 2nd ed. (London: I.B. Tauris, 2006), 125. See especially "The Diffusion

of Columbus's Letter through Europe, 1493–1497," at The Osher Map Library & Smith Center for Cartographic Education at the University of Southern Maine: https://oshermaps.org/special-map-exhibits/columbus-letter/iv-diffusion-columbuss-letter-through-europe-1493-1497.

49 Laurence Bergreen, *Columbus: The Four Voyages, 1492–1504* (New York: Penguin Books, 2011), 379.

50 See the press release of The United States Attorney's Office, District of Delaware, May 18, 2016, available at https://www.justice.gov/usao-de/pr/stolen-letter-christopher-columbus-historic-voyage-americas-repatriated-italian.

51 On the presumed eagerness of eastern rulers to learn of European affairs, see Samuel Eliot Morison, *Admiral of the Open Sea: A Life of Christopher Columbus* (Boston: Little, Brown, and Company, 1942), 107–8.

52 Columbus's name is spelled with the *chrismon* abbreviation. See Morison, *Journals and Other Documents*, 30, 31.

53 A *caravela*, a quick and agile ship that draws a shallow draught, was developed by the Spanish and the Portuguese for fishing and exploration. The origins of the name are obscure, but they may lie in the Latin *carabus* (= Greek κάραβος) and/or the Arabic qârib. See George Robert Schwarz, "The History and Development of Caravels" (master's thesis, Texas A & M University, 2008).

54 There is a mistake here, most likely involving the place name. According to his journal (Morison, *Journals and Other Documents*, 49, 51, 64), Columbus departed Cádiz on August 3, 1492 and Gomera (in the Canary Islands) on September 6, and he sighted land on October 12. Therefore the crossing from Cádiz to the Bahamas took about seventy days.

55 This ceremony and Columbus's initial thoughts upon encountering the inhabitants of Guanahaní are described more fully in his journal. See Morison, *Journals and Other Documents*, 64–65.

56 At 2 a.m. on Friday, October 12, 1492, land was first spotted by Rodrigo de Traina, who was on board the *Pinta*. For more than a century this land has been identified as Watling's or San Salvador Island. See Morison, *Journals and Other Documents*, 64–66, and William F. Keegan, "Columbus's 1492 Voyage and the Search for His Landfall," in Milanich and Milbrath, *First Encounters*, 27–40.

57 On the practice of renaming as well as retaining indigenous names, see Gene Rhea Tucker, "Place-Names, Conquest, and Empire: Spanish and Amerindian Conceptions of Place in the New World" (PhD diss., University of Texas at Arlington, 2011), esp. 300–5.

58 Morison, *Journals and Other Documents*, 69–70 identifies these as

follows: Sancta Maria Conceptionis = Rum Cay; Fernandina = Long Island; Isabela = Crooked Island; Ioanna = Cuba.

59 Columbus reached Cuba on October 28, 1492.

60 Columbus thought that he had reached Cathay, which was the name for a province as well as the capital of China.

61 Columbus is thought to have abducted more than twenty Native Americans on his first voyage, six of whom survived the crossing back to Europe and were presented before Ferdinand and Isabella at the Alcázar. Columbus's intent, as is evident from his journal entry of October 14, 1492, was eventually to return them to their homes. See Andrés Reséndez, *The Other Slavery: The Uncovered Story of Indian Enslavement in America* (Boston: Mariner, 2017), 17–28, esp. 22, who remarks that "strictly speaking" they were "showpieces" rather than slaves, intended to corroborate Columbus's discovery and to become translators.

62 The original can be seen through PARES: http://pares.mcu.es/ParesBusquedas20/catalogo/show/1931496?nm. fol. 136r of Fernando II el Católico. Diversorum Sigilli Secreti 9 [Cathalonie et Insularum], Archivo de la Corona de Aragón, ACA, Cancillería, Registros, Núm 3569. It was reproduced in L. Gallois, "Histoire de la géographie travaux récents," *Annales de Géographie* 37 (1928): 208. A slightly different text is found in Morison, *Journals and Other Documents*, 31.

63 As a result of Portuguese opposition, this line was soon adjusted by the Treaty of Tordesillas (June 7, 1494) to 370 leagues (1185 miles) west of the Cape Verde Islands. See "Treaty of Tordesillas" at britannica.com.

64 Herman Vander Linden, "Alexander VI and the Demarcation of the Maritime and Colonial Domains of Spain and Portugal, 1493–1494," *The American Historical Review* 22 (1916): 1–20.

65 Quoted in Vander Linden, "Alexander VI and the Demarcation," 18.

66 The easternmost islands in the Azores (São Miguel, Santa Maria) have the same longitude (25°) as the westernmost Cape Verde island (Santo Antão). See Vander Linden, "Alexander VI and the Demarcation," 9.

67 A league was the equivalent of four Roman miles; therefore the line of demarcation would be at 31° latitude. See Davenport, *European Treaties* (see Source), 74. See also Vander Linden, "Alexander VI and the Demarcation," 9, who explains that the phrase *versus occidentem et meridiem* means "to the west and in the Ocean Sea," the latter being thought to lie to the south, near the Equator.

68 Alexander VI had not yet completed his first year as Pope, having been elected on August 11, 1492.

69 Quinn, *North America from Earliest Discovery* (note 37 above), 109, 132.

70 See John R. Hébert, "The Map that Named America: Library Acquires 1507 Waldseemüller Map of the World," *Library of Congress Information Bulletin* 62 (September 2003), available at https://www.loc.gov/loc/lcib/0309/maps.html.
71 *Bibliotheca Americana Vetustissima* (see Source), 94.
72 *Woodstock Letters* 30 (1901): 457.
73 I.e., Ameri(ci) γῆ. Similarly, Waldseemüller had called himself Hylacomylus, from ὕλη + lacus + μύλος. See Edward Gaylord Bourne, *Spain in America 1450–1580* (New York: Harper & Brothers, 1904), 99–100.
74 Quinn, *North America from Earliest Discovery* (note 37 above), 112–35. On the Cabot voyages, see James A. Williamson with R.A. Skelton, *The Cabot Voyages and Bristol Discovery under Henry VII* (Cambridge: University Press, 1962; rept. New York: Routledge, 2016), and Heather Dalton, *Merchants and Explorers: Roger Barlow, Sebastian Cabot, and Networks of Atlantic Exchange 1500–1560* (Oxford: Oxford University Press, 2016).
75 A school text of Peter Martyr's passages on Columbus has been published: Constance P. Iacona and Edward V. George, *Columbus' First Voyage: Latin Selections from Peter Martyr's* De Orbe Novo (Wauconda, IL: Bolchazy-Carducci, 2005). On the influence of Peter Martyr's depiction of indigenous peoples, see D.A. Brading, *The First America: The Spanish Monarchy, Creole Patriots and the Liberal State, 1492–1867* (Cambridge: Cambridge University Press, 1991), 16–18.
76 See Francis A. MacNutt, *De Orbe Novo: The Eight Decades of Peter Martyr d'Anghera*, 2 vols. (New York: G.P. Putnam's Sons, 1912), 1:46–50, 254. Towards the end of the seventh chapter of the seventh decade Peter Martyr acknowledges his unusual Latinity: *Vulgaribus utor vocabulis, quando illis caret vetus lingua latina, et liceat quae de novo emergunt, novis induere tegminibus, cum id negantium bona venia, volo intelligi*, "I use vulgar words, for no suitable expression can be found in the ancient Latin, and it is permissible to clothe new facts in new words. I trust those who do not share this opinion will pardon me" (MacNutt trans., *De Orbe Novo* 2:296). I have benefited greatly from MacNutt's translation.
77 "Eas" refers to "glaciales oras" from the previous sentence.
78 Later in life Cabot maintained that on this voyage he was at 67° 30', which is inside the Arctic Circle. See Quinn, *North America from Earliest Discovery*, 134.
79 The Outer Banks of North Carolina have approximately the same latitude as the Straits of Gibraltar (Herculei freti).
80 According to Quinn, *North America from Earliest Discovery*, 135, this word could refer to Newfoundland or to North America in gener-

al. MacNutt (*De Orbe Novo*, 1:347) mentions that the word may be of Basque origin.

81 MacNutt translates (*De Orbe Novo* 1:347): "It is not merely probable, therefore, but becomes even necessary to conclude that between these two hitherto unknown continents there extend large openings through which the water flows from east to west."

82 Demogorgon is an arch-demon.

83 Charles V was successor to King Ferdinand, who died in January 1516.

84 Henry VII died on April 21, 1509.

85 Cabot and Peter Martyr were co-workers in the Council of the Indies.

86 In 1518 he gained employment as Pilot Major with the Casa de la Contratación in Seville, and in 1525 he received permission from the Council of the Indies for a multi-year expedition to the Far East, which he undertook in April 1526.

87 The Cantino map (1502), drawn in Portugal, includes a land mass to the northwest of Cuba, which some have identified as Florida. For a recent and succinct discussion of scholarly opinion on the pre-Ponce de León knowlege of Florida, see Paul E. Hoffman, "The Historiography of Sixteenth-Century La Florida," *Florida Historical Quarterly* 91 (2013): 316–18.

88 For accounts of the successive Spanish explorations of Florida, see Michael V. Gannon, *The Cross in the Sand: The Early Catholic Church in Florida* (Gainesville: University of Florida Press, 1965), 1–19, and Quinn, *North America from Earliest Discovery* (note 37 above), 137–51, and for translations of original narratives see John E. Worth, *Discovering Florida: First-Contact Narratives from Spanish Expeditions along the Lower Gulf Coast* (Gainesville: University Press of Florida, 2014). For recent scholarship on Ponce's Florida venture, see Samuel Turner, "Juan Ponce de León and the Discovery of Florida Reconsidered," *Florida Historical Quarterly* 92 (2013): 1–31.

89 Worth, *Discovering Florida*, 8, 17.

90 See T. Frederick Davis, "Ponce de Leon's First Voyage and Discovery of Florida," *Florida Historical Society Quarterly* 14 (1935): 45.

91 Worth, *Discovering Florida*, 10, 11.

92 Sacchini wrote Latin biographies of various saints and three pedagogical works in Latin. See Carlos Sommervogel, *Bibliothèque de la Compagnie de Jésus*, vol. 7 (Brussels: Oscar Schepens, 1896), 362–68.

93 This refers to lands discovered to the north of Hispaniola.

94 On this passage, and on the story of the fountain in general, see Leonardo Olschki, "Ponce de León's Fountain of Youth: History of a Geographical Myth," *The Hispanic American Historical Review* 21

(1941): 361–85, and see especially Worth, *Discovering Florida*, 9–13.
95 Pope Leo X (*r.* 1513–21).
96 Cf. MacNutt's translation (note 76 above), 1:275: "Unless, that is to say, we are prepared to believe the Colchian fable concerning the renewal of Aeson and the researches of the Sibyl of Erythraea." The syntax of the Latin is obscure.
97 Elsewhere Peter Martyr identifies one of his authorities as Alvares de Castro, the Dean of the Cathedral of Concepción in Hispaniola. See MacNutt, *De Orbe Novo*, 2:258. Another authory was Lucas Vázques de Ayllón.
98 The Lucaya were the native residents of the Bahamas.
99 The Romans used to frequent mineral springs in Puteoli (in Campania). Cicero had a villa nearby.
100 I have benefited from the transcription of this passage given by Eugène Beauvois in *Le Muséon* 3 (1884): 408.
101 30° latitude is just north of St. Augustine.
102 Sacchini, following other early sources, gives the date of the voyage as 1512, but modern research has shown that the year was 1513. See Davis, "Ponce de Leon's First Voyage and Discovery of Florida," 47–48.
103 Sacchini has in mind here the Jesuit martyrs who would be killed in Florida (see section 11).
104 See Quinn, *North America from Earliest Discovery* (note 37 above), 154–59.
105 Excerpts from a translation by Susan Tarrow of Verrazzanno's letter can be found at http://nationalhumanitiescenter.org/pds/amerbegin/contact/text4/verrazzano.pdf; original = Lawrence C. Wroth, ed., *The Voyages of Giovanni da Verrazzano, 1524–1528* (New Haven: Yale University Press, 1970).
106 34° is the latitude of Wilmington, North Carolina.
107 The Hudson.
108 Verrazzano named the island Louise (Aloysia), after the mother of King François, but geographers mistakenly gave the island the name Claudia, after the King's first wife. The identity of this island is not certain, but many suspect it denotes Block Island rather than Martha's Vineyard.
109 This harbor is thought to be in present-day Rhode Island. 41°40' passes through Martha's Vineyard and New London, Connecticut.
110 This region is thought to be Cape Cod.
111 The exceptions allowed for the enslavement of cannibals, prisoners taken in a just war, and those who were already slaves. See Reséndez, *The Other Slavery* (note 61 above), 41–42.
112 For context, see Lewis Hanke, "Pope Paul III and the American

Indians," *The Harvard Theological Review* 30 (1937): 65–102. An earlier letter, *Pastorale Officium* (May 29, 1537), had imposed the penalty of excommunication on those who reduced Indians to slavery or deprived them of their possessions.

113 In addition to Reséndez, *The Other Slavery*, see Alan Gallay, *The Indian Slave Trade: The Rise of the English Empire in the American South, 1670–1717* (New Haven: Yale University Press, 2002) and Brett Rushforth, *Bonds of Alliance: Indigenous and Atlantic Slaveries in New France* (Chapel Hill: University of North Carolina Press, for the Omohundro Institute of Early American History and Culture, 2012).

114 Reséndez, *The Other Slavery*, 5.

115 Documents in Spanish and Italian are collected in Richard Flint and Shirley Cushing Flint, *Documents of the Coronado Expedition, 1539–1542: "They Were Not Familiar with His Majesty, nor Did They Wish to Be His Subjects"* (Albuquerque: University of New Mexico Press, 2005). For earlier syntheses see John Francis Bannon, *The Spanish Borderlands Frontier 1513–1821* (Albuquerque: University of New Mexico Press, 1974), 15–21; David J. Weber, *The Spanish Frontier in North America* (New Haven: Yale University Press, 1992), 14–29, 45–49, and John L. Kessell, *Kiva, Cross, and Crown* (Albuquerque: University of New Mexico Press, 1987), 1–27. For a map of Coronado's route, see https://www.nps.gov/coro/planyourvisit/upload/COROExpeditionmap2.pdf.

116 For the identities of these friars, see Angélico Chavez, *Coronado's Friars* (Washington, DC: Academy of American Franciscan History, 1968).

117 See Flint and Flint, *Documents*, 424, 481.

118 Canice Mooney, "The Writings of Father Luke Wadding, O.F.M.," *Franciscan Studies* 18 (1958): 225–39. Wadding published a compendium of all Franciscan authors, *Scriptores Ordinis Minorum* (1650), a sixteen-volume edition of the works of John Duns Scotus (1639), the complete annotated writings of St. Francis (1623), and two volumes defending the dogma of the Immaculate Conception of the Virgin Mary (1641, 1655).

119 Charles V became Holy Roman Emperor in 1519; Paul III was Pope from 1534 to 1549; the Franciscans were founded in 1209.

120 Wadding had already introduced Coronado in his chronicle of the year 1539.

121 A region in northwest New Mexico populated by the Zuni, which, according to Fray Marcos's report, contained seven fabulously wealthy cities, one of which was larger than Mexico City.

122 "Minorita" is a term for a Franciscan friar. On the significance of this designation, see Regis J. Armstrong, "Franciscus: Inter minores

minimus," *Collectanea Franciscana* 85 (2015): 401–26.
123 According to Chavez, *Coronado's Friars*, 29, the place name "Escalona," was misattributed to Fray Luis de Úbeda.
124 Juan de Padilla, from Andalusia, had founded Franciscan convents in Tzapotlán, Tuchpán, and Tulancingo.
125 In 1536, one year after he arrived in the New World, Coronado married Beatriz de Estrada, the daughter of the former treasurer of New Spain.
126 Tiguez is the region around present-day Albuquerque.
127 On the identities of those who remained behind with the friars and on the death of Fray Juan de Padilla, see the accounts of Castañeda de Nájera and Juan Jaramillo, which are printed and translated in Flint and Flint, *Documents of the Coronado Expedition*, 427, 517–18. On the death of Fray Luis de Úbeda, see Chavez, *Coronado's Friars*, 72–74, who notes that "nobody ever returned to New Spain to tell how or when he died" (72), but that chroniclers early on began to state that he had been martyred.
128 For accounts of the French settlements, see Gannon, *Cross in the Sand* (note 88 above), 20–29; Bannon, *Spanish Borderlands Frontier* (note 115 above), 43–46; Eugene Lyon, *The Enterprise of Florida: Pedro Menéndez de Avilés and the Spanish Conquest of 1565–1568* (Gainesville: University Press of Florida, 1976), 21–22, 33, 67–69, 100–30; Weber, *Spanish Frontier in North America* (note 115 above), 60–64; W.J. Eccles, *The French in North America 1500–1783* (Markham, Ontario: Fitzhenry & Whiteside, 1998), 8–10; Paul E. Hoffman, *A New Andalucia and a Way to the Orient: The American Southeast During the Sixteenth Century* (Baton Rouge: Louisiana State University Press, 2004), 205–30. On the images, see Jerald Milanich, "The Devil in the Details," *Archaeology* 58 (May-June 2005): 27–31.
129 Quinn, *North America from Earliest Discovery* (note 37 above), 556.
130 An *orgyia* is a unit of measurement equivalent to the distance between the outstretched hands.
131 For an account of the ballgame among the Apalachee people, see the description by Juan de Paiva, available at https://earlyfloridalit.net/juan-de-paiva-the-ball-game-manuscript/.
132 For a translation by William Appleton see *Narrative of Le Moyne, an artist who accompanied the French Expedition to Florida under Laudonnière, 1564* (Boston: James R. Osgood, 1875).
133 The primary documents for the Jesuit presence in Florida are contained in Felix Zubillaga, *Monumenta Antiquae Floridae (1566–1572)* (Rome: Monumenta Historica Societatis Iesu, 1946).
134 See Brendan Wolfe, "Don Luís de Velasco/Paquiquineo (fl.

1561–1571)," *Encyclopedia Virginia* (online), for an excellent timeline of Paquiquineo's life. Prior to his involvement with the Jesuits, Paquiquineo had been associated with two failed Dominican missions to the Chesapeake (1562, 1566).

135 The other primary sources for this episode are printed and translated in Clifford M. Lewis and Albert J. Loomie, *The Spanish Jesuit Mission in Virginia, 1570–1572* (Chapel Hill: University of North Carolina Press, 1953). For scholarship on this episode, see Frank Marotti, "Juan Baptista de Segura and the Failure of the Florida Jesuit Mission, 1566–1572," *Florida Historical Quarterly* 63 (1985): 267–79; Charlotte M. Gradie, "Spanish Jesuits in Virginia: The Mission that Failed," *Virginia Magazine of History and Biography* 96 (1988): 131–56; Seth Mallios, *The Deadly Politics of Giving: Exchange and Violence at Ajacan, Roanoke, and Jamestown* (Tuscaloosa: University of Alabama Press, 2006); Anna Brickhouse, *The Unsettlement of America: Translation, Interpretation, and the Story of Don Luis de Velasco, 1560–1945* (New York: Oxford University Press, 2014).

136 For a bibliography of his writings, see Carlos Sommervogel, *Bibliothèque de la Compagnie de Jésus*, vol. 5 (Brussels: Oscar Schepens, 1894), 1237–38.

137 For an acount from a Franciscan martyrology of the 1597 death of five friars in present-day Georgia, see *Martyrologium Franciscanum*, 2nd ed. (Paris 1653), 438–39. For an account from a Dominican martyrology of the 1549 death of Fray Luis de Cancer near Tampa, Florida, see Petrus Malpaeus, *Palma Fidei S. Ordinis Praedicatorum* (Antwerp: Typis Ioannis Cnobbari, 1630), 126–28.

138 The Jesuits regularly spoke of fellow Jesuits as "ours."

139 This account, unlike other ancient sources, indicates that Spanish soldiers sought out Don Luis as a valuable interpreter.

140 In fact two Jesuit priests were in Ajacán: Juan Bautista Segura and Luis de Quirós. The other Jesuits on the mission were Brothers Gabriel de Solís, Juan Bautista Méndez, Pedro de Linares, Sancho Zaballos, Gabriel Gómez, and Cristóbal Redondo.

141 According to the best modern assessment (Lewis and Loomie, *The Spanish Jesuit Mission*), the Jesuit mission was located on the south shore of the York River.

142 Don Luis was perhaps a member of the Kiskiak tribe, who lived about a day and a half's journey from the Jesuit mission.

143 Other sources give the dates of the two attacks as February 4 and February 9 or 10, 1571.

144 Early sources mention the sudden death of those natives who opened an *arca* that the Jesuits had brought as a repository for their vestments and sacred objects.

145 Alonso Olmos.
146 See note 144 above.
147 Paestum, in southern Italy, was famous for its rose gardens (cf. Vergil *G.* 4.119; Ovid, *Met.* 15.708; et al.).
148 Weber, *Spanish Frontier in North America* (note 115 above), 62. See also Bannon, *Spanish Borderlands Frontier* (note 115 above), 33, 49–51; Hans P. Kraus, *Sir Francis Drake: A Pictorial Biography* (Amsterdam: Israel, 1970).
149 Andrew Lawler, "Did Francis Drake Really Land in California?" *Smithsonian*, September 26, 2019.
150 Harry Kelsey, "Did Francis Drake Really Visit California?" *Western Historical Quarterly* 21 (1990): 455.
151 James W. Covington, "Drake Destroys St. Augustine: 1586," *Florida Historical Quarterly* 44 (1965): 81–93.
152 See the introduction to the hypertext critical edition by Dana F. Sutton, available at The Philological Museum, http://www.philological.bham.ac.uk/bigges/.
153 The California-Oregon border is at 42°.
154 Drake's Bay is at 38°.
155 Several early accounts refer to Nova Albion as an island. For extensive discussion of these, see Kelsey, "Did Francis Drake Really Visit California?" 452–54.
156 In February 1937 a California store clerk claimed to have discovered near San Francisco Bay a brass plate bearing the date June 17, 1579, Drake's name, and language claiming New Albion for Queen Elizabeth, but in the 1970s this was shown to be a forgery. See John Sugden, *Sir Francis Drake* (London: Pimlico, 2006), 134–35, and see also Lawler, "Did Francis Drake Really Land in California?"
157 This, the sixth fort to be constructed at St. Augustine, was named San Juan de Pinos and was located slightly to the north of today's Castillo San Marcos. The English viewed the fort from Anastasia Island, across the Matanzas River.
158 Nicholas Borgoignon, a French fifer who had been in St. Augustine since 1565, rowed out to the English to alert them that the fort was abandoned.
159 Pedro Menéndez Marqués, the Governor of Florida from 1577 to 1594 (and the nephew of the founder of St. Augustine), had arranged for the evacuation of women and children from the city and for expedited construction on the fort.
160 Prior to abandoning the fort, the Spanish had thrown two bronze falcons into the moat and had attempted to bury fourteen bronze cannon.

161 The Spanish had neglected to take with them the chest that contained the *situado*, the annual subsidy from Mexico City that supported the Spanish settlement in St. Augustine.
162 An image can be seen at http://international.loc.gov/service/rbc/rbdk/d031/02600013.jpg. For discussion of DeBry's text, see https://bodmerlab.unige.ch/recits-et-images/debry/#/grands-voyages/GVVIII.
163 Images of this text can be seen at https://www.loc.gov/resource/rbdk.d020/?sp=17.
164 Valuable early studies of this episode include: J. Lloyd Mecham, "The Martyrdom of Father Juan de Santa María," *Catholic Historical Review* 6 (1920): 308–21, esp. 317–18; idem, "The Second Spanish Expedition to New Mexico," *New Mexico Historical Review* 1 (1926): 265–91; idem, "Supplementary Documents Relating to the Chamuscado-Rodríguez Expedition," *Southwestern Historical Quarterly* 29 (1926): 224–31. A more recent narrative is found in chapter 2 of Kessell, *Kiva, Cross, and Crown* (note 115 above). The Rodríguez expedition is briefly discussed in Weber, *Spanish Frontier in North America* (note 115 above), 78–79, 95 and Bannon, *Spanish Borderlands Frontier* (note 115 above), 30–32. See also the entries in *Handbook of Texas Online*: "Rodríguez, Agustín," (Christopher Long); "Sánchez, Francisco" (John G. Johnson); "Rodríguez-Sánchez Expedition" (W. H. Timmons).
165 A biographical notice of Gonzaga is in *American Ecclesiastical Review* 32 (1905): 80–81. For discussion of Gonzaga's sources, see Chavez, *Coronado's Friars* (see note 116), viii-xvii.
166 In 1534 the Franciscans established the Province of the Holy Gospel, based in Mexico City. The three Franciscans on this mission had been in residence at the convent of San Francisco, in Mexico City.
167 Zacatecas, currently a state as well as a diocese in northern Mexico, was inhabited by the Chichimeca tribe.
168 Rodríguez was stationed in San Bartolomé, not far from Santa Bárbara.
169 Rodríguez, likely prompted by Sánchez, obtained a license from the Viceroy Lorenzo Suarez de Mendoza (*r.* 1580–83) to undertake this exploration to the north.
170 Francisco López, a native of Seville, was designated superior of the Franciscans on this mission. Juan de Santa María was a native of Catalonia. According to other accounts, one of which was written by one of soldiers, there were nine soldiers on this expedition.
171 For a detailed account of the sizes and locations of the pueblos encountered, see Mecham, "The Second Spanish Expedition to New Mexico."
172 On September 7, 1581 Santa María left the expedition when it was

in the Santa Fé region.
173 For the circumstances of Santa María's death, who was killed by the Tiguas in the pueblo of San Pablo in the Monzano Mountains (Sierra Morena), see Mecham, "The Martyrdom of Father Juan de Santa María."
174 For background on this episode and the personalities involved, see Quinn, *North America from Earliest Discovery* (note 37 above), 360–61 and Quinn's biographies of Parmenius and Gilbert in *Dictionary of Canadian Biography*, University of Toronto/Université Laval, vol. 1 (online version).
175 David B. Quinn and Neil M. Cheshire, *The New Found Land of Stephen Parmenius* (Toronto: University of Toronto Press, 1972) 36, refer to Leicester Bradner, *Musae Anglicanae: A History of Anglo-Latin Poetry, 1500–1925* (New York: Modern Language Association of America, 1940).
176 *De navigatione illustris et magnanimi aurati Humfredi Gilberti, ad deducendam in novum orbem coloniam suscepta, carmen* Επιβατικον (London 1582), which is printed in *Collections of the Massachusetts Historical Society* 9 (1804): 55–75.
177 Quinn and Cheshire, *New Found Land of Stephen Parmenius*, 14.
178 I am indebted for most of the notes below to the excellent commentary on this letter in Quinn and Cheshire, *New Found Land of Stephen Parmenius.*
179 The five vessels were the *Delight*, the *Bark Raleigh*, the *Golden Hind*, the *Swallow* (which carried Parmenius), and the *Squirrel.* The *Bark Raleigh*, commanded by Walter Raleigh, Gilbert's half-brother, turned back to Plymouth after a few days.
180 The southern tip of Newfoundland lies at 46° latitude, the northern tip at 51°.
181 This is Funk Island, located to the west of Newfoundland; the birds are Great Auk.
182 St. John's, Newfoundland lies at 47° latitude.
183 Maurice Brown, the son of a London merchant, had once worked for Sir Francis Walsingham (d. 1590), who was Queen Elizabeth's chief spy; he later became a supporter and publicist for Gilbert's expedition.
184 Some crewmembers of the *Swallow* raided and pillaged a fishing vessel that was returning to France, but they drowned while trying to return to the *Swallow* with the spoils.
185 The admiral in charge of the port of St. John's, although an Englishman, attempted to deny Gilbert entry, but Gilbert was able to gain access by showing the commission he had received from Queen Elizabeth.
186 On August 5 Gilbert claimed Newfoundland and all lands 200 leagues to the north and south for England. This involved a formal

assembly in front of Gilbert's tent and the erection of a wooden marker with the royal coat of arms. The laws forbade any public expression of religion apart from Anglicanism and any disrespect or opposition to the queen.

187 The charter can be found at the Avalon Project: https://avalon.law.yale.edu/17th_century/va01.asp.

188 On John Popham, see Douglas Walthew Rice, *The Life and Achievements of Sir John Popham 1531–1607: Leading to the Establishment of the First English Colony in New England* (Madison, NJ: Fairleigh Dickinson University Press, 2005). Rice treats the American settlement on pp. 231–60. I have not found a monograph on George Popham.

189 Early accounts include Henry S. Burrage, *The Beginnings of Colonial Maine. 1602–1658* (Portland, ME: printed for the state by Marks Printing House, 1914) and Charles E. Banks, "New Documents Relating to the Popham Expedition, 1607," *Proceedings of the American Antiquarian Society* 39 (1929): 307–34. A more recent account is Pat Higgins, "Popham Colony," *The Maine Story*, found at http://mainestory.info/maine-stories/popham-colony.html.

190 Archaeological excavations conducted at Maine's Popham Beach State Park in the 1990s revealed several structures, which had been known from a contemporary map of the settlement drawn by John Hunt. See Myron Beckenstein, "Maine's Lost Colony," *Smithsonian*, February 2004. See also Bilodeau (note 193 below) and William H. Tabor, "Maine's Popham Colony," *Athena Review* 3 (2000): 84–89.

191 The letter was discovered by the American historian George Bancroft (1800–1891) in the middle of the nineteenth century while he was doing research in the State Paper Office in London. He presented it to the Maine Historical Society as the "oldest extant letter written on the soil of Maine." See *Collections of the Maine Historical Society* 5 (1857): 355.

192 *Collections of the Maine Historical Society* 5 (1857): 352.

193 Christopher J. Bilodeau, "The Paradox of Sagadahoc: The Popham Colony, 1607–1608," *Early American Studies* 12 (2014): 1–35 (p. 28).

194 Aysha Pollnitz, *Princely Education in Early Modern Britain* (Cambridge: Cambridge University Press, 2015), 277.

195 According to Native Americans kidnapped by the English on an earlier voyage (see next note), this region of present-day Maine was called Mawooshen.

196 During an exploratory voyage in 1605 George Waymouth had seized five Native Americans from the Penobscot and Wawenocke tribes with the hope that they would serve as translators for future expeditions. See Rice, *Life and Achievements*, 234–36.

197 Ballard, *Memorial Volume* (see Source), conjectures that "myristicas" (nutmegs) rather than "amisticas" (which is not a Latin word) may be meant. The other commodities mentioned are mace (from the hazel-nut), cinnamon, pitch, Brazil wood, cochineal, and ambergris.
198 Ballard also includes an annotated translation. A facsimile is in Henry O. Thayer, *The Sagadahoc Colony, Comprising the Relation of a Voyage into New England* (Portland, ME: for the Gorges Society by Stephen Berry, 1892), after 116.
199 See the work of The New Netherland Institute: https://www.newnetherlandinstitute.org.
200 Rolf H. Bremmer, "The Correspondence of Johannes De Laet (1581–1649) as a Mirror of his Life," *Lias* 25 (1998): 139–64. I am much indebted to Bremmer for biographical information on De Laet.
201 Bremmer, "The Correspondence of Johannes De Laet," 150–51.
202 This debate is summarized in Herbert F. Wright, "Origin of American Aborigines: A Famous Controversy," *Catholic Historical Review* 3 (1917): 257–75.
203 Cf. De Laet, *Responsio ad dissertationem secundam Hugonis Grotii, de origine gentium Americanarum* (Amsterdam: Elsevier, 1644), 111, where he acknowledges that he was not as proficient in Latin as Grotius.
204 Hudson originally attempted to sail northeast, above Russia, but he reversed his course and headed west instead.
205 44°15' is the latitute of southern Nova Scotia (near the town of Liverpool).
206 A *scrupulus*, which DeLaet abbreviates here and below, was a unit of measurement originally equivalent to the 24th (or the 288th) part of something.
207 This is probably the southeastern portion of Cape Cod, which has a latitude of 41°54'.
208 Newport News, Virginia and New York City, respectively.
209 The latitude of Albany is 42°65'.
210 An English translation of this passage is in Wright, "Origin of American Aborigines," 267–68.
211 The exact location of the Jesuit mission in uncertain, but it may have been on Mount Desert Island, Maine. See Quinn, *North America from Earliest Discovery* (note 37 above), 412. The primary sources for this event are in Lucien Campeau, *Monumenta Novae Franciae*, vol. 1: *La première mission d'Acadie (1602–1616)* (Rome: Monumenta Historica Societatis Iesu, 1967), who provides a critical text of this letter on pp. 414–21. See also the entries in *Dictionary of Canadian Biography*, vol. 1 (online version) for Samuel Argall (W. Austin Squires), Pierre Biard (Lucien Campeau), Gilbert Du Thet (Lucien Campeau), and the Bien-

courts (Huia Ryder), and the entry in *Encyclopedia Virginia* (online) for Argall (J. Frederick Fausz).

212 In addition to the letter printed here, the other Latin letters, all addessed to Aquaviva, are dated January 21, 1611; June 11, 1611; January 31, 1612. They are printed in Campeau, *Monumenta Novae Franciae*, vol. 1, 116–21, 151–53, 203–25.

213 The priests Pierre Biard, Enemond Massé, and Jaques Quentin, and the Brother Gilbert Du Thet.

214 The commander of the Saint-Sauveur settlement was René Le Coq de la Saussaye, on whom see Lucien Campeau's sketch in *Dictionary of Canadian Biography*, vol. 1 (online version).

215 In early July 1613 Samuel Argall arrived on the 130-ton, 14-gun *Treasurer* along with sixty soldiers and made a surprise attack on the French settlement.

216 The names of the two who were killed were LeMoyne (from Dieppe) and Nepveu (from Beauvais).

217 Gilbert Du Thet, born in Chantelle (France) arrived in New France in January 1612, but he returned to France that summer to clear himself of an accusation leveled by the French agent in Port-Royal, Simon Imbert. The exonerated Du Thet returned to New France in the fall of 1612 to found the new settlement at Saint-Sauveur. He was on board the French ship *Jonas* when Argall attacked. Du Thet attempted to man the guns of the ship, but he was mortally wounded and died the next day.

218 Most likely these were Wabanaki.

219 A pilot nicknamed Bailleur, from Rouen, was not captured because he was away from his ship reconnoitering in a smaller boat when Argall attacked.

220 King Louis XIII (*r.* 1610–1643).

221 Jacques Quentin, a native of Abbeville, was ordained a priest in 1599 and entered the Jesuits in 1604.

222 Dirou is the reading in Campeau. Originally an agent for a French merchant, Dirou (1582–1641) became a Jesuit novice while at Saint-Sauveur or while in captivity.

223 William Crito. He was subsequently taken to London and sent back to his father.

224 Campeau suggests that these were the Pemaquid Islands, south of Mount Desert Island.

225 The marshal in Jamestown at the time was Sir Thomas Dale (d. 1619).

226 See Luca Codignola, *The Coldest Harbour of the Land: Simon Stock and Lord Baltimore's Colony in Newfoundland, 1621–1649*, trans. Anita Weston (Kingston: McGill-Queen's University Press, 1988).

227 This is available in a student text: Barbara Lawatsch-Boomgaarden, ed., with Josef IJsewijn, *Voyage to Maryland (1633): Relatio Itineris in Marilandiam* (Wauconda, IL: Bolchazy-Carducci, 1995).
228 An early translation was done by Nathan C. Brooks (1809–98), who also authored *Vitae Virorum Illustrium Americae, a Columbo ad Jacksonum* (New York: Barnes and Burr, 1864).
229 Hughes (1849–1939) was born in Liverpool and joined the Jesuits in England but soon moved to the Missouri Province. For context to his scholarship see Robert Emmett Curran, *Shaping American Catholicism: Maryland and New York, 1805–1915* (Washington, DC: Catholic University of America Press, 2012), 52–68.
230 Queen Henrietta Maria (1609–69).
231 King Charles I (*r.* 1625–49).
232 The charter for Maryland had originally been drawn up for George Calvert, the first Lord Baltimore, but he died before it was signed. A few months later Calvert's son, Cecil, the second Lord Baltimore, was granted this charter, which was sealed on June 20, 1632.
233 Cf. Bede, *Ecclesiastical History* 2.1.
234 Seville is at 37° latitude, Sicily lies roughly between 36° and 38°, Beijing lies at 40°, but Jerusalem and Arabia are much lower.
235 Cf. the title of Robert J. Brugger's history: *Maryland: A Middle Temperament, 1634–1980* (Baltimore: Johns Hopkins University Press, 1988).
236 The Chesapeake Bay is 200 miles long and its width ranges from about 3 to 30 miles.
237 Delaware Bay.
238 "Asellus" denotes either cod or haddock.
239 See also Thomas Hughes, *History of the Society of Jesus in North America, Colonial and Federal: Text*, vol. 1 (London: Longman, Green, 1908), 249–53.
240 See the biography of Jogues by Georges-Émile Giguère in *Dictionary of Canadian Biography*, vol. 1 (online version).
241 Cf. Lucien Campeau, *Monumenta Novae Franciae*, vol. 5, *La bonne nouvelle reçue*, 1641–1643 (Rome: Institutum Historicum Societatis Iesu, 1990), 592: "C'est un exposé de son état d'âme qu'un jésuite fait à son supérieur. C'est une pièce intime, qui justifie l'usage du latin. Car les jésuites de Nouvelle-France écrivaient d'ordinaire en français à leur provincial."
242 See Arthur Melançon, ed., *Memoires Touchant la Mort et las Vertus des Pères Isaac Jogues . . .* (Montréal: n.p., 1930), 68–75, 145–46. A critical edition is Lucien Campeau, *Monumenta Novae Franciae*, vol. 4: *Les*

grandes épreuves (1638–1640) (Rome: Institutum Historicum Societatis Iesu, 1989), 43–46.

243 See John Gallucci, "'I began to teach [...]': Emotion and Performance in Isaac Jogues's Letter to Father Jean Filleau," in Yasmin Haskell and Raphaële Garrod, eds., *Changing Hearts: Performing Jesuit Emotions Between Europe, Asia, and the Americas* (Leiden: Brill, 2019), 167–86, who highlights the strategic aspect of Jogues's choice of Latin for this letter. For Neo-Latin in Canada, in addition to the survey by Jean-François Cottier and Haijo Westra in *Oxford Handbook of Neo-Latin* (note 29 above), 541–47, see Cottier's edited collections of articles in *Tangence* 92 (2010): À la recherche d'un signe oublié: le patrimonie latin du Québec et sa culture classique and *Tangence* 99 (2012): Nova Gallia: recherches sur les écrits latins de Nouvelle-France.

244 S.P.N. = Sancto Patre Nostro

245 The feast of St. Ignatius is July 31.

246 Eustache Ahatsistari (b. 1602), a Huron warrior, was baptized on Holy Saturday 1642 and died in August of that year after being tortured. See the biographical sketch by Thomas Grassmann in *Dictionary of Canadian Biography*, vol. 1 (online version).

247 René Goupil was a surgeon and Jesuit brother who was imprisoned with Jogues. He was killed in Auriesville on September 29, 1642.

248 A more recent, critical text of the entire letter is found in Campeau, *Monumenta Novae Franciae*, vol. 5, 588–625.

249 See now Mark L. Thompson, *The Contest for the Delaware Valley: Allegiance, Identity, and Empire in the Seventeenth Century* (Baton Rouge: Louisiana State University Press, 2013), 74–77 and 83–84. Earlier accounts include Christopher Ward, *The Dutch & the Swedes on the Delaware, 1609–64* (Philadelphia: University of Pennsylvania Press, 1930), 118–22; Amandus Johnson, *The Swedish Settlements on the Delaware: their History and Relation to the Indians, Dutch and English, 1638–1664,* vol. 1 (New York: University of Pennsylvania/Appleton, 1911), 380–404; Carl K.S. Sprinchorn (trans. Gregory B. Keen), "The History of the Colony of New Sweden," *Pennsylvania Magazine of History and Biography* 7 (1883): 395–419; Samuel Hazard, *Annals of Pennsylvania, from the Discovery of the Delaware, 1609–1682* (Philadelphia: Hazard and Mitchell, 1850), 73–76.

250 See, for example, Johan Danielson Svedberg, *Dissertatio Gradualis de Svionum in America Colonia* (Uppsala: Werneriana, 1709) and Tobias Biörk, *Dissertatio Gradualis de Plantatione Ecclesiae Svecanae in America* (Uppsala: Werneriana, 1731), and cf. Justin Winsor, *Narrative and Critical History of America*, vol. 4 (Boston: Houghton Mifflin, 1884), 493.

251 The words from *se* to *possis* are underlined in the original (see next note).
252 An image of the original document can be seen in Kidder (see Source), after p. 13.
253 On Le Moyne, see the biographical sketch by Léon Pouliot in *Dictionary of Canadian Biography*, vol. 1 (online version). On Stuyvesant, see the entry at: https://www.newnetherlandinstitute.org/history-and-heritage/dutch_americans/peter-stuyvesant/.
254 The French placed upon the Dutch conditions similar to what the Dutch had placed upon them, viz., that the Dutch not trade with Native Americans and that they not publicly practice their religion in French territory.
255 Still extant is correspondence in Latin between Le Moyne and Jan Megapolensis concerning religious questions. See *Reply of Rev. Johannes Megapolensis, Pastor of the Church of New Amsterdam, to a Letter of Father Simon Le Moyne, a French Jesuit Missionary of Canada, 1658* (New York: Collegiate Church, 1907).
256 Le Moyne enclosed a letter written in French by Governor Louis D'Ailleboust, dated Quebec, February 18, 1658, consenting to Dutch trade in the St. Lawrence. This letter is printed in O'Callaghan's *History of New Netherland* (see Source) beneath Le Moyne's Latin letter.
257 Louis D'Ailleboust de Coulonge et D'Argentenay (c. 1612–60), on whom see the entry by Marie-Claire Daveluy in *Dictionary of Canadian Biography*, vol. 1 (online version).
258 D'Ailleboust had ended his governorship on October 13, 1651, but on August 26, 1657 he had assumed the role of acting Governor when Charles de Lauson left for France.
259 Cf. John A. Gallucci, "Latin Terms and Periphrases for Native Americans in the Jesuit Relations," in Juanita F. Ruys and Yasmin A. Haskell, eds., *Latinity and Alterity in the Early Modern Period* (Tempe: Arizona Center for Medieval and Renaissance Studies, 2010), 259–72.
260 See the entries in *Dictionary of Canadian Biography*, vol. 1 (online version): Frontenac (W.J. Eccles), Jolliet (André Vachon), Dablon (Marie-Jean-d'Ars Charette), Albanel (Georges-Émile Giguère), and Marquette (J. Monet), and see the entry on Marquette in *New Catholic Encyclopedia*, 2nd ed. (Detroit: Thomson-Gale) (E. Burrus).
261 In 1671 and again in 1672 the Jesuit priest Charles Albanel (d. 1696) undertook missions to explore the area around the Northern Sea (Hudson Bay).
262 The Outauais Missions were located in the northern Great Lakes region. Immediately before his Mississippi venture, Marquette had been at St. Ignace, near Mackinac Island. He entered the Mississippi River at

Prairie du Chien, Wisconsin, which is about 500 miles distant from St. Ignace.
263 33° latitude would put Marquette at the present-day border of Louisiana and Arkansas.
264 Although Hernando De Soto had crossed the lower Mississippi as early as 1541, at the time of Marquette's voyage the westernmost Spanish settlements in Florida were located in Apalachee (near present-day Tallahassee).
265 Jolliet's papers, log book, and map of the Mississippi exploration were lost when his canoe capsized near Montreal in late spring 1674. He had left copies of these papers with the Jesuits at Sault Ste. Marie, but they were lost in a fire.
266 Following the Mississippi trip Marquette went to the mission of St. Francis Xavier near De Pere, Wisconsin. In 1675, shortly before his death, he revisited the Illinois tribe. Jacques Gravier would later assume this mission (see section 29).
267 Alvord (see Source) suggests that this is a mistaken transcription for "Conceptionis." Marquette called the Mississippi the (Immaculate) Conception.
268 The date is problematic, because Marquette died on May 18, 1675. Alvord believes that the transcriber mistook 1673 for 1675.
269 Alvord speculates that the transcriber mistook the "rque" of the original for "cpu."
270 Judith S. Graham, *Puritan Family Life: The Diary of Samuel Sewall* (Boston: Northeastern University Press, 2000), 260n35.
271 M. Halsey Thomas, *The Diary of Samuel Sewall 1674–1729*, 2 vols. (New York: Farrar, Strauss and Giroux, 1973), 1:65.
272 Notes in Thomas, *Diary of Samuel Sewall*, explain that these references are to Joseph Davis, Joseph Tappin, and Ephraim Savage.
273 "Wherein ye greatly rejoice, though now for a season, if need be, ye are in heaviness through manifold temptations" (King James Version).
274 John Hull (1624–83) was a merchant as well as the mintmaster and treasurer of the Massachusetts Bay Colony. For an interpretation of this passage, see Samuel Sewall (a descendant of the diarist), *The Diaries of John Hull, Mint-master and Treasurer of the Colony of Massachusetts Bay* (Boston: Wilson, 1857), 252–54.
275 "Trust in the Lord, and do good; So shalt thou dwell in the land, and verily thou shalt be fed. Delight thyself also in the Lord; And he shall give thee the desires of thine heart. Commit thy way unto the Lord; Trust also in him, and he shall bring it to pass" (King James Version).
276 Newburyport
277 Roxbury and Dorchester

278 Elizabeth was one of Sewall's fourteen children.
279 Juan Baptista Segura to Francis Borgia, Havana, November 18, 1568, printed in Zubillaga, *Monumenta Antiquae Floridae* (note 133 above), 362. On Segura, see section 11.
280 See Jerome V. Jacobsen, *Educational Foundations of the Jesuits in Sixteenth Century New Spain* (Berkeley: University of California Press, 1938).
281 See Andrew Laird, "Nahuas and Caesars: Classical Learning and Bilingualism in Post-Conquest Mexico; An Inventory of Latin Writings by Authors of the Native Nobility," *Classical Philology* 109 (2014): 150–69, and see his surveys in *Oxford Handbook of Neo-Latin* (note 29 above), 525–40, esp. 529–32 and *Brill's Encyclopedia of the Neo-Latin World* (note 29 above), 993–94.
282 Robert Ricard, *The Spiritual Conquest of Mexico: An Essay on the Apostolate and the Evangelizing Methods of the Mendicant Orders in New Spain: 1523–1572*, trans. Lesley Byrd Simpson (Berkeley: University of California Press, 1966), 222.
283 See Louise M. Burkhart, *Holy Wednesday: A Nahua Drama from Early Colonial Mexico* (Philadelphia: University of Pennsylvania Press, 1996), 68–70, and cf. the prologue to the Franciscan Juan Bautista's *Sermonario en lengua Mexicana*, Primera Parte (Mexico City: Diego López Davalos, 1606). Yet the practice of educating Native Americans faced significant opposition. Still extant are the texts of two Latin greetings given in 1584 by Native American students at the school in Tlatelolco to the visiting commissary general of the Franciscans, Fray Alonso Ponce. These constitute a sort of "small symbolic play" which, as Robert Ricard argues, amounts to a satirical but "eloquent commentary" on the notions of those who sought to restrict Native Americans's access to the study of Latin. See Ricard, *Spiritual Conquest of Mexico*, 227. Texts from this play are printed in *Coleccion de Documentos Inéditos para la historia de España*, vol. 57 (Madrid: La Viuda de Calero, 1872), 22–24.
284 In recent decades this poem has received scholarly attention. See, for example, Leo M. Kaiser, "Thirteen Early American Latin Elegies: A Critical Edition," *Humanistica Lovaniensia* 23 (1974): 358–60 and Wolfgang Hochbruck and Beatrix Dudensing-Reichel, "Honoratissimi Benefactores" Native American Students and Two Seventeenth-Century Texts in the University Tradition," in Helen Jaskoski, ed., *Early Native American Writing: New Critical Essays* (Cambridge: Cambridge University Press, 1996), 1–14.
285 Thacher published the first medical work in the American colonies, *A Brief Rule to Guide the Common People of New-England How to Order Themselves and Theirs in the Small Pocks, or Measels* (Boston:

John Foster, 1677). This can be seen at https://www.loc.gov/resource/rbpe.03300900/?sp=1.

286 Corydon Ireland, "Harvard's Indian College Poet," *The Harvard Gazette*, September 16, 2013. The poem has been printed in Thomas Keeline and Stuart M. McManus, "Benjamin Larnell, The Last Latin Poet at Harvard Indian College," *Harvard Studies in Classical Philology* 108 (2015): 621–42.

287 Natalie Panther, "'To Make Us Independent': The Education of Young Men at the Cherokee Male Seminary, 1851–1910" (PhD diss., Oklahoma State University, 2013), 142–45.

288 *An Illustrated Souvenir Catalog of the Cherokee National Female Seminary, Tahlequah, Indian Territory 1850 to 1906* (Chilocco, OK: Indian Print Shop, 1906).

289 See *Cherokee Advocate* (Tahlequah, OK), August 8, 1884; cf. also *Daily American* (Nashville), July 29, 1884; *Memphis Daily Appeal*, July 18, 1884. The wedding, which took place at Monteagle on July 17, 1884, was of Dr. James H. Warren and Lucie Frank Ransom.

290 See William G. McLoughlin, *Cherokee Renascence in the New Republic* (Princeton: Princeton University Press, 1986), 367.

291 Four Greek lines follow.

292 See John A. Donohue's biographical sketch in *New Catholic Encyclopedia.*

293 See Ernest J. Burrus, ed., *Kino Writes to the Duchess: Letters of Eusebio Francisco Kino, S. J., to the Duchess of Aveiro* (Rome: Jesuit Historical Institute, 1965), 20. For a recent study see George Antony Thomas, "The Death of the Duchess of Aveiro: The Life and Legacy of María de Guadalupe de Lencastre," *Dieciocho* 39 (2016): 29–42.

294 The treatise was *Exposicion astronómica de el cometa, que el año de 1680 . . .* (México: Francisco Rodríguez Lupercio, 1681).

295 Most of Sor Juana's literary works, which fill four volumes in a modern edition, are in Spanish, but they contain frequent references to classical themes and authors—poets as well as historians and philosophers. But she also wrote several Latin poems, notably the *Neptuno alegórico*, a series of Horatian epigrams designed to be inscribed in a triumphal arch commemorating the arrival in New Spain of the new Viceroy, Tomás de la Cerda (1680–86). See Tarsicio Herrera Zapién, *Historia del humanismo mexicano: sus textos y contextos neolatinos en cinco siglos* (México: Editorial Porrúa, 2000), 97–119 and George Antony Thomas, "'La Décima Musa' and the Classical Tradition: Sor Juana Inés and the Poetry of Empire," *Letras Femeninas* 35 (2009): 255–70. Sor Juana also wrote a few Latin villancicos—poems of popular origin set to music and

incorporated into religious feasts. Classicists and scholars of Neo-Latin have been increasingly drawn to her Latin works. See especially Jane Stevenson, *Women Latin Poets: Language, Gender, & Authority from Antiquity to the Eighteenth Century* (New York: Oxford University Press, 2005), 401–6. Until September 2019 her image was on Mexico's 200-peso note.

296 Eymer was one of a number of Jesuits from central Europe to work in New Spain during the seventeenth and eighteenth centuries. For a catalogue of their writings and for brief biographies, see Bernd Hausberger, *Jesuiten aus Mitteleuropa im kolonialen Mexico* (Vienna: Verlag für Geschichte und Politik, 1995). Kino's extensive writings are catalogued on pp. 204–18.

297 Baltasar de Mansilla (1638–92), a Spanish Jesuit, was treasurer (1677–86) of the Philippine Province of Jesuits in Mexico, which was also responsible for the Mariana Islands.

298 Rev. Bernardo Pardo, S.J. was the Provincial at the time.

299 According to Burrus, this was Fr. Matías Goñi, S.J.

300 See note 294 above, and see Burrus, *Kino Writes to the Duchess*, 9, and Ellen Shaffer, "Father Eusebio Francisco Kino and the Comet of 1680–1681," *The Historical Society of Southern California Quarterly* 34 (1952): 57–70.

301 On this image, see Herbert Eugene Bolton, *Rim of Christendom: A Biography of Eusebio Francisco Kino, Pacific Coast Pioneer* (Tucson: University of Arizona Press, 1936, rept. 1984), 60–61. Kino later sent the Duchess an image of Our Lady of Guadalupe. The Duchess in turn sent Kino another image of the Virgin Mary.

302 The Duchess's children were Joachin, Gabriel, and Elizabeth.

303 *Deipara sine labe concepta* = the Mother of God, conceived without sin.

304 Kino and other Jesuits had entrusted the success of their missionary endeavors to *Regina Lauretana* (Our Lady of Loreto). In his memoirs, Kino speaks of carrying an image of Our Lady of Loreto that had been painted by Juan Correa.

305 Juan Maria Salvatierra (1648–1717), a Spanish Jesuit, arrived in Mexico in 1675 and was later appointed Visitor of the northwestern Jesuit missions.

306 Sir Francis Drake (see section 12).

307 Bolton gives Angli[c]o. "Anglia" is the reading printed in Emilio Bose and Francisco Fernández del Castillo, eds., *Las Misiones de Sonora y Arizona*, Publicaciónes del Archivo General de la Nación VIII (Mexico: Editorial Cultura, 1913–1922), 137.

308 The syntax is not entirely clear. Bolton translates: "Away now with

British temerity, with her English Drake, and let him keep silent who boasts that he has circumnavigated California, as if, by a foolish fiction, California were the Atlantis of the West."

309 I benefited from the transcription in Burrus, *Kino Writes to the Duchess*, 236–37, who includes the entire text of this letter as well as the other Latin letters in this correspondence.

310 See the article at https://www.wisconsinhistory.org/Records/Article/CS318 and W.J. Eccles, *The Canadian Frontier, 1534–1760*, rev. ed. (Albuquerque: University of New Mexico Press, 1983), 106–12, 130 idem, *The French in North America* (note 128 above), 112–14.

311 Maurice Ries, "The Mississippi Fort, Called Fort de la Boulaye," *The Louisiana Historical Quarterly* 19 (1936).

312 Henri de Tonty (c. 1649–1704), born in Italy, was a trader and military officer who accompanied French expeditions in North America. See the notices by E.B. Osler in *Dictionary of Canadian Biography*, vol. 2 (online version) and by Robert S. Weddle in *Handbook of Texas Online*.

313 Zenobius Membré (1645–89) was a Recollect priest (a branch of the Franciscan Order).

314 I have retained the orthography and punctuation of the printed text. The journal of Du Ru, which includes this inscription, is printed in Marc de Villiers, "Extrait d'un journal de voyage en Louisiane du Père Paul du Ru (1700)," *Journal de la Société des américanistes*, n.s. 17 (1925): 119–35.

315 See the biographical notice for the Francis Daniel Pastorius Papers (collection 0475), Historical Society of Philadelphia, http://www2.hsp.org/collections/manuscripts/p/Pastorius0475.html. On Penn, see the article at www.loc.gov/item/today-in-history/october-14/.

316 An image of the title page of his thesis, *De rasura documentorum*, which was published (Altdorf 1676), as well as biographical details about Pastorius, can be found in Samuel Whitaker Pennypacker, *The Settlement of Germantown Pennsylvania and the Beginning of German Emigration to North America* (Philadelphia: Campbell, 1899), 53–74.

317 This is printed in Patrick M. Erben, ed., *The Francis Daniel Pastorius Reader: Writings by an Early American Polymath* (University Park, PA: Pennsylvania State University Press, 2019), 396–401.

318 Pastorius held a number of positions in Germantown, including justice of the peace. At the time of this letter he was still the agent of the colony, although he would be relieved of this responsibility in 1700.

319 In 1688 Pastorius married Ennecke Klostermanns (1658–1723), and they had two sons: Johann Samuel (1690–1722) and Heinrich (1692–1726).

320 Penn returned to Pennsylvania in 1699.

321 Melchior Adam Pastorius was 74 years old at the time of this writing. He lived for another three years.
322 Cf. Luke 2:25–35.
323 It is also printed in Myers, *Narratives of Early Pennsylvania* (note 1 above), 444–45.
324 *The History of the College of William and Mary from its Foundation, 1660, to 1874* (Richmond: Randolph & English, 1874), 3, 15.
325 E.M. Counsell, "Latin Verses Presented by Students of William and Mary College to the Governor of Virginia, 1771, 1772, 1773, and 1774," *William and Mary Quarterly* 10 (1930): 269–74.
326 On Nicholson, see the notice by Natalie Zacek in *Encyclopedia Virginia* (online).
327 In the Royal Charter, the crown granted the trustees of the College two 10,000-acre tracts of land, one on the south side of the Blackwater Swamp, another in Pamunkey Neck (near the York River).
328 Perhaps this should be "dabitur" or "debetur."
329 See the sketch on Gravier by Charles E. O'Neill in *Dictionary of Canadian Biography*, vol. 2 (online version).
330 Gravier is writing from Paris.
331 Kaskaskia.
332 Fr. Pierre-Gabriel Marest (1662–1716), who had earlier served as chaplain to the French expedition that captured the English fort at Hudson's Bay, was stationed among the Illinois.
333 Fr. Jean Mermet (1664–1718) had worked at Guardian Angel mission (the site of present-day Chicago) and then along the St. Joseph River (in Michigan). He came to Kaskaskia in about 1705 or 1706. See the entry by Donald Chaput in *Dictionary of Canadian Biography*, vol. 2 (online version). For Mermet's account of Gravier's wounding, see Reuben Gold Thwaites, ed., *Jesuit Relations and Allied Documents: Travels and Explorations of the Jesuit Missionaries in New France 1610–1791*, 73 vols. (Cleveland: Burrows Bros., 1896–1901), 66:50–65.
334 Ann M. Little, *Abraham in Arms: War and Gender in Colonial New England* (Philadelphia: University of Pennsylvania Press, 2007), 186.
335 See Thomas Charland, "Sébastien Ralc" in *Dictionary of Canadian Biography*, vol. 2 (online version).
336 John Pickering, ed., "A Dictionary of the Abnaki Language, in North America; by Father Sebastian Rasles. With an Introductory Memoir and Notes," *Memoirs of the American Academy of Arts and Sciences*, n.s. 1 (1833): 370–574.
337 "Letter-Book of Samuel Sewall," *Collections of the Massachusetts Historical Society*, ser. 6, vol. 2 (1888): 174.
338 For Ralé's own account of this exchange, see *Jesuit Relations and*

Allied Documents 67:98, 100. For a bibliography of Baxter's writings, see H.C. Schuyler, "The Apostle of the Abnakis: Father Sebastian Rale, S.J. (1657–1724)," *Catholic Historical Review* 1 (1915): 164–65. See also Thomas O'Gorman, *A History of the Catholic Church in the United States* (New York: Christian Literature, 1895), 140–44.
339 Cf. Horace, *C.* 4.7.19–20.
340 Ambrose, *Expositio evangelii secundum Lucam* 4:64 (*PL* 15:1631d).
341 This expression is found in early Latin dictionaries such as Thomas Holyoke, *A Large Dictionary in Three Parts* (London: W. Rawlins, 1677), s.v., amicus, but no classical passage is listed.
342 A saying used of Pythagoras (cf. Cicero, *N.D.* 1.10.5).
343 Cf. Terence, *Ph.* 1014: culpam meritum.
344 Cf. Apuleius, *Met.* 4.8.
345 Cf. Luke 17:2.
346 Baxter cites this and the following scriptural passages not according to the Vulgate but according to the version of Theodore Beza (Geneva, 1556).
347 Beza's translation reads *ne respondeto stolido . . .*
348 Following his initial studies in Carpentras, Ralé taught grammar, humanities, and rhetoric at Nîmes before completing his theological formation at Lyons.
349 My transcription differs from what Baxter (who is a descendant of Rev. Baxter) provides on pp. 399–404 (see Source). Baxter also provides a translation.
350 *Aberdeen Democrat*, February 25, 1913; *Citizen-Republican* (Scotland, SD), February 27, 1913; *Boston Globe*, March 4, 1913; *Washington Post*, March 30, 1913 (reprinted from the *New York Sun*); *Omaha World-Herald*, March 30, 1913; *Sioux City Journal*, June 15, 1913.
351 On the Vérendrye brothers, see the articles by Antoine Champagne in *Dictionary of Canadian Biography*, vols. 3 and 4 (online version).
352 See Antoine Champagne's biography of Pierre Gualtier de la Vérendrye de Boumois (1714–55) in *Dictionary of Canadian Biography*, vol. 3 (online version).
353 Champagne, "Louis-Joseph Gaultier de La Vérendrye," *Dictionary of Canadian Biography.*
354 Louis XV was King of France from 1715 to 1774.
355 The Marquis de Beauharnois was Governor of New France from 1726 to 1747.
356 Although the Latin inscription gives the date as 1741, French writing on the reverse of the plate indicates that it was placed on March 30, 1743.
357 Harriette Eliza Noyes, *A Memorial of the Town of Hampstead, New*

Hampshire (Boston: Reed, 1899), 321–22.
358 Edward P. Hamilton, *The French and Indian Wars: The Story of Battles and Forts in the Wilderness* (Garden City, NJ: Doubleday, 1962), 263–76.
359 Fort Edward, named after a son of King George II, was constructed on the upper Hudson River in 1755. See the entry by Alexander V. Campbell in *The Encyclopedia of New York State*, ed. Peter Eisenstadt (Syracuse: Syracuse University Press, 2005), 587.
360 I have not been able to locate any information concerning Robert Makane.
361 "An Enquiry into the Utility of the Knowledge of the Greek and Latin Languages as a Branch of Liberal Education, with Hints of a Plan of Liberal Instruction without Them," *American Museum* 5 (June 1789): 525–35. It is also printed, with Rush's response to an objection he received, in *Essays, Literary, Moral and Philosophical*, 2nd ed. (Philadelphia: Thomas and William Bradford, 1806), 21–56. On Rush's attitude toward the classics and education, see Harry G. Good, *Benjamin Rush and His Services to American Education* (Berne, IN: Witness, 1918); Meyer Reinhold, "Opponents of Classical Learning in America during the Revolutionary Period," *Proceedings of the American Philosophical Society* 112 (1968): 228–32.
362 Benjamin Rush to John Adams, Philadelphia, July 21, 1789, printed in Lyman H. Butterfield, *Letters of Benjamin Rush*, 2 vols (Princeton: Princeton University Press for the American Philosophical Society, 1951), 1:524.
363 *American Museum* 5 (1789): 525.
364 Rush to Adams, Philadelphia, July 21, 1789 (Butterfield, *Letters*, 1:524).
365 Rush to Adams, Philadelphia, July 21, 1789 (Butterfield, *Letters*, 1:524).
366 Rush to Adams, Philadelphia June 15, 1789 (Butterfield, *Letters*, 1:516).
367 Rush to Adams, Philadelphia, July 21, 1789 (Butterfield, *Letters*, 1:524). See David Freeman Hawke, *Benjamin Rush: Revolutionary Gadfly* (Indianapolis: Bobbs-Merrill, 1971), 367–69.
368 Rush to Adams, Philadelphia, July 2, 1789 (Butterfield, *Letters*, 1:517–18).
369 Rush to Adams, Philadelphia, October 2, 1810 (Butterfield, *Letters*, 2:1067).
370 David Ramsay, *An Eulogium upon Benjamin Rush, M.D.* (Philadelphia: Bradford and Inskeep, 1813), 16.
371 Benjamin Rush to Ebenezer Hazard, Philadelphia, June 27, 1765

(Butterfield, *Letters*, 1:17).

372 Several English letters from Rush to Hazard survive. See Butterfield, *Letters,* 1:5–25, 56, 67–68. Later Hazard was Postmaster General of the United States (1782–89).

373 Rush to Hazard, Philadelphia, November 8, 1765 (Butterfield, *Letters*, 1:18).

374 Lyman H. Butterfield, "Further Letters of Benjamin Rush," *Pennsylvania Magazine of History and Biography* 78 (1954): 6.

375 Some students, however, paid to have their theses translated into Latin. In his autobiography Rush notes with satisfaction that he was successful in his efforts to end the practice of writing inaugural dissertations in Latin at the Medical College of Philadelphia. See George W. Corner, ed., *The Autobiography of Benjamin Rush, His "Travels Through Life," together with his* Commonplace Book *for 1789–1813* (Princeton: Princeton University Press for The American Philosophical Society, 1948; rept. Westport, CT: Greenwood, 1970), 89.

376 John Rodgers (1727–1811), Boston-born but Philadelphia-reared, was a Presbyterian minister as well as a Trustee of the College of New Jersey (Princeton). In early 1765 he accepted a call to pastor a congregation on Wall Street in New York, where he arrived on July 24, 1765. Later he was Vice-Chancellor of The Regents of the University of New York and Moderator of the Presbyterians in the United States. See Samuel Miller, *Memoirs of the Rev. John Rodgers, D.D.: Late Pastor of the Wall-Street and Brick Churches in the City of New-York* (New York: Whiting and Watson, 1813) and Robert T. Handy, "John Rodgers, 1727–1811: 'A Life of Usefulness on Earth,'" *Journal of the Presbyterian Historical Society* 34 (1956): 69–82.

377 Rev 3:7 mentions the (ancient) city of Philadelphia.

378 In May 1765 John Murray (1742–93), born in County Antrim, Ireland, succeeded Gilbert Tennent (1703–64) as pastor of Second Presbyterian in Philadelphia, but due to questions concerning the authenticity of his credentials, in June 1766 the presbytery of Philadelphia suspended him, and in 1767 they dismissed him. See Robert E. Cray, "The Reverend John Murray and the Eighteenth Century Presbyterian Church, *The Journal of Presbyterian History* 88 (2010): 59–67; Ashbel G. Vermilye, "Memoir of the Rev. John Murray, First Minister of the Church in Boothbay," *Collections of the Maine Historical Society* 6 (1859): 153–70.

379 John Brainerd (1720–81), a graduate of Yale (1746), who followed his brother David (1714–47) in becoming a Presbyterian missionary to Native Americans, married Elizabeth Price of Philadelphia (d. 1783). (His first wife, Experience Lyon, had died in 1757.) The date of John's marriage to Elizabeth is often given as 1766, but Rush's letter indicates

that it took place in 1765. See Thomas Brainerd, *The Life of John Brainerd* (Philadelphia: Presbyterian Publication Committee, 1865).

380 Cf. Vergil, *A.* 1.73, 4.126.

381 Hazard's response (in Latin) survives (Rush Family Papers, Library Company of Philadelphia), dated New York, July 27, 1765, in which he identifies several of Rush's errors: "temporibus meis" should be accusative; "funerem" is wrong because the word is neuter; "pallidi" ought to be feminine to agree with "mortis;" "obsecrat" is not an appropriate word for the context;" "peracti" ought to be feminine to agree with "ceremoniae;" "praenosceri" ought to be "praenosci." Hazard, for his part, requests that Rush reciprocate this "opus iniucundum."

382 Cf. Horace, *C.* 2.14.1.

383 Two and a half months earlier, on May 3, 1765, John Morgan (1735–89) was elected chair of the Theory and Practice of Physic at the College of Philadelphia, the first Medical School in the United States, which Morgan himself had founded. Born in Philadelphia, Morgan was in the first graduating class of the College of Philadelphia; he earned an M.D. from Edinburgh (1763), and he was honored with memberships in various European societies and academies. When Morgan died in 1789 Rush succeeded him as chair of Medicine at the College of Philadelphia. See the biographical sketch by Howard A. Kelly, *A Cyclopedia of American Medical Biography*, vol. 2 (Philadelphia: Saunders, 1912), 188–91 and the sketch at Penn University Archives and Records Center (archives.upenn.edu). Morgan was one of the dedicatees of Rush's Edinburgh thesis, but see Stephen Fried, *Rush: Revolution, Madness and the Visionary Doctor Who Became a Founding Father* (New York: Crown, 2018), 58–60, for the controversy this dedication engendered.

384 Horace, *S.* 1.5.32–33: "ad unguem/ factus homo."

385 Vergil, *A.* 1.408–9: "cur dextrae iungere dextram/ non datur ac veras audire et reddere voces." In an earlier (English) letter to Hazard, dated Philadelphia, September 27 [1762], Rush had quoted these verses in Latin. See Butterfield, *Letters*, 1:6.

386 Samuel Treat (1739–1814) obtained medical faculties on September 1, 1765 and practiced in New Jersey and New York. See the note in Butterfield, *Letters*, 1:7.

387 For biographical details about Hazard's mother, Catharine (Clarkson) Hazard (1720–88), and his sisters, see Thomas R. Hazard, with Willis P. Hazard, *Recollections of Olden Times: Rowland Robinson of Narragansett and His Unfortunate Daughter* (Newport: Sanborn 1879), 232–33. One of his sisters, Mary Hazard (1750–72), who is mentioned below, married Cornelius Turk in 1770 and died in childbirth.

388 Thomas Hazard (d. 1787), a sailor, was Ebenezer's distant cousin

(Butterfield, *Letters*, 1:11).
389 Rush often mentions a "Mrs. Flint" in his letters, but nothing is known about her apart from her marriage to Thomas Flint, a ship-captain. See Butterfield, *Letters* 1:8.
390 For a biographical sketch and bibliography of Ducrue, see Hausberger, *Jesuiten aus Mitteleuropa im kolonialen Mexico* (note 296 above), 136–39. His surviving writings are in Spanish, German, and Latin.
391 See Peter M. Dunne, "The Expulsion of the Jesuits from New Spain," *Mid-America* 19 (1937): 3–30, esp. 18–21.
392 On Murr, see Claudia von Collani, "The German Protestant Scholar Christoph Gottlieb von Murr (1733–1811) and his Defence of the Suppressed Society of Jesus," *Archivum Historicum Societatis Iesu* 85 (2016): 43–96. On Jesuit Latin in eighteenth-century Mexico, see Andrew Laird, "Patriotism and the Rise of Latin in Eighteenth-Century New Spain: Disputes of the New World and the Jesuit Construction of a Mexican Legacy," *Renaessanceforum* 8 (2012): 231–62.
393 The sixth ferial day is Friday, and it has traditionally been an occasion for devotion to the Most Sacred Heart of Jesus. The Jesuits were early promoters of this devotion.
394 The Litany of Loreto.
395 For an annotated text and translation see Ernest J. Burrus, *Ducrue's Account of the Expulsion of the Jesuits from Lower California, 1767–1769* (Rome: Jesuit Historical Institute, 1967).
396 Benjamin Franklin to Deborah Franklin, London, June 13, 1766, printed in Sparks, 7:320 (see Source).
397 Benjamin Franklin to Erich Raspe, London, September 9, 1766. Printed in Robert L. Kahn, "Three Franklin-Raspe Letters," *Proceedings of the American Philosophical Society* 99 (1955): 399.
398 Beatrice M. Victory, *Benjamin Franklin and Germany* (Philadelphia: University of Pennsylvania, 1915), 49–50. But see Andre Wakefield, "The Practical Enlightenment: German Cameralists and Yankee Economists," in Hans Erich Bödeker and Martin Gierl, eds., *Jenseits der Diskurse: Aufklärungspraxis und Institutionenwelt in europäisch komparativer Perspektive* (Göttingen: Vandenhoeck & Ruprecht, 2007), 149–65. And see Glenn Weaver, "Benjamin Franklin and the Pennsylvania Germans," *William and Mary Quarterly* 14 (1957): 536–59.
399 Victory, *Benjamin Franklin and Germany*, 52–53.
400 On Franklin's language learning, see J.A. Leo Lemay, *The Life of Benjamin Franklin*, vol. 2, *Printer and Publisher, 1730–1747* (Philadelphia: University of Pennsylvania Press, 2006), 17–20.
401 See Thomas Woody, ed., *The Educational Views of Benjamin Franklin* (New York: McGraw-Hill, 1931), 210–17 and Gummere, *The Ameri-*

can Colonial Mind (note 26 above), 125–31.

402 Especially to be noted are the following: Giambatista Beccaria to Franklin, December 24, 1757; Giambatista Beccaria to Franklin, October 11, 1766; Michaël Kôváts de Fabricÿ to Franklin, January 13, 1777; J.B. Janek to Franklin, January 25, 1778; Andreas Christian Knoepffel to Franklin, March 4, 1778; Abbé Jacob Hemmer to Franklin, September 24, 1778; Johann Adolf Behrends to Franklin, October 28, 1778. These can be read at franklinpapers.org, and annotated resumes may be found at founders.archives.gov.

403 *M.T. Cicero's Cato Major, or his Discourse of Old-Age: with explanatory notes* (Philadelphia: Franklin, 1744), v. Yet more than a century earlier George Sandys had translated Ovid's *Metamorphoses* (1626, 1632), much of which was completed while Sandys was en route to, or working in, Jamestown. On the Americanism of this work, see Richard Beale Davis, "America in George Sandys' 'Ovid,'" *William and Mary Quarterly* 4 (1947): 297–304.

404 I. Bernard Cohen, *Benjamin Franklin's Science* (Cambridge, MA: Harvard University Press, 1990), 157. See also Cohen's other contributions on this topic, and for an older treatment see "Franklin's Celebrated Line—'Eripuit Coelo Fulmen,' etc.," *The United States Magazine and Democratic Review*, n.s. 15 (1844): 625–26.

405 See Peter W. van der Pas, "The Latin Translation of Benjamin Franklin's Letters on Electricity," *Isis* 69 (1978): 82–85.

406 According to editors (see note 409), this may be a reference to Prince Friedrich Karl (1736–93), who regularly corresponded with natural scientists.

407 Franklin began to experiment with electricity and lightning in 1747; in June 1752 he undertook his kite experiment, and in June or July 1752 the first lightning rods were installed in Philadelphia.

408 Hartmann published *Die angewandte Electricität ben Krankheiten des menschlichen Körpers* (Hanover 1770).

409 A translation by Claude-Anne Lopez with annotation is available at *Founders Online*, National Archives, https://founders.archives.gov/documents/Franklin/01-14-02-0156. [Original source: *The Papers of Benjamin Franklin*, vol. 14, *January 1 through December 31, 1767*, ed. Leonard W. Labaree (New Haven: Yale University Press, 1970), 264–65].

410 Peter Guilday, "Father John McKenna: A Loyalist Catholic Priest," *Catholic World* 133 (1931): 21–27; Edward Kelly, "Father John McKenna: Loyalist Chaplain," *Canadian Catholic Historical Association* 1 (1933/34): 31–44; Richard K. MacMaster, "Parish in Arms: A Study of Father John MacKenna and the Mohawk Valley Loyalists, 1773–1778," *Historical Records and Studies* 45 (1957): 107–25.

411 MacMaster, "Parish in Arms," 121.
412 See the biographical sketch by Lucien Lemieux in *Dictionary of Canadian Biography*, vol. 4 (online version).
413 William L. Stone, *The Campaign of Lieut. Gen. John Burgoyne and the Expedition of Lieut. Col. Barry St. Leger* (Albany: Munsell, 1877); Gavin K. Watt, *Rebellion in the Mohawk Valley: The St. Leger Expedition of 1777* (Toronto: Dundurn, 2002).
414 See https://www.nps.gov/fost/learn/historyculture/the-battle-at-oriska.htm.
415 Based on events described in the letter, the actual date of the letter must be a few weeks later. For example, General Herkimer did not die until August 16. MacKenna may have begun the letter on the 16th but completed it later.
416 = septima *die* huius *mensis*
417 Sir John Johnson (1741–1830) was the son and heir of Sir William Johnson, on whose New York estate the immigrants had initially settled.
418 Modern estimates give the size of the British force as between 1500 and 1800 and the size of the defending patriot force as between 750 and 800. The companies defending the fort were from New York and Massachusetts, under the command of Col. Peter Gansevoort.
419 The battle of Oriskany took place about eight miles from Ft. Stanwix.
420 General Nicholas Herkimer (1728–77), who died as a result of a wound suffered during the battle of Oriskany.
421 Modern estimates give the losses as follows: on the patriot side up to 500 were killed, wounded, or captured; on the loyalist side sightly more than 60 were wounded or killed, most of whom were Native Americans, including several chiefs and warriors. See also Watt, *Rebellion in the Mohawk Valley*, 315–24.
422 Capt. Hertel de Rouville, who commanded a company in the Royal Regiment of New York.
423 Ignace-Michel-Louis-Antoine d'Irumberry de Salaberry (1752–1828).
424 The identities of St. Ours, Vasal, and Bazin are unclear.
425 Reverendissimae Dominationis Vestrae.
426 Fr. Bernard Well (1724–91) was the last Jesuit remaining in Canada following the 1773 suppression of the order.
427 The Latin text, with slight variations, is also printed in Kelly, "Father John McKenna: Loyalist Chaplain," 31–44.
428 The Latin text of this commendation may be found in Anthony Pelzer Wagener, "The Adaptation of the Ancient Philosophy of Medicine to the New World by Jean-François Coste," *Journal of the History of*

Medicine and Allied Subjects 7 (1952): 10–67 (pp. 13–14).
429 Although Rev. Madison indicates that Coste's speech was to be published in Philadelphia, this appears not to have happened; instead it was published the following year in Leiden (1783). Coste's work was not altogether unique. Dr. John David Schöpf (1752–1800), field surgeon to Hessian troops during the Revolutionary War, published *Materia Medica Americana Potissimum Regni Vegetabilis* (Erlangen: Jacob Palm, 1787).
430 Rev. James Madison to James Madison, Williamsburg, June 15, 1782, *Founders Online*, National Archives, https://founders.archives.gov/documents/Madison/01-04-02-0154 [Original source: *The Papers of James Madison*, vol. 4, *1 January 1782–31 July 1782*, ed. William T. Hutchinson and William M.E. Rachal (Chicago: University of Chicago Press, 1965), 337–39].
431 For a biography of Coste see John E. Lane, *Jean-François Coste: Chief Physician of the French Expeditionary Forces in the American Revolution* (Somerville, NJ: 1928) = *Americana* 22 (1928); and see Wagener, "The Adaptation of the Ancient Philosophy of Medicine to the New World," 12–17 and *The Medical Pickwick* 6 (1920): 47–48.
432 For a facsimile of this book see John E. Lane, "Coste's Compendium Pharmaceuticum," *Bulletin of the Society of Medical History of Chicago* 3 (1923–25): 214–20, and for discussion and a translation see Harold J. Abrahams, "The Compendium Pharmaceuticum of Jean François Coste," *Economic Botany* 24 (1970): 374–98.
433 Washington to Coste, October 7, 1782, George Washington Papers, Library of Congress: https://www.loc.gov/resource/mgw4.088_0195_0196/?st=gallery.
434 I am particularly indebted to the helpful translation of Coste's exuberant and at times challenging Latin given by Wagener, "The Adaptation of the Ancient Philosophy of Medicine to the New World."
435 The printed text frequently includes suspension points.
436 Wagener translates: "This has won its bright fame from joining experience to learning."
437 Wagener's note explains: "The appointment, in the reorganization of the College in 1779, of Dr. James McClurg as Professor of Anatomy and Medicine."
438 In an endnote Coste elaborates: "Dicabantur Gallorum militum nosocomio maiori, aedes universitatis et professorum . . . ducibus aegrotis aut vulneratis academiae Praesidis ipsiusmet domus tota.
439 Harvard Medical School began in 1782, the year of Coste's speech; the University of Pennsylvania's began in 1765 and Columbia's (King's College) in 1767; William & Mary added a professorship of anatomy

and medicine in 1779, but this was discontinued in 1785.
440 Cf. Vergil, *A.* 6.869.
441 A note that Coste appends to this line begins: "In nova quam dixerant Anglia, si monumentorum inscriptionibus fides, constat hunc esse medium, ut dicunt, terminum vitae in Orbe Novo Boreali." But he indicates that he has encountered exceptions, especially in the mountains of Connecticut.
442 See John Rothensteiner, "Paul de Saint Pierre, The First German-American Priest of the West" *Catholic Historical Review* 5 (1919): 195–222.
443 This letter is addressed to Fr. Louis Payet (1749–1801), who was a priest in Detroit from 1781 to 1786. Payet had made at least one missionary visit to Cahokia and Kaskaskia, where he likely met Saint Pierre.
444 John Carroll (1735–1815) was appointed Apostolic Prefect of the American colonies in 1784.
445 John Carroll's first official act as Apostolic Prefect was the proclamation of a Jubilee year to last from November 28, 1784 to November 28, 1785. Due to the Revolutionary War, the colonies had been unable to celebrate a jubilee in 1775, so the Pope allowed them to celebrate this later. See Peter Guilday, *The Life and Times of John Carroll: Archbishop of Baltimore, 1735–1815* (New York: Encyclopedia, 1922), 205.
446 Anne-César, Chevalier de la Luzerne, the second French minister to the United States (1779–84).
447 For some account of De Saint Pierre's encounters with local politicians and businessmen, see Rothensteiner, "Paul de Saint Pierre, The First German-American Priest of the West," 203.
448 Louis-Philippe Mariauchau d'Esgly was Bishop of Québec from 1784 to 1788.
449 Jacques Marquette (see section 22) had founded Immaculate Conception mission in 1673. It later moved south to Kaskaskia.
450 On the sculpture, see Francis Henry Taylor, "Jean-Antonie Houdon: 1828–1928," *Bulletin of the Pennsylvania Museum* 24 (1928): 13–21; John S. Hallam, "Houdon's Washington in Richmond: Some New Observations," *American Art Journal* 10 (1978): 72–80; Garry Wills, "Washington's Citizen Virtue: Greenough and Houdon," *Critical Inquiry* 10 (1984): 420–41; Peter E. Bondanella, *The Eternal City: Roman Images in the Modern World* (Chapel Hill: University of North Carolina Press, 1987); Tracy L. Kamerer and Scott W. Nolley, "Rediscovering an American Icon," *Colonial Williamsburg Journal* (2003), available at https://history.org/Foundation/journal/Autumn03/houdon.cfm.
451 Jefferson to Washington, July 10, 1785, Thomas Jefferson Papers, Library of Congress: https://www.loc.gov/resource/

mtj1.003_1040_1041/?sp=1.
452 Madison, in fact, was present at Mt. Vernon along with Houdon. See Stuart Leibiger, *Founding Friendship: George Washington, James Madison, and the Creation of the American Republic* (Charlottesville: University Press of Virginia, 1999), 51.
453 Jefferson to Madison, Paris, February 8, 1786, *Founders Online*, National Archives, https://founders.archives.gov/documents/Jefferson/01-09-02-0229 [Original source: *The Papers of Thomas Jefferson*, vol. 9, *1 November 1785—22 June 1786*, ed. Julian P. Boyd (Princeton: Princeton University Press, 1954), 264–71].
454 For a discussion of the authorship of this inscription, see the notations in Boyd (see previous note) and see Irving Brant, *James Madison: The Nationalist, 1780–1787* (Indianapolis: Bobbs-Merrill, 1948), 321–22. According to an early biographer of Madison, Jefferson's proposed text was "singularly jejune and pompous . . . and was almost ludicrous by the bathos of its termination." William C. Rives, *History of the Life and Times of James Madison*, vol. 1 (Boston: Little Brown, 1859), 572.
455 Lafayette to Jefferson, before February 8, 1786, *Founders Online*, National Archives, https://founders.archives.gov/documents/Jefferson/01-09-02-0226. [Original source: Boyd (see note 453), 261–62].
456 Madison to Jefferson, Orange, Virginia, May 12, 1786: https://www.loc.gov/resource/mjm.02_0649_0652/?sp=1.
457 Jefferson explains to Madison that this portion "may be translated as follows . . ." but he does not provide the original Latin for these beginning lines.
458 Jefferson has crossed out "devictis."
459 Jefferson has crossed out "debellatis."
460 Washington was elected the first President of the Society of the Cincinnati, which was founded in 1783 for former officers (French and American) who served in the Revolutionary War.
461 L. Junius Brutus enjoyed great popularity in late eighteenth-century-Europe. He was the subject of a famous painting by Jacques Louis David (1789) and of the drama *Bruto Primo* by Vittorio Alfieri (1788), which was dedicated to George Washington.
462 Washington was familiar with the so-called Fabian Strategy from his reading (in translation) of Plutarch, Livy, and Polybius, but scholars are divided on the extent to which he employed this approach during the Revolutionary War. See Gregory J. Dehler, "Fabian Strategy," *Digital Encyclopedia of George Washington*.
463 Jefferson appends a note to this last line: "or [civica fer meritis serta, America, comis.]" This alternative reading is also found in *Journal historique et littéraire* 176.1 (1787): 393.

464 These four lines do not appear in Jefferson's letter to Madison of February 8, 1786, but they as well as the previous four lines (passage 3) are found in *Journal encyclopédique ou universel* (February 1788, vol. 2 part 1): 180.
465 https://www.loc.gov/resource/mtj1.005_0343_0344/?sp=1.
466 See "A Bishop for the Indians in 1790," *Catholic Historical Review* 3 (1917): 79–89; John Gilmary Shea, *Life and Times of the Most Rev. John Carroll* (New York: John G. Shea, 1888), 373–74. On Penet, see Franklin B. Hough, *Notices of Peter Penet, and of His Operations among the Oneida Indians* (Louisville: n.p., 1866).
467 Luca Codignola, "The Holy See and the Conversion of Aboriginal Peoples in North America, 1760–1830," in Anthony Gregg Roeber, ed., *Ethnographies and Exchanges: Native Americans, Moravians, and Catholics in Early North America* (University Park, PA: Pennsylvania State University Press, 2008), 80. See also Codignola's summaries of the relevant documentation in his *Calendar of Documents Relating to North America (Canada and the United States) in the Archives of the Sacred Congregation "De Propaganda Fide" in Rome 1622–1846*, 6 vols. (Library and Archives Canada and the Research Centre for Religious History in Canada of Saint Paul University, 2012), 5.132–33, 6.143–44.
468 This word is uncertain in the manuscript, according to the printed version.
469 Archibald Henderson, *Washington's Southern Tour 1791* (Boston: Houghton Mifflin, 1923); Warren L. Bingham, *George Washington's 1791 Southern Tour* (Charleston, SC: History, 2016).
470 P.A. Strobel, *The Salzburgers and Their Descendants* (Baltimore: Kurtz, 1855); Charles C. Jones, *The Dead Towns of Georgia* (Savannah: Morning News, 1878); George Fenwick Jones, *The Salzburger Saga: Religious Exiles and Other Germans along the Savannah* (Athens: University of Georgia Press, 1984); James Barlament, "Salzburgers," *New Georgia Encyclopedia* (online); Shane A. Runyon and Robert S. Davis, "Ebenezer," *New Georgia Encyclopedia* (online).
471 Strobel, *The Salzburgers and Their Descendants*, 221, 222, 226.
472 The identity of this friend is unknown.
473 Series 4, General Correspondence 1697–1799, MSS 44693: Reel 100: https://www.loc.gov/resource/mgw4.100_0771_0772/?st=gallery.
474 Margaret Bingham Stillwell, *Washington Eulogies: A Checklist of Eulogies and Funeral Orations on the Death of George Washington, December, 1799–February, 1800* (New York: Public Library, 1916).
475 Willard, *An Address in Latin* (see Source), iv.
476 The program for Harvard's 1799 Commencement Exercises is preserved in the Library of Congress: https://www.loc.gov/item/

rbpe.04601400/.
477 See Willard's letter to Washington, January 1, 1790, *Founders Online*, National Archives, https://founders.archives.gov/documents/Washington/05-04-02-0339. [Original source: *The Papers of George Washington*, Presidential Series, vol. 4, *8 September 1789–15 January 1790*, ed. Dorothy Twohig (Charlottesville: University Press of Virginia, 1993), 503–505].
478 George Washington to Joseph Willard, December 23, 1789, George Washington Papers, Library of Congress, https://www.loc.gov/resource/mgw2.022/?sp=245. This portrait, by Edward Savage, is currently in the Harvard University Portrait Collection.
479 https://www.harvard.edu/about-harvard/harvard-glance/history-presidency/joseph-willard. See also Sidney Willard's sketch in William B. Sprague, *Annals of the American Pulpit; or Commemorative Notices of Distinguished American Clergymen of Various Denominations*, vol. 2 (New York: Robert Carter & Brothers, 1859), 23–30.
480 *The Monthly Magazine, and American Review* 3 (1800): 47–50 (p. 50).
481 The reviewer in *The Monthly Magazine* faults this title: a Roman would have said "Praesidis concio brevis," "Concio brevis a Praeside habita," or "Concio brevis quam Praeses habuit."
482 *The Monthly Magazine* says that "casus" would be more appropriate than "eventum," which signifies rather "a *result* or *issue* of a train of causes; and, therefore, cannot express what we presume to be the author's meaning."
483 James 1:17.
484 *The Monthly Magazine* dubs this "a gross *anglicism*."
485 Cf. Horace *C.* 3.30.
486 George Thomas, *The Founders and the Idea of a National University: Constituting the American Mind* (New York: Cambridge University Press, 2015), 2–4.
487 J. Wilfrid Parsons, "Rev. Anthony Kohlmann, S.J. (1771–1824)," *Catholic Historical Review* 4 (1918): 38–51.
488 Thaddeus Brzozowski (1749–1820), the General of the Jesuits, was in Russia, where the Jesuit Order had not been suppressed.
489 P.C. = Pax Christi
490 Vergil, *A.* 1.204.
491 Ireland.
492 John Carroll (1735–1815), the Bishop and then Archbishop of Baltimore. Carroll had entered the Jesuits in 1753.
493 Reverendissimam Vestram.
494 The city of Georgetown, established in 1751, was independent until

1878, when it was annexed to the city of Washington, which was then made co-extensive with the District of Columbia.
495 Initially Georgetown was separated from Washington by Rock Creek, which, as early maps show, was spanned by two bridges: https://www.loc.gov/resource/g3852g.la002257/?r=0.632,0.52,0.357,0.18,0.
496 Baltimore is 40 miles distant from Georgetown.
497 At this time Georgetown College consisted of three buildings, Old South, Old North (still standing), and an infirmary. Modeled after Princeton's Nassau Hall, Old North (opened 1797) contained a chapel, classrooms, and dormitories. As Georgetown's historian comments, "there was nothing in the town to compete with Old North, and in the rising federal city, only the capital itself promised to be grander." See Robert Emmet Curran, *The Bicentennial History of Georgetown*, vol. 1, *From Academy to University, 1789–1889* (Washington, DC: Georgetown University Press, 1993), 46, 59. When Kohlmann arrived Old North was still incomplete.
498 Cf. Bob Arnebeck, *Through a Fiery Trial: Building Washington 1790–1800* (Lanham, MD: Madison Books, 1991), 3: "The salient feature of the terrain that impressed almost all visitors in the 1790s was the forest-covered hills." The bracketed word is printed with brackets in *Woodstock Letters.*
499 McLoughlin, *Cherokee Renascence in the New Republic* (note 290 above), 92–108.
500 See McLoughlin, *Cherokee Renascence in the New Republic*, 72–78 and his earlier article "Thomas Jefferson and the Beginning of Cherokee Nationalism, 1806 to 1809," *William and Mary Quarterly* 32 (1975): 547–80.
501 Guilday, *Life and Times of John Carroll* (note 445 above), 723–28.
502 This letter, dated April 19, 1806 can be seen at https://www.loc.gov/resource/mtj1.035_1113_1119/?sp=1. (Thomas Jefferson Papers, Library of Congress).
503 Henry Dearborn (1751–1829) was Secretary of War under President Thomas Jefferson.
504 Col. Return Meigs (1740–1823), an agent to the Cherokee Nation, was stationed at Southwest Point, the site of present-day Kingsport, Tennessee.
505 https://www.loc.gov/item/mtjbib016447/. A statement (in English) from Return Meigs attesting to Reuter's character and his conduct while among the Cherokees accompanies this letter.
506 Alison Reed Ross, *The Bedford Springs Hotel* (Charleston, SC: Arcadia, 2012).
507 Rob Lukens and Sandra S. Momyer, *Yellow Springs* (Charleston, SC:

Arcadia, 2007).
508 On Ross, see Philip N. Lockhart's sketch in *Database of Classical Scholars*. See also *The Historical Magazine, and Notes and Queries Concerning the Antiquities, History and Biography of America* 6 (1862): 228, 261–62, 324–325, 357; J. Smith Futhey and Gilbert Cope, *History of Chester County, Pennsylvania, with Genealogical and Biographical Sketches* (Philadelphia: Everts, 1881), 716–17; James Henry Morgan, *Dickinson College: The History of One Hundred and Fifty Years 1783–1933* (Carlisle: Dickinson College, 1933), 98–104.
509 "Sanis" is the reading in the *Bedford Gazette*, August 23, 1867. The text in *New York Medical Repository* reads "salus."
510 This poem is also printed with a translation in Fortescue Cuming, *Sketches of a Tour to the Western Country* (Pittsburgh: Cramer, Spear & Eichbaum, 1810), 51.
511 "Rupibus" is the reading in Futhey and Cope (see note 508); *The Medical Repository* (Source) prints "Rupei."
512 William S. Prince, "St. George Tucker: Bard on the Bench," *Virginia Magazine of History and Biography* 84 (1976): 268, 280. See idem, *The Poems of St. George Tucker of Williamsburg, Virginia 1752–1827* (New York: Vantage, 1977). For a biographical sketch, see the entry "St. George Tucker (1752–1827)" by Davison M. Douglas in *Encyclopedia Virginia* (online).
513 Carl Dolmetsch, *The Collected Essays of St. George Tucker*, manuscript available at https://digitalarchive.wm.edu/handle/10288/18950.
514 Prince, "St. George Tucker: Bard on the Bench," 279.
515 It was only later, for example, that Tucker, rather than Philip Freneau, was determined to be the author of "The Probationary Odes of Jonathan Pindar, Esq." published in the *National Gazette* (1793).
516 See the notes at *Founders Online*, National Archives, https://founders.archives.gov/documents/Jefferson/03-01-02-0486-0002. [Original source: *The Papers of Thomas Jefferson*, Retirement Series, vol. 1, *4 March 1809 to 15 November 1809*, ed. J. Jefferson Looney (Princeton: Princeton University Press, 2004), 617–19].
517 Anne Elizabeth McCorkle, "St. George Tucker's 'Old Bachelor' Letter on Language and Literature in America: A Critical Edition" (master's thesis, College of William & Mary, 1971).
518 John Pendleton Kennedy, *Memoirs of the Life of William Wirt, Attorney-General of the United States*, 2nd ed., vol. 2 (Philadelphia: Blanchard and Lea, 1856), 382.
519 Cf. Anya Jabour, "Male Friendship and Masculinity in the Early National South: William Wirt and His Friends," *Journal of the Early Republic* 20 (2000): 92.

520 The manuscript reads "ter," which must be a mistake.
521 In his notebook Tucker says that the fourth stanza refers to Napoleon and George III.
522 This is the manuscript reading, but it must be a mistake. Perhaps "pollet" was intended (see notes 516, 524).
523 The cover letter is dated Williamsburg, November 16, 1814.
524 https://www.loc.gov/resource/mtj1.044_0338_0341/?sp=3. An annotated text, as well as a translation by John F. Miller, is available at *Founders Online* (see note 516).
525 Richard A. Harrison, *Princetonians, 1769–1775: A Biographical Dictionary* (Princeton: Princeton University Press, 1980), 240–43.
526 Luckey to Madison, December 8, 1812, James Madison Papers, Library of Congress.
527 Luckey to Madison, June 12, 1809, James Madison Papers, Library of Congress.
528 Luckey to Madison, August 26, 1810, James Madison Papers, Library of Congress.
529 Luckey to Madison, June 12 1809; August 10, 1809, James Madison Papers, Library of Congress.
530 Samuel Davies Alexander, *Princeton College During the Eighteenth Century* (New York: Randolph, 1872), 155. See also Robert Lorenzo Clark, *History of Centre Presbyterian Church, New Park, Pa. 1780–1903* (Lancaster, PA: New Era, 1903), 3–17.
531 Ralph Ketcham, *James Madison: A Biography* (Charlottesville: University Press of Virginia, 1971, with reprint 1990), 19–20, 29, (quotation on p. 46).
532 The other Latin letter was dated April 1, 1812. On Luckey's correspondence with Madison, see Garrett Ward Sheldon, "Religion and the Presidency of James Madison," in Gastón Espinosa, ed. *Religion and the American Presidency: George Washington to George W. Bush with Commentary and Primary Sources* (New York: Columbia University Press, 2009), 133–34.
533 https://www.loc.gov/resource/mjm.13_0637_0639/?sp=1. An English summary of this letter is at *Founders Online*, National Archives, https://founders.archives.gov/documents/Madison/03-03-02-0580. [Original source: *The Papers of James Madison*, Presidential Series, vol. 3, *3 November 1810–4 November 1811*, eds. J.C.A. Stagg, Jeanne Kerr Cross, and Susan Holbrook Perdue (Charlottesville: University Press of Virginia, 1996), 490].
534 On Flaget, see the article by J.H. Schauinger in *New Catholic Encyclopedia.*
535 William E. Foley, *Wilderness Journey: The Life of William Clark* (Co-

lumbia: University of Missouri Press, 2004), 44, 201.
536 St. Anne's parish (now the Basilica of Sainte Anne de Detroit), located near the waterfront in Detroit, was established in 1701.
537 St. Anthony of Padua parish.
538 Fr. Gabriel Richard (1767–1832) founded Michigan's first newspaper, contributed to the founding of the University of Michigan, and served in the U.S. House of Representatives.
539 Prairie du Chien, Wisconsin.
540 Perhaps Green Bay, Wisconsin.
541 Isaiah 6:8.
542 The chair was endowed by Sir Benjamin Thompson, the Count of Rumford (1753–1814), a Massachusetts-born inventor. Some of Bigelow's lectures are printed in Bigelow, *Elements of Technology* (Boston: Hilliard, Gray, Little, and Wilkins, 1829).
543 Ellis, *Memoir of Jacob Bigelow* (see Source), 21.
544 Bigelow, *An Address on the Limits of Education* (Boston: E.P. Dutton, 1865), 17.
545 Bigelow, *Remarks on Classical and Utilitarian Studies* (Boston: Little Brown, 1867), 55–56. Bigelow is here expanding on his MIT lecture (see previous note).
546 See Richard, *Golden Age of the Classics in America* (note 26 above).
547 John Thornton Kirkland (1770–1840) became President of Harvard in 1810.
548 Harvard's campus at the time included three College Houses as well as Massachusetts Hall (1720), Holden Chapel (1744), Hollis Hall (1763), Stoughton Hall (1805), Holworthy Hall (1812), and the recently completed University Hall (1815).
549 Among the faculty members at the time were Edward Everett (1794–1865) and John Snelling Popkin (1771–1852), the first two holders of the Eliot Professorship of Greek Literature. Moreover, Harvard had recently added a Divinity School (1816) to join its Medical School (1783). The Law School was added the following year (1817).
550 I treat this essay in "Latin and the American Civil War," *Classical Journal* 113 (2018): 229–30.
551 For a brief overview of the congressional debate, see https://www.senate.gov/artandhistory/history/minute/Missouri_Compromise.htm.
552 In 1818 the House of Representatives approved along sectional lines an amendment prohibiting slavery in Missouri, which had applied for statehood, but in the Senate the statehood bill passed only after senators from slave states had removed this amendment. The bill then returned to the House, but representatives declined to pass it without the amendment.

553 Clay's proposed Missouri Compromise admitted Missouri as a slave state and Maine as a free state and also established a line of division at 36° 30', above which no future slave state would be admitted.
554 Nettleship cites Harriet Martineau, *A History of the American Compromises*. He likely had in mind the following text from p. 11 of the 1856 edition (London: John Chapman): "The Missouri Compromise was believed by all but the most far-sighted of the citizens of the Union to have settled 'the Difficulty' for ever."
555 For this paragraph Nettleship cites Cornelis de Witt, *Thomas Jefferson, étude historique sur la démocratie américaine* (Paris: Didier, 1861), 365 and Martineau, *History of the American Compromises*.
556 Arkansas and Florida became territories, respectively, in 1819 and 1822, and states in 1836 and 1845.
557 The notice appears to have been printed first in the *Wilmington Spectator*. It was reprinted in the *Dayton Watchman*, March 9, 1824, and in April it appeared throughout the nation. See, for example, the *National Gazette* (Philadelphia), April 7, 1824.
558 Francis Glass, *A Life of George Washington, in Latin Prose*, ed., J.N. Reynolds (New York: Harper & Brothers, 1835). An inner page bears the Latin title: *Georgii Washingtonii, Americae Septentrionalis Civitatum Foederatarum Praesidis Primi, Vita, Francisco Glass, A.M. Ohioensi, litteris Latinis conscripta*. Two later editions of the work were published.
559 Cf. Revilo P. Oliver, "A Voice in the Wilderness," in Charles Henderson, ed., *Classical Mediaeval and Renaissance Studies in Honor of Berthold Louis Ullman*, vol. 2 (Rome: Edizioni di Storia e Letteratura, 1964), 515–35 (p. 520), who considers it "*possible*" though "improbable" that Glass's work is an "elaborate hoax" contrived by Reynolds and the Vice-Provost of the University of Pennsylvania, "with the connivance (if not the active complicity) of Professor Charles Anthon."
560 Robert W. Steele, "Francis Glass, A.M.," *Magazine of Western History* 2 (1885): 291–93; Henry Howe, *Historical Collections of Ohio*, vol. 2 (Columbus: Henry Howe & Son, 1891), 293–94; A. W. Drury, *History of the City of Dayton and Montgomery County Ohio*, vol. 1 (Chicago: Clarke, 1909), 427–429; R. H. Eckelberry, "Francis Glass, Master Teacher," *Educational Research Bulletin* 13 (1934): 107–12, 132. See also *Lebanon* (Ohio) *Western Star*, October 29, 1908.
561 But cf. Oliver, "A Voice in the Wilderness," 523 nn.1, 3, who thinks that Glass must have assisted Ross with the latter's work on Greek, rather than Latin, grammar; moreover, despite two inquiries with the Registrar, Oliver found no evidence that Glass studied or taught at the University of Pennsylvania.
562 According to the *Dayton Watchman*, June 15, 1824, Glass spent

"some years" in France.
563 *Lebanon* (Ohio) *Western Star*, July 11, 1820.
564 Arthur Harold Weston, "The *Vita Washingtonii* of Francis Glass," *Classical Journal* 28 (1933): 410–11.
565 Glass, *Life of George Washington*, 221.
566 Glass, *Life of George Washington*, xi-xii.
567 Glass, *Life of George Washington*, 214.
568 Only six weeks earlier Glass had posted an announcement (dated July 13, 1824) in newspapers in the mid-Atlantic and as far south as Georgia seeking employment. See *Constitutional Whig* (Richmond, VA), September 10, 1824.
569 *Wilmington* (Ohio) *Spectator*, reprinted in *Dayton Watchman*, March 9, 1824. J.P. Foote of Cincinnati was a partner with Reynolds in the purchase of the copyright.
570 *Scioto* (Chillicothe, Ohio) *Gazette*, September 23, 1824.
571 A curious episode occurred in this interval. In April 1829 a letter appeared in Washington DC's *Daily National Intelligencer* (April 10, 1829) announcing that the author had recently discovered the manuscript of Glass's work, and that it would soon be sent to Carey & Lea of Philadelphia for publication. For Reynolds's extraordinary activities from 1824 on, including his venture towards Antarctica and his experiences in Chile, see Aaron Sachs, *The Humboldt Current: A European Explorer and His American Disciples* (Oxford: Oxford University Press, 2007), 115–76.
572 In 1836 another Latin life of Washington was published: William Lance, *Georgii Washingtonis Vita* (Charleston: Dowling, 1836). According to a letter of Lance published in the *Charleston Courier* on November 11, 1835, this work had initially been submitted to Harper's in 1834. According to a description in William S. Baker, *Bibliotheca Washingtoniana: a Descriptive List of the Biographies and Biographical Sketches of George Washington* (Philadelphia: Lindsay, 1889), 77–78, Lance's work ended with the Battle of Princeton and he died in Texas in 1840 without completing a subsequent part. Lance's work received comparatively little attention when it was published. See *Richmond Enquirer*, November 3, 1835; *Charleston Courier*, November 3, 1835.
573 The appendix to Glass's work contains testimonials from several college presidents, literary magazines, et al., including one from former President John Quincy Adams.
574 *Southern Literary Messenger* 2 (1835/36): 52–54.
575 *The North American Review* 43 (1836): 28–52. A rebuttal to Kingsley is in *The Knickerbocker* 8 (1836): 473–76. Kingsley responds in *The North American Review* 44 (1837): 270–72 For later assessments of

Glass's Latinity, see Weston, "The *Vita Washingtonii* of Francis Glass;" see also Oliver, "A Voice in the Wilderness," 529–32, who is responsible for identifying the author of the *The North American Review* articles.
576 Baker, *Bibliotheca Washingtoniana*, 75.
577 *La Civiltà Cattolica* 1.3 (1850): 316.
578 Madison to Glass, Montpelier, April 8, 1821, printed in *Letters and Other Writings of James Madison, Fourth President of the United States*, vol. 3, *1816–1828* (Philadelphia: Lippincott, 1867), 208.
579 Eckelberry, "Francis Glass, Master Teacher," 112. Howe, *Historical Collections of Ohio*, 294 quotes the preface to this ode: "To the academicians and scholars in the United States of America, especially of those who delight in literary pursuits, Francis Glass, A. M., wishes much health."
580 Cf. *Richmond Enquirer*, November 3, 1835: "The Charleston author [William Lance] has followed the analogy of the Latin Language better, in declining Washington in *Washingtonis*, &c., like Cimon, Cimonis—Agamemnon, Agamemnonis, &c."
581 This is perhaps a reference to the effects of the Panic of 1819.
582 I have not found the expression "Sociae Civitates Americae Septentrionalis" used elsewhere.
583 Series 1, General Correspondence, 1723–1859. http://hdl.loc.gov/loc.mss/mjm.19_0789_0790. A translation of this letter made by students at St. Andrew's Episcopal School in Potomac, Maryland is available at latinprimarysourceproject.weebly.com.
584 *Novus orbis pictus juventuti instituendae et oblectandae*, vol. 7 (Vienna: Typis Antonii Puchler, 1808), no. 41; J.F. Gmelin, *Caroli a Linné, Systema Naturae per Regna Tria Naturae*, 13 ed., vol. 1 (Leipzig: George Emanuel Beer, 1788), 470.
585 The history of the Catholic mission and the reasons for the forced departure of Bachelot and Short are given in Reginald Yzendoorn, *History of the Catholic Mission in the Hawaiian Islands* (Honolulu: Honolulu Star-Bulletin, 1927), 26–75. See more generally George Verne Blue, "The Project for a French Settlement in the Hawaiian Islands, 1824–1842," *Pacific Historical Review* 2 (1933): 85–99. And see also Reginald Yzendoorn, "Alexis John Augustine Bachelot," in *Catholic Encyclopedia*.
586 Carlo Maria Pedicini was Cardinal Prefect of the Sacred Congregation Propaganda Fide from 1831 to 1834.
587 Bachelot was at Mission San Gabriel from 1832 to 1837. Patrick Short spent six months at Mission San Gabriel and then went north to Carmel and Monterey.
588 Captain James Cook, on his third journey around the world, arrived in Oahu in January 1778.

589 Kamehameha ruled most of the Big Island; Keoua ruled the remaining part of the Big Island; Kahekili ruled Maui, Lanai, Oahu, and Molokai; Kaeo ruled Kauai and Niihau.
590 Dissension followed the death of Kahekili in 1794, and by 1810 Kamehameha emerged as ruler of all the islands, a position that he retained until his death in 1819.
591 Kauikeaouli, the second son of Kamehameha, ruled from 1825 to 1854.
592 A French vessel visited Hawaii in the summer of 1819 (see below note 596), but Bachelot is referring to the Protestant missonaries from New England who reached Hawaii in early April 1820.
593 Keopuolani (c. 1778–1823), of royal birth, was captured in the Battle of Kepaniwai in 1790. She married Kamehameha in 1795.
594 Liholiho (*c.* 1797–1824), known as Kamehameha II, inherited the kingdom when Kamehameha I died in 1819, but Kaahumanu, one of the wives of Kamehameha I, acted as his regent. Liholiho died from measles while visiting London in 1824.
595 Kauikeaouli (1814–1854) was ten when his older brother, Liholiho (Kamehameha II) died. Kauikeaouli ruled as Kamehameha III.
596 Since Kauikeaouli was young, Boki (or Poki), the Governor of Oahu, exercised great influence. Boki, who had been baptized in 1819 by a chaplain onboard a visiting French ship, was favorable to the Catholic mission. But following Boki's disappearance at sea in 1830 the Catholic mission was increasingly vulnerable.
597 The "praedicatores" are the Protestant missionaries.
598 On April 2, 1831, Bachelot and Short appeared before an assembly of chiefs presided over by Kaahumanu and were given a letter containing a decree of banishment.
599 My transcription is uncertain here.
600 On the morning of Christmas Eve, Kekuanaoa, the commander of the troops, arrived at Bachelot's and Short's house and escorted them to the *Waverley*, which was waiting in the harbor.
601 *Woodstock Letters* 33 (1904): 23, 318.
602 Georgetown's Irish-born tailor, Brother Edmund McFadden (b. 1784), was a legendary figure in the college's early years—a confidant of President Millard Fillmore and dispenser of pithy wisdom but a lousy mender of garments. For sketches of McFadden see *Woodstock Letters* 62 (1933): 323–24; *Georgetown College Journal* 26 (1897): 117.
603 Anthony Leifer is listed as tailor in the *Catalogus Provinciae Marylandiae Societatis Jesu, ineunte anno MDCCCXXXVI* (Georgetown: Langtree and O'Sullivan, 1836).
604 In addition to Anthony Leifer (see previous note) the following

brothers ("coadjutores") are listed in the 1836 *Catalogus Provinciae Marylandiae*: Daniel Connolly (b. 1807), Christian DeSmett (b. 1771), Edward Clifford (b. 1808), Thomas Moore (b. 1790), Joseph West (b. 1764), Auden McGirr (b. 1796), William Mullen (b. 1786), Thomas Hickey (b. 1807), John Gavin (b. 1780), John Sparks (b. 1801), Joseph Flaut (b. 1805), William Smith (b. 1801), Maurice Staunton (b. 1795), Sylvester Clarke (b. 1800). Marbury and Fitzgerald are not listed. The Catalogue lists other brothers, whose names, perhaps, could not be accommodated into Latin verse.

605 Joseph A. Lopez, S.J. (b. 1779) was for a brief time president of Georgetown (1839–40). See *Woodstock Letters* 33 (1904): 16–17. In 1836 he was teaching Spanish.

606 The instructor of logic and metaphysics was Fr. Stephen Gabaria (b. 1794).

607 Brother Thomas Mead (1785–1848), born in Ireland, entered the Jesuits in 1817 and was infirmarian at Georgetown.

608 See, for example, the essays in *U.S. Catholic Historian* 37.2 (2019).

609 See also Matthew Quallen, "Slavery Inextricably Tied To Georgetown's Growth," *The Hoya*, October 23, 2015, and see *Report of the Working Group on Slavery, Memory, and Reconciliation to the President of Georgetown University* (Washington, DC: Georgetown University, Summer 2016).

610 For narrative and analysis, see inter alia Curran, *Shaping American Catholicism* (note 229 above), 92–110 and Cornelius Michael Buckley, *Stephen Larigaudelle Dubuisson, S.J. (1786–1864) and the Reform of the American Jesuits* (Lanham, MD: University Press of America, 2013), 149–72, 180–81.

611 Mulledy and McSherry swapped positions in 1837 as this transaction was being negotiated. Mulledy was President from 1829 to 1837 and Provincial from 1837 to 1840, McSherry was Provincial from 1833 to 1837 and President from 1837 to 1839.

612 Robert K. Judge, "Foundation and First Administration of the Maryland Province," *Woodstock Letters* 88 (1959): 392–401.

613 Francis Vespré, S.J. (1783–1860) was the procurator of the Maryland Province of Jesuits.

614 This document is visible at slaveryarchive.georgetown.edu. This site includes a transcription and translation made by students and Josiah Osgood, Professor of Classics at Georgetown; I looked at the translation, but I have made my own transcription.

615 For an account of this mission, see Rothensteiner, "The Flat-head and Nez Perce Delegation," *St. Louis Catholic Historical Review* 2 (1920): 183–97.

616 See also the discussion in Alvin M. Josephy, *The Nez Perce Indians and the Opening of the Northwest* (Boston: Mariner, 1997), 93–98, 124–25.
617 Rothensteiner, "The Flat-head and Nez Perce Delegation," 186.
618 This letter is printed in *Concilia Provincialia Baltimori Habita ab anno 1829 usque ad annum 1849*, 2nd ed. (Baltimore: John Murphy, 1851), 55–59. On Rosati, see John E. Rybolt, "Joseph Rosati, C.M. (1789–1843): Pioneer American Bishop," *Vincentiana* 48 (2004): 394–403.
619 The traditional Catholic liturgical calendar marks the Sundays of summer and fall by their distance from Pentecost.
620 Those who were to receive the Sacrament of Confirmation.
621 Carlos E. Castañeda, *Our Catholic Heritage in Texas 1519–1936*, vol. 7, *The Church in Texas Since Independence 1836–1950* (Austin: Von Boeckmann-Jones, 1958), 9.
622 Charles G. Deuther, *The Life and Times of the Rt. Rev. John Timon, D.D. First Roman Catholic Bishop of the Diocese of Buffalo* (Buffalo: by the author, 1870); Patrick Foley, "Timon, John" in *Handbook of Texas Online.*
623 Ralph Francis Bayard, *Lone-Star Vanguard: the Catholic Re-Occupation of Texas, 1838–1848* (St. Louis: Vincentian, 1945), 152.
624 Arthur Ikin, *Texas: Its History, Topography, Agriculture, Commerce, and General Statistics* (London: Sherwood, Gilbert, and Piper, 1841), 77. See also Joseph W. Schmitz, "Diplomatic Relations of the Republic of Texas," in *Handbook of Texas Online.*
625 See Patrick Foley, *Missionary Bishop: Jean-Marie Odin in Galveston and New Orleans* (College Station: Texas A&M University Press, 2013), 87–91.
626 The preface which introduces this transcription reads: "His denique Epistolam clarissimo Texanae Reipublicae Praesidi a D. Tua exhibendam adiungo, ut praesto tibi sit, ac Missionis bona quae sunt, resignare iubeat. Hinc . . ."
627 Dominatione.
628 In the 1839-40 session, the Congress of the Republic of Texas, newly-moved to Austin, consisted of forty representatives and fourteen senators.
629 Sacrae Congregationis.
630 Dominationem.
631 The letterbook does not give the full benediction, but an early English version of the original Latin reads: "I most earnestly beseech God that he may long preserve and bless Your Excellency, and enrich you with his heavenly gift" (Ikin, *Texas*, 78).

632 Laura Dassow Walls, *Henry David Thoreau: A Life* (Chicago: University of Chicago Press, 2017), 97.
633 Walter Harding, *The Days of Henry Thoreau* (New York: Knopf, 1966), 86–87.
634 Harding, *Days of Henry Thoreau*, 163, quoting Isaac Hecker.
635 *A Catalogue of the Officers and Students of Harvard University, for the academical year 1833–4* (Cambridge, MA: Brown and Shattuck, 1833), 23–25.
636 F.B. Sanborn, *The Life of Henry David Thoreau* (Boston: Houghton Mifflin, 1917), 260.
637 "Aulus Persius Flaccus," *Dial* 1 (July 1840): 117–21.
638 John Paul Pritchard, "Cato in Concord," *Classical Weekly* 36 (1942): 3–5.
639 Clarence Gohdes, "Henry Thoreau, Bachelor of Arts," *Classical Journal* 23 (1928): 323–36 (p. 330).
640 Sanborn, *Life of Henry David Thoreau*, 186. See also K.W. Cameron, "Thoreau's Early Compositions in the Ancient Languages," *The Emerson Society Quarterly* 8.3 (1957): 20–29.
641 Harding, *Days of Henry Thoreau*, 183.
642 Linda Beaulieu, "Helen Thoreau," *The Concord Saunterer* 14.4 (1979): 15–20.
643 Archibald MacMechan, "Thoreau," in William Peterfield Trent, John Erskine, Stuart P. Sherman, Carl van Doren, eds., *A Short History of American Literature* (New York: Putnam, 1924), 131.
644 Gerri L. Herrick, "Sophia Thoreau—'Cara Sophia,' *The Concord Saunterer* 13.3 (1978): 5–12; Thomas Blanding, "Sophia Thoreau," *The Concord Saunterer* 14.4 (1979): 22–30.
645 Anne McGrath, "Cynthia Dunbar Thoreau," *The Concord Saunterer* 14.4 (1979): 8–14.
646 Walls, *Henry David Thoreau*, xvii.
647 Cf. Vergil, *A.* 2.774, et al.
648 Cf. Horace, *C.* 1.9.6.
649 Horace, *C.* 1.4.3–5. Other references to Horace, in particular, are noted in John Paul Pritchard, "Horace's Influence upon American Criticism," in *Transactions and Proceedings of the American Philological Association* 68 (1937): 228–63 (pp. 235–36).
650 Fairhaven.
651 Walden Pond.
652 Edward Bulwer-Lytton (1803–73) was an English author and politician.
653 Juvenal 7.51–52.
654 The steamboat *SS Lexington* caught fire and sank off the coast of

Bridgeport, Connecticut during the night of January 13, 1840 while en route from New York City to Stonington, Connecticut. For another mention of this disaster in a familial Latin letter, see Taylor, *Memoir of the Rev. Oliver Alden Taylor* (note 15 above), 326–27.
655 The Thoreau family cat.
656 The printed text has a (?) after this word.
657 Sophia Dunbar (1781–1868).
658 See now Robert N. Hudspeth, ed., *The Correspondence of Henry D. Thoreau*, vol. 1, *1834–1848* (Princeton: Princeton University Press, 2013), 58–63.
659 John Niven, *Martin Van Buren: The Romantic Age of American Politics* (New York: Oxford University Press, 1983), 452–53.
660 General Francis E. Spinner, a prominent banker, held a number of positions in New York politics before being elected to the U.S. Congress and later being appointed Treasurer of the United States under President Lincoln. See the biographical sketch by Isaac S. Hartley, "General Francis E. Spinner the Financier," *Magazine of American History* 25 (1891): 185–200.
661 *Albany Argus*, October 4, 1839 (reprinting an article from the *Mohawk Courier*).
662 For biographical notices, see George A. Hardin and Frank H. Willard, eds., *History of Herkimer County, New York* (Syracuse: Mason, 1893), 186–87 and William R. Cutter, ed., *Genealogical and Family History of Western New York*, vol. 2 (New York: Lewis, 1912), 616.
663 Spinner to Van Buren, November 23, 1840, Martin Van Buren Papers, Library of Congress: https://www.loc.gov/resource/mss43828.024_0012_0346/?sp=186.
664 Van Buren received visitors in Mr. Couch's Hotel, on Second Street, and later at the homes of local lawyers and judges.
665 Spinner's speech is printed in the *Albany Argus*, October 4, 1839.
666 Spinner was educated at the gymnasium in Bishofsheim and then he attended the University of Mainz.
667 Van Buren, the first President whose native language was not English, spoke Dutch as a child.
668 Martin Van Buren Papers, 1787–1910, Library of Congress: https://www.loc.gov/resource/mss43828.022_0361_0392/?sp=29.
669 J. Orin Oliphant, "Old Fort Colville," *The Washington Historical Quarterly* 16 (1925): 29–48.
670 See the summary in Robert C. Carriker and Eleanor R. Carriker, *Guide to the Microfilm Edition of the Pacific Northwest Tribes Missions Collection of the Oregon Province Archives of the Society of Jesus* (Wilmington, DE: Scholarly Resources, 1987), 32–33.

671 *Life, Letters and Travels of Father Pierre-Jean de Smet, S.J. 1801–1873*, 4 vols. (New York: Harper, 1905), 2.482.
672 Still extant is an 1858 letter (in French) sent by Chief Michael of the Kettle tribe and addressed to the "Blackrobe head chief" at Rome, in which he requests more priests and attributes the collapse of the mission to the poor habits introduced by gold miners. See Robert Ignatius Burns, *The Jesuits and the Indian Wars of the Northwest* (New Haven: Yale University Press, 1966), 316.
673 On St. Paul's Mission, see https://www.nps.gov/laro/learn/history-culture/mission-point.htm; Wilfred P. Schoenberg, *Paths to the Northwest: A Jesuit History of the Oregon Province* (Chicago: Loyola University Press, 1982), 64–66, 76, 94; William N. Bischoff, *The Jesuits in Old Oregon* (Caldwell, ID: Caxton, 1945), 153–56.
674 De Smet visited Fort Colville in 1841 and 1842, although Catholic missionaries from Canada (François Norbert Blanchet and Modeste Demers) had visited the region a few years earlier.
675 According to Bischoff, *The Jesuits in Old Oregon*, 153, the Jesuits were motivated in part by rumors of a projected Presbyterian mission at Kettle Falls.
676 This is likely a mistake for 1875, which is the date of the last recorded Mass at St. Paul's.
677 "Canal History," canals.ny.gov.
678 Biographical notices of Skolla appear in Chrysostom Verwyst, *Life and Labors of Rt. Rev. Frederic Baraga, First Bishop of Marquette, Mich.* (Milwaukee: Wiltzius, 1900), 393–409 and Antoine Ivan Rezek, *History of the Diocese of Sault Ste. Marie and Marquette*, vol. 1 (Houghton, MI: n.p., 1906), 359–74.
679 John Dubois (1764–1842) was Bishop of New York from 1826 to his death.
680 Skolla is writing several decades after his 1842 trip.
681 In 1847 Lansing became the capital of Michigan.
682 Anthony J. Kuzniewski, "'Our American Champions:' The first Generation of American Jesuit Leaders after the Restoration of the Society," *Studies in the Spirituality of Jesuits* 46.1 (2014).
683 Willard Thorp, "Catholic Novelists in Defense of Their Faith, 1829–1865," *Proceedings of the American Antiquarian Society* 78 (1968): 25–117 (Pise is discussed on pp. 25–38).
684 So far as I can determine, this poem was first published in *The Washington Sentinel*, January 20, 1855.
685 Henry A. Brann, "Rev. Charles Constantine Pise, the Only Catholic Chaplain of the Congress of the United States," *Historical Records and Studies* 2 (1900): 357.

686 Mary M. Meline and Edward F. X. McSweeny, *The Story of the Mountain: Mount St. Mary's College and Seminary*, vol. 1 (Emmitsburg, MD: Weekly Chronicle, 1911), 127–28.
687 *Baltimore Gazette and Daily Advertiser*, September 19, 1827. A translation, by eighteen-year-old Neilson Poe (1809–84), a cousin of Edgar Allan Poe, was published three days later in the same paper. See https://collections.digitalmaryland.org/digital/collection/poe/id/181/. Another translation is in Pise's *The Pleasures of Religion and Other Poems* (Philadelphia: Carey & Hart, 1833), 224.
688 *Baltimore Gazette and Daily Advertiser*, February 29, 1828.
689 *The Catholic Expositor and Literary Magazine* 3 (1843): 208–9. An English translation follows.
690 *The Jubilee at Mount Saint Mary's, October 6, 1858* (New York: Dunigan, 1859), 88–92.
691 Pise also includes a Latin translation of one of his Italian poems, "From Metastasio," in *The Pleasures of Religion*, 207. This six-line elegiac poem begins "Et montem, vallemque vagi lavit aequoris unda."
692 M. Eulalia Teresa Moffatt, "Charles Constantine Pise," *Historical Records and Studies* 20 (1931): 64–97.
693 See especially Gigliotti, "*Musae Americanae*," (note 32 above).
694 Helen Doe, *The First Atlantic Liner: Brunel's* Great Western *Steamship* (Gloucestershire: Amberley, 2017).
695 "Horae Vagabundae," *The Catholic Expositor and Literary Magazine* 3 (1843): 116–17.
696 John Loughery, *Dagger John: Archbishop John Hughes and the Making of Irish America* (Ithaca: Cornell University Press, 2018), 140.
697 See Robert F. Trisco, *The Holy See and the Nascent Church in the Middle Western United States, 1826–1850* (Rome: Gregorian University Press, 1962), 84.
698 This letter is printed in Brann, "Rev. Charles Constantine Pise," 355.
699 The printed version reads "descedenti."
700 Cf. Genesis 6:14.
701 In fact the *Great Western* typically made its last eastern crossing in November and resumed its western service anytime between late February and early April.
702 The *Great Western* had four masts.
703 In May 1842 the *Great Western* made the crossing from New York to England in 12 1/2 days. See *Leicester Chronicle*, May 14, 1842. The western crossing took two or three days longer.
704 The *Great Western* was propelled by two side paddle-wheels.
705 A note to the English translation specifies: "Capt. Hoskins to whom, I am glad of this opportunity of awarding my tribute of respect as a gen-

tleman, and my admiration as a seaman." The reading "Et bona cuncta" rather than "favoremque" is found in the *Catholic Expositor* 3 (1842): 155.

706 The *Great Western*'s final transatlantic voyage was in September 1855. After transporting soldiers to the Crimean War, it was scrapped in 1857.

707 The British built Fort Mackinac on Mackinac Island in 1780 to replace Fort Michillimackinac, which had been located on the mainland at the site of present-day Mackinaw City.

708 Ste. Anne's Church originally stood in present-day Mackinaw City, but it was moved to Mackinac Island in 1780. Skolla drew a still-extant sketch of St. Anne's in 1845.

709 In July 1845 General Zachary Taylor led troops into Texas, which in December of that year was admitted into the Union as a state; the House and Senate voted to go to war against Mexico in May 1846.

710 In 1670/71 Claude Dablon (see section 22) founded the Catholic mission of St. Ignace on Mackinac Island. It was relocated to the north shore (the present-day town of St. Ignace, on the upper peninsula), and much later to the south shore (present-day Mackinaw City, but at the time Skolla wrote it was back in St. Ignace (in the upper peninsula).

711 In September 1845 Skolla traveled by boat to Sault Ste Marie and then to L'Anse (in present-day Baraga County, in the upper peninsula of Michigan), where he met Baraga. Together they traveled by canoe to La Pointe (on Madeline Island), arriving on October 3.

712 A translation by Thomas J. Shanahan is in *Acta et Dicta* 7 (1936): 217–68.

713 Zappone's biography can be reconstructed from contemporary newspaper accounts and advertisements, but see also Gerald McKevitt, *Brokers of Culture: Italian Jesuits in the American West, 1848–1919* (Stanford: Stanford University Press, 2007), 70.

714 See John C. Pinheiro, *Missionaries of Republicanism: A Religious History of the Mexican-American War* (Oxford: Oxford University Press, 2014), 72–85.

715 James Wynne, "Memoir of the Rev. Anthony Rey, S.J.," *United States Catholic Magazine and Monthly Review* 6 (1847): 543–52. Correspondence concerning Rey's wartime activities is in *Woodstock Letters* 17 (1888): 3–12, 149–63.

716 *Carmen Panegyricum, a Poetical Address to General Zachary Taylor, President of the United States of America* (Washington, DC: Robert A. Waters, 1849); reprinted in *Latin Poems . . . Addressed to his Friends on Particular Occasions and Respectfully Dedicated to his Pupils*, 2nd ed. (Washington, DC: Waters, 1849). In addition to the panegyric for Tay-

lor, this volume contains the ode to Fr. Rey and an elegiac poem "Puero Corporis Egregii," as well as an English poem about Taylor.

717 The title in the (later) version published in *Latin Poems* is "Clarissimo Amico. In Bellum Contra Mexicum Profecturo. Ode."

718 A reference to the founder of the Jesuits, St. Ignatius Loyola. In the later version the word "Magnanimum" appears instead.

719 The later version reads "viri" here.

720 Curtis Carroll Davis, *That Ambitious Mr. Legaré: The Life of Mr. James M. Legaré of South Carolina, Including a Collected Edition of His Verse* (Columbia: University of South Carolina Press, 1971), 70–72. On Legaré, see also R. Bruce Bickley, "James Mathews Legaré," in Joseph M. Flora and Amber Vogel, eds., *Southern Writers: A New Biographical Dictionary* (Baton Rouge: Louisiana State University Press, 2006), 251–52.

721 *Boston Evening Transcript*, April 13, 1848.

722 Davis, *That Ambitious Mr. Legaré*, 54.

723 E.g., "Thanatokallos," which he published in *The Knickerbocker* 34 (1849): 204–6.

724 Richard A. Macksey, quoted in Davis, *That Ambitious Mr. Legaré*, 306.

725 Davis suggests that the original reading was "spoliantes."

726 Davis suggests that the original reading was "cirrusque."

727 For the Causten tomb, see the three articles collected by Carlton Fletcher at https://gloverparkhistory.com/estates-and-farms/weston/the-causten-tomb/.

728 *Washington Union*, March 23, 1851.

729 *Washington Republic*, March 25, 1851.

730 Other children were Eliza Carvallo (1836–53) and Washington Carvallo (d. 1865).

731 The 1850 *Washington and Georgetown Directory* lists the Carvallo address as 7th Street, across from the city Post Office.

732 *New York Tribune*, May 30, 1880.

733 *Sermons Delivered During the Second Plenary Council of Baltimore, October, 1866* (Baltimore: Kelly & Piet, 1866), 9–10.

734 *Baltimore Sun*, May 10, 1852.

735 This appears to be a mistake. Easter Sunday in 1852 was April 11. Therefore May 9 would be considered the fourth, rather than the third, Sunday after Easter.

736 A.S. = Anno Salutis

737 A reference to the superiors of various religious congregations: Augustinians, Dominicans, Benedictines, Franciscans, Jesuits, Redemptorists, Vincentians, Sulpicians.

738 "In the streets in the vicinity there was a dense mass of human beings, blocking up every avenue for squares around—the windows, doorways, and every other prominent point from which a view could be obtained, being filled with interested and curious spectators" (*Baltimore Sun*, May 10, 1852).
739 The Cathedral of the Assmumption, designed by Benjamin Henry Latrobe, the architect of the U.S. Capitol, was dedicated in 1821. It is designated a metropolitan church because Baltimore was (and is) an archdiocese.
740 In attendance were six archbishops and twenty-five bishops.
741 A cope, worn by bishops and certain abbots.
742 The mitre, worn by bishops and certain abbots.
743 St. Mary's de Trappe denotes Our Lady of Gethsemani Abbey near Bardstown, Kentucky, which had recently been founded (1848); the abbot was Eutropius Proust (1809–74).
744 A hat.
745 A chasuble.
746 Cf. *Baltimore Sun*, May 10, 1852: "The services, indeed, of the Young Catholic's Friend, throughout the day, were very deserving, being both efficient and courteous, and serving, by their judiciousness, to the best interest and convenience of all concerned, both among the clergy and the very large congregation in attendance."
747 The Archbishop of Baltimore was Francis Patrick Kenrick (1797–1863), who had been designated the Apostolic Delegate, i.e., the representative of Rome.
748 Francis L'Homme (1794–1860), a native of France, was a Sulpician who was superior of the Seminary in Baltimore.
749 Alexius J. Elder (1791–1871) was a Maryland native who entered the Sulpicians and taught in Baltimore and Emmitsburg.
750 Charles Voirdye (1819–80) was a Sulpician who briefly taught at St. Mary's College (Baltimore). After serving in various dioceses, he became a Benedictine monk.
751 Henry B. Coskery (1808–72), the rector of the Baltimore Cathedral in 1852, refused an appointment to be Bishop of Portland (Maine) and instead spent many years as Vicar-General of the Archdiocese of Baltimore.
752 Rev. Thomas Foley (1822–79) was secretary to Archbishop Francis Patrick Kenrick and Chancellor of the Archdiocese; later he became coadjutor Bishop of Chicago.
753 John Hughes (1797–1864), the Archbishop of New York (see section 70, and cf. section 61).
754 Lewis Cass Jr. to Edward Everett, Rome, March 20, 1853, printed

in Leo Francis Stock, ed., *United States Ministers to the Papal States: Instructions and Despatches 1848–1868* (Washington, DC: Catholic University Press, 1933), 96–97.

755 For Bedini's visit, see especially James F. Connelly, *The Visit of Archbishop Gaetano Bedini to the United States of America, June 1853–February 1854* (Rome: Editrice Pontificia Università Gregoriana, 1960), but see also Howard R. Marraro, *American Opinion on the Unification of Italy, 1846–1861* (New York: Columbia University Press, 1932), 138–48; Peter Guilday, "Gaetano Bedini: An Episode in the Life of Archbishop John Hughes," *Historical Records and Studies* 23 (1933): 87–170; David Endres, "Know-Nothings, Nationhood, and the Nuncio: Reassessing the Visit of Archbishop Bedini," *U.S. Catholic Historian* 21 (2003): 1–16; Andrew Mach, "Transatlantic Tales and Democratic Dreams: Archbishop Gaetano Bedini, Alessandro Gavazzi, and the Struggle to Define Republican Liberty in a Revolutionary Age, 1848–1854" (master's thesis, West Virginia University, 2014).

756 Franklin Pierce Collection, George J. Mitchell Department of Special Collections & Archives, Hawthorne–Longfellow Library, Bowdoin College.

757 Bedini was appointed titular Archbishop of Thebes on March 15, 1852.

758 On March 18, 1852 Bedini was appointed Apostolic Nuncio to the Imperial Court of Pedro II of Brazil at Rio de Janeiro.

759 Piux IX was elected Pope on June 16, 1846.

760 P.P. = Papa

761 The text is also found in Henry de Courcy, *The Catholic Church in the United States: A Sketch of its Ecclesiastical History*, trans. John Gilmary Shea (New York: Dunigan, 1856), 505–6 as well as in Appendix D of Connelly, *Visit of Archbishop Gaetano Bedini.*

762 Paul Johnson, *A History of the American People* (New York: HarperPerennial, 1997), 427–30 (p. 429). See also the resources at the Kansas State Historical Society, https://www.kshs.org/kansapedia/kansas-nebraska-act/15159.

763 Gilbert J. Garraghan, *The Jesuits of the Middle United States* (New York: America, 1938), 1.558–64.

764 A vicariate, administered by a Vicar Apostolic, was a forerunner to a diocese.

765 John Baptist Miège, S.J. (1815–84) was appointed Vicar Apostolic of Indian Territory east of the Rocky Mountains in 1850.

766 Kansas and Nebraska.

767 The pro-slavery *Kansas Weekly Herald* (Leavenworth) and *Kansas Pioneer* (Kickapoo City), and the free-soil *Herald of Freedom* (Wakaru-

sa), all of which were founded in 1854.
768 The Missouri Compromise, which admitted Missouri as a slave state and Maine as a free state and prohibited slavery beyond 36° 30' latitude.
769 Kansas was admitted into the Union as a free state in 1861.
770 Beginning in 1829 with the Delaware Indians, various tribes moved from regions east of the Mississippi River into Kansas in the face of encroaching European settlement. In 1854, contrary to earlier pledges by the federal government, these tribes were forced to leave Kansas as white settlers encroached once again.
771 A transcription is also found in Garraghan, *Jesuits of the Middle United States*, 1.559.
772 Walter R. Agard, "Classics on the Midwest Frontier," *Classical Journal* 51 (1955): 103–110 (p. 108). See also the address by Laura McClure, "'Classics on the Midwest Frontier': The Legacy of Walter Ray Agard," at the 114th Annual Meeting of CAMWS: https://camws.org/2018banquet.
773 On St. Francis Seminary, see Peter Leo Johnson, *Halcyon Days: Story of St. Francis Seminary, Milwaukee, 1856–1956* (Milwaukee: Bruce, 1956).
774 On Loras, see Thomas E. Auge, *Man of Deeds: Bishop Loras and the Upper Mississippi Valley Frontier*, ed. Amy Lorenz (Dubuque: Loras College Press, 2008) and Mathias M. Hoffmann, *Centennial History of the Archdiocese of Dubuque* (Dubuque: Columbia College Press, 1938). Loras's outgoing letters are printed in R.F. Klein, ed., assisted by Benvenuta Bras, *Foundations: The Letters of Mathias Loras, D.D., Bishop of Dubuque* (Dubuque: Loras College Press, 2004), hereafter = *FLML*. His incoming correspondence is in Loras C. Otting, ed., *Letters to a Pioneer Bishop: Correspondence to Mathias Loras, D.D., First Bishop of Dubuque* (Dubuque: Loras College Press, 2009), hereafter = *LPB*.
775 The Joseph Salzmann Papers, 1847–1898 in the Archdiocese of Milwaukee Archives do not contain any Latin letters by Salzmann, although his surviving German letters contain much interspersed Latin.
776 For Loras's knowledge of German, see *FLML*, 410, 538, 542, 611, 687–688. Only six of the roughly 400 surviving letters from Loras, and fourteen of the 621 surviving letters to him, are in German.
777 Yet likely unbeknownst to Salzmann, Loras was not comfortable in Latin. Shortly after becoming bishop, he apologized for writing the Pope in French rather than Latin (*FLML* 186). He requested Latin-French and French-Latin dictionaries to facilitate his episcopal correspondence (*FLML* 253), but years later he still had such anxiety about making embarrassing mistakes that he wrote the Propaganda Fide in French (*FLML* 544). Yet despite his anxiety, Loras did have a working knowledge of Latin: he required priests to use it when completing ques-

tionnaires (*FLML* 587–588, *LPB* 406), and it often appears when his correspondents cite theological definitions/decrees (*LPB* 573, 589, 888), or when they discuss discrete matters (*LPB* 227, 356, 375, 732, 850). For remarks on the languages used by midwestern American bishops in their correspondence with Rome, see Trisco, *The Holy See and the Nascent Church in the Middle Western United States* (note 697 above), 6–7.

778 Loras to Orth, Dubuque, January 1, 1858 (*FLML* 923).

779 For an account of the dedication ceremonies, see the *Milwaukee Journal*, September 30, 1897.

780 Joseph Rainer, *A Noble Priest: Joseph Salzmann, D.D. Founder of the Salesianum*, trans. Joseph William Berg (Milwaukee: Olinger & Schwartz, 1903).

781 *The National Cyclopaedia of American Biography* (New York: White, 1899 and 1907), 9.505.

782 The orthography and punctuation of the original have been retained.

783 The superlatives "Reverendissime" and "Illustrissime" were commonly paired in salutations for prelates, but the use of "praesul" as well as "episcope" is somewhat fulsome and is a sign of Salzmann's ingratiating respect for Loras.

784 The classical citation serves as a *captatio benevolentiae*, designed to secure Loras's sympathy as a fellow admirer of the classics, although Salzmann mistakenly attributes these lines to Horace rather than to Vergil (*A*. 3.56–57). This is surprising, because Horace was said to have been his favorite poet. See Rainer, *Noble Priest*, 168.

785 A striking application to Horace of language that in Scripture is used of God (1 Chron 28:9, Wis 1:6, Ps 7:10, Rom 8:27).

786 Matt 5:6, cf. Ps 106:5.

787 Little information is known about George Schneider. He attended seminary in St. Louis and spent the summer prior to his 1856 ordination in Guttenberg, a haven for German immigrants. He later served at the parishes of Holy Trinity and St. Elizabeth, but his name drops out of the Catholic Almanac in 1865.

788 James Orth (1818–97), a priest of the Diocese of Dubuque, spent the latter years of his life as chaplain to St. Joseph's Hospital in Keokuk, Iowa.

789 New Vienna, about thirty miles west of Dubuque, had been settled in 1843 by five German families relocating from Ohio, whom Loras had directed to an area on the North Fork of the Maquoketa River known as Wilson's Grove. Loras's correspondence from the 1850s reveals that his relationship with the parish in New Vienna was strained.

790 The adjective "rigorosis" modifies an implicit "examinibus" and de-

notes the four examinations required for the doctoral degree in Austria. Following his ordination, Salzmann earned a scholarship to attend the prestigious Institute of St. Augustine (also known as the Frinaneum) in Vienna from 1843–1846. See William David Bowman, *Priest and Parish in Vienna, 1780–1880* (Boston: Humanities Press, 1999), 104–5.

791 "Neo-Mysta," derived from the Greek νέος μύστης, denotes a newly-ordained priest.

792 Lucien Galtier (1812–66) was one of the first priests Loras recruited for Dubuque, but against Loras's wishes he later requested and received his *exeat*. He moved to the diocese of Milwaukee and was stationed in Prairie du Chien.

793 Louis DeCailly (1832–98) was Loras's grand-nephew. From early 1856 to March 1858 he served as the first missionary priest at McGregor, the western terminus of the ferry from Prairie du Chien, where he would have met Salzmann.

794 The quotation marks around "peccavi" indicate that Salzmann is citing 2 Kings 12:13: "And David said to Nathan, 'I have sinned (peccavi) against the Lord.'"

795 Patrick McCabe (1828–97), a native of Ireland, was stationed at the Cathedral of St. Raphael in Dubuque.

796 As penance for his misdeed, Salzmann offers Loras the opportunity of sending a Dubuque seminarian to the Salesianum. Although Salzmann does not specify the terms, it is likely that such a student would attend at a reduced rate or even free of charge.

797 Salzmann echoes King David: "Miserere mei, Deus, secundum magnam misericordiam tuam" (Ps 50:3).

798 According to an old proverb, the ministry of a bishop is "onus angelicis humeris formidandum" or "tremendum." Salzmann modifies this by inserting the name of Croesus, the archetypical rich man of the Greek world (cf. Herodotus 1.30; Bacchylides 3 [Snell]).

799 At a retreat for German priests of the diocese in July of 1853 Salzmann pledged $1,000 of his own money toward the seminary, an amount that far exceeded the other pledges received that day. Nonetheless, the seminary struggled with sizable debt in the first years of its existence.

800 The expression "necessitas extrema" is a technical term in moral theology for a circumstance that might excuse theft. The locus classicus is St. Thomas Aquinas, *Summa Theologiae* IIaIIae 66.7.

801 The fifth ferial day is Thursday. To foster contributions to the Salesianum, in August 1853 Salzmann had founded the Salesian Society, whose members contributed one dollar each year and were remembered in a daily Rosary and a Mass every Thursday. Now that Loras had, albeit

unwittingly, joined this Society (by virtue of his flock's contributions), he too would receive the benefits of membership.

802 The feast of St. Denis is October 9.

803 The patron of St. Francis Seminary is St. Francis de Sales (1567–1622), the Bishop of Geneva.

804 Salzmann's epitaph—he is buried beneath the seminary chapel—identifies him as the "fundator" of St. Francis Seminary.

805 In 1877 Pope Pius IX proclaimed Francis de Sales a Doctor of the Universal Church.

806 Originally the ten-foot statue was positioned on the apex of the seminary roof. Now it stands on the ground in front of the main building.

807 The statue depicts St. Francis de Sales wearing a bishop's mitre.

808 Cf. Mark 1:3.

809 Another transcription (as well as translation) is in *LPB*, 790–92, but I have adopted several different readings.

810 For the history of the cable, see http://atlantic-cable.com//Field/.

811 *New York Herald*, August 6, 1858.

812 John M. Farley, *History of St. Patrick's Cathedral* (New York: Society for the Propagation of the Faith, 1908). See also George J. Marlin and Brad Miner, *Sons of Saint Patrick: A History of the Archbishops of New York from Dagger John to Timmytown* (San Francisco: Ignatius Press, 2017), 77–78.

813 *New York Herald*, August 16, 1858.

814 Sam Roberts, "At St. Patrick's, a Cornerstone That Has Long Eluded Searchers," *New York Times*, October 12, 2011.

815 "Ad Maiorem Dei Gloriam" was the motto of the Jesuits but it was used as an epigraph in many ecclesiastical contexts.

816 The feast of the Assumption of the Virgin Mary is celebrated on August 15.

817 The laying of the cornerstone was preceded by a Pontifical High Mass.

818 Hughes, a native of Ireland, was the fourth Bishop and first Archbishop of New York.

819 At the time the ecclesiastical province of New York included the dioceses of Albany, Boston, Brooklyn, Buffalo, Burlington (Vermont), Hartford, Newark, and Portland (Maine).

820 Pius IX was Pope from 1846 to 1878.

821 James Buchanan was President from 1857 to 1861.

822 John Alsop King was Governor of New York in 1857 and 1858.

823 Daniel Fawcett Tiemann was Mayor of New York City from 1858 to 1860.

824 James Renwick (1818–95) was a prominent late nineteenth-century American architect, known especially for his design of the Smithsonian Castle. William Rodrigue (1800–67), the brother-in-law of Archbishop Hughes, designed the Church of St. John the Evangelist in Philadelphia as well as St. John's Seminary (located on the grounds of present-day Fordham).
825 Cyrus W. Field (1819–92) was a Massachusetts-born businessman whose resources and commitment made possible the laying of the cable. Archbishop Hughes was one of the initial stockholders of the Atlantic Telegraph Company that Field founded. Following the successful laying of the cable in 1858, Hughes sent Field the following letter: "Under the blessing of Almighty God you have accomplished the work. But your merit, if not your human glory, would have been the same in my estimation if you had returned to us what they would call a disappointed man in whose scales of judgment enthusiasm had preponderated over 'common sense.'" See Isabella Field Judson, ed., *Cyrus W. Field: His Life and Work, 1819–1892* (New York: Harper, 1896), 70, 102.
826 Spaeth, *Charles Porterfield Krauth, D.D., LL.D*, 1.39–40 (see Source). See also the biographical summary at Penn University Archives & Records Center: https://archives.upenn.edu/exhibits/penn-people/biography/charles-porterfield-krauth.
827 Diedrich Henry Steffens, *Doctor Carl Ferdinand Wilhelm Walther* (Philadelphia: Lutheran Publication Society, 1917), 392–93. But cf. the sharp criticism of Krauth's Latin in *American Catholic Quarterly Review* 2 (1877): 750.
828 For a biography of Walther, see Daniel Waldschmidt, "C.F.W. Walther 1811–1897," at https://studiumjournal.com/author/walther-bio.
829 C.D.W. (Carl Ferdinand Wilhelm) Walther (1811–1887) Papers, c. 1828–1887, at Concordia Historical Institute: https://concordiahistoricalinstitute.org/m-0004/.
830 Steffens, *Doctor Carl Ferdinand Wilhelm Walther*, 157.
831 For example, Walther edited *Joh. Guilielmi Baieri Compendium Theologiae Positivae*, 3 vols. (St. Louis: Lutheran Concordia Press, 1879).
832 Krauth was pastor of the First English Lutheran congregation on Seventh Street in Pittsburgh. This sermon was delivered on November 26, 1857.
833 Kaiser, "Contributions to a Census of American Latin Prose" (note 28 above), 168.
834 For an example of resistance to the use of Latin, see John Talbot Smith, *Our Seminaries: An Essay on Clerical Training* (New York: Young, 1896), 258–65.
835 Mazzella (1833–1900), born in Vitulano (Italy), arrived in Ameri-

ca in 1867 and taught theology at Woodstock College. In 1878 he was appointed chair of theology at the Gregorian (Rome). De Augustinis (1829–99), born in Naples, arrived in America in 1869. He was the founding editor of *Woodstock Letters* and later rector of the Gregorian.

836 *Theologia moralis novissimi ecclesiae doctoris S. Alphonsi* (New York: Benziger, 1876).

837 *American Catholic Quarterly Review* 3 (1878): 380.

838 *Theologia Dogmatica*, 2nd ed. (Mechelen: Dessain, 1858), ix.

839 I.e., English Common Law differs from Roman Law (ius caesareum).

840 Kenrick treats slavery in Tractate 5, chapter 6, citing the work of Hyacinthe Sigismond Gerdil, *Opere edite ed inedite del Cardinale Giacinto Sigismondo Gerdil*, vol. 7 (Rome: Vincenzo Poggioli, 1807).

841 Kenrick's footnotes, frequently in English, cite civil laws as well as commentaries such as James Kent, *Commentaries on American Law*, 4 vols. (New York: Halsted, 1826–30).

842 The first edition of the *Theologia Moralis* was published in Philadelphia by Eugene Cummiskey. Similarly, the *Theologica Dogmatica* was initially published in Philadelphia (Johnson). But the second editions of both were published in Belgium.

843 The Nativity of the Blessed Virgin Mary (Beatae Mariae Virginis) is celebrated on September 8.

844 Morton H. Prince, "History of Football at Harvard, 1800–1875 (June)," in John A. Blanchard, ed., *The H Book of Harvard Athletics, 1852–1922* (Cambridge, MA: Harvard Varsity Club, 1923), 316. See also Vivekae M. Kim, "Harvard's Bloody Monday," *Harvard Crimson*, March 29, 2018.

845 Prince, "History Football at Harvard, 1800–1875," 320.

846 The authorship of the Latin inscription is uncertain. In Harvard's copy of vol. 7 (1861) of the *Magazine* (visible at GoogleBooks) "Garrison '61" appears to be handwritten at the top of the article containing the inscription. Wendell Phillips Garrison (1840–1907) was one of the senior editors of the *Magazine* for 1861, the others being Oliver Wendell Holmes, Jr., and Albert Stetson. See Prince, "History of Football at Harvard," 339 who also provides an English translation by E.K. Rand.

847 Prince, "Football at Harvard, 1800–1875," 338 gives a slightly different order of these lines, and he comments on the lifespan of LX years, which would imply a surprisingly early birthdate: "Perhaps the students of the time had information lost to written history."

848 Juvenal 4.2–3.

849 An example of a Latin theological work published by a Redemptorist in the United States has already been noted in section 72.

850 A summary of this incident may be found at https://www.nps.gov/fomc/learn/historyculture/the-pratt-street-riot.htm.
851 *Pittsburgh Gazette*, April 22, 1861.
852 St. Alphonsus Church on West Saratoga Street, dedicated in 1845, was the Redemptorist foundation in Baltimore.
853 The Irish-born Michael O'Connor (1810–72), was consecrated Bishop of Pittsburgh in 1843. One month after the incident described here, O'Connor resigned his episcopal see and entered the Jesuits. An excellent Latinist, at the First Plenary Council of Baltimore (cf. section 66) he was commissioned to write the Latin letter to the Pope on behalf of the hierarchy.
854 In New York Archbishop John Hughes raised the flag at St. Patrick's Cathedral and at his residence, and in Philadelphia Bishop James Wood ordered the flag to be flown over the new cathedral, while in St. Louis Archbishop Peter Richard Kenrick (see section 78) chose not to comply with a request from the provost marshal to do the same. See John Rothensteiner, *History of the Archdiocese of St. Louis in its Various Stages of Developement from A. D. 1673 to A .D. 1928*, 2 vols. (St. Louis: Blackwell Wielandy, 1928), 2:213–14.
855 For a biographical notice of Muench see Walter D. Kamphoefner in *Dictionary of Missouri Biography*, eds., Lawrence O. Christensen, William E. Foley, Gary R. Kremer, Kenneth H. Winn (Columbia: University of Missouri Press, 1999), s.v., "Muench, Friedrich (1799–1881)," and see also Don Heinrich Tolzmann, "Recollections of Friedrich 'Far West' Muench, German-American Nestor of Missouri," *The Report: A Journal of German-American History* 46 (2011): 79–102.
856 See the essays in *Utopia: Revisiting a German State in America* (note 16 above).
857 This seems to be a reference to Louise Muench, who was born to Friedrich's son Julius on January 13, 1863. Friedrich Muench's second wife, Hugo's mother, was also named Louise. See the extensive genealogy at https://www.muenchfamilyassociation.com/uploads/1/3/1/0/13104486/outline_descendant_report_for_friedrich_muench1.pdf.
858 Dr. Johann Bernhard Bruns (1801–64), born in Hanover, Germany, was mayor of Jefferson City during the early years of the Civil War. When the Senate met in 1864 Muench and Hugo boarded at the Bruns home, which was located opposite the capitol. The diary of Bruns's wife, Jette (1813–99) has been published: Adolf E. Schroeder and Carla Schulz-Geisberg, eds., *Hold Dear, As Always: Jette, a German Immigrant Life in Letters* (Columbia, MO: University of Missouri Press, 1988), see esp. p. 197. See also Kenneth Luebbering and R.D. Anderson in *Dic-*

tionary of Missouri Biography, s.v., "Bruns, Anna Elisabeth Henriette Geisberg (1813–1899)."

859 I discuss a portion of another one of Muench's letters to his son in "Latin and the American Civil War" (note 550 above), 221–22. Two of Muench's letters to his son are visible at https://mohistory.org/collections/item/resource:103707.

860 Thomas Joseph Peterman, *The Cutting Edge: The Life of Thomas Andrew Becker: First Catholic Bishop of Wilmington and Sixth Bishop of Savannah (1831–1899)* (Devon, PA: William T. Cooke, 1982), 6–8. Peterman notes that Becker's affiliation with Saint Xavier and the University of Virginia, reported in early biographical accounts, is not supported by records from either school.

861 Becker had care for Catholic churches in Martinsburg, Bath, Berkeley Springs, Fairfax, and Winchester. See Peterman, *Cutting Edge*, 42.

862 Peterman (*Cutting Edge*, 63 n.96) notes that in addition to failing to include the prescribed prayer, Becker was also charged with aiding the Confederate guerilla Col. John S. Mosby.

863 "The Classical Education of the Day," *American Catholic Quarterly Review* 1 (1876): 34.

864 "Shall We Have a University," and "A Plan for the Proposed Catholic University," *American Catholic Quarterly Review* 1 (1876): 230–53, 655–79. See also Peterman, *Cutting Edge*, 247–54.

865 An English translation is in Peterman, *Cutting Edge*, 49.

866 The Prefect of the Sacred Congregation (S.C.) Propaganda Fide at this time was Cardinal Alessandro Barnabò (1801–74).

867 Cf. Vergil, *A*. 6.86.

868 John McGill (1809–72) was the Bishop of Richmond from 1850 until his death.

869 This may be a reference to the church in Winchester, which had been used as a stable for federal cavalry. It may also refer to St. Vincent de Paul in Bath (now Berkeley Springs), which had been used as quarters by Confederate soldiers and accidentally burned to the ground.

870 The Diocese of Richmond was in the ecclesiastical province of Baltimore, whose Archbishop was Francis Patrick Kenrick.

871 Becker cites the common ecclesiastical formulation for "an archdiocese with its suffragan sees," i.e., an archdiocese and those dioceses that depend juridically and administratively upon it.

872 Quoted in Stephen L. Dyson, *The Last Amateur: The Life of William J. Stillman* (Albany: State University of New York Press, 2014), 124.

873 The letter and inscription were printed widely in American newspapers. See, for example, *Providence Evening Press*, September 15, 1865. The origin of the stone can be traced from *Cronaca della guerra d'Italia*

1864-1865-1866, vol. 7 (Rieti: Trinchi, 1866), 409–10.

874 It is curious to note that despite the original anti-papal intentions of the stone's donors, the invocation at the 1936 dedication was given by the Catholic Bishop of Springfield (Illinois), James Aloysius Griffin.

875 The odyssey of the stone is summarized by John Lockwood, "Stone for Lincoln nearly lost," *Washington Times*, January 23, 2004; Ray Serati, "Lincoln's Old Roman Stone," *Daily Illinois State Journal*, August 26, 1973; Howard R. Marraro, "Italy and Lincoln," *The Abraham Lincoln Quarterly* 3 (1944): 3–16. See also the collection of newspaper clippings and the brief narrative assembled in *The Assassination of Abraham Lincoln, Springfield Tomb, Stone from the Wall of Servius Tullius*, available at https://archive.org/stream/assassinatisprlinc#page/n1/mode/2up.

876 *Region[um] Foederat[arum] Americ[ae]*. This use of *regio*, which originally denoted a ward or district of the city of Rome or the surrounding territory, is unusual. But another instance is found in a letter of Pope Pius IX to Archbishop John Hughes, October 18, 1862, which is printed in *Pii IX Pontificis Maximi Acta, Prima Pars*, vol. 3 (Rome: Ex Typographia Bonarum Artium, 1864), 530.

877 *II*: by the convention of classical Roman inscriptions, the Roman numeral indicates that Lincoln held this office twice.

878 *Aggere*: Servius Tullius was credited with building a 50' wide *agger* to protect the northeastern part of the city of Rome; his famous wall ran along the top of the *agger*.

879 *Adsertoris*: a technical term in Roman Law to describe one who asserts or vindicates the freedom of a slave.

880 See William B. Faherty in *Dictionary of Missouri Biography* (note 855 above), s.v., "Cummings, John A. (1840–1873)."

881 Examples of signed oaths may be seen at https://www.nps.gov/jeff/blogs/oath-of-loyalty-book-1868-1871-artifact-of-the-month-for-september-2011.htm.

882 For discussions of this episode, see Rothensteiner, *History of the Archdiocese of St. Louis* (note 854 above), 2:215–19; Harold Charles Bradley, "John A. Cummings and the Missouri Test Oath 1865" (master's thesis, St. Louis University, 1958); John Niven, *Salmon P. Chase: A Biography* (Oxford: Oxford University Press, 1995), 406–7; Harold Charles Bradley, "In Defense of John Cummings," *Missouri Historical Review* 57 (1962): 1–15.

883 E.g., *Philadelphia Age*, August 31, 1865; *Pittsburgh Daily Commercial*, August 30, 1865; *Burlington* (Vermont) *Weekly Sentinel*, September 8, 1865.

884 E.g., *Evansville Daily Journal*, August 31, 1865.

885 *San Francisco Pacific*, October 12, 1865.

886 *New York Tribune*, August 25, 1865.
887 *Star of the North* (Bloomsburg, PA), September 6, 1865 (reprinting an article from the *Illinois State Register*).
888 This letter is also printed in Mary Emmanuel White, "Archbishop Peter Richard Kenrick and the Civil War" (master's thesis, St. Louis University, 1948).
889 The only biography of Corcoran is Mary Marcian Lowman, "James Andrew Corcoran: Editor, Theologian, Scholar (1820–1889)" (PhD diss, St. Louis University, 1958). See also my article, "Far From a Fossil: Msgr. James Andrew Corcoran and the Latin Language," *American Catholic Studies* 131 (2020): 25–51.
890 Andreas Niedermayer, *Das Concilium in Baltimore* (Frankfurt: Verlag für Kunst und Wissenschaft, 1867), 36.
891 Peter Richard Kenrick was the Archbishop of St. Louis (see section 78).
892 John Baptist Purcell (1800–83) was the Archbishop of Cincinnati.
893 Richard Vincent Whelan (1809–74) was the Bishop of Wheeling.
894 Thomas Grace (1814–97) was Bishop of St. Paul.
895 John Timon (1797–1867) was the Bishop of Buffalo (see section 56).
896 Thaddeus Amat (1810–78) was the Bishop of Monterey.
897 Martin John Spalding (1810–72), the Archbishop of Baltimore, was the Apostolic Delegate to the Second Plenary Council.
898 John McCloskey (1810–85) was the Archbishop of New York.
899 Cf. Cic. *Phil.* 3.1.
900 James Cardinal Gibbons, "Personal Reminiscences of the Vatican Council," *The North American Review* 158 (1894): 388–89.
901 Leon Dehon, *Diario del Concilio Vaticano I*, ed. Vincenzo Carbone (Rome: Tipografia Poliglotta Vaticana, 1962), 43. See also Françoise Waquet, *Latin, or the Empire of a Sign*, trans. John Howe (London: Verso, 2002), 155.
902 Gibbons, "Personal Reminiscences of the Vatican Council," 399.
903 Gibbons, "Personal Reminiscences of the Vatican Council," 396. Kenrick, a prominent opponent during the council of the definition of papal infallability, did not have the opportunity to address the council on this issue; accordingly he published his remarks: *Concio Petri Ricardi Kenrick archiepiscopi S. Ludovici in Statibus Foederatis Americae Septentrionalis in Concilio Vaticano Habenda et non Habita* (Naples: Angeli Brothers, 1870).
904 For a biography of Verot see Michael V. Gannon, *Rebel Bishop: The Life and Era of Augustin Verot* (Milwaukee: Bruce, 1964).
905 Dehon, *Diario del Concilio Vaticano I*, 66.
906 Gannon, *Rebel Bishop*, 207.

907 Dehon, *Diario del Concilio Vaticano I*, 78–79.
908 *A Tract for our Times* (New Orleans: Catholic Propagator Office, 1861).
909 Marcianne Kappes, "Bishop Augustin Verot: 'L'Enfant Terrible' of Vatican I," *American Catholic Studies* 111 (2000): 64.
910 Ariel [Buckner H. Payne], *The Negro: What is His Ethnological Status*, 2nd ed. (Cincinnati: for the proprietor, 1867). I was led to this reference by James Leo Garrett, *Systematic Theology*, 4th ed., vol. 1 (Eugene, OR: Wipf & Stock, 2014, rept).
911 At the time Vincent was the former chief of the Coeur d'Alenes, having been succeeded in 1865 by Andrew Seltis (of the family of Emote). For brief illustrated biographical sketches, see C. Wood, "Famous Indians. Portraits of Some Indian Chiefs," *The Century* 46 (1893): 439–41. Two years later Seltis (or Seltice) sent a petition to President Ulysses S. Grant, dated July 28, 1873, and in 1887 he traveled to Washington, DC and met with President Grover Cleveland. For his role in the 1877 war, see R. Ignatius Burns, "Coeur d'Alene Diplomacy in the Nez Perce War of 1877," *Records of the American Catholic Historical Society of Philadelphia* 63 (1952): 37–60. Bronze plaques with relief busts of both of these leaders are in the National Museum of the American Indian (New York).
912 Gannon, *Rebel Bishop* (note 904 above), 235. Verot found fourteen of the original fifteen volumes. The last volume was discovered in 1938.
913 Jacinto Maria Martínez y Sáez (1812–73), a Franciscan, was consecrated Bishop of San Cristobal de la Habana in 1865.
914 Benigno Merino y Mendi was the Vicar General of the Diocese. He wrote *Instrucción pastoral que sobre el espiritismo moderno* (Havana: Imp. Militar de la Viuda de Soler y Comp., 1875).
915 For biographical notices of Selden Jennings Coffin, see *The Lafayette Weekly* 18 (1891): 136–37. A brief sketch of his father is found in the introduction to the James H. Coffin Papers, 1829–1911 at Lafayette: https://sites.lafayette.edu/coffinpapers/.
916 William T. Smithers, *Memoir of Nathaniel B. Smithers* (Wilmington: The Historical Society of Delaware, 1899).
917 *Translations of Latin Hymns of the Middle Ages* (Dover, DE: Kirk, 1879).
918 *The Lafayette Monthly* 1 (1871): 288–90, and see Smithers, *Memoir*, 15-20, and *Potter's American Monthly* 13 (July 1879): 117–18.
919 William B. Owen, Alden March, Selden J. Coffin, *The Men of Lafayette, 1826–1893: Lafayette College, Its History, Its Men, Their Record* (Easton: West, 1891), 49–55.
920 Nathaniel B. Smithers

921 Suo
922 Selen[o] = Selden
923 Coffin taught astronomy at Lafayette, and his father, James Henry Coffin (1806–73), was instrumental in establishing the college's astronomical observatory.
924 According to the *Lafayette College Journal* (see Source), the newlyweds received numerous fancy gifts, including a $500 check from someone in Utah, a set of silver spoons, an oil painting, furs, and some exquisitely bound books.
925 The bride's surname was Angle.
926 The wedding ceremony took place in Belvidere, New Jersey (Second Presbyterian), some fifteen miles north of Lafayette.
927 Winterer, *Culture of Classicism* (note 26 above), 77–98.
928 *Woodstock Letters* 64 (1935): 94, which is a review of Francis Donnelly, *Cicero's Milo—A Rhetorical Commentary* (New York: Bruce, 1935). Cf. also *Woodstock Letters* 65 (1936): 273; 66 (1937): 387–95; 71 (1942): 126, and see my article, "*Woodstock Letters* and the Jesuit Commitment to Latin," *Humanistica Lovaniensia* 66 (2017): 478–80.
929 See McKevitt, *Brokers of Culture* (note 713), 77–90.
930 See Gerald L. McKevitt, "Italian Jesuits in Maryland: A Clash of Theological Cultures," *Studies in the Spirituality of Jesuits* 39.1 (2007): 33.
931 A biographical sketch of Piccirillo is in *Woodstock Letters* 17 (1888): 339–50 (p. 341).
932 *Woodstock Letters* 56 (1927): 94–95.
933 *Woodstock Letters* 17 (1888): 347.
934 *Woodstock Letters* 13 (1884): 207–10.
935 Here Piccirillo cites the following names: Guido Ferrari (1717–91), Louis Antoine Lanzi (1732–1810), Antonio Francesco Zaccaria (1714–95), Stefano Antonio Morcelli (1737–1822), Joseph Marchi (1795–1860), Antonio Angelini–Rota (1809–92). One name is illegible, but it appears to be Voghera. Piccirillo also identifies works written by these authors, which I have omitted here. Additionally, a blank space appears between the names of Marchi and Angelini-Rota, where Piccirillo clearly intended to supply another name.
936 For an example of one of Piccirillo's Latin inscriptions, composed upon the death of the Jesuit Father General Peter Beckx, see *Woodstock Letters* 16 (1887): 123.
937 See the biographical notice by Ward W. Briggs in *Database of Classical Scholars*.
938 He wrote *Ten Discourses on Orthodoxy* and *Hebrew Men and Times*; he co-edited the *Christian Examiner* and edited the *Unitarian Review*. In addition to his Latin grammar, Allen published *Latin Composition*,

Greek Reader, and school texts on Sallust, Virgil, Caesar, Ovid, and Cicero.

939 Allen (see Source), 9.

940 Gábor Almási and Lav Subaric, "Introduction," in Almási and Subaric, *Latin at the Crossroads of Identity: The Evolution of Linguistic Nationalism in the Kingdom of Hungary* (Leiden: Brill, 2015), esp. 4–20.

941 Eph 4:3, but the Vulgate reads *pacis* rather than *fidei*.

942 Peter Guilday, *John Gilmary Shea: Father of American Catholic History, 1824–1892* (New York: United States Historical Society, 1926). At some point in his youth he took the name Gilmary (servant of Mary).

943 Gen. John Newton (1822–95), a West Point graduate, distinguished himself in combat and as an engineer in the Civil War. He was awarded the Laetare medal in 1886.

944 Thomas Addis Emmet (1826–1919), born in Charlottesville, Virginia, was a New York physician who worked among Irish immigrants on Ward's Island and wrote *The Principles of Gynecology* (1879). He was awarded the Laetare medal in 1897.

945 Charles O'Conor (1804–84) was a New York lawyer who, inter alia, served as counsel to Jefferson Davis and prosecuted William M. "Boss" Tweed.

946 Gen. William Rosecrans (1819–98), a Catholic convert, led the Army of the Cumberland to victory at Stones River, Tennessee and later served as Congressman from California. He was awarded the Laetare medal in 1896.

947 John LaFarge (1835–1910) was an artist whose work adorns churches and municipal buildings in Boston, New York, Minneapolis, and Baltimore.

948 Msgr. James Andrew Corcoran (1820–89) was regarded by many as the most learned theologian and most elegant Latinist of his day. Shea contributed articles to the *American Catholic Quarterly Review*, which Corcoran edited. See section 79.

949 Maurice Francis Egan (1852–1924) was a prolific author and Literature professor (The Catholic University of America, University of Notre Dame) who become ambassador to Denmark. In 1883 he was associate editor of the *Freeman's Journal* (New York). Egan, in fact, made the presentation of the Laetare medal to Shea on behalf of Notre Dame. He himself was awarded the Laetare medal in 1910.

950 It is also printed in the *Notre Dame Scholastic* 16 (May 26, 1883): 584–85. Rev. Fitte's Latin address is printed in the *Scholastic* 16 (March 3, 1883): 392–93.

951 *Woodstock Letters* 23 (1894): 322. See also Dinan, "*Woodstock Letters* and the Jesuit Commitment to Latin" (note 928 above), 471–73,

476–77.
952 *Brooklyn Daily Eagle*, April 20, 1928.
953 Stefano Villani, "Le tre vite di Costantino Stauder (1841–1913), la chiesa episcopale italiana di New York e la comunità italiana di Londra tra la fine dell'Ottocento e i primi del Novecento," *Altreitalie* 49 (2014): 48–79.
954 Five lines from Horace *C.* 4.30 appear as an epigraph.
955 Cf. Horace, *C.* 1.2.1.
956 The East River.
957 Brooklyn and New York.
958 The Brooklyn Bridge replaced regular ferry service between Brooklyn and Manhattan.
959 Cf. Montgomery Schuyler, "The Brooklyn Bridge as a Monument," in *American Architecture: Studies* (New York: Harper & Brothers, 1892), 72: "'A Roman work,' we often hear it said of the bridge, and it is in many ways true."
960 As President Chester Arthur completed his inaugural walk across the bridge into Brooklyn, the boats in the river staged a "mimic bombardment" that was "the sight of a lifetime." See *New York Sun*, May 25, 1883.
961 Footnotes in *Latine*, vol. 3 (see note 967 below) clarify that these refer, respectively, to the inventions of gunpowder, printing-types, musical notes, bales, double-stitching sewing, and gas.
962 These refer, respectively, to the inventions of steam power, electricity, electric light, telephone, and electric engines.
963 This refers to the double-track railroad on the bridge.
964 References to prominent New York newspapers: *Herald, Times, Sun, Eagle, Tribune, World, Critic, Graphic, Argus.*
965 The mayor of Long Island City was George Petry (1833–90).
966 The later version prints "reddere."
967 The poem is reprinted with the addition of explanatory glosses in *Latine* 3 (1884): 39–41.
968 Cedric Cummins, *The University of South Dakota, 1862–1966* (Vermillion: Dakota Press, 1975), 11, 13, 23; "Dr. Ephraim M. Epstein, First Head of the University," *The Alumni Quarterly of the University of South Dakota* 7.3 (1911): 63–74 (p. 70).
969 Epstein apparently appended a note to his name: "Germanice 'Epstein,' quo 'Ep' pro 'Epheu' stat, hinc multi et "Eppstem" scribunt, et hoc genus "Hedera" latine dicitur." To this the editor of *Latine* responded "Te doctarum hederae praemia frontium Dis miscent."
970 Accounts of this celebration are in the *Baltimore Sun*, May 14, 16, 1884. See also John Gilmary Shea, *Memorial of the First Century of*

Georgetown College (Washington, DC: P.F. Collier for the College, 1891), 129–34. Georgetown's Philodemic Society still awards a Merrick Medal for the winner of the annual Merrick Debate.

971 Leonard Calvert was the first Governor of Maryland (1633–47).

972 Although Maryland was named after Queen Henrietta Maria (1609–69), the wife of Charles I, some have long associated the name with the Virgin Mary.

973 In the Litany of Loreto, the Virgin Mary is invoked as "Stella Matutina;" elsewhere she is invoked as "Stella Maris."

974 The *Dove* was battered by a massive storm on the night of Monday, November 25, and it became separated from the *Ark* for six weeks, during which time it was assumed to have sunk.

975 The syntax of this stanza as printed is obscure.

976 The English translation of Coad's ode, printed in the *Baltimore Sun* (May 16, 1884), is sixty lines in length and begins "O citizens! let us consecrate this day."

977 Eugene Schuyler, "Italian Immigration into the United States," *Political Science Quarterly* 4 (1889): 485.

978 See the articles by Edward C. Stibili in the special issue "What Can Be Done to Help Them? The Italian Saint Raphael Society, 1887–1923," *Center for Migration Studies* 16.1 (2000); Michael F. Lombardo, "The Italian Problem: Immigration and Inculturation in the American Catholic Context," in Derek C. Hatch and Timothy R. Gabrielli, eds., *Weaving the American Catholic Tapestry: Essays in Honor of William L. Portier* (Eugene, OR: Pickwick, 2017), 125–44; Richard N. Juliani, "Italian Americans and Their Religious Experience," in William J. Connell and Stanislao G. Pugliese, eds., *The Routledge History of Italian Americans* (New York: Routledge, 2018), 193–211.

979 Biff Rocha, "'De Concilio's Catechism,' Catechists, and the History of the *Baltimore Catechism*" (PhD diss., University of Dayton, 2013), 130–34.

980 James J. McGovern, *The Life and Life-Work of Pope Leo XIII* (Chicago: Catholic Publications, 1903), 47–48, 57–58, 65–66.

981 H.T. Henry, *Poems, Charades, Inscriptions of Pope Leo XIII* (New York: Dolphin, 1902), 44.

982 *New York World*, June 6, 1897.

983 Francis T. Furey, *Life of Leo XIII and History of His Pontificate* (New York: Catholic Educational, 1903), 571.

984 One interesting episode involving Pope Leo XIII and Latin is his recording of a Latin message to be played at the World's Columbian Exposition in 1893. I have not located the Latin text, but an English translation is in the *Pittsburgh Post Gazette*, October 19, 1893. The re-

cording was made by Stephen Moriarty (d. 1907) of the English branch of Edison Phonograph Company. See *Scientific American* 68 (May 20, 1893): 308; *The Shorthand Review* 5 (1893): 99–100.
985 Some biographical details are found in a notice of his retirement in the *Jersey Journal*, April 24, 1939.
986 David Shakow, "Grace Helen Kent," *Journal of the History of the Behavioral Sciences* 10 (1974): 275–80. An obituary is in the *Bennington Banner*, October 1, 1973.
987 Two other Latin letters from the Kent family survive. One, dated Atlanta, Georgia, August 29, 1888, is from Ernest to his father; another, whose postmark reads Eldora, Iowa, October 2, 1891, is addressed to Ernest, but the author signs his or her name "Occido."
988 *Catalogue of Iowa College XLIVth Year, 1890–1891* (Grinnell, IA: n.p.), 17, 19, 20.
989 See "History of the College," at https://catalog.grinnell.edu/content.php?catoid=26&navoid=4405.
990 "Quattuor-in-manu," is a literal translation of "four-in-hand," an old name for a necktie.
991 Christopher Polt, "Anti-Catholicism, Classical Curriculum, and the Beginnings of Latin Drama in the United States," blog post, July 18, 2019, Society for Classical Studies. Press notices of this production are sparse, but see the recollection in the *Boston College Stylus* 13 (March 1, 1899): 155.
992 A bilingual libretto was printed, which can be seen at HathiTrust: *P. Terenti Adelphoe. Latin and English. Acted by Students of the University of Michigan. June. 1882.*
993 *University of Michigan Chronicle*, June 10, 1882.
994 *St. Louis Post-Dispatch*, May 24, 1884.
995 *New York Herald*, May 16, 1890.
996 *Woodstock Letters* 19 (1890): 285; see also 129–30.
997 See the *Fall River Daily Evening News*, June 17, 1890. The play was written by Mabel Barrows (1873–1931), a student at Boston Latin School. Six years later this play was staged at Boston University. See *Boston Globe*, May 1, 1896. In 1904 Barrows directed the *Ajax* of Sophocles at Hull House in Chicago. The music to the *Ajax* was composed by Willys Peck Kent (1877–1957), whose siblings were mentioned in section 91. See *Christian Register* 83 (February 11, 1904): 155.
998 *Buffalo Courier*, May 17, 1895.
999 *San Francisco Chronicle*, April 16, 1899. See also *San Francisco Chronicle*, May 10, 1899.
1000 *Boston Globe*, May 16, 1896.
1001 *Brooklyn Daily Eagle*, July 4, 1897.

1002 *Montgomery Advertiser*, June 11, 1897.
1003 *Classical Weekly* 20 (1927): 122 (Hamilton); 9 (1916): 127–28 (Wilson); 7 (1914): 224 (Smith); 9 (1915): 39–40 (Union); 4 (1911): 111 (Jamaica High School); 11 (1917): 8 (Western High School); 9 (1916): 135 (Chicago); 10 (1917): 200 (Hollywood High School); 9 (1916): 112 (Catskill High School); 8 (1915): 200 (Wadleigh High School); 8 (1914): 24 (Oakwood Seminary); 7 (1913): 8 (Canajoharie High School).
1004 *Classical Weekly* 5 (1911): 1–2. These plays were published: *Two Latin Plays for High-School Students* (Boston: Ginn, 1911). See also Mildred Dean, "Three Latin Playlets," *Classical Weekly* 14 (1920): 71–72. Dean was a Latin teacher at Central High School in Washington, DC.
1005 See Gonzalez Lodge, "Dramatic Interpretation in the Teaching of the Classics," *Classical Weekly* 14 (1921): 73–77, 81–85.
1006 *Classical Weekly* 5 (1912): 158.
1007 See Dinan, "*Woodstock Letters* and the Jesuit Commitment to Latin" (note 928 above), 460–62.
1008 *Chicago Record*, October 20, 1893.
1009 "The Latin Play at Chicago," *Woodstock Letters* 23 (1894): 188–90.
1010 Two episodes are worth mentioning: 1) A few months prior to the 1893 performances of *Captivi*, the faculty of Harvard Law School, with President Eliot's support, had decided to limit regular admission to graduates from a list of select colleges, which included no Jesuit institution. 2) A few years after the production of *Captivi*, The Regents of the University of the State of New York, the body responsible for accreditation, decided that students graduating from Jesuit schools did not have sufficent credits to gain entrance to the state's Law, Veterinary, Dental, or Medical schools. When the Jesuits protested, representatives from the Regents visited the College of St. Francis Xavier. Among the matters that particularly impressed them was the give-and-take in Latin between teacher and students in the classroom. See Kathleen A. Mahoney, *Catholic Higher Education in Protestant America: The Jesuits and Harvard in the Age of the University* (Baltimore: Johns Hopkins University Press, 2003), and see also "The Regents of the University and Our Colleges," *Woodstock Letters* 25 (1896): 124–34.
1011 *New York Tribune*, April 20, 1894.
1012 *Boston Herald*, April 20, 1894.
1013 See Henry W. Haynes, "The Latin Play," *The Harvard Graduates' Magazine* 2 (1894): 515–24.
1014 *P. Terenti Afri Phormio/The Phormio of Terence* (Cambridge, MA: John Wilson and Son, 1894). Photographs of these images had been obtained through the courtesy of Bishop John J. Keane, the founding rector of The Catholic University of America, to whom Harvard granted

an honorary doctorate two months later.
1015 According to *New York World*, October 13, 1893, the attendance was 1500.
1016 Satolli and Plautus were both natives of Umbria.
1017 Satolli was appointed titular archbishop of Naupactus in June 1888.
1018 In January 1893 Satolli was appointed the first Apostolic Delegate to the United States.
1019 Fr. René Holaind (1836–1906), a native of France, worked at times in Boston, New York, Alabama, and Louisiana, and he served as a chaplain during the Spanish-American War.
1020 "In the music there was no attempt to make use of Grecian modes or to keep the instrumentation within the limitations of a Greek orchestra, but strains in the Aeolian, Phrygian and Lydian scales were introduced, without excluding modern chromatic harmony." *The College of St. Francis Xavier: A Memorial and a Retrospect, 1847–1897* (New York: Meany, 1897), 177.
1021 A footnote explains: "Vulgo: 50 cents."
1022 Frederic DeForest Allen (1844–97), a professor of Classical Philology at Harvard, wrote the music for the production.
1023 The performance took place in Sanders Theatre.
1024 The first performance was given on April 19, which had only recently been designated Concord Day (or Patriots' Day).
1025 The journalist who covered this event for the *Boston Globe* remarked: "This refers to the Cambridge electric cars, and is probably the first time that these vehicles have ever been mentioned in the Latin language" (April 20, 1894). Another account contrasted this phrase with the corresponding phrase that accompanied Harvard's 1881 production of *Oedipus Tyrannus*: Μετὰ τὴν θέαν ἅμαξαι ἱπποσιδηροδρομικαὶ ἑτοῖμαι ἔσονται τοῖς εἰς ἄστυ πορεύεσθαι μέλλουσιν (Haynes, "The Latin Play," 524).
1026 Heinz Hofmann, "*Adveniat tandem Typhis qui detegat orbes:* Columbus in Neo-Latin Epic Poetry (16th–18th Centuries)," in Haase and Reinhold, *The Classical Tradition and the Americas* (note 26 above), 420–656; Maya Feile Tomes, "News of a Hitherto Unknown Neo-Latin Columbus Epic, Part I: José Manuel Peramas's *De invento Novo Orbe inductoque illuc Christi sacrificio (1777)," International Journal of the Classical Tradition* 22 (2015): 1–28; see also 223–57 for Part II.
1027 Francis Griffin, *Remains of the Rev. Edmund D. Griffin*, vol. 1 (New York: Carvill, Swords, Bliss, Halsted 1831), 87–90.
1028 For another example, see Octavio Cagnacci, "Carmen Seculare 12 Octobris 1892," *Woodstock Letters* 22 (1893): 1–2.
1029 An obituary of Alizeri is in the *Buffalo Catholic Union and Times*,

August 10, 1893. For his other poetry, see *History of the Seminary of Our Lady of the Angels* (Buffalo: Matthews-Northrup, 1906), 59–61; *Buffalo Catholic Union and Times*, May 8, 1890, October 2, 1890, and cf. also October 8, 1891; *Carmen Leoninum Leoni XIII P.M. Laus et Jubilatio Sacra Liturgia* (Buffalo: Press Times and Union, 1893).
1030 C.M. = Congregatio Missionis, a religious congregation founded by St. Vincent de Paul in 1625; also known as the Vincentians.
1031 Alizeri, like Columbus, was from Genoa.
1032 Alizeri was seventy years old when he composed this poem.
1033 This line occurs in a hymn from the Roman Breviary "Saepe, dum Christi populus cruentis."
1034 Genoa is the capital city of Liguria.
1035 In 1500 Columbus was imprisoned by Francisco de Bobadilla, who had been sent by the Spanish crown to investigate conditions in Hispaniola. Columbus was sent back to Spain in chains.
1036 A reference to the large number of Italian immigrants (see section 90).
1037 Horace, *C.* 3.11.35.
1038 Vergil, *A.* 3.57.
1039 Columbus intended to recover the Holy Land, and particularly the Holy Sepulchre, for Christians. See Abbas Hamdani, "Columbus and the Recovery of Jerusalem," *Journal of the American Oriental Society* 99 (1979): 39–48.
1040 Matt 8:26.
1041 Pope Leo XIII devoted the encyclical *Quarto Abeunte Saeculo* (July 16, 1892) to the fourth centenary of Columbus's first voyage, and he decreed that a solemn Mass of the Holy Trinity be celebrated in Italy, Spain, and the Americas on October 12.
1042 Deward E. Walker and Peter N. Jones, "The Nez Perce," https://content.lib.washington.edu/aipnw/walker.html.
1043 https://www.nezperce.org/about/history/.
1044 Edward S. Curtis, *The North American Indian*, vol. 8, ed. Frederick Webb Hodge (Norwood, MA: Plimpton Press, 1911), 157.
1045 See Bischoff, *Jesuits in Old Oregon* (note 673 above), 141–52, and see the summary in Carriker and Carriker, *Guide to the Microfilm Edition* (note 670 above), 29–30.
1046 The Dawes Act (February 8, 1887), "An Act to Provide for the Allotment of Lands in Severalty to Indians on the Various Reservations," had effectively left open for white settlement those lands that had not been parcelled out specifically to individual Native Americans.
1047 The proclamation granted to those religious societies working among the Nez Percé the right for two years of purchasing tracts of

tribal lands for $3 per acre.
1048 Frederick Peterson, "Obituary: Dr. Charles Loomis Dana, 1852–1935," *Bulletin of the New York Academy of Medicine* 12 (1936): 27–30. See also the sketch at the Charles Loomis Dana Papers, 1876–1932, available online at the New York Academy of Medicine.
1049 *Proceedings of the Charaka Club* 1 (1902), v. For a summary of the club's history, see https://www.nyam.org/library/collections-and-resources/archives/finding-aids/ARC-0004.html/.
1050 "The Costume of the Ancient Greek Physician," and "The Cult of Aesculapius," *Proceedings of the Charaka Club* 1 (1902); "The Medicine of Horace," *Proceedings* 2 (1906); "'When Apollo Strikes the Lyre.' A Study of the Canticles of the Old Anatomists," *Proceedings* 3 (1910); "Military and Civil Surgery Among the Ancient Romans, with Remarks on their Surgical Instruments," *Proceedings* 5 (1919).
1051 *New York Times*, February 2, 1895.
1052 *Boston Herald*, February 3, 1895.
1053 *New York Times*, February 10, 1895.
1054 *Boston Herald*, February 11, 1895.
1055 The sumptuous French menu for the occasion is printed in the *New York Times*, February 2, 1895.
1056 Apollinaris, a natural spring water first bottled in Germany in 1852, had been imported to the United States at least since the late 1870s.
1057 Horace, *C.* 3.2.13, 4.12.28.
1058 The first Delmonico's was established on William Street in 1827.
1059 Dana had been elected President of Dartmouth's New York Alumni Association in 1894.
1060 According to the *New York Times* (February 10, 1895), the Dartmouth alumni were particularly impressed with this line, "in which the doctor adapted to the occasion the college motto, 'Vox clamantis in deserto'" (Mark 1:3, John 1:23).
1061 The speeches, which lasted more than two hours, included: "Old Dartmouth," by Rev. William J. Tucker, Dartmouth's President from 1893 to 1909; "Greek or Football," by Rev. M. Woolsey Stryker, the President of Hamilton College from 1892 to 1917; and "Reminiscences," by Dr. Samuel C. Bartlett, Dartmouth's President from 1877 to 1892. For a summary of Stryker's speech, see the *New York Times*, February 2, 1895 and *Hamilton Literary Monthly* 29 (1895): 199, and for Stryker's advocacy of the classics, see *Classical Weekly* 4 (1911): 223.
1062 *America* 18 (February 23, 1918): 503. The review is signed F.M.C., probably denoting the Jesuit Francis M. Connell (1866–1935).
1063 *Praeco Latinus* 2.1 (October 1895): 4.

1064 Patrick M. Owens, "Arcadius Avellanus: Neo-Latin Works of the Early 20th Century," paper delivered at American Philological Association (AANLS panel), January 5, 2014, published at linguae.weebly.com/arcadius-avellanus.html.
1065 *Classical Review* 12 (1898): 430.
1066 *Boston Herald*, July 3, 1897, although the letter is dated June 18, 1897. The author is John McDonald of New York, who says that he visited the monument with "our 7th regiment."
1067 On the origin of this term, which dates back to the first decade of the nineteenth century, see Thomas H. O'Connor, *The Athens of America: Boston 1825–1845* (Amherst: University of Massachusetts Press, 2006).
1068 This is a mistake. The inscription reads SERVARE.
1069 This was Avellanus's term for his Latin pedagogy, but his methodology had parallels in other disciplines. See his discussion of music education earlier in the same volume, *Praeco Latinus* 3 (December 1896): 7.
1070 *The Springfield* (MA) *Republican*, October 22, 1901.
1071 The University of Freiburg sent one letter in German and another in Latin.
1072 Yet the tradition of using Latin on such occasions appeared to be waning. By way of comparison, when Princeton celebrated its sesquicentennial three years earlier, about two thirds (or 75 out of 112) of the congratulatory letters printed in the *Memorial Book* were in Latin. See *Memorial Book of the Sesquicentennial Celebration of the Founding of the College of New Jersey and of the Ceremonies Inaugurating Princeton University* (New York: Charles Scriber's Sons, 1898), 187–316.
1073 *New Haven Morning Journal and Courier*, October 25, 1901.
1074 Vergil, *A.* 9.6–7.
1075 Rev. Francis Landey Patton (1843–1932) was Princeton's President from 1888 to 1902.
1076 Nassau Hall, constructed in 1756, was Princeton's first building.
1077 See the work of Michele Valerie Ronnick, especially "Twelve Black Classicists," *Arion*, 3rd ser. 11 (2004): 85–102 and the touring exhibit Black Classicists: Fifteen Portraits. Ronnick also has brought back into print *First Lessons in Greek* (1881) by William Sanders Scarborough (1852–1926), who is considered the "first professional classicist of African descent in the United States." See Ronnick's biographical sketch of Scarborough in *Database of Classical Scholars.*
1078 *Catalogue of the Officers and Students of Howard University, District of Columbia, 1868–'69* (Washington, DC: Judd & Detweiler, 1869), 22–24; *Catalogue of the Officers and Students of Harvard University for the Academical year 1868–69. First Term* (Cambridge, MA: Sever and

Francis, 1868), 25, 28–32.
1079 *Catalogue of the Officers and Students of Lincoln University 1877–'78* (Philadelphia: Ashmead, 1878), 12–14.
1080 *Lincoln University Herald* 3.2 (February and March 1896): 3; 3.4 (June 1896): 9–10.
1081 *Biennial Catalogue of the Officers and Students of Storer College, Academic and Normal Departments, located at Harper's Ferry, West Virginia, October 7, 1879; May 30, 1881* (Dover, NH: Morning Star, 1881), 16–17.
1082 *Catalogue of the Officers and Students of Shaw University 1878–'79* (Raleigh: Edwards, Broughton, & Co., 1879), 13, 15–16.
1083 Edward R. Carter, *The Black Side: A Partial History of the Business, Religious and Educational Side of the Negro in Atlanta, GA.* (Atlanta: n.p. 1894), 135.
1084 *Lincoln University Herald* 19.6 (June 1915): 4.
1085 In 2015 a plaque honoring Selden was placed in Silverman Hall at Penn Law School. https://www.law.upenn.edu/live/news/5331-penn-law-pays-tribute-to-theodore-selden-class-of.
1086 Stephen J. Ochs, *Desegregating The Altar: The Josephites and the Struggle for Black Priests, 1871–1960* (Baton Rouge: Louisiana State University Press, 1990), 96. For the classical curriculum at Epiphany, which moved to New York in 1925, see p. 412.
1087 For a biography of Aggrey see Edwin William Smith, *Aggrey of Africa: A Study in Black and White* (New York: Richard R. Smith, 1930) and Sylvia M. Jacobs, "James Emman Kwegyir Aggrey: An African Intellectual in the United States," *The Journal of Negro History* 81 (1996): 47–61. A brief notice is in Frank Lincoln Mather, *Who's Who of the Colored Race: A General Biographical Dictionary of Men and Women of African Descent*, vol. 1 (Chicago: n.p., 1915), 2.
1088 Fonvielle (see Source), 102.
1089 This poem was printed in the *Columbia Student* (August 14, 1914), but thus far I have not been able to obtain this issue, much less to determine how it compares to the poem printed here, which also ends with "Bene valete."
1090 See the introduction to Mark Riley, ed., *Raphael Thorius, Hymnus Tabaci (1626): A Hypertext Edition* at http://www.philological.bham.ac.uk/thorius/intro.html#z1716.
1091 Printed in *Opera Omnia*, vol. 2 (Leiden: John Arnold Langerak, 1725), 420–21.
1092 Bradner, *Musae Anglicanae* (note 175 above), 73 (cited in Riley).
1093 See the biographical sketches by John Francis Latimer at *Database of Classical Scholars* and Gertrude Smith in *Classical Journal* 41 (1946):

360–62. A translation of Bonner's ode by James S. Sprague, M.D., appeared in *Dominion Medical Monthly and Ontario Medical Journal* 20 (1903): 206–7.

1094 *Eighteenth Catalogue of John B. Stetson University, DeLand, Florida 1902–1903* (DeLand: Painter, 1903), 133.

1095 The printed text reads "paliuit."

1096 Cyprian Davis, "The Holy See and American Black Catholics. A Forgotten Chapter in the History of the American Church," *U.S. Catholic Historian* 7 (1988): 172.

1097 Ochs, *Desegregating The Altar* (note 1086 above), 123. Not long after delivering this homily, Slattery left for Europe. Subsequently he left the Catholic Church. Ochs provides valuable and detailed context.

1098 *Baltimore Sun*, July 25, 1902.

1099 For a description of this school see the *Topeka Plaindealer*, April 14, 1905.

1100 Édouard Brion, "Un défenseur des droits des noirs aux États-Unis: l'abbé Joseph Anciaux (1858–1931)," *Revue d'histoire ecclésiastique* 100 (2005): 43–82.

1101 The date of Anciaux's arrival in the United States is not entirely clear, but the document giving his bishop's placet to leave the diocese of Namur (Belgium) is dated April 15, 1895. After spending time in New Orleans, Anciaux was in Oklahoma as least as early as June 1897.

1102 A special session following the Second Plenary Council of Baltimore (1866) had been devoted to pastoral care of newly-emancipated slaves. See Edwardo J. Misch, *The American Bishops and the Negro from the Civil War to the Third Plenary Council of Baltimore* (Rome: Pontificia Universitas Gregoriana, 1968).

1103 Luke 10:31–32.

1104 Lam. 4:4.

1105 A reference to the 15th Amendment, which was ratified on February 3, 1870.

1106 Matt 25:21.

1107 On October 16, 1901 Booker T. Washington joined President Roosevelt for dinner at the White House, an event that was stridently criticized throughout the south as well as by some in the north. Relying on Washington's judgment, Roosevelt appointed African Americans to federal posts: Robert Heberton Terrell (1857–1925) as Justice of the Peace of the District of Columbia; Samuel Vick (1863–1946) as Postmaster of Wilson, North Carolina; William D. Crum (1859–1912), a Charleston physician, as Collector of the Port of Charleston (1902). Vick and Crum were rejected by the Senate, but the latter obtained office through a series of interim appointments. See Seth M. Scheiner,

"President Theodore Roosevelt and the Negro, 1901–1908," *The Journal of Negro History* 47 (1962): 169–82.

1108 Matt 5:22.

1109 In a lengthy footnote he acknowledges that there were exceptions to this, but he concludes: "Haec omnia vera sunt et cum laude refero, sed de abusis et iniustitiis *generali modo* loquor. Vastissima regio est America et, ut comparatione utar dicam: multae sunt ecclesiae multique sacerdotes in *civitate* Romae, ex eo tamen totam Europam catholicam dicere non licet."

1110 Winterer, *Culture of Classicism* (note 26 above), 99–151. See also Richard, *Golden Age of the Classics in America* (note 26 above), 204–9.

1111 Winterer, *Culture of Classicism*, 101; Turner, *Philology* (note 26 above), 276–77.

1112 Carl-Henry Geschwind, "Embracing Science and Research: Early Twentieth-Century Jesuits and Seismology in the United States," *Isis* 89 (1998): 49.

1113 Mahoney, *Catholic Higher Education in Protestant America* (note 1010 above), 195–238; Philip Gleason, *Contending with Modernity: Catholic Higher Education in the Twentieth Century* (New York: Oxford University Press, 1995), 55–61.

1114 *Woodstock Letters* 56 (1927): 217–18.

1115 "The Golden Jubilee 1869–1919," *Woodstock Letters* 49 (1920): 1–112.

1116 *Woodstock Letters* 17 (1888): 342; 58 (1929): 68–76; 59 (1930): 82; 77 (1948): 23; 70 (1941): 38–50.

1117 For an obituary, see *Georgetown College Journal* 58 (1929): 129–30.

1118 The Jesuits were particularly committed to the emerging field of seismology. In 1909 they established the Jesuit Seismological Service, and by 1911 they were maintaining 15 of the 54 seismological stations in the United States. See Geschwind, "Embracing Science and Research," 28.

1119 *The Georgetown Hoya*, December 4, 1929.

1120 *Washington Evening Star*, January 27, 1929.

1121 Francis A. Tondorf, SJ papers, (Booth Family Center for Special Collections, Georgetown University Library, Washington DC).

1122 *Woodstock Letters* 60 (1931): 426–32.

1123 Christopher Donesa, "History of the *Georgetown College Journal*," in Joseph Durkin, ed., *Swift Potomac's Lovely Daughter: Two Centuries at Georgetown through Students' Eyes* (Washington, DC: Georgetown University Press, 1990), 3–29. Another Latin poem published in the *College Journal* [58 (1929): 112–19], facetious in tone, described a football game between Georgetown and New York University.

1124 See *Georgetown College Journal* 33 (1905): 254, 319: "Querela hiemalis—Why?," attributed to "Senior Corridor" and dated February 26, 1905; "A Palinode inspired by the 'Querela Hiemalis'" attributed to "Mt. Rascal" and dated February 22, 1905; "A Parody," attributed to "Querelans Hiemaliter." See also the complimentary notice in *The Fordham Monthly* 23 (1905): 213.
1125 *New Haven Morning Journal and Courier*, March 19, 1907.
1126 *New Haven Morning Journal and Courier*, March 16, 1907.
1127 Ralph D. Paine, "Taft at Yale: His Four Years in New Haven," *The Outing Magazine* 53 (1908): 141.
1128 Brief biographical sketches are in J.A. Spalding, ed., *Illustrated Popular Biography of Connecticut* (Hartford: Case, Lockwood & Brainard, 1891), 317; *Yale Alumni Weekly* 31 (1921/22): 273, 299, 392–93; Grant Showerman, "In Memoriam: Tracy Peck of Yale, 1838–1921," *Classical Journal* 17 (1921): 339–40; *Database of Classical Scholars* (Meyer Reinhold).
1129 Lamberton (see Source), 18.
1130 "Latin Pronunciation," *The Cornell Review* 3 (1876): 385–97.
1131 *Addresses at the Induction of Professor Timothy Dwight, as President of Yale College, Thursday, July 1, 1886* (New Haven, n.p., 1886), 11–14.
1132 I have not located this text, but it is mentioned in *1861–1911, The Fiftieth Anniversary of The Class of 1861, Yale College, with Biographical Sketches* (Philadelphia: Allen, Lane & Scott, 1912), 132.
1133 *New York Times*, February 27, 1910.
1134 *New Haven Morning Journal and Courier*, October 2, 1905. Tennyson's "but something ere the end, some work of noble note may yet be done, not unbecoming men that strove with gods" was rendered "prius autem sunt facienda/ Quae nos cum Divis mortales esse renisos/ Nec post degenerasse per aevum testificentur," and his "to strive, to seek, to find, and not to yield," was rendered "Conari, petere ac reperire, et cedere nusquam."
1135 "Ad Fortunam," *Class of 1861 Yale College Biographical Notes 1912–1916, Supplementary to the Fiftieth Anniversary Report* (Philadelphia: n.p., 1916), 7.
1136 *New Haven Morning Journal and Courier*, October 7, 1904.
1137 Brooks Mather Kelley, *Yale: A History* (New Haven: Yale University Press, 1974), 267.
1138 "The Classics and the Yale Curriculum," *The New Englander and Yale Review* 44 (1885): 257–58.
1139 Andrew Fleming West, *Value of the Classics* (Princeton: Princeton University Press, 1917), 133–34.
1140 Frederick Rudolph, *Curriculum: A History of the American Under-*

graduate Course of Study Since 1636 (San Francisco: Jossey-Bass, 1977), 214, who cites multiple works by the Yale historian George Wilson Pierson. Cf. also *Time* 1 (March 3, 1923): 17 and the *Bridgeport* (CT) *Telegram*, February 9, 1923.

1141 Daniel O. Levine, *The American College and the Culture of Aspiration, 1915–1940* (Ithaca: Cornell University Press, 1986), 94.

1142 From 1904 to 1908 Taft was Secretary of War under President Theodore Roosevelt.

1143 A decade earlier the United States had gone to war against Spain (1898), which led to Taft's assignment to the Philippines.

1144 Among Taft's prior accomplishments were: Assistant Prosecutor in Hamilton County (Ohio), Superior Court Judge in Ohio, U.S. Solicitor General, Judge on the 6th U.S. Circuit Court of Appeals, Professor and Dean at the University of Cincinnati School of Law, President of the Civil Commission administering the Philippines. Following his one presidential term he taught at Yale Law School and then was appointed by President Harding Chief Justice of the U.S. Supreme Court. For a biography of Taft, see Peri E. Arnold's articles at millercenter.org.

1145 Cf. Livy, 39.40.5, said of Marcus Porcius Cato.

1146 The printed speech, *Allocutio habita inter convivium sollemne societatis Phi beta kappa yalensis a Tracy Peck in hospitio Neo-Portuensi a.d. XV Kal. apriles MCMVII* (n.p., n.d.), is in Yale University Library, but I have not seen a copy.

1147 *Classical Weekly* 1 (1907): 58. For Peck's career, see Meyer Reinhold's sketch in *Database of Classical Scholars*. And for a Latin ode he wrote in commemoration of Columbia's transition from a College to a University, see *Praeco Latinus* 2.8 (1896): 1.

1148 *Classical Weekly* 3 (1910): 238–39. I have not been able to locate the original printing of the poem in the *Milwaukee Journal*. (It was originally said, in fact, to have appeared in the *Wilwaukee Journal*, which must be a mistake.)

1149 Hennepin County Bar Association, *Memorial to Edward Welles Hawley (1867–1952)*, available at http://www.minnesotalegalhistoryproject.org/assets/Hawley,%20Edward.pdf. See also *Harvard College Class of 1889, Secretary's Report No. II* (Andover: Andover Press, 1892), 32–33; *Harvard College Class of 1889, Secretary's Report No. VI* (Boston: Rockwell and Churchill, 1909), 98–99.

1150 Catullus 62.54 (quotation marks in the original).

1151 *Columbia Spectator*, June 21, 1888. But for a recent reevaluation, see Stephen Wu, "Et tu, Columbiae?" *Columbia Daily Spectator*, April 20, 2011, who argues that the absence of a Latin address "represents a sad concession that modern scholarship is somehow fundamentally different from that of the classical tradition, which forms the basis of our society."

1152 *Boston Globe*, July 1, 1909.

1153 The simultaneous conferral of two honorary degrees upon one person may be a unique event in American higher education. See R. Andrew Lady, "Honoris Causa: An Examination of the Doctor of Philosophy Degree," *The Journal of Higher Education* 38 (1967): 205.

1154 *Boston Herald*, July 1, 1909.

1155 Cicero, *Or.* 3.57.215.

1156 Abbott Lawrence Lowell was the president of Harvard from 1909 to 1933. For recent assessments of Lowell's tenure at Harvard, see Amit R. Paley, "The Secret Court of 1920," *Harvard Crimson*, November 21, 2002, and Shera S. Avi-Yonah and Delano R. Franklin, "Renovated Lowell House will not Display Portrait of Controversial Former University President Abbott Lawrence Lowell," *Harvard Crimson*, March 26, 2019.

1157 In his speech on commencement day, Lowell warned of the danger of "social disintegration" in large colleges and expressed the belief that a college ought to be "a community." See also the biographical sketch at https://www.harvard.edu/about-harvard/harvard-glance/history-presidency/abbott-lawrence-lowell.

1158 The members of the Corporation and of the Board of Overseers for the academic year 1908–1909 are printed in *Harvard University Catalogue, 1908–1909* (Cambridge, MA: by the University, 1909), 3–4. One member of The Board of Overseers was William Watson Goodwin (1831–1912), Harvard's Eliot Professor of Greek from 1860 to 1901.

1159 Ebenezer Sumner Draper (1858–1914) was Governor of Massachusetts from 1909 to 1911.

1160 Charles W. Eliot.

1161 The deans are listed in *The Harvard University Catalogue, 1908–1909*, xiii–xiv. The Acting Dean of the Graduate School of Arts and Sciences that year was Herbert Weir Smyth, who was Eliot Professor of Greek from 1902 to 1925.

1162 Among Harvard's Classics professors in 1908–9 were Clifford Herschel Moore (1866–1931), Morris Hicky Morgan (1859–1910), Edward Kennard Rand (1871–1945), John Williams White (1849–1917), and two future Eliot Professors of Greek, Charles Burton Gulick (1868–1962) and Carl Newell Jackson (1875–1946). For biographical details of these classicists see the entries in *Database of Classical Scholars*.

1163 See note 1155 above.

1164 Cicero, *Off.* 1.30.109.

1165 Wolfgang Jenniges, "Vox Urbis (1898–1913) quid sibi proposuerit," *Melissa* 139 (2007): 8–11; Alexius Slednikov, "Schola Latinitatis Vivae

Italo-Vaticana (ab saec. XIX exeunte ad saec. XXI iniens) quomodo explorari possit," *Vox Latina* 55 (2019): 430–36. See also Dirk Sacré, "Neo-Latin Prose in the Twilight Years," in *Brill's Encyclopedia of the Neo-Latin World* (note 29 above), 898, and David Butterfield, "Latin and the Social Media," ibid., 1014–16.

1166 *The Classical Review* 12 (1898): 430; 23 (1909): 28.

1167 Leonori, the editor, designed several American buildings, including St. Joseph's Cathedral (Buffalo), the interior of the Bishop's Chapel in Mount Carmel Cemetery (Chicago), The All Saints' Chapel and The Lady Chapel in the Cathedral-Basilica of St. Louis, and the Franciscan Monastery of the Holy Land in America (Washington, DC).

1168 *Vox Urbis* 15 (1912): 1, 25.

1169 The headquarters of the Equitable Life Assurance Society of the United States (founded 1859), located at 120 Broadway, was destroyed by fire on January 9, 1912.

1170 On February 21, 1912, following the Mardi Gras parade, a fire swept through Houston's Fifth Ward. No one perished but it was the city's largest fire to date.

1171 More than seventy men were killed in an explosion at the San Bois Coal Company's mine in McCurtain, Oklahoma on March 20, 1912.

1172 This likely refers to a March 26, 1912 explosion at a mine in Jed, West Virginia, in which eighty workers died.

1173 The Mississippi River flood of 1912 was one of the worst to date. The first levee broke on the morning of April 6 on the Atchafalaya River.

1174 The RMS *Titanic* sunk in the Atlantic Ocean on the morning of April 15, 1912 on its maiden voyage from Southampton to New York.

1175 Numerous tornadoes occurred in Oklahoma in late April 1912. This may refer to one near Kingfisher and Hennessey on April 20, 1912.

1176 See above note 1173. The Mississippi crested in New Orleans on May 11, 1912 at 21 feet.

1177 On May 30, 1912 Wilbur Wright, age 45, died in Dayton from typhoid fever.

1178 On June 8 1912 a statue of Christopher Columbus was unveiled in front of Washington DC's Union Station.

1179 On July 4, 1912 thirty-nine persons died and eighty-eight were injured near East Corning, New York when one passenger train ran into the rear of another.

1180 On July 11, 1912 an explosion in the Panama mine of the Ben Franklin Coal Company in Moundsville, West Virginia killed eight workers. The words "autem" and "eidem" refer to the previous entry, not included here, which mentioned a mining disaster in England.

1181 On October 14, 1912 while campaigning in Milwaukee for a third presidential term, Theodore Roosevelt was shot in the chest by John Schrank, a New York saloonkeeper. Roosevelt nonetheless persisted in delivering extemporaneously an hour-long speech.

1182 On November 12, 1912 a freight train rear-ended a passenger train on the Yazoo & Mississippi Valley Railroad near Montz, Louisiana.

1183 In 1951 the mission was relocated to the Andreafsky River. See the online history of St. Mary's mission in Akulurak at http://dioceseof-fairbanks.org/joomla/index.php/parishes/profiles-of-former-mission-churches/93-akulurak-saint-marys-mission. See also *Woodstock Letters* 58 (1929): 445–47, and Segundo Llorente, *Memories of a Yukon Priest* (Washington, DC: Georgetown University Press, 1990).

1184 The other priest in residence at this time was John Lucchesi (1858–1937), born in Genoa, who came to Alaska in 1899 and served as general superior of the Alaskan mission for about twenty years. Also in residence were two Jesuit brothers: Alfred Murphy (1886–1954), born in Calgary, who was responsible for catching the 20,000 fish eaten each year and gathering the wood necessary to heat the mission during the winter; Bartholomew Keogh, or Chiaudano (d. 1940), born in Italy, who arrived in Alaska in 1900 and served as cook.

1185 In the sisters's convent, the stars reportedly could be seen through the porous roof. See Suzanne H. Schrems, *Uncommon Women, Unmarked Trails: The Courageous Journey of Catholic Missionary Sisters in Frontier Montana* (Norman, OK: Horse Creek Publications, 2003), 99.

1186 NN. = nostrorum, which was the Jesuit convention for referring to themselves.

1187 The Ursuline sisters arrived in 1905 to staff a boarding school in Akulurak.

1188 The *Fairbanks Daily Times*, January 5, 1916 reports that along the Bering Coast (where the Jesuit mission was located) the storm was "one of the worst that that part of the country has ever known at this time of the year."

1189 *Brooklyn Times Union*, May 15, 1918.

1190 *New York Evening World*, May 15, 1918.

1191 *Washington Times*, May 15, 1918.

1192 C.V. Glines, "The Day the Airmail Started," *Air Force Magazine* 72 (December 1989): 98–101.

1193 On *America*, see Michael F. Lombardo, *Founding Father: John J. Wynne, S.J. and the Inculturation of American Catholicism in the Progressive Era* (Leiden: Brill, 2017), 231–94. *America* lent regular support to classical studies. See, for example, Reville's article cited below in section 110, note 1208, as well as the reviews of Leo T. Butler's works on Latin Verse Composition, *America* 10 (February 14, 1914): 451 and *America*

18 (October 20, 1917): 43. Cf. especially "The Worth of Latin Composition" in *America* 13 (April 17, 1915): 22–23.

1194 It was reprinted in *Classical Weekly* 12 (1918): 8.

1195 A brief synopsis of this mission is in Bischoff, *Jesuits in Old Oregon* (note 673 above), 207–11. See also various notices in *The Indian Sentinel* 2.4 (1920).

1196 In 1885 sisters of the Third Order of St. Francis from Philadelphia arrived in the Pacific Northwest and assumed responsibility for several schools in Oregon. See "Sisters of the Third Order of St. Francis, 1855–1928," *Records of the American Catholic Historical Society of Philadelphia* 40 (1929): 226–48.

1197 Joseph Giraudi (1865–1953) and Aloysius Veraldi (1861–1938) were the two Jesuit brothers who assisted the mission. Giraudi was in charge of the garden (hortulanus) and Veraldi, who had recently arrived from Montana to replace Bernard Collins (b. 1862), was in charge of the field and flock (custos agri et armentorum).

1198 Joseph Francis McGrath (1871–1950) was Bishop of Baker City (now Baker), Oregon from 1918 to 1950. In 1919 the feast of Corpus Christi fell on June 19.

1199 Cf. Matt 8:26–27, Ps 88:10.

1200 See Donna W. Hurley, "Alfred Gudeman, Atlanta, Georgia, 1862—Theresienstadt, 1942," *Transactions of the American Philological Association* 120 (1990): 355–81.

1201 *Classical Journal* 7 (1912): 312–14. Rolfe's ode, "Salvete, O comites, sollemnia qui celebrantes," is printed on p. 314.

1202 Evidently this is a reference to William Jennings Bryan (1860–1925), a noted proponent of Prohibition.

1203 See the biographical notice on Rolfe by Ward W. Briggs in *Database of Classical Scholars*. A bibliography of Rolfe's writings is in George D. Hadzsits, ed., *Classical Studies in Honor of John C. Rolfe* (Philadelphia: University of Pennsylvania Press, 1931), 345–52.

1204 See also "Andreae Dickson White, Annis Feliciter Peractis LXXX," *Classical Weekly* 6 (1913): 87 (White was the first President of Cornell); "Seni Iuveni Decano Artis Chirurgicae Illustrissimo Annis LXXXIV Feliciter Peractis S.P.D. Io. Carew Rolfe," *Classical Weekly* 14 (1921): 128 (in honor of Dr. W.W. Keen of Philadelphia).

1205 Hurley, "Alfred Gudeman," 365–66, discusses Gudeman's motivation for becoming a German citizen.

1206 Vergil, *A.* 1.203.

1207 Abraham Flexner, *A Modern School* (New York: General Education Board, 1916), 18.

1208 John C. Reville, "The Second Battle of Princeton," *America* 17 (June

16, 1917): 231.
1209 The conference addresses are printed in *Value of the Classics* (note 1139 above).
1210 "The Classics for America," *The Phi Beta Kappa Key* 4 (1921): 483–90.
1211 *De disputationibus inter allegoricas personas habitas quas ante Christum natum finxerunt Graeci.*
1212 "Some Features of the Allegorical Debate in Greek Literature," *Harvard Studies in Classical Philology* 23 (1912): 1–46; "The Form of the Early Etruscan and Roman House," *Classical Philology* 9 (1914): 113–33; "The Meaning of the 'Dokana'" *American Journal of Archaeology* 23 (1919): 1–18; "Satura Rediviva," *American Journal of Philology* 40 (1919): 308–16; "The Nature of the Lares and Their Representation in Roman Art," *American Journal of Archaeology* 24 (1920): 241–61; "The Deities of the Sacred Axe," *American Journal of Archaeology* 27 (1923): 25–56.
1213 *Rockford* (Illinois) *Morning Star*, May 5, 1912.
1214 "Performance of the Phormio, in Latin, at Mount Holyoke College," *Classical Weekly* 10 (1917): 104.
1215 *Classical Journal* 12 (1917): 341–42. Cf. also her note "Latin an End in Itself," *Classical Weekly* 16 (1923): 134
1216 A full account is in the *Boston Globe*, May 22, 1921.
1217 "Report of the President, 1920–1923," *Mount Holyoke College Bulletin* 17.2 (1923): 5.
1218 "The China Educational Commission," *The Phi Beta Kappa Key* 4 (1922): 687–89.
1219 *Springfield Republican*, March 16, 1923. See also *Springfield Republican*, March 18, 1923, for an account of the memorial service for Waites and a summary of the eulogy delivered for her.
1220 In the copy in the archives of Mt. Holyoke the words in the last line of each strophe are repeated.
1221 Horace, C. 2.16.40.
1222 *Classical Weekly* 14 (1920): 54.
1223 "A Giant Air Liner from Germany," *Current Opinion* 77 (November 1924): 621–23.
1224 *Washington Evening Star*, October 17, 1924.
1225 A footnote explains: "'Los Angeles;' nomen ab Americanis Zeppelinio aerostato impositum."
1226 Roy C. Flickinger, "The King is Dead. Long Live the King!" *Classical Journal* 26 (1931): 339–40. For a biographical notice of Flickinger, see Archie C. Bush's entry in *Database of Classical Scholars*. In addition to work on ancient drama and the accusative of exclamation, Flickinger compiled *Carmina Latina* (Chicago: University of Chicago Press, 1919).

1227 Roy C. Flickinger, "Horace's First Bimillennium," *Classical Journal* 32 (1936): 65–91 (p. 72). See also Willis A. Ellis, "Horace and his Bimillennium," *Classical Journal* 28 (1933): 643–56.
1228 The contest regulations are given in *Classical Journal* 30 (1935): 575–76.
1229 An obituary appeared in *New York Times*, January 17, 2007.
1230 Her dissertation was "An Unpublished Commentary on Ovid's 'Fasti' by Arnulfus of Orléans" (1940).
1231 Among her many publications is *Diseases of the Cat: Medicine and Surgery* (Philadelphia: Saunders, 1987).
1232 *Bryn Mawr Alumnae Bulletin* 16.3 (March 1936), 7–8.
1233 John Richmond, "Classics and Intelligence: Part I," *Classics Ireland* 8 (2001): 98.
1234 *Some Oxford Compositions* (Oxford: Clarendon Press, 1949). See also *More Oxford Compositions* (Oxford: Clarendon Press, 1964).
1235 J.F.C. Richards in *American Journal of Philology* 72 (1951): 440.
1236 *The Classical Review*, n.s. 37 (1987): 92.
1237 *Orationes Oxonienses Selectae*, 1960.
1238 Richard T. Bruère in *Classical Philology* 56 (1961): 214. See also W.K.C. Guthrie's review (in Latin) in *Classical Review*, n.s. 11 (1961); 157–58.
1239 May 8, 1945, known as V-E day, was, in the words of Winston Churchill, "the signal for the greatest outburst of joy in the history of mankind." See Stephen E. Ambrose, *Eisenhower: Soldier and President* (New York: Simon & Schuster, 1990), 205.
1240 Ovid, *Tr.* 3.12.47–48.
1241 On June 12, 1943, King George VI flew to North Africa and bestowed on Eisenhower the insignia of Knight, Grand Cross, Order of the Bath, which had been established by King George I in 1725. At the time Eisenhower was preparing for the allied invasion of Italy.
1242 Dudley Kirk and Earl Huyck, "Overseas Migration from Europe Since World War II," *American Sociological Review* 19 (1954): 447–56.
1243 Data available at Migration Policy Institute: https://www.migrationpolicy.org/programs/data-hub/charts/net-number-migrants-country-1950-2015-five-year-intervals.
1244 A.M. Melville, "St. Francis Xavier Cabrini," in *New Catholic Encyclopedia*.
1245 Castel Gandolfo, built by Pope Urban VIII (*r.* 1623–44), has long been the summer residence of popes.
1246 I have cited the text from http://www.vatican.va/content/pius-xii/la/briefs/documents/hf_p-xii_apl_19500907_superiore-iam-aetate.html. It is also printed in *Apostolicae Sedis Commentarium Officiale*, ser. 2, vol.

18 (1951): 455–56.

1247 Lincoln Sesquicentennial Commission, *Abraham Lincoln Sesquicentennial 1959–1960: Final Report* (Washington, DC: n.p., 1960), 46–47.

1248 Cf. Jared Peatman, *The Long Shadow of Lincoln's Gettysburg Address* (Carbondale: Southern Illinois University Press, 2013), 153–54.

1249 *Congressional Record, Proceedings and Debates of the 86th Congress, First Session*, vol. 105, part 15 (Washington, DC: United States Government Printing Office, 1959), 19600 (September 14, 1959). The translation had recently been published in the Cosmos Club *Bulletin* 12.5 (1959), 3.

1250 *The Church in the South American Republics* (Milwaukee: Bruce, 1952).

1251 *A College Handbook to Newman* (Washington, DC: Catholic Education Press, 1930); *Candles in the Roman Rite* (Baltimore: A. Gross Candle, 1934); "Medieval Latin in the Secondary School," *Classical World* 52 (1959): 144–47.

1252 *Gettysburg Times*, June 19, 1959; *Syracuse Post-Standard*, June 27, 1959.

1253 Kleist published widely on the pedagogy of Latin Prose Composition, and he was founding editor of *The Classical Bulletin*. See the sketch and bibliography in Richard E. Arnold, ed., *Classical Essays presented to James A. Kleist, S.J.* (St. Louis University: Classical Bulletin, 1946), ix–xx.

1254 In his *Aids to Latin Prose Composition* (New York: Schwartz, Kirwin & Fauss, 1912), 91–93, Kleist gives two other slightly different versions of the Gettysburg Address, both of which are annotated.

1255 John W. O'Malley, *What Happened at Vatican II* (Cambridge, MA: Belknap Press of Harvard University Press, 2008), 25.

1256 "A Letter of Very Reverend Father General to All Major Superiors on the Study and Use of Latin," *Woodstock Letters* 92 (1963): 3–12 (p. 4).

1257 For a negative evaluation of the efficacy of Latin at the Council, see Xavier Rynne [= Francis X. Murphy], *Vatican Council II* (New York: Farrar, Strauss and Giroux, 1968), 59–60. Cf. also Andrew Chandler and Charlotte Hansen, eds., *Observing Vatican II: The Confidential Reports of the Archbishop of Canterbury's Representative, Bernard Pawley, 1961–1964* (Cambridge: Cambridge University Press, 2013), 113.

1258 Ralph M. Wiltgen, *The Rhine Flows into the Tiber: The Unknown Council* (New York: Hawthorn Books, 1967), 150–51.

1259 The course was taught by Aloys Kennerknecht, who co-authored *Introductio in stenographiam latinam* (Darmstadt: Winklers, 1962). For brief recollections by one of the stenographers, see Gerald E. Bensman,

"Recollections of Vatican Council II," *The Athenaeum Magazine* [published by Mount Saint Mary's Seminary of the West] (Summer 2012): 9.

1260 O'Malley, *What Happened at Vatican II*, 233.

1261 Pope John XXIII had stated seven months earlier (*Pacem in Terris*, April 11, 1963): "Quare iustitia, recta ratio, humanaeque dignitatis sensus instanter requirunt . . . ut atomica arma interdicantur."

1262 Philip Hannan, with Nancy Collins and Peter Finney, *The Archbishop Wore Combat Boots: From Combat, to Camelot, to Katrina—Memoir of an Extraordinary Life* (Huntington, IN: Our Sunday Visitor, 2010), 452. In November 2019 Pope Francis expressed his intent to insert language into the Catechism of the Catholic Church declaring that not only the use but also the possession of nuclear weapons is immoral. See https://www.vaticannews.va/en/pope/news/2019-11/pope-francis-press-conference-japan-airplane.html.

1263 Wiltgen, *The Rhine Flows into the Tiber*, 278–82. See also *Acta Synodalia Sacrosancti Concilii Oecumenici Vaticani II*, vol. 4.3 (Rome: Typis Polyglottis Vaticanis, 1977), 811–812.

1264 According to a footnote, which reflects the written rather than the spoken text, Hannan clarifies: "Haec arma praeparantur ut immanes ruinae ex largioribus nuclearibus instrumentis erumpentes evitentur et ut certo ictu destinata singillatim deleri possint."

www.ingramcontent.com/pod-product-compliance
Lightning Source LLC
LaVergne TN
LVHW020516100826
845148LV00010B/1255

9781734018981